Theatre and Playhouse

An illustrated survey of theatre building from Ancient Greece to the present day

Helen and Richard Leacroft have collaborated on numerous books on the history of theatres and the architecture of early times. Richard trained as an architect, and while practising architecture he also studied stage decor under Michel St. Denis at the London Theatre Studio. Helen trained as an actress at R.A.D.A., played at Bradford, Folkestone and the Theatre Royal, Leicester, where Richard was working as designer and scenic artist, and where Helen became Company Manager during the war years.

Both later turned to teaching. Helen specializing in Drama and History, while Richard became a Principal Lecturer in the Leicester School of Architecture, teaching Design and History of Architecture. In 1954 he was awarded the R.I.B.A. Athens Bursary for the study of early Greek theatres, followed in 1960 by the R.I.B.A. Rose Shipman Studentship with which he undertook a study tour of experimental theatres in the United States and Canada.

The present book is designed to complement Richard's *Development of the English Playhouse*, which was awarded an Honourable Mention in 1973 by the American Theater Library Association, in the George Freedley Award, for an outstanding contribution to the literature of the theatre. It is now looked upon as standard work on its subject.

The Leacrofts have a son and daughter and seven grand-daughters.

The drawing on the front cover is a reconstruction of Ledoux's Theatre at Besançon in France in 1778. The drawings on the back of the hardback edition are of Sparrow Hill Theatre, Loughborough, in 1822 and The Forum, Billingham, in 1968, both in England. All three drawings are by Richard Leacroft.

1 Actors and audience: their architectural expression at Delos, Greece

Richard and Helen Leacroft

THEATRE AND PLAYHOUSE

An illustrated survey of theatre building from Ancient Greece to the present day

with isometric reconstructions by Richard Leacroft, ARIBA, MSIAD

Methuen LONDON AND NEW YORK

For Jo and Robert, Kate and Bob

also by Richard Leacroft

CIVIC THEATRE DESIGN

THE DEVELOPMENT OF THE ENGLISH PLAYHOUSE

THE THEATRE ROYAL, LEICESTER

also by Helen and Richard Leacroft

THE THEATRE

First published in 1984
in simultaneous hardback and paperback editions
by Methuen London Ltd,
11 New Fetter Lane, London EC4P 4EE
and by Methuen Inc, 733 Third Avenue,
New York, NY 10017.

Design by Christopher Holgate

ISBN 0 413 52930 4 (Hardback)
0 413 52940 1 (Paperback)

Filmset and printed by BAS Printers Limited,
Over Wallop, Stockbridge, Hampshire

Contents

Preface

'Don't talk to me of frames and pictures. If I can't make myself heard within the frame, I'll come out of it – and out of it he came.'

William Dowton (comic actor, 1764–1851)

How did Old Dowton get into the frame, and what happened to him when he stepped out?

Theatres represent the built environments resulting from a number of actor-audience relationships, which are varied by many conditions. In elemental form: dance may be viewed by an enclosing audience, while an actor telling a story needs a directional approach if he is to take full advantage of the use of facial expression; but both may be affected by the impact of social conditions, as when one member of an audience – say a tribal chief or a prince – receives extra attention.

Conditions will vary to suit differing situations; a large audience may require the actor to be raised if he is to be seen, or alternatively the audience may be raised if it is to appreciate the pattern of movement on the stage. Conventions regarding the entrances and exits of performers will affect actor-audience relationships, as will the inclusion in the performance of sacred objects, or various forms of scenic representation. The need to protect the protagonists from the weather by enclosing them within a covered building will introduce new problems, which will be further complicated by the need to continue existing customs under differing architectural conditions.

Adaptations of existing buildings to theatrical purposes impose further limitations, and the resurrection of misunderstood conventions and architectural forms, as happened in the Renaissance era, adds to the problems. Social conditions which require one section of an audience to be separated from another, or to enjoy additional facilities related to its social status, complicate theatre design; as also do the uses of new forms of lighting, and the need to protect the participants from the effects of fire.

In recent years many new theatres have been built in Britain and elsewhere, and it would require several large volumes to include them all. The majority of these theatres, however, fall into one or other of a limited number of actor-audience relationships; and so, in this book, we have chosen to illustrate, through a series of cut-open isometric drawings, those theatres which we have selected as being the precursors of the various forms of theatre that have been developed through the ages, and which have set the patterns for the presentation of modern drama.

We wish to take this opportunity to thank the many people who have, in one form or another, contributed towards the preparation of this book. Our thanks are due especially to the staffs of the many libraries and museums that we have consulted, for their help with all the problems of research, not forgetting those unknown staff who work behind the scenes in Inter-Library Loan. More particularly our thanks are due to Miss Catherine Dembsky of the British Architectural Library; Miss Sarah Woodcock of the Theatre Museum; Shirley Hind of the Architectural Press; Mrs. Marjorie Williams and Mrs. Christine Jordan of the Leicester Polytechnic Library; Richard Brinkley of the University of Wales; John Farrell of the University, Bristol; Marjorie Maynard of the Central Library, Ipswich; Enrico Alfieri, Coadiutore Principale, Galleria Nazionale, Parma; the Director of the Musei Civici, Pinacoteca di Vicenza; Miss Birgitta Walin of the Drottningholms Teatermuseum; Le Conservateur, Archives Municipales de Bordeaux; Mme. G. Mathieu, Conservateur, Bibliothèque Municipale, Ville de

Besançon; and Mme. Chantal Morel, Head Librarian, Institut Français du Royaume-Uni.

Particular thanks are due to those architects who so kindly made copies of the working drawings for their theatres available to us, and to the staffs of theatres and others who helped in a similar manner. To W. Kelly Oliver of Oliver and Hellgren, for the Kalita Humphreys Theater, Dallas; Elidir L. W. Davies, FRIBA, for the Mermaid, Puddle Dock; Norman Branson, RIBA, and John Roake, FRIBA, of W. S. Hattrell and Partners, and Alfred Emmet, for the Questors, Ealing; R. J. Murphy, ARIBA, of HKPA, for Christ's Hospital, Horsham; Law and Dunbar-Nasmith, for Eden Court, Inverness; Jack Gustafsson of Frank Welch Associates, for Midland, Texas; T. A. Lester, RIBA, of Elder Lester Associates, for the Forum, Billingham; Geoffrey H. Brookes, RIBA, for the Octagon, Bolton; and J. McM. Abbott, RIBA, for the Theatre Royal, Bury St. Edmunds; Mrs. and Mr. R. H. Harvey, ARIBA, for the Royal Shakespeare Theatre, Stratford-upon-Avon; Ulricke Schnappat, for the National Theatre, Mannheim; Ian Emmerson, for the Maddermarket Theatre, Norwich; the Headmaster of Bradfield College, for their Greek Theatre; James Hull Miller, for the various theatres for which he was consultant; George C. Izenour, for his project for Yale; Daniel W. Ladell, Archivist of the Stratford Shakespearean Festival Foundation of Canada; Richard Bauer, of the Malmo Stadsteater; Terry Clarke of Horsham and Tony Rushforth, Head of Drama, for St. Mary's College, Twickenham.

Thanks are also due to all those who gave permission for the use of material, including Edward Craig, for his photograph of the Teatro Farnese and for information on this theatre and SS. Giovanni e Paolo; Sir Denys Lasdun, for the photograph of the Olivier Theatre; Professor E. A. Langhans, for his reconstruction of Lincoln's Inn Fields; Lionel Nazareth of Levitt Bernstein Associates, for the Manchester Royal Exchange; Lady Miles, for the drawing of the Royal Exchange Mermaid; Peter Cheeseman, for the Victoria Theatre, Stoke on Trent; Nancy Gronlund of the Guthrie Theatre, Minneapolis; Jose Ferrandez Cruz, Presidente Geste, Patranato Nacional del Mysterio de Elche; Albert M. Koga, for the use of drawings prepared for Hub Electric's publications; Kommunalborgmastare S. Schultz of the Vadstena Kommun, for kindly making photographs available of his theatre; Thomas W. L. Porter, General Manager of the Adelphi Theatre; Anthony Loynes, of the Mermaid Theatre; John Gardiner, Administrator of the Haymarket, Leicester; James Sargant, Administrator of the Barbican Theatre; Jason Barnes and Tony Bond, of the National Theatre; Bill Clancy of the Belgrade Theatre, Coventry; T. K. Whitelaw, Theatre Manager of the New Fortune Theatre, University of W. Australia; the Rt. Hon. Viscount De L'Isle, for the Barons Hall at Penshurst Place, Kent; O. B. Hardison, Jr., of the Folger Shakespeare Library, for slides of the Mystery of Elche; and Mike Flannigan, Secretary of the University of Oxford Royal Tennis Court.

We must also thank Miss Sybil Rosenfeld of the Society for Theatre Research; Mike Kilburn; John Marlow, RIBA; Dr. Albert Hoffler; Peter Gardner; Dr. A. Keller; Iain Mackintosh; Professor Ben Farmer; and Professor O. A. W. Dilke for their help; and James H. Jacques for translations. Last, but by no means least, we must acknowledge our debt to the late Hope Bagenal, RIBA, who most kindly made available to us a copy of the manuscript of the relevant chapters of his unpublished work on *The History of the Auditorium*, with particular reference to the place of Greek 'carpentry' orders in scenic design.

We would also like to thank those members of the publisher's team whose efforts have contributed so much to this work, in particular Nick Hern and Simon Trussler for their editorial advice, and Christopher Holgate for typography and layout.

HELEN AND RICHARD LEACROFT
Keven Lodge, Countesthorpe

I Early Greece: rectangular and timber theatres

Primitive man and Dionysiac festivals. Minoan palaces. Earliest theatres. Thespis and the first actor. Ikaria. Timber benches. Thorikos. Rectangular orchestras. Theatre of Dionysus, Athens: earliest evidence. The skene and painted scenery. Phlyakes stages. Temporary structures and post-holes. Corinth and Oropus. Vase paintings and paraskenia. Earliest theatre at Eretria.

Primitive man sang, danced, and performed mimes to please the gods and ensure the fertility of his family, or the success of his hunting or harvests. [2] Such rituals were performed in many places, ranging from an open space in a settlement to a circle surrounding a sacred stone, post, or tree. Sometimes the whole community took part, on other occasions particular tribesmen performed for the benefit of the rest, who gathered around to watch. From that time until the present, every type of performance has created its own environmental conditions of performer-audience relationship, and these have varied from a patch of beaten earth to complicated built structures.

The Ancient Greeks disguised themselves and performed dances to the spirits of nature, and by the sixth century BC festivals in honour of Dionysus, the god

2 Indian tribal dance

of the vine, were taking place each year, when priests, accompanied by flute players, singers, and dancers, made sacrifices at an altar. The festivals took place on any flat, open space in a village, which in many instances would be the local threshing floor, [3] while the market place – the *agora* – could be used in the cities.

In the Athenian *agora* there was reputedly a place called the *orchestra* with a poplar tree close to the wooden benches or scaffolding – the *ikria* – from which the audience could watch. Evidence for timber seating of necessity comes from literary or artistic sources, but stone steps from later periods may still be seen in various *agoras*. In the Minoan palaces of Crete [4, 5] there are steps facing on to open spaces, and although the nature of the performances given there is unknown, these could have been used as stands by the nobles. At Lato [6–8] a flight of steps, facing an open space

Cretan theatral areas:
4 Palace of Gournia
5 Palace of Knossos
6, 7, 8 Lato

3 Threshing floor near Bassae, Greece

4

5

6

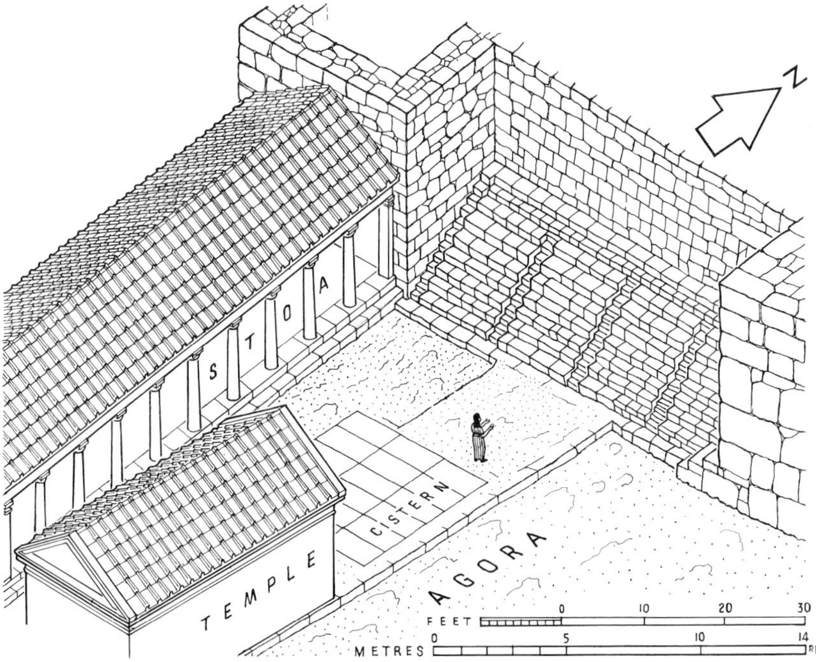
N
STOA
TEMPLE
CISTERN
AGORA
FEET 0 10 20 30
METRES 0 5 10 14
RL

7

8

9 Vase painting by Sophilus

in front of a small temple of Artemis, is similar in size and shape to the steps seen in a vase painting, [9] which shows how an audience could have been seated. Further examples of stone steps by temples and on processional ways are to be found on mainland Greece, [10] but none can really be classed as theatres.

The development of a specifically theatrical environment – as distinct from the *agora* – may have been hastened by the collapse of the *ikria* in Athens, which led to the performances being moved to the precinct of Dionysus on the south face of the Acropolis, where the theatre still stands. An example of such a theatre adjoining an *agora* may be seen in the sanctuary of Dionysus at Ikaria, [11] which may even have been the place where Thespis, by tradition the first actor, interposed spoken verse into the songs and dances performed by a chorus. It is said that Thespis, wearing a mask of painted linen and standing on a sacrificial table so that he could be distinguished from the chorus, introduced this most primitive form of 'drama' to Athens in 534 BC, and that he took a statue of Dionysus

10 Steps on processional way, Eleusis, Greece

11 Sanctuary of Dionysus, Ikaria, Greece

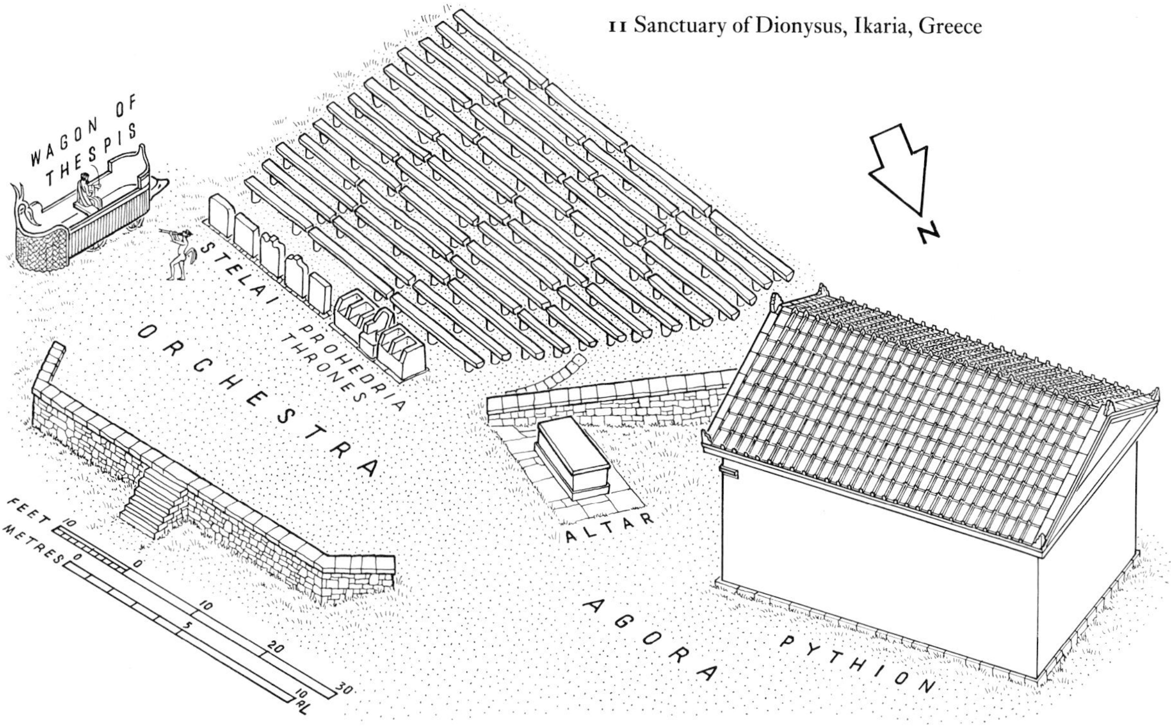
WAGON OF THESPIS
STELAI
PROHEDRIA THRONES
ORCHESTRA
ALTAR
AGORA
PYTHION
FEET
METRES
N

and his band of performers round the countryside in a cart, which he also used as a platform.

At Ikaria a retaining wall was built on the hillside adjoining the *agora*, and the space was infilled to form a flat rectangular dancing place, or *orchestra*. The hillside made an ideal *cavea* or *theatron* – this word originally describing the space where the audience sat, mainly on the ground, only the elders sitting on timber benches. Later, similar benches could have been set up for the rest of the spectators, at which time the seats of honour – the *prohedriai* – were probably made of stone.

A similar theatre may be seen at Rhamnous. [12] Rows of benches set one behind another up the slope of a hill would have been adequate until larger audiences had to be accommodated. Flanking units of straight benches could then be added, angled-in so that a larger audience could sit within reasonable distance of the performers on what could be called a 'trapeze-shaped' *orchestra*.

12 Rhamnous, Greece

6 : Early Greece : rectangular and timber theatres

Three stages of development may be seen in the theatre at Thorikos. At first [13a] the *cavea* probably consisted of straight timber benches set on the hillside, adjoining a rectangular *orchestra* supported by a stone retaining wall. Sometime during the fifth century BC, [13b] the timber benches were replaced by straight stone steps, flanked by wings which curved or angled forward to enclose a larger *orchestra*, formed by the construction of an additional retaining wall. The front step of the centre block – *kerkis* – is subdivided by marks to form a simple *prohedria* bench for the priests and elders. A temple of Dionysus was built at the same time, separated from the seating by a narrow passageway, the *parodos*. Directly opposite was an altar, and beyond were two rooms built against the rock-face. [14].

When further accommodation was needed in the fourth century BC, [13c] the *cavea* was almost doubled in size by additional seating at the rear. The slope of the hill was not adequate to take this addition, so it had to be built up, the new height being marked by the surrounding wall, or *analemma*, together with two entry ways at either end of the north section. [15] The next stage of *cavea* development can be seen at

13a

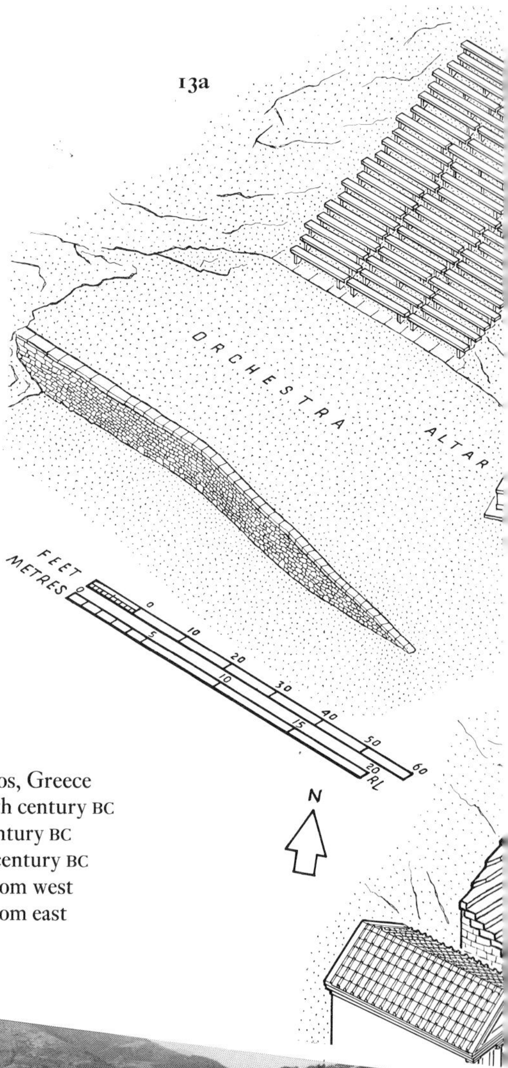
ORCHESTRA
ALTAR
FEET
METRES
0
10
20
30
40
50
60
0
5
10
15
20
N

13 Thorikos, Greece
a : late sixth century BC
b : fifth century BC
c : fourth century BC
14 View from west
15 View from east

14

15

13b

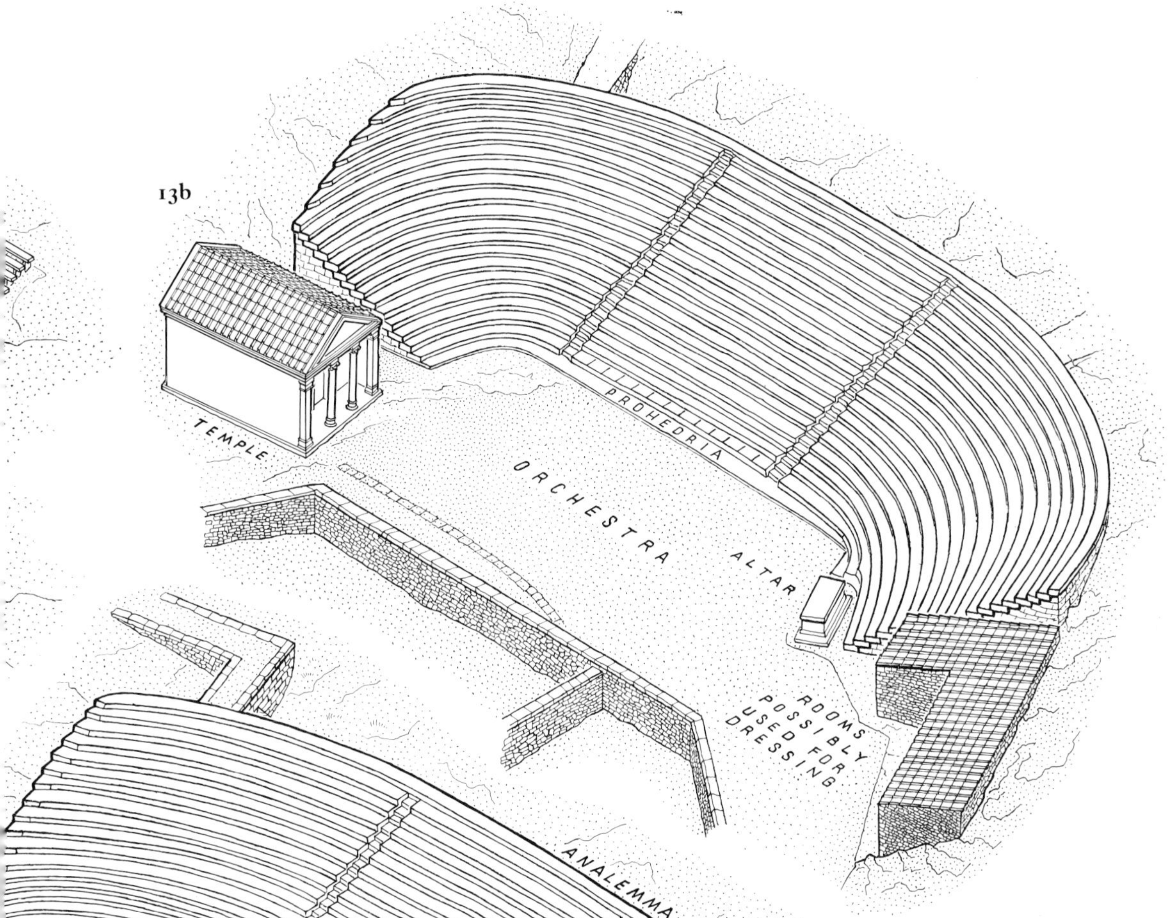
TEMPLE
PROHEDRIA
ORCHESTRA
ALTAR
ROOMS POSSIBLY USED FOR DRESSING

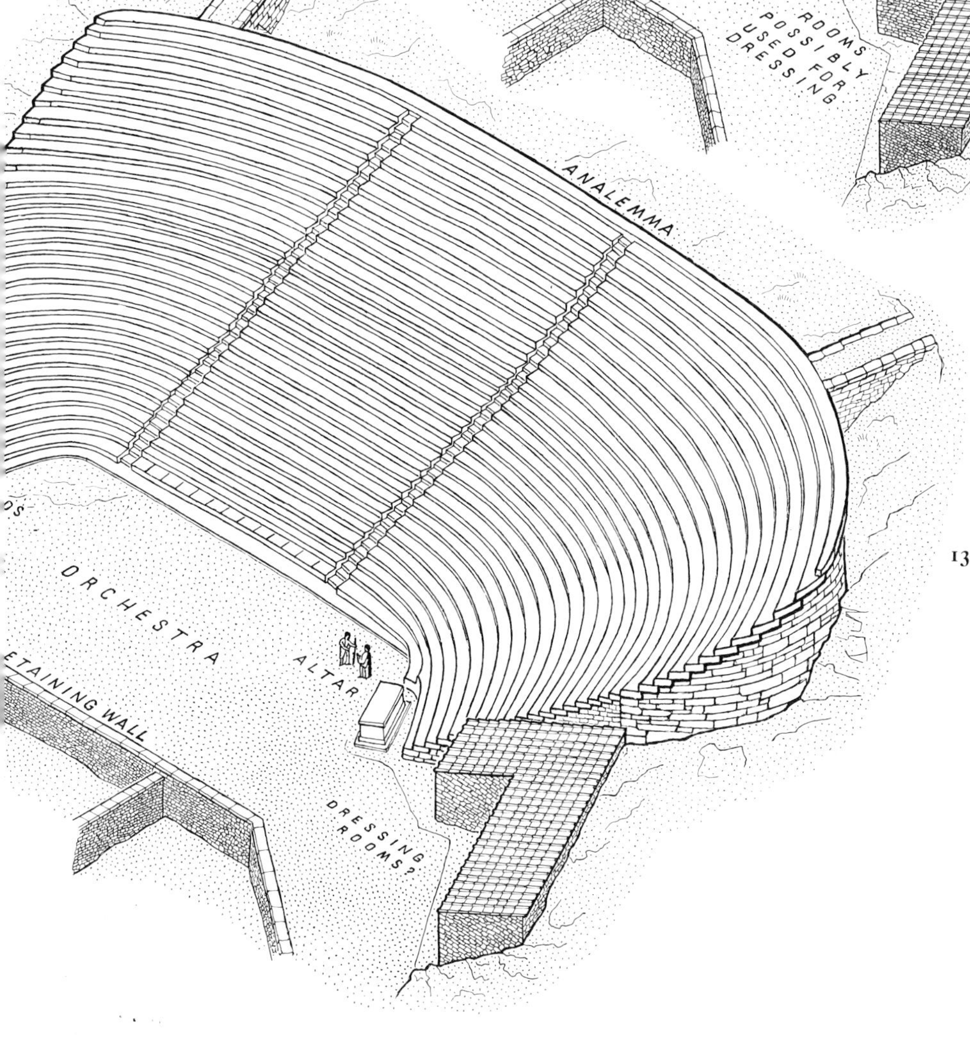
ANALEMMA
ORCHESTRA
ALTAR
ETAINING WALL
DRESSING ROOMS?

13c

8 : Early Greece: rectangular and timber theatres

16 Chaeronea, Greece

17 Greek dancers at Delphi

Chaeronea, [16] where the rock-cut seats have an elliptical form.

Contrary to previously held theories that the circular *orchestra* of the developed Greek theatre had been present from the earliest times, the known use of timber benches, with their straight lines, in early theatres suggests that consideration should now be given to the idea that the Greek theatre may equally well have developed from a free or 'rectangular' form, as retained in the formation of the dramatic chorus. Although the chorus of the dithyrambic dance was circular, it should be appreciated that even a circular dance need not necessarily take place in a circular space, as the photograph [17] of Greek dancers shows.

In the Theatre of Dionysus in Athens [18] a portion of the earliest evidence, consisting of six stones (marked A: see also fig. 21), is generally accepted as forming part of the retaining wall to the first *orchestra*, which is now presumed to have followed a free shape. There does not seem to be any direct evidence as to the shape of this *orchestra*; many authorities have attempted to fit a circle to the available evidence, but the form may

FEET
METRES
TEMPLE OF DIONYSUS
ALTAR
ALTAR
A
B
N

18 Theatre of Dionysus, Athens, phase I

equally well have been roughly 'rectangular' or polygonal, especially as early records indicate the use of timber benches on a raised bank of earth.

A temple was situated below the level of the *orchestra*, to which it was connected by a track along the base of the wall. Within the *orchestra* were an altar and a sacrificial table, the latter perhaps serving as a raised stage for the actor, a use which could later have been superseded by the introduction of a low platform with steps.

The shape of the *orchestra* which resulted from later alterations is also in doubt, but it is known to have been backed by a long, straight retaining wall. [21] The earth bank was raised again, a move which necessitated the building of supporting stone walls on the southern ends and on the eastern and western sides of the *cavea*. Timber benches were still in use, with stone *prohedria* benches at the front.

About 30 years after the traditional date for the introduction of the actor, Greek tragedy began to assume its familiar form. It was the poet Aeschylus (525–456 BC) who introduced the second actor, while a third was used by Sophocles (496–406 BC). When the classical theatre was at its height, these three actors portrayed all the characters, including the women, different masks being required for changes of character: thus, it became necessary for the actors to have a changing room, or *skene*.

10 : Early Greece: rectangular and timber theatres

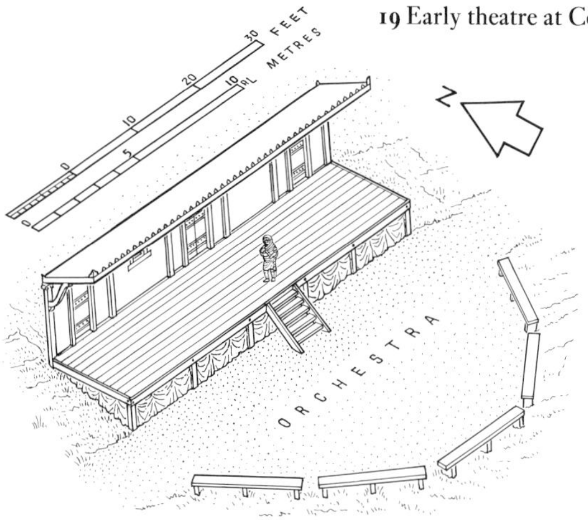

FEET
METRES
ORCHESTRA

19 Early theatre at Corinth, Greece

20 Stage for *phlyax* comedy

As the drama developed the need arose for scenic backgrounds. The early plays of Aeschylus, who is generally credited with the introduction of the *skene* and of painted scenery, required only simple settings, such as an altar with surrounding statues, or a simple building with a single door – possibly similar to the structure which may have existed at Corinth, [19] where extant post-holes could have held timbers supporting a low stage backed only by a wall or screen with entry doors.

This arrangement is similar to the examples seen in the vase paintings [20] of stages used for the *phlyakes* by the players of these popular farces, whose stages were raised on timber posts – sometimes left bare, but more usually hung about with cloths, or with the spaces between the posts filled with painted panels. Steps at the front, varying in number from six to eight, suggest a stage height of from 3 to 4 feet (0.91–1.22m).

The stage was backed by curtains, or a wall containing variously a door, a window, or other openings. It was often roofed by a canopy carried on brackets projecting from posts, sometimes decorated as one of the classical orders. Although the vase paintings depict the stages of strolling players, it is a feature of architectural development that as each building type is superseded by a more advanced design, the replaced type moves slowly down the social scale; so it is likely that these illustrations of later, common stages from Southern Italy may depict the form of stage once in use in the main theatres of Greece during the fifth century BC.

In the Theatre of Dionysus, temporary structures could have been built in front of the new retaining wall to the *orchestra*. A central opening in its upper courses gave access to a timber stair for actors to reach the *orchestra* from the lower level. On the *orchestra* side, a series of grooves are cut in the wall, [21] and it is generally agreed that there were originally five such grooves on either side of the opening; in addition it has been suggested that there were two further rows of holes in the orchestra floor in front of the wall chases.

Similar holes may be seen at Pergamon [22] where temporary scene buildings were erected on an access way between the temple of Dionysus and the market place. Here there is a grid of 64 holes each cut from a solid stone, rebated to take a capping piece into which timber posts could be set. The holes in the front row were not so deep as the others, suggesting that the front posts were of less height and could have supported the front of a low stage. Smaller, usually rounded holes in

21 Theatre of Dionysus, Athens: straight retaining wall with post grooves; stones from earlier wall in foreground

22 Pergamon, Asia Minor: stone sockets for timber posts

FEET
METRES
0
10
20
30
5
10
RL
15
TEMPLE OF DIONYSUS
N
SCENIC HOLES
ORCHESTRA
PROHEDRIAI
ALTAR
RETAINING WALL
WATER CHANNEL
PROHEDRIAI

23 Theatre of Dionysus, Athens, phase II

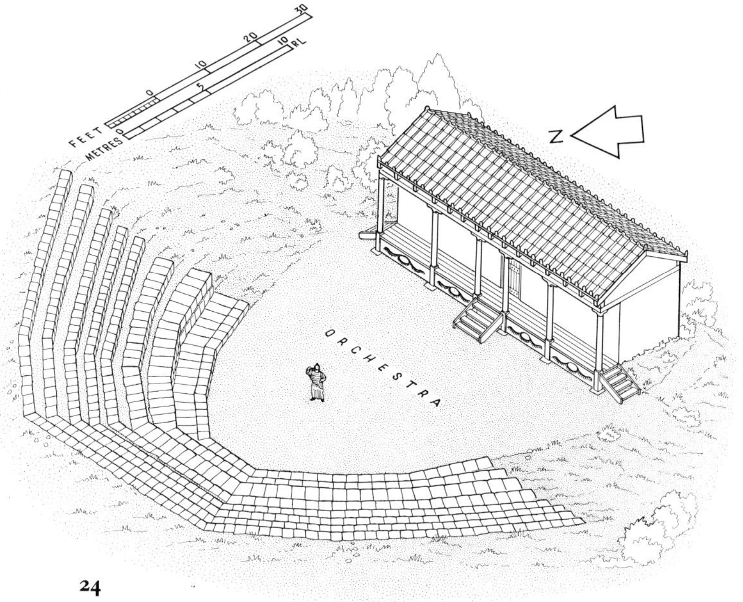
FEET
METRES
0
10
20
30
5
10
RL
N
ORCHESTRA

Oropus, Greece.
24 Early theatre
25 *Skene* with *breccia* wall, left and post holes 2,3,4,5,6

the paving stones may have been bored as and when required for minor variations to the standard scene building.

A simple building with a single door could have been built in the manner shown here. [23] At first temporary changing rooms were perhaps provided at the lower level, but soon after the erection of the wall a long room was built adjoining it, which formed a more permanent backing to the timber structures. The floor of the hall was some 8 feet (2.44m) below orchestra level, with a colonnade on the south side opening onto the temple precinct. A small room at the west end perhaps served as a dressing room and as a store for scenery.

A similar arrangement to that at Corinth may be seen in the *skene* at Oropus, [24] where a wall of rough breccia has survived from an earlier structure. This has a series of holes at an approximate height of 3 feet (0.91m), into which horizontal beams could have been inserted. Further stones with holes in them were partly covered by the front wall of the later *skene*, and posts set in these would have supported the front of a low stage. [25] For the reconstruction, it has been assumed that the breccia wall was the front wall to a small *skene* related to a *cavea* of timber benches, these being replaced at some later date by stone steps, following the same three-sided pattern as the benches.

In many instances temporary timber structures depicted on vases of the fourth century BC [26, 27] have open columned porticoes in front of a rear wall and doorway. Others show an arrangement with a long back wall covered by a tiled roof, and with two projecting wings, with doors beneath the pedimented ends to the roof. The grid pattern of holes at Athens suggests that quite considerable buildings may have been erected, with walls of canvas or wooden panels – *pinakes* – set between timber posts. When this was the case, the enclosed areas could provide additional space for use as dressing rooms.

6
5
4
3
2

25

26

26 Orestes and Iphigenia in Tauris

27

27 Vase painting from Tarentum

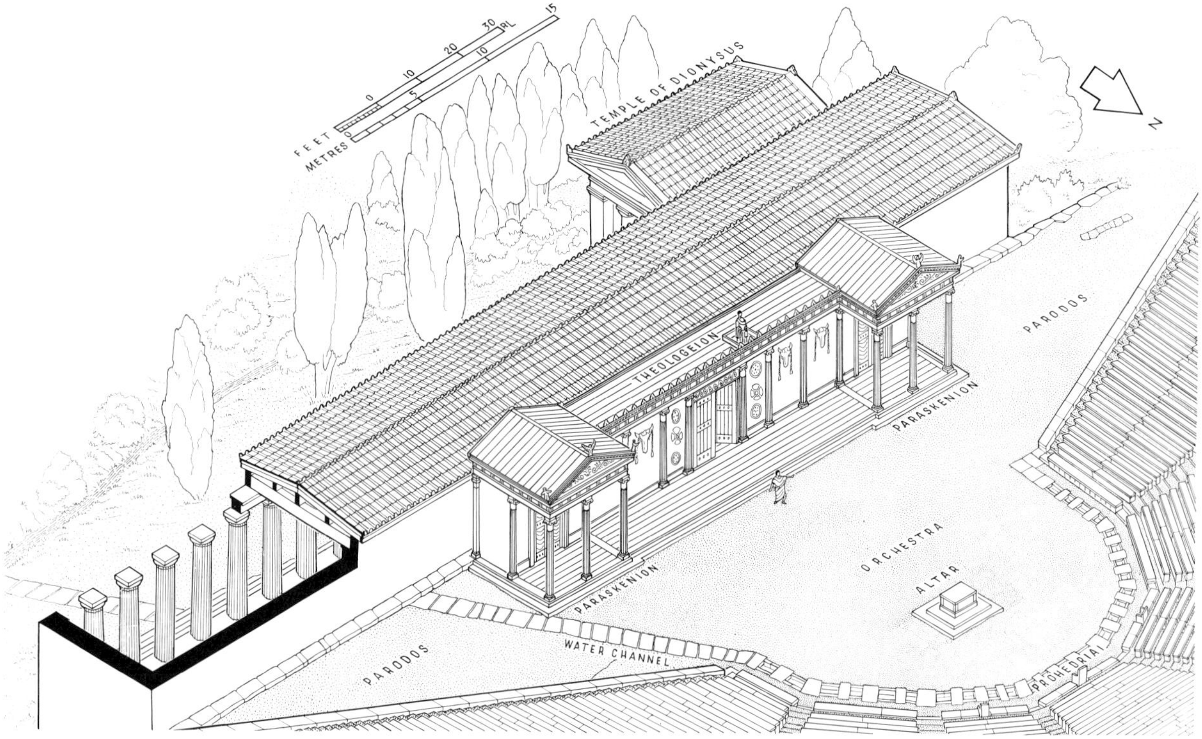
FEET
METRES
TEMPLE OF DIONYSUS
THEOLOGEION
PARASKENION
PARASKENION
PARODOS
PARODOS
ORCHESTRA
ALTAR
WATER CHANNEL
PROHEDRIA
N

28 Theatre of Dionysus, Athens, phase III

The reconstruction [28] is based on the vase paintings, and shows a building with a central opening with double doors, on either side of which an enclosed corridor gives access to two minor doors set within porticoes which project forward at each end – *paraskenia*. A flat roof over the central corridor section, reached by a ladder and trap-door, provided for the possibility of an upper acting area, or *theologeion*, for use by gods and similar personages, whose dramatic ascents or descents could be contrived by a simple crane, or *mechane* (whence the Latin *deus ex machina*).

The central doors could reveal an inner group of actors, or (more likely) a group on a sliding platform – *ekkuklema* – which was pushed out into view as occasion demanded. To make this possible the floor levels of the side porches have been continued across the intervening space to form a low stage. The Roman architect Vitruvius, describing the developed Greek

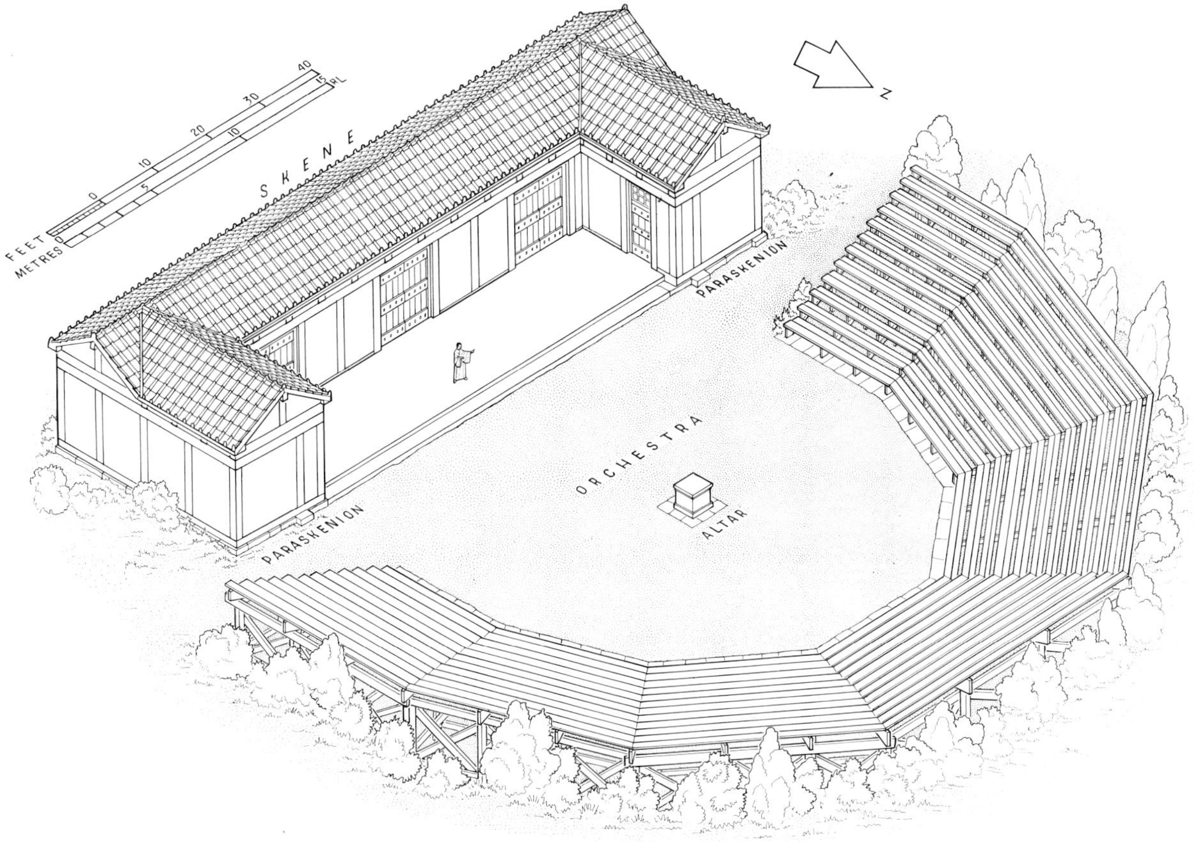
SKENE
FEET
METRES
0
10
20
30
40
0
5
10
15
PARASKENION
ORCHESTRA
ALTAR
PARASKENION
N

theatre, tells us that the central doors represented the palace or home of the protagonist, the side doors representing the homes of other characters.

The theatre at Eretria in its earliest form [29] had a simple timber and mud-brick *skene* with projecting *paraskenia*. There were three doorways in the front wall of the *skene*, while the inner faces of the *paraskenia*, originally open, were later rebuilt with doors at their outer ends, making in all a total of five doors. The rectangular space enclosed by these buildings may have been raised by one or two steps above the level of the *orchestra*. At this time the *cavea* is thought to have been made up of timber seats on scaffolding. Such a *paraskenia* setting must generally have proved eminently suitable, since it was this arrangement which was translated into stone when the Theatre of Dionysus underwent radical alterations, *c*.338–326 BC, under Lycurgus.

29 Eretria, Greece, early theatre

2 Circles, sight-lines, and raised stages

Acoustics and geometry. Athens under Lycurgus. New Comedy. Eretria and the proskenion. Epidaurus. Problems of sight lines. Fan-shaped cavea.

Theories relating to acoustics and the Greek preoccupation with geometry probably led to a desire to develop a perfect form of *cavea*, and in the Lycurgan alterations to the Theatre of Dionysus the timber benches were replaced by stone seating, and, because this material could be more easily and economically cut and shaped than timber, it was possible to arrange these seats as a portion of a circle. Many of the lower seats of this *cavea* may still be seen today.

Two cross gangways – *diazomata* – divided the *cavea*; the upper, on the line of an existing track, may for a while have formed the limits of the theatre, but the seating was eventually extended to the base of the Acropolis, [30] some seats being cut from the rock itself. The front row of seats consisted of individual thrones, those seen today [31] being generally dated to the second or first centuries BC. The circular *orchestra* of beaten earth was surrounded by a water channel 3 feet (0.91m) wide, the large size being necessary to accommodate the extra volume of water running down from the stone *cavea*, which would previously have been absorbed by the earth banking.

Theatre of Dionysus, Athens
30 general view of *cavea*
31 central thrones

30

31

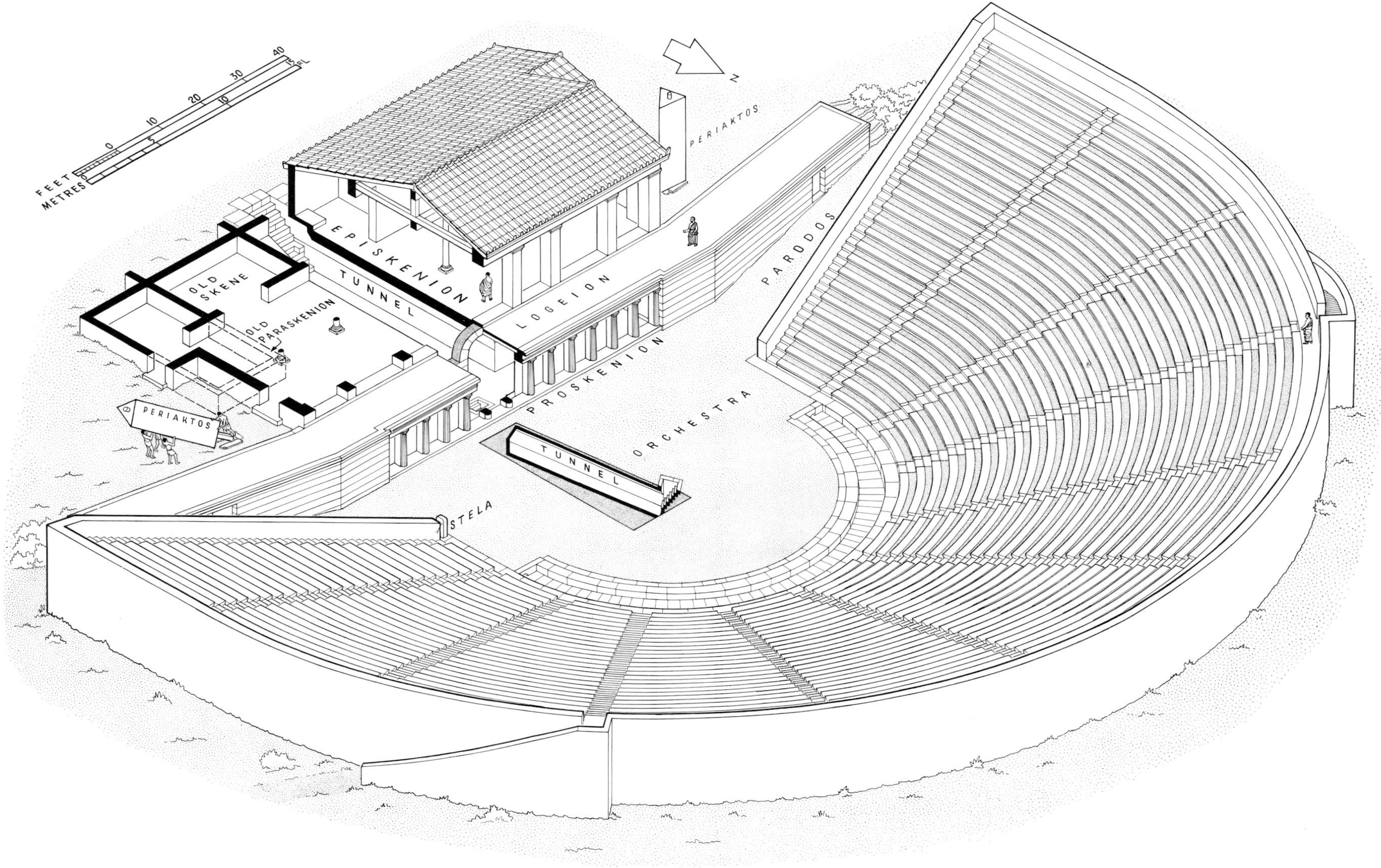
FEET
METRES
0
10
20
30
40
5
10
15
N
PERIAKTOS
EPISKENION
TUNNEL
OLD SKENE
OLD PARASKENION
LOGEION
PARODOS
PROSKENION
PERIAKTOS
ORCHESTRA
TUNNEL
STELA

32 Eretria, Greece. The Hellenistic theatre

18 : Circles, sight-lines, and raised stages

In primitive performances, when song and dance were the main ingredients, the performers could be viewed by a surrounding audience for their three-dimensional qualities, but the introduction of the actor required a directional relationship. In the early 'rectangular' theatres the attention of the audience had been directed towards both chorus and actor, a relationship which was maintained in the 'trapeze'-shaped auditoria, but as these were replaced by the geometrically perfect *cavea*, the focus of the audience was concentrated on the chorus in the circular *orchestra* – at precisely the time when the actors were moving to an area beyond it.

The introduction of scenic backgrounds with a central doorway, and the subsequent development of these into the three-doored *skene* and low stage enclosed by *paraskenia* with their additional doorways, presented the actors with new points of entry. Their use – notably of that most useful of dramatic features the opening centre back – meant that the playing of the actors (as opposed to that of the chorus) began to centre on these areas, and inevitably directed the attention of the audience towards them. A rearrangement was thus needed to restore the clear view which the earlier forms had permitted. That the rectangular *paraskenia* were no longer fully satisfactory in that they obstructed the view is suggested by the arrangement adopted in the theatres of the second century BC at Segesta and Tyndaris, where the end walls of the *paraskenia* were sloped obliquely towards the central doorway, so opening up the view of this enclosed space.

Eretria
33 (*above*) *skene* area
34 (*below*) the *orchestra*

The shift to a more individualistic focus in the tragedies of Euripides (*c*.485–406 BC) was continued in the co-called New Comedy of the later fourth century BC, with its domestic rather than social emphasis. More importance thus devolved on the individual actors at the expense of the chorus, and raised stages were introduced to make it easier for the more remote members of the audience to identify the characters. Early in the third century BC, it became necessary to increase the size of the *cavea* at Eretria [32], which unlike most Greek theatres, was on a flat site, so a new orchestra [34] was excavated and the spoil was heaped up to form an enlarged *cavea*. To support the *skene*, [33] now extended forward, a retaining wall was built, concealed behind a timber framework – *proskenion* – supporting a timber stage – *logeion* – for the actors. They could, however, still appear in the *orchestra* through doors in

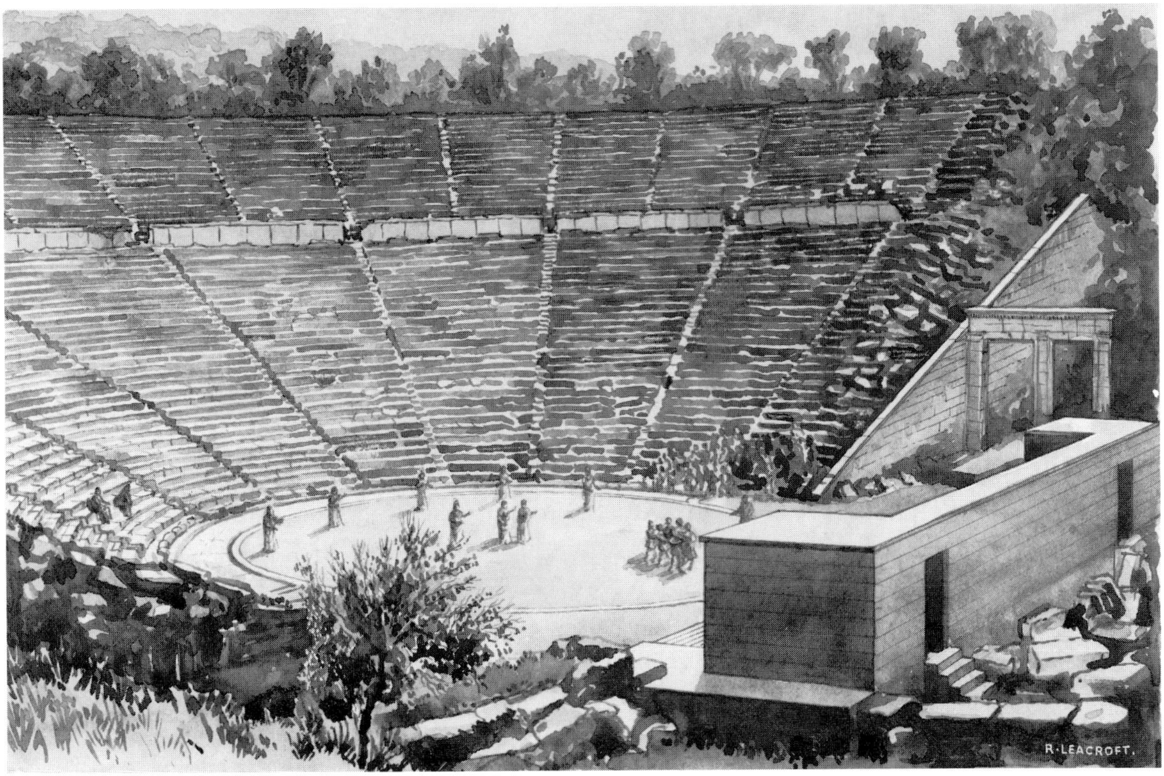
R·LEACROFT.

35 (*above*) Epidaurus, Greece. 1954 production of the *Hippolytus*

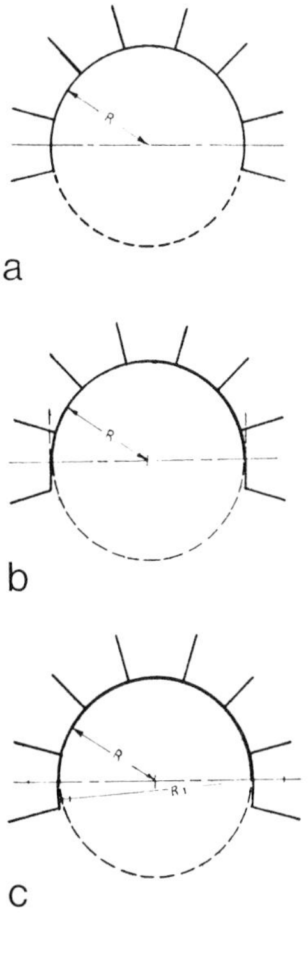
a
b
c

36 *Cavea* ends:
a: Megalopolis
b: Athens
c: Epidaurus

the *proskenion* approached by a tunnel built under the *skene*. The lowering of the *orchestra* meant that the entrance ways – *parodoi* – between the *proskenion* and the surrounding wall, the *analemma*, had to be ramped.

The theatre at Epidaurus, *c*.350–340 BC, [35] is an excellent example of the developed *cavea*, but little is known regarding the original *skene*, which may well have resembled the early building at Eretria. The *cavea* was still focused on the *orchestra*, in spite of the movement of the actors to the space between the *paraskenia*, but some features suggest that the sight-line problems were at least recognized. Unlike the *cavea* at Megalopolis [36a, 37] where the extensions of the seats beyond a semi-circle were continued on the same radius as the main body of the seating, or at Athens [36b] where the extensions were straight lines parallel with one another, the extended portions of seating at Epidaurus [36c, 38] were struck as segments of larger circles with their centres situated in the opposing block of seats or *kerkis*, while the end sections of seating at the upper level were omitted. Such concessions were, however, a compromise, and it is interesting to note

37

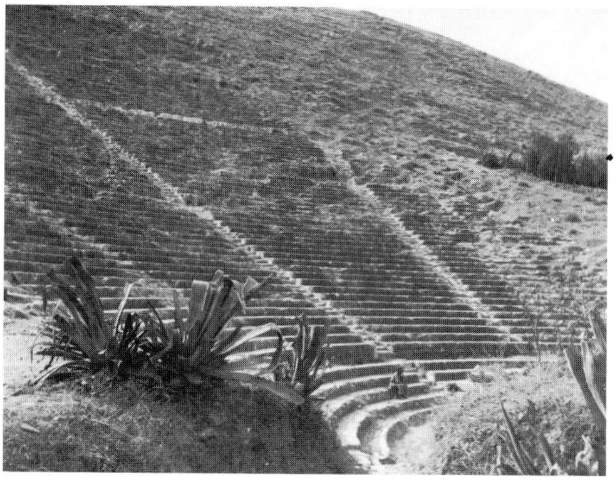

40

38

that the Greeks looked upon the outermost *kerkides* [39] as being the worst seats in the house, and reserved their use to foreigners, latecomers and women.

Ideally, the *cavea* should now have taken a fan-shape, such as may be seen at Argos [40] and Pergamon. [41] But a fan-shaped *cavea*, having the same capacity as a circular one, placed a larger proportion of the audience much further from the actors, and so increased the acoustic problems inherent in all open-air theatres – problems which already required the use of masks in part to reinforce the actors' voices. On balance the typical *cavea* of the developed Greek theatre [42] was probably the most satisfactory solution.

Cavea ends:
37 Megalopolis
38 Epidaurus

39

39 Epidaurus. Restored outer *kerkides*

The fan-shaped *cavea*:
40 Argos
41 Pergamon

41

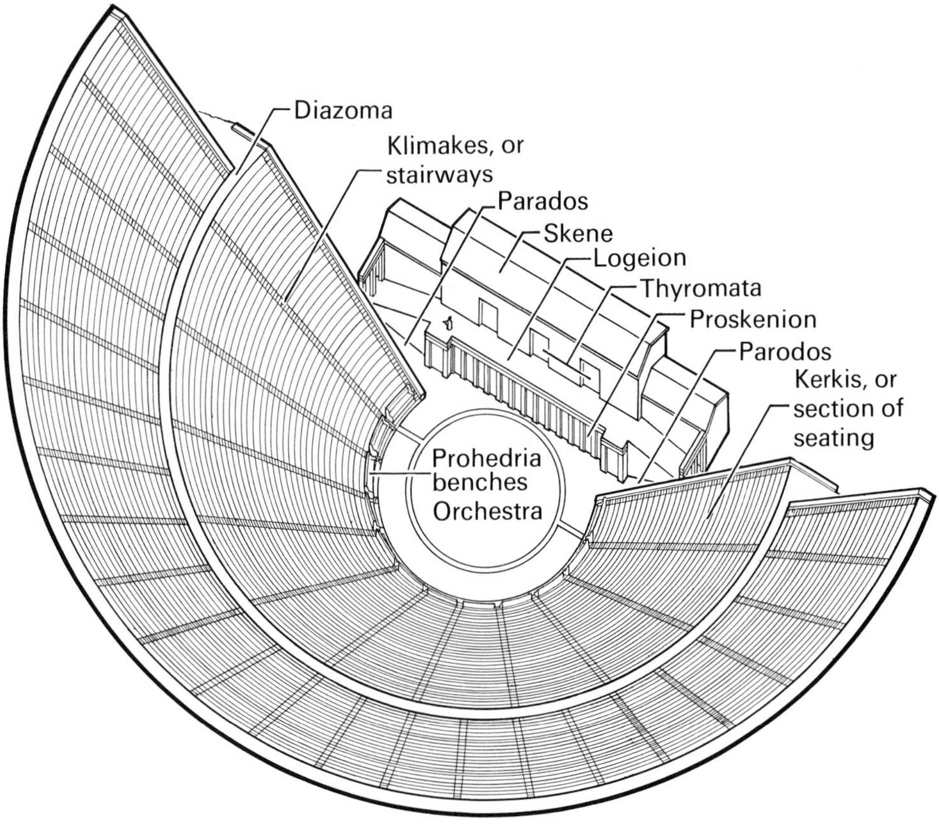
Diazoma
Klimakes, or stairways
Parados
Skene
Logeion
Thyromata
Proskenion
Parodos
Kerkis, or section of seating
Prohedria benches
Orchestra

42 Typical theatre of the early Hellenistic period

3 Stages and scenery

Timber and stone proskenia. Oropus and episkenion, pinakes, and thyromata. The logeion. Hellenistic Priene. Vitruvius' Greek theatre. Perspective and scenic items.

The introduction of timber *proskenia* had brought the actors forward, and placed them within the sight-lines even of those members of the audience seated in the outermost *kerkides*. That this new *proskenion* arrangement was found to be generally acceptable is suggested in the replacement of the timber structures by more permanent stone buildings. But the construction of a *proskenion* concealed the *skene*, with its entrances for the actors, and these now had to be provided at the upper level, giving access to the new raised stages.

At Eretria this had not been necessary, as the extended *skene* remained in place at the upper level, but at Oropus it was necessary to build an upper floor, or *episkenion*. The *proskenion* here [43] was adapted in stone *c.*200 BC, a colonnade [44] of Doric half-columns being attached to piers, with recesses into which painted *pinakes* could be set, and held in place with wedges and bars. A later inscription states that additional *pinakes* were provided at the upper level, which were probably required when the three original doors were replaced by five wider openings, or *thyromata*.

These *thyromata* could well have been used as a form of inner stage, even though this would have reintroduced the sight-line problems: it may be, however, that the *ekkyklema* continued in use to overcome them. When the *skene* at Epidaurus was rebuilt in the second century BC, [45] five *thyromata* were included, but seven are suggested for Eretria, when this was finally rebuilt in stone, [32] with the second, third, and fifth openings being wider than the remainder.

The *logeion* could also be approached from either end; at Eretria the approach-ways were level, but at

43

Oropus: 43 Polygonal stone *cavea*, restored *proskenion* and thrones;
44 *Proskenion* and western *parados*

44

Epidaurus [39] they took the form of ramps leading from ground level. Here, two portals on either side linked the scene building to the *cavea*, one portal leading to the ramp, the other to the *parodos*. The ramps at Sikyon [46] may still be seen, as here they were cut from solid rock.

46 Sikyon, Greece. Rock-cut ramp to *logeion*

45 Late Hellenistic theatre with painted scenery

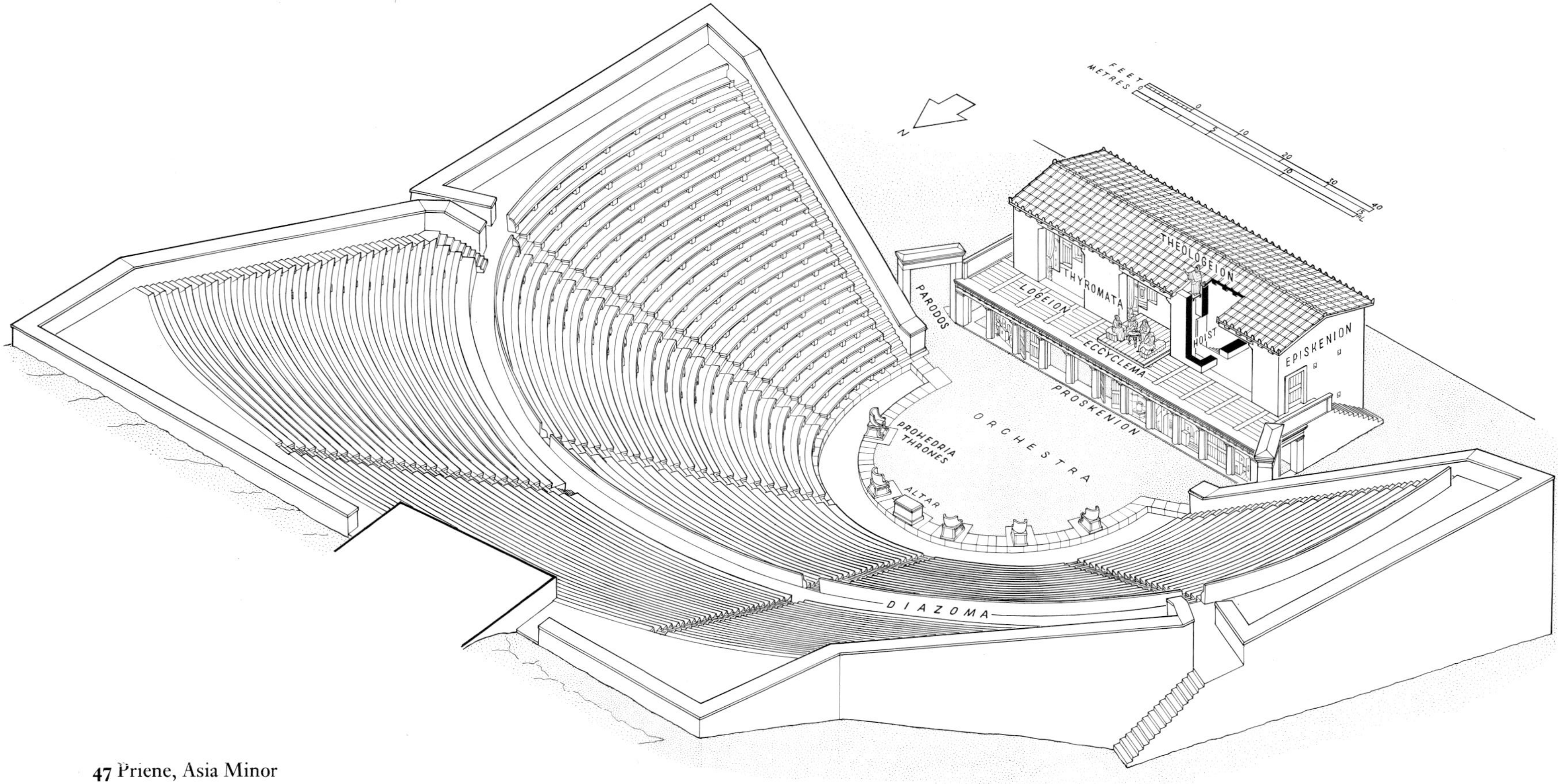
FEET
METRES
0
5
10
20
10
30
40
N
THEOLOGEION
THYROMATA
LOGEION
HOIST
EPISKENION
ECCYCLEMA
PARODOS
PROSKENION
ORCHESTRA
PROHEDRIA
THRONES
ALTAR
DIAZOMA

47 Priene, Asia Minor

48

49

The best remaining example of a theatre of the Hellenistic period (generally dated from the occupation of Athens by Alexander the Great in 336 BC) may still be seen in the city of Priene. [47–50] By the mid-second century BC the theatre had taken on the appearance seen in the reconstruction. The stone *proskenion* had three doors and recesses for *pinakes*, with three *thyromata* above. The *episkenion* was divided into three rooms, with one partition containing a staircase; a shaft at the front end of this could have accommodated a hoist to the roof, which may then have been used as a *theologeion*. Instead of the usual ramps, the ends of the *logeion* returned along the sides of the *skene*, so that entrances could be made from doors in the end walls and by an external flight of steps at the west end.

With the actors appearing in relief on the narrow upper stage, it could be assumed that less importance was now placed on the *orchestra*, a view which is perhaps borne out by the siting of the thrones [51] – both here and at Oropus [43] – inside rather than outside the orchestral circle. But the inclusion of doors in the *proskenion* and the retention of the *parodoi* suggest that the use of the *orchestra* was still of sufficient importance to warrant their inclusion.

At some time the space between the thrones was infilled by *prohedria* benches, and a number of statues were introduced. An additional *prohedria* bench was also constructed in the centre of the fifth row of seating, which would have permitted some dignitaries a better view of the actors on their raised stage.

50

51

Priene, late Hellenistic theatre
48 general view; **49** *logeion*; **50** *proskenion*; **51** orchestra with seats of honour

26 : Stage and scenery

The Greek theatre at Priene corresponds closely to the Greek theatre described by Vitruvius, [52] with its circular *orchestra* and inscribed square, one side of which determines the position of the *proskenion*, while the parallel front wall of the *skene* forms a tangent to the circle; it differs only in having less stairways to its *cavea*. Regarding the height of the stage, Vitruvius says only that 'The height of this "logeum" ought to be not less than ten feet nor more than twelve' – dimensions which vary considerably in practice.

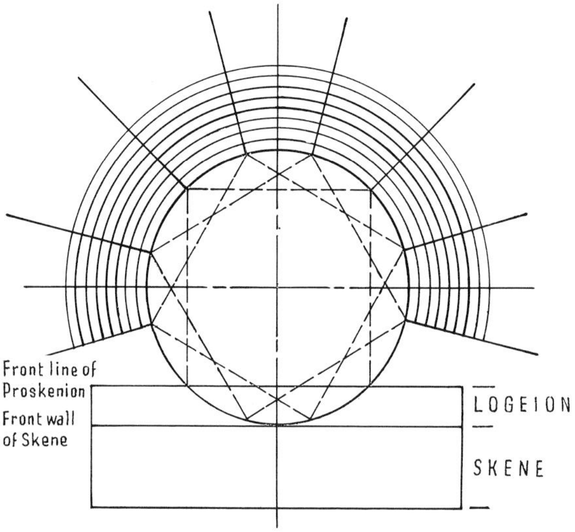
Front line of Proskenion
Front wall of Skene
LOGEION
SKENE

52 Vitruvius' Greek theatre

Painted decorations on the *pinakes* may have been no more than a representation of panelling or decorative symbols, but Vitruvius suggests that scenes may have been painted in perspective 'so that by this deception a faithful representation of the appearance of buildings might be given in painted scenery'. In addition to providing for scenic illusion, he suggests that the *pinakes*, being made of wood, provided an essential source of resonance for the voice in an otherwise stone building. Vitruvius comments on this point in some detail when he considers the use of resonating jars in the Roman theatre, and to the *pinakes* he adds the value of the timber boards forming the floor of the *logeion*.

In speaking of scenery, Vitruvius mentions the use of *periaktoi*, [32] which he describes as 'triangular pieces of machinery which revolve, each having three decorated faces. When the play is to be changed, or when gods enter to the accompaniment of sudden claps of thunder, these may be revolved and present a face differently decorated.' Vertical movement for such characters as gods was provided by the *deus ex machina*, thought to have been some sort of crane situated at the upper level of the *skene*, and possibly reached from the *theologeion*. Ladders may have been set up against the *proskenion* to give access to the *logeion*.

Further scenic items such as tombs, statues, hills, rocks, or cliffs depicted on vase paintings would appear to have been used, at least in the earlier classical theatre, but it is not known if these continued into the Hellenistic period. That some characters may still have performed in the *orchestra* is suggested by the presence at Phillipi, Segesta, and Eretria of underground tunnels [53] (Charon's tunnels, after the ferryman of the underworld), leading from the *skene* to an opening in the *orchestra* floor.

So it will be seen that the Greeks were instrumental in developing many of the actor-audience relationships which were to become the basis of the theatrical experience down to the present day.

53 (*right*) Eretria. Charon's tunnel

4 The Roman theatre

Graeco-Roman theatres. Paved orchestras. Terence, Plautus, and Menander. Pompey's theatre. The Theatre of Marcellus. Mass concrete and the frons scaenae. Aspendos, the Colosseum, and amphitheatres.

In many respects Greek – and more notably Hellenistic – theatres were adapted by the Romans, with the *cavea* continuing the Greek form, but sometimes cut short, and with new stages and scene buildings advanced closer to the audience. The *orchestra* in the Roman theatre was semicircular and paved, unlike that of the Greeks, and where Greek theatres were adapted it is normal to find that the *orchestra* had not only been paved, but was also enclosed by a parapet. [54–56] This protected the audience when the *orchestra* was used for gladiatorial fights, or was flooded for nautical spectacles – *naumachiae* – or water ballets. In some instances the front seats were removed to give the impression that the level of the *orchestra* had been dropped to form a sunken area, as at Miletus. [57]

From the middle of the third century BC, Greek tragedies and comedies were being translated and adapted for presentation to the Romans, the writers Plautus and Terence basing some of their work on the New Comedies of the Greek Menander. But the popular, farcical, and acrobatic entertainments, which had existed alongside 'serious' drama in ancient Greece, now tended to become the dominant forms of theatre in the hands of the *mimi* – troupes of itinerant players, including women, who set up their portable wooden stages wherever they could gather an audience.

In 155BC, when it was intended to build a stone theatre near the Palatine in Rome, its completion was prevented; and it has been suggested that seating at the temporary theatres was also denied – the spectators being forced to stand on the scaffolding provided, on the premise that if they were allowed to sit they would idle away whole days in the theatre. Whatever the truth of the matter, no theatres with permanent stone seating

The paved Roman *orchestra* and protective walls: **54** Theatre of Dionysus, Athens

55 Delphi

28 : The Roman theatre

56 Perge, Asia Minor. Protective balustrade

57 Miletus, Asia Minor. 'Sunken *orchestra*'

58 Theatre of Pompey, Rome, 55 BC

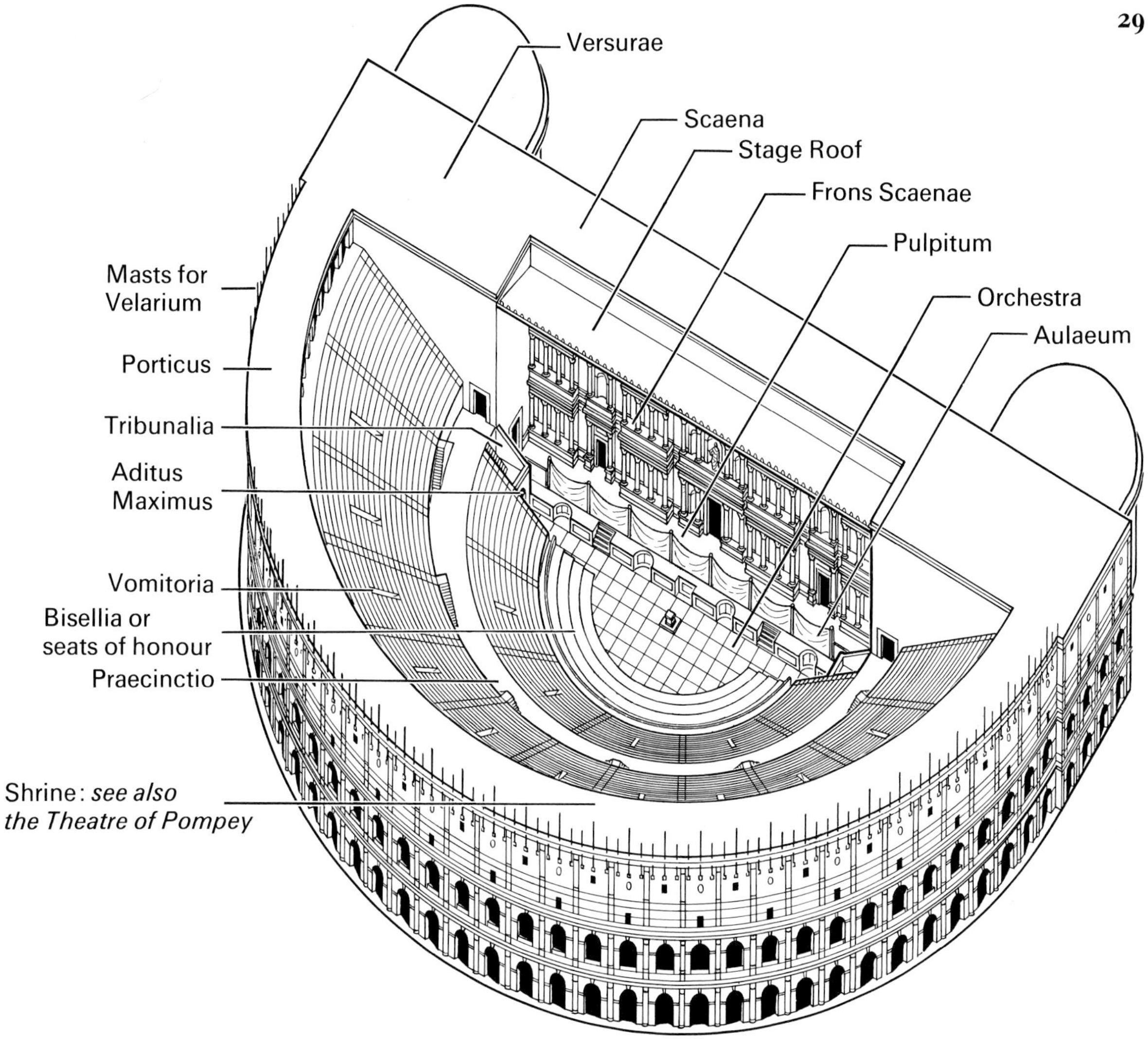
Versurae
Scaena
Stage Roof
Frons Scaenae
Pulpitum
Orchestra
Aulaeum
Masts for Velarium
Porticus
Tribunalia
Aditus Maximus
Vomitoria
Bisellia or seats of honour
Praecinctio
Shrine: *see also the Theatre of Pompey*

59 Theatre of Marcellus, Rome, 13–11 BC

were erected in Rome until 55 BC, when the theatre of Pompey [58] was constructed with a temple to Venus Victrix at the upper level of the *cavea* on its central axis, approached by a wide flight of steps.

Evidence of Pompey's theatre is seen on a fragment of the Severan marble plan of Rome. This shows a semicircular *cavea* divided by a *diazoma* or *praecinctio* into two parts, which are further subdivided into sixteen wedges. There is no indication of a wide flight of steps, and it is possible that the whole semicircle of seats was so described as a means of overcoming the prohibition on stone seating. Tertullian describes the theatre as a temple of Venus, 'under which we have placed steps for watching games'.

A reconstruction of the theatre of Marcellus [59] illustrates the essential differences between the Greek and Roman theatres. Unlike the Greeks, the Romans normally built their theatres on flat sites, and their answer to the problem thus created was to unify the two parts of the theatre – the scene building or *scaena*, and the *cavea* or auditorium – into a single architectural unit. The auditorium, in the form of a semicircle, was built on a series of arches and barrel-vaults, an arrangement made possible by the use of mass concrete. This hollow, vaulted, structure had an added advantage in that it permitted ready access for the audience to the main areas of seating by means of arched openings, or *vomitoria*. [60]

30 : The Roman Theatre

60 Aspendos, Asia Minor. Vaulted passage

61 Reconstruction based on the theatre of Aspendos

The Roman stage was long and narrow, [61] backed by the richly decorated *frons scaenae* – the front wall of the *scaena,* which housed the dressing rooms, and had from three to five doorways. The main, central door – *aula regia* – played a similar role to that in the Greek theatre, the side doors – *hospitalia* – representing the homes of minor characters. Further doorways gave access to the ends of the stage from enclosing side wings, or *versurae*, while a roof over the stage protected the actors and the sculptured and painted *frons scaenae* from the sun and rain.

In some theatres a trench at the front of the stage provided space into which a curtain – *aulaeum* – could be lowered on telescoping posts, and such curtains were apparently decorated with paintings appropriate to the play. Smaller curtains, or *siparia*, were used on the stage, possibly for purposes of concealment during the action of the play, or to hide a particular scenic object until it was required.

Both stage and stage roof were of timber, and painted panels added further and varied decoration to the *frons scaenae*, while on occasions realistic scenery would also appear to have been used. The height of the stage was seldom more than 5 feet (1.52m), being restricted by the need for the audience, sometimes seated in the semicircular *orchestra*, to see the actors. The entry way – *aditus maximus* – to the *orchestra* on either side was roofed with a barrel-vault, and a balcony was provided above for the magistrates financing the performance. A *porticus* or colonnade surrounded the upper levels of the *cavea*, and usually contained a small temple on its central axis, reminding us that the Roman theatre,

62 Aspendos. Second century AD theatre

like the Greek had a religious function. The whole building was enclosed by a fine facade, with three levels of arched openings articulated by the three Roman orders.

A well-preserved variant on the developed Roman theatre is to be seen at Aspendos, [62] where the *cavea* is set on a hillside in the Greek manner, but with the upper walls to the *cavea* and the scene building following the Roman pattern. While small theatres like that at Pompeii, *c.*75 BC, were permanently roofed, larger theatres were open to the sky, the audience being protected from the weather by a canvas *velarium* suspended from masts around the circumference of the theatre.

Theatrical entertainments were also staged in amphitheatres, although their principal use was for gladiatorial contests, animal baiting, and similar amusements. The Colosseum in Rome and other late amphitheatres [63] were equipped with rooms and passages below the level of the arena, with lifts to raise scenic devices to ground level. They were oval in shape, with tiers of seating enclosing the arena, from which they were separated by a parapet. Simpler, earth-banked amphitheatres were built outside many towns in the Roman Empire: employed by the army for training purposes, they could also be used for entertainment. They underline well the difference between the theatres, with their semi-directional relationship of actor and audience, and the total surround of an audience related to the three-dimensional activities of the participants in the arena.

63 Verona, Italy. Amphitheatre

5 Churches, places, and pageants

Circular rounds. The Quem Quaeritis trope. Resurrection and Jeu d'Adam. Brunelleschi and the Mystery of Elche. The Martyrdom of S. Appollonia. Mansions and 'places'. The Cornish Ordinalia. Valenciennes. The Mysteries of Villingen and Lucerne. Scaffolds and pageants. Ballet Comique de la Reyne. Medieval manor houses. Penshurst.

With the fall of the Roman Empire during the third and fourth centuries AD, it is often held that organized theatre in Western Europe fell into decay and finally disuse, but it is virtually certain that theatrical performances of one form or another continued throughout the so-called Dark Ages, and it is only the lack of information which has led historians to suggest a total disintegration of organized theatre. In England, a fan-shaped structure supporting seating found at Yeavering in Northumberland was certainly a place of assembly, and could have been used for some form of theatrical performance, while circular rounds, found in various parts of the country, (notably at St. Just and Perranzabuloe in Cornwall), may have continued the traditions set by the amphitheatres of Roman Britain. As late as 1602, Richard Carew was to describe the use of such rounds for the presentation of miracle plays, equipped with 'devils and devices', which had their birth in the Christian church.

Because literacy was limited to the clergy, most of our written evidence concerning the development of a 'serious' medieval drama comes from ecclesiastical sources. Thus, the earliest example we have of a quasi-dramatic presentation is that of the *Quem Quaeritis* trope – a sung dialogue occurring during the Easter Mass – since directions for its staging were given in the *Concordia Regularis* written during the tenth century AD by Ethelwold, Bishop of Winchester. From these early beginnings, further portions of the services developed into plays performed within churches, many being presented in a most realistic and spectacular manner, while in others simple scenic devices sufficed.

A twelfth-century play of the *Resurrection* suggests that the play was performed in various parts of the church building, and as the choir was separated from the public areas of the church by a rood screen, it may perhaps be argued that the performance would have been given within the nave. The prologue details the places of action known as *houses* or *mansions* – some like Paradise and Emmaus, being described as raised, presumably so that the actors might be seen above the heads of a standing audience.

A twelfth-century Anglo-Norman play, *Jeu d'Adam*, requires that 'Paradise be set up in a somewhat lofty place', be set with 'curtains and silken hangings', and be equipped with 'fragrant flowers and leaves' and 'diverse trees and hanging fruit'. By this time, such plays had moved outside the church, as is suggested by the directions that 'the Figure shall go back into the church' and 'the devils shall go forth, and run to and fro in the square'.

In 1493 there are records of a performance given on a scaffold erected in the nave of the Church of the Annunciation in Florence, the congregation crowding round to marvel at the Throne of God surrounded by hundreds of lights, with children dressed as angels playing on cymbals, flutes, and harps. A special contrivance permitted the angel Gabriel to descend from Heaven, and there were other devices designed by Filippo Brunelleschi – 'although some assert that they were introduced long before' – for use in the church of S. Felice, Florence.

A domed heaven, with lights and small children dressed as angels, was hung from the rafters of the church,

Mystery of Elche, Spain
64 *araceli*; 65 *granada*

64

65

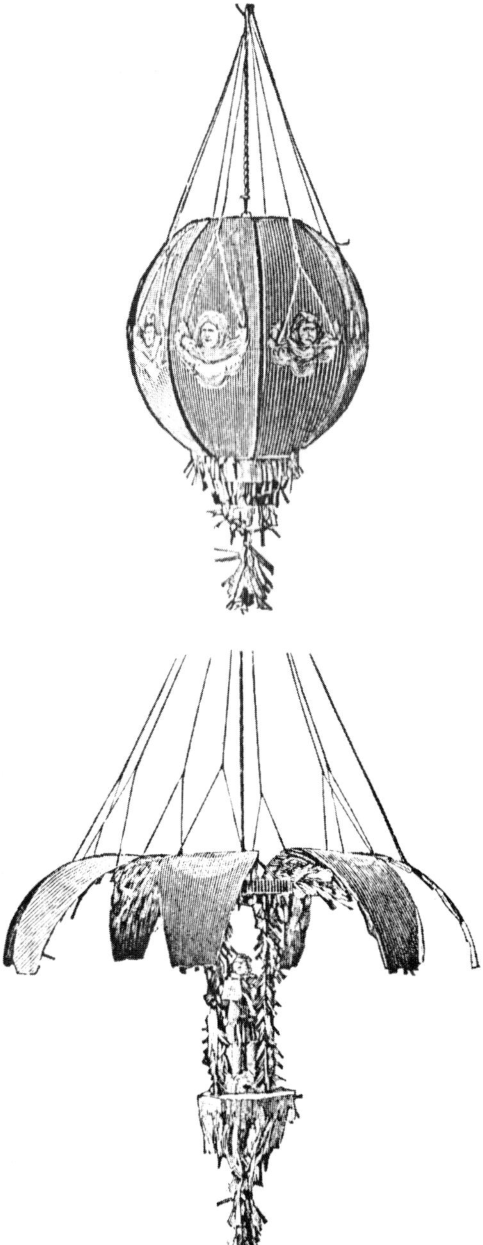

and from this descended a copper ball containing a youth costumed as an angel. The ball settled on a throne raised on steps above a stage, on which the main performance took place, and the angel then stepped down and approached other characters on the stage. Just such machines may be seen in use today in the performances of the Mystery presented in the Church of Santa Maria in Elche, Spain.

The play is largely performed on a raised stage set beneath the dome, and approached down the length of the nave. High above the stage the dome is floored in to provide a 'machine room'. The underside is lined with cloth painted to represent heaven and an opening allows for the passage of devices: the *Araceli* [64] to which actors are lashed, and the *Granada* [65], or golden pomegranate, which opens in sections to reveal an angel. Ropes bound with blue cloth are fastened to windlasses within the dome, which are used to lower and raise these machines.

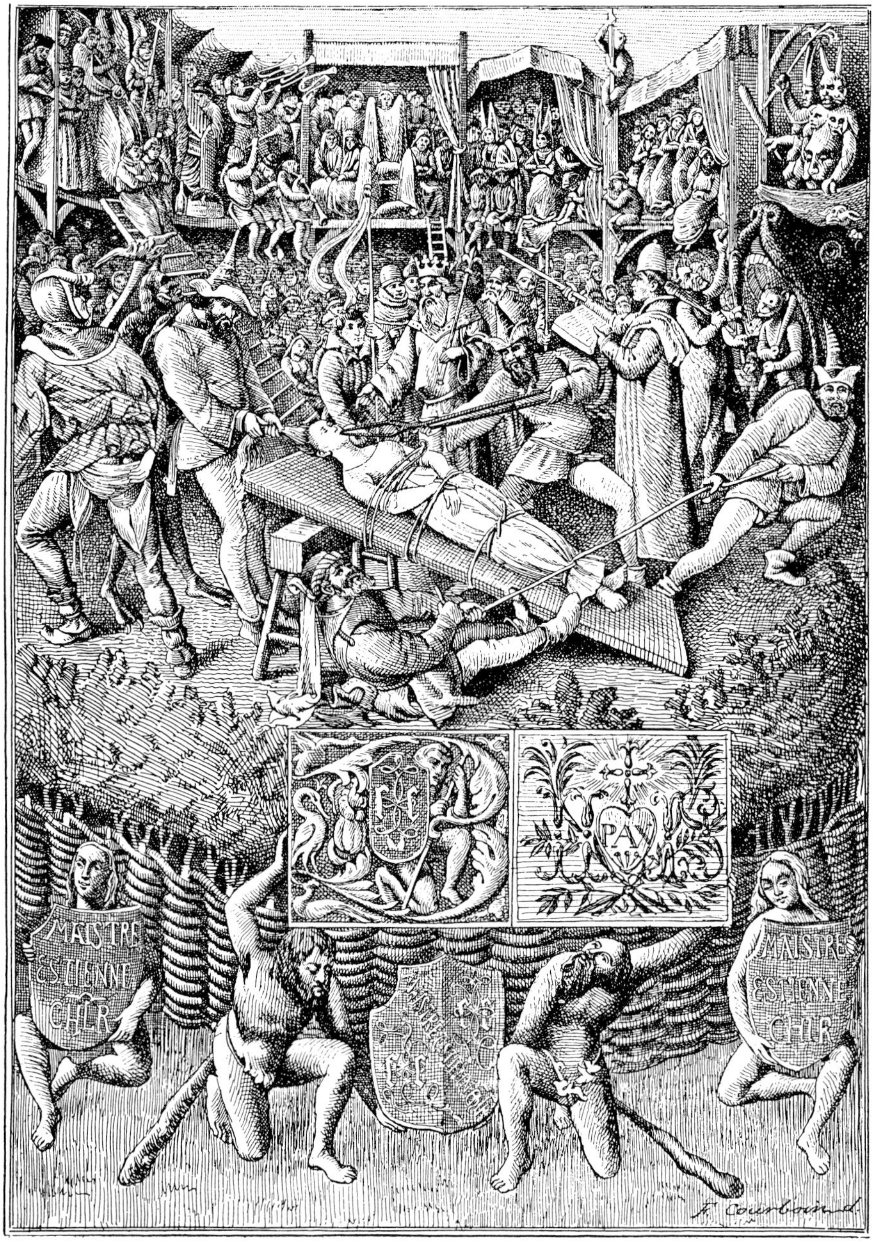
MAISTRE
ESTIENNE
CHLR
PAX
MAISTRE
ESTIENNE
CHLR

66 The Martyrdom of S. Apollonia

The mid-fifteenth century illustration of the *Martyrdom of S. Apollonia* [66] shows each 'house' or 'mansion' set on its own raised stage. Steps lead down from two of these to the arena, 'place' or *platea* – the generalized playing area (as distinguished from the localized 'mansions'), which is circular and enclosed by a wattle fence and hedge. Actors not immediately engaged in the performance sit in their mansions, while the main action proceeds in the 'place', surrounded by the audience (those in the foreground have probably been omitted by the artist so that the action may be seen).

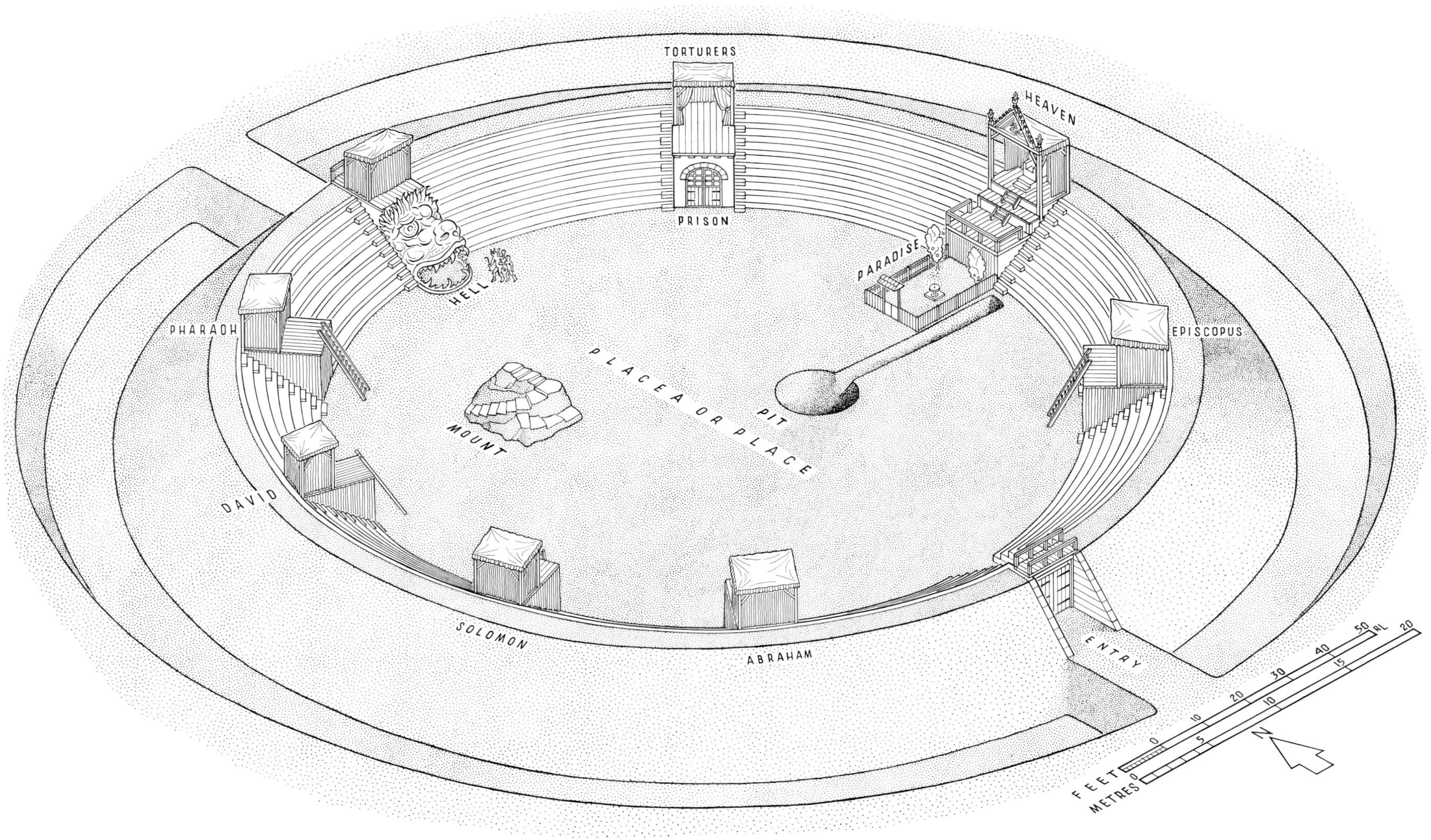
TORTURERS
HEAVEN
PRISON
PARADISE
HELL
PHARAOH
EPISCOPUS
PLACEA OR PLACE
PIT
MOUNT
DAVID
SOLOMON
ABRAHAM
ENTRY
FEET
METRES
0
10
20
30
40
50
0
5
10
15
20
N

67 Piran Round, Cornwall. Day One of the Cornish *Ordinalia*

A similar disposition is shown in the reconstruction of the arrangements for the first of the three-day Cornish *Ordinalia* [67] as it may have been staged in the Piran Round near Perranzabuloe. [68] Houses are arranged on a raised stage in the illustration of the *Mystère de la Passion* at Valenciennes, [69] staged on a platform in the grounds of the chateau of the Duke of Arschot in 1547. Here the spectacle lasted for 25 days, and the mansions were changed as the drama progressed. In addition to the architectural 'houses', there were also built-up representations of hills, countryside, and distant towns.

A plan, *c.*1585–1600, [70] shows the arrangement of the various places of action for the Mystery given in the main square at Villingen. The space is divided into three parts, with arched openings reminiscent of the divisions of a church. The setting for the Mystery in and around the market square at Lucerne [71] is shown in drawings of 1583 depicting the first and second days' performances. Heaven is at one end, and at the other is a large, raised stage, approached from the 'place' by steps, with Hell to one side. Practical mansions are set on the stage and in the square, which is enclosed by additional stations – open, fenced platforms, whose use

68 Piran Round

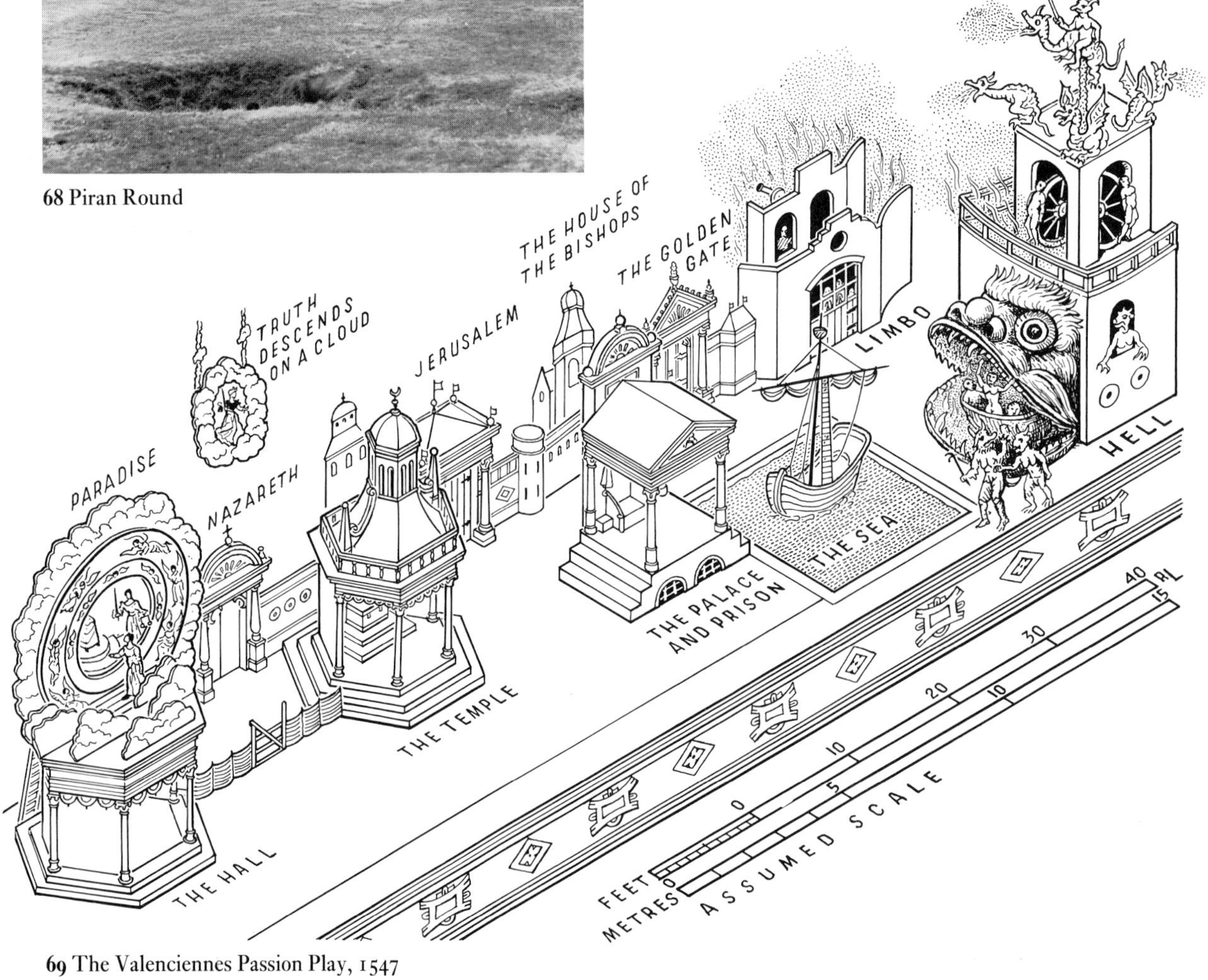
PARADISE
NAZARETH
TRUTH DESCENDS ON A CLOUD
JERUSALEM
THE HOUSE OF THE BISHOPS
THE GOLDEN GATE
LIMBO
HELL
THE SEA
THE PALACE AND PRISON
THE TEMPLE
THE HALL
FEET
METRES
ASSUMED SCALE

69 The Valenciennes Passion Play, 1547

70 The Villingen Passion

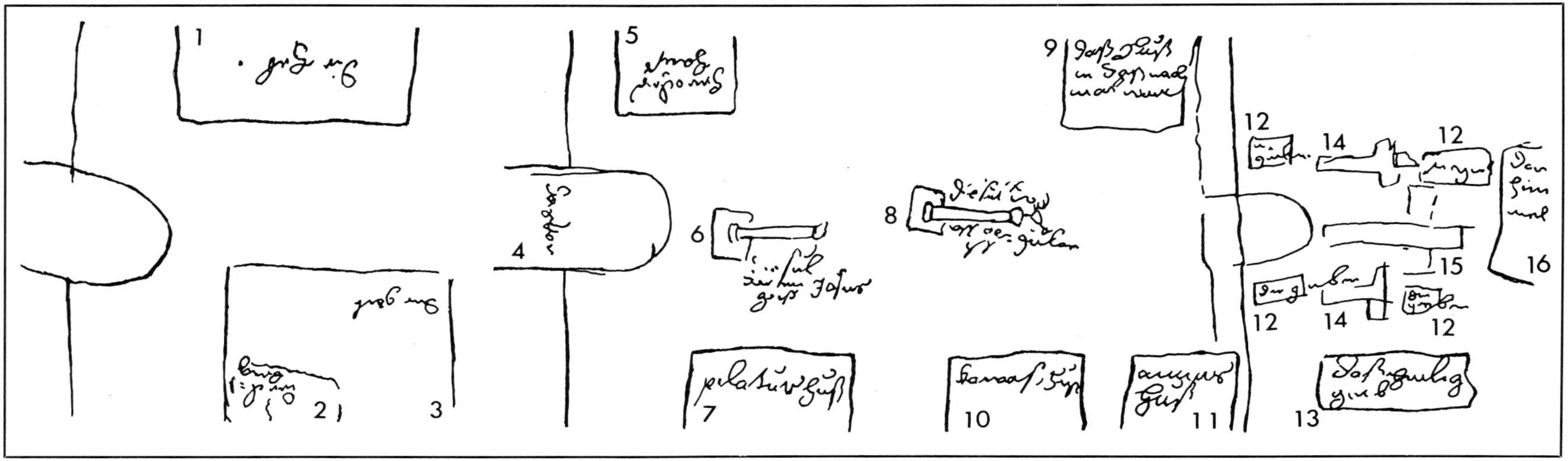
1
2
3
4
5
6
7
8
9
10
11
12
13
14
15
16

1: Hell 2: Mount of Olives 3: Garden of Gethsemane 4: The Door 5: Herod's Palace 6: Pillar of scourging 7: Pilate's Palace 8: Pillar of the Cock 9: House of the Last Supper 10: House of Caiaphas 11: House of Annas 12: Graves from which the dead arise 13: Holy Sepulchre 14: The Thieves crosses 15: The Cross of Christ 16: Heaven

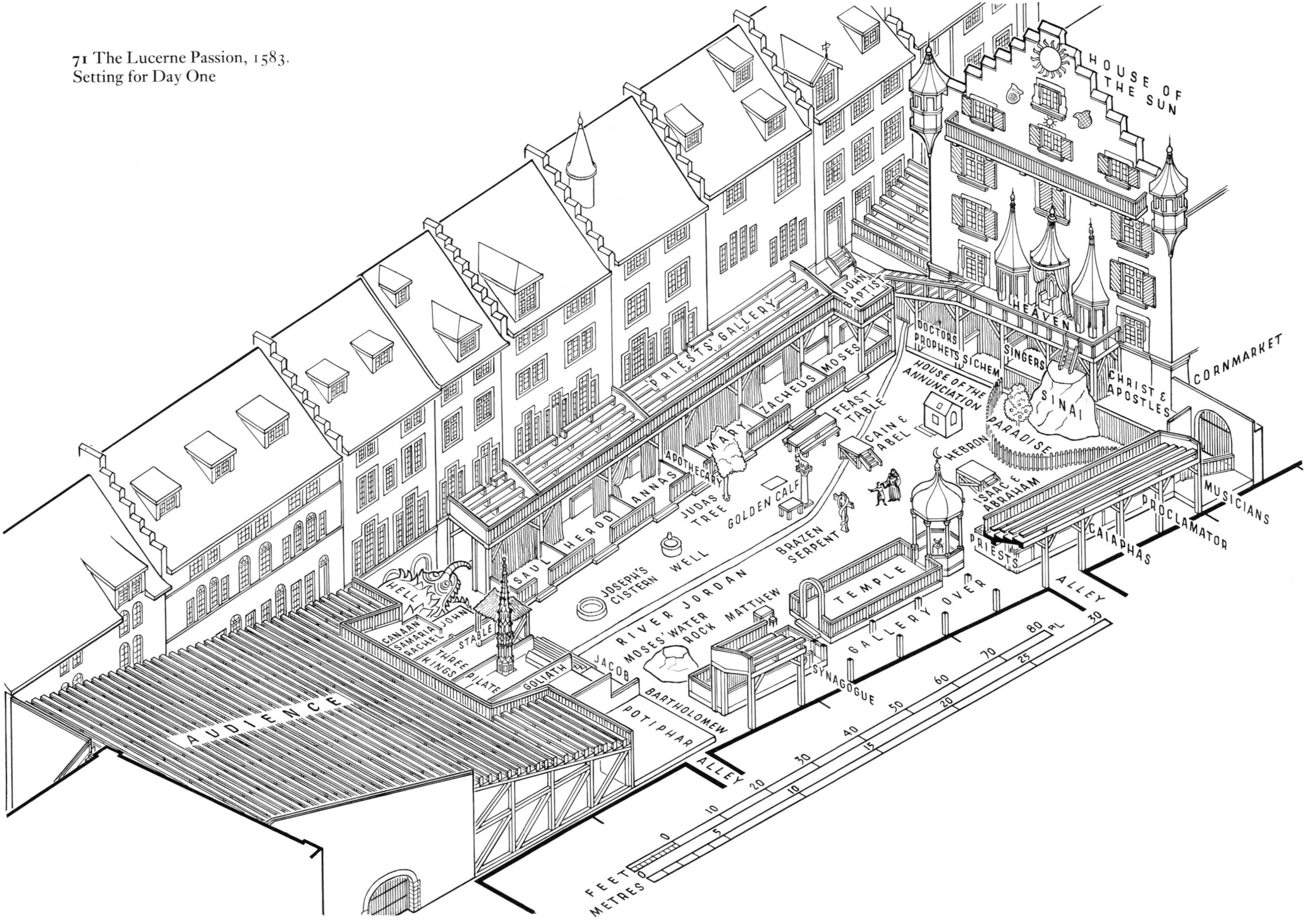
HOUSE OF THE SUN
CORNMARKET
CHRIST & APOSTLES
HEAVEN
SINGERS
SICHEM
DOCTORS
PROPHETS
HOUSE OF THE ANNUNCIATION
SINAI
PARADISE
JOHN BAPTIST
PRIESTS' GALLERY
MOSES
ZACHEUS
FEAST TABLE
CAIN & ABEL
HEBRON
MARY
APOTHECARY
ANNAS
JUDAS TREE
GOLDEN CALF
ISAAC & ABRAHAM
MUSICIANS
PROCLAMATOR
CAIAPHAS
PRIESTS
HEROD
SAUL
JOSEPH'S CISTERN
WELL
BRAZEN SERPENT
TEMPLE
ALLEY
HELL
CANAAN
SAMARIA
RACHEL
JOHN
STABLE
THREE KINGS
PILATE
GOLIATH
JACOB
RIVER JORDAN
MOSES' WATER ROCK
MATTHEW
GALLERY OVER
SYNAGOGUE
BARTHOLOMEW
POTIPHAR
ALLEY
AUDIENCE
FEET
METRES
0 10 20 30 40 50 60 70 80
0 5 10 15 20 25 30

71 The Lucerne Passion, 1583.
Setting for Day One

varied from day to day. Scaffolds for the audience enclosed the 'place', with one main block of seating giving a directional view of the performances.

The *platea* or 'place' could take on the character of whichever mansion or station was in use, in addition to providing space for the activities of devils and other characters, or for processions from one stage to the next. Such an arrangement of scenic units is usually called a 'simultaneous setting'.

A further variant was to make each of the mansions mobile, building them on 'pageant' wagons so that they could move from place to place within the city or town. [72, 73] As one play was completed, the pageant was wheeled to the next station and its place taken by another. Information concerning these pageants is limited to a description by the sixteenth-century Archdeacon Rogers who writes of them (possibly at second-hand) as being enclosed below and open above. Stage directions suggest that the open space could be curtained so that performers might be concealed or revealed during the action of the play.

RL

72 (*right*) A medieval pageant
73 Isabella's Triumph, 1615

74 *Ballet comique de la Reyne*

Further directions indicate that provision for ascents to Heaven and descents to Hell were made within the different structures, which varied from Noah's Ark to Hell's Mouth. While descents could be made into the curtained space below, ascents into Heaven would require a roof, or even an upper stage. The plays were presented with realistic detail: earthquakes, thunderbolts, miracles, floods, and fires were common features, the Mouth of Hell being constructed with massive jaws through which the devils prodded the damned amid smoke and flames belching forth.

The space around the pageant was also used by the actors, Herod, for example, raging both on the pageant and in the street. The devils, too, ran among the audience and played practical jokes on them. Some authorities suggest that more than one pageant was in use at each staging point at the same time; it is possible that these were grouped around an open stage set before the scaffolding.

Entertainments were also given in the halls of palaces and houses, often here in the form of the more secular 'interludes' of the later middle ages, performed by itinerant professional players. An illustration of the *Ballet Comique de la Reyne* [74] shows a performance in the Petit Bourbon in Paris on 15 October 1591. The king, seated at one end of the hall, faced a Garden of Circe, with two mansions arranged on either side of the open floor – the plain, one representing a 'gilded vault for musicians', the other the 'Grove of Pan', while between the two, hanging from the roof, was a cloud. The size of the hall permitting, pageants were introduced into the entertainments, as happened on the occasion of the wedding of Prince Arthur and Katherine of Aragon in 1501, when three great pageants were wheeled into Westminster Hall representing a castle, a ship sailing on the sea, and a great hill.

In the smaller halls forming the nucleus of most medieval manor houses the entertainment was simpler. The average hall had a raised dais at the upper end on which the family sat at a table set across the width of the hall. At the lower end a passage crossed the hall from an outer to an inner court, separated from the hall by a screen with two openings. This 'screens' passage was ceiled just above head height, the space above being open to the hall in the form of a gallery. Tables for the retainers were set lengthwise in the body of the hall.

For performances these tables and benches could be moved to either side to leave an open plain, as may be seen in the model of Penshurst.[75] The doorways in the screens were used by the performers as mansions, or simply for their entrances and exits, and additional mansions could be set around the plain. When a pageant could not be brought into a hall, it became necessary to make other arrangements for ascents, descents, or discovery spaces, and so raised stages, with trap-doors, were located adjoining the screens, the whole disguised in any appropriate manner. [76–78]

The medieval theatre, then, can be seen to present a number of different actor-audience relationships in addition to those introduced in the classical period. In the church and market place, it would seem that audience and performers sometimes mixed freely in the open space, the spectators moving from place to place as the action of the play moved from one raised mansion to another, with actors descending to an open space at ground level where they performed surrounded by their audience.

Some of the simultaneous settings, however, were also presented on raised platforms, before an audience who all faced in one direction towards the stage, and the basis for a similar directional relationship is to be seen in the arrangements in the medieval halls where the stages were set up facing the lord of the manor on his dais at the upper end of the hall. Raised stages not only made the actors visible above the heads of a standing audience, but also provided the mechanics of vertical movement.

75

76

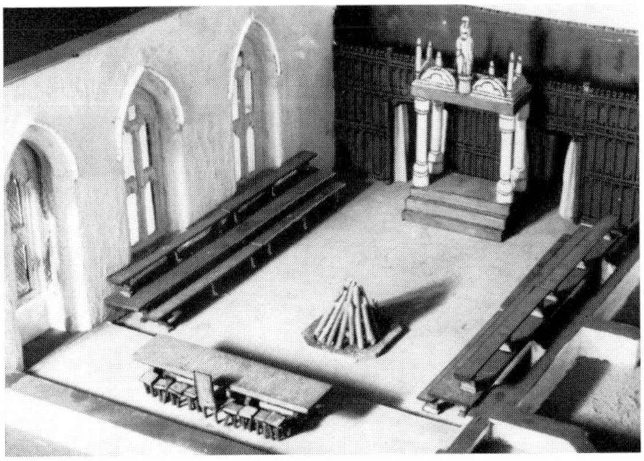

The Great Hall, Penshurst, Kent
75 open *platea* before the screens
76 with small stage
77 stage in the form of a 'city'
78 practical mansions and curtained throne

77

78

6 Classical rebirth and the perspective scene

Roman Academies. Revivals of Terence and Plautus. Vitruvius and Sebastiano Serlio. Mansions and the perspective scene. Palladio and the Teatro Olimpico, Vicenza. Scamozzi and Sabbioneta. Nicola Sabbattini. The Commedia dell'Arte.

Up to the thirteenth century, the Church had been largely responsible for thought and learning, but during the fourteenth century the ideas of the scholars of Ancient Greece and Rome were reborn in Italy. It became fashionable for the princes of the various states to surround themselves with as many treasures from the ancient world as they could lay their hands on, and to collect about them learned men, architects, and artists, who were – or who considered themselves to be – authorities on classical ideas.

While church performances continued, and the popular forms of theatre were enjoyed in the market place, a different form of theatrical presentation thus began to develop for the productions staged by princes at their courts, or under the patronage of learned societies like the mid-fifteenth-century Roman Academy of Pomponius Laetus.

The discovery in 1427 of a manuscript including comedies by Plautus and Terence led to attempts to present these and other classical plays in what was thought to be their original manner, based on interpretations of the descriptions of Greek and Roman theatres by Vitruvius. But it must be appreciated that no drawings had survived relating to his writings, and the Renaissance designers had to base their reconstructions on the text alone, interpreted in terms of the contemporary medieval forms of setting.

The *Menaechmi* of Plautus was thus performed in Ferrara in 1491 with scenery consisting of four to five houses, each with a door and a window, an arrangement which suggests the use of medieval-style mansions. [79] But in 1513 the followers of Laetus presented a performance of the *Poenulus* in Rome on a stage which was

almost a hundred feet wide, twenty-four feet deep and about eight feet high. . . . At the back of the stage was a highly decorated arcade screen divided into five sections by columns with gilded bases and capitals, each section framing an opening covered with curtains of gold cloth. Above was a frieze of beautiful paintings and a gilded cornice. At the ends of the screen were two great towers with doors, one marked 'via ad forum'.

Obviously this setting was an attempt to reproduce what was thought to be the correct appearance of a Roman theatre. Illustrations to various editions of Terence [80] show arrangements of similar arcade screens, more reminiscent of Hellenistic *thyromata* than of the doorways of a Roman *frons scaenae*. Each opening is curtained, with a name displayed above indicating the place it was intended to represent. When curtains are shown open, it appears that each interior was decorated to represent the locale it depicted, and actors are shown within.

Many manuscript copies of Vitruvius are known to have been available between the ninth century and 1485, when a copy from the Convent of St. Gall was printed and published in Rome. Vitruvius described

three kinds of scenes, one called the tragic, second, the comic, third, the satyric. Their decorations are different and unlike each other in scheme. Tragic scenes are delineated with columns, pediments, statues, and other objects suited to kings. Comic scenes exhibit private dwellings, with balconies and views representing rows of windows, after the manner of ordinary dwellings. Satyric scenes are decorated with trees, caverns, mountains, and other rustic objects delineated in landscape style.

79 Medieval mansions, after Tèrence des Ducs

The perfection of the science of perspective in the early fifteenth century provided artists and architects with a means of representing scenes in a limited space, either on a single or on multiple canvas screens; and in a book on perspective published in 1545, Sebastiano Serlio illustrated the three scenes, and described methods by which they could be lit and activated.

Phœbus

80 The *Andria* of Terence, 1493

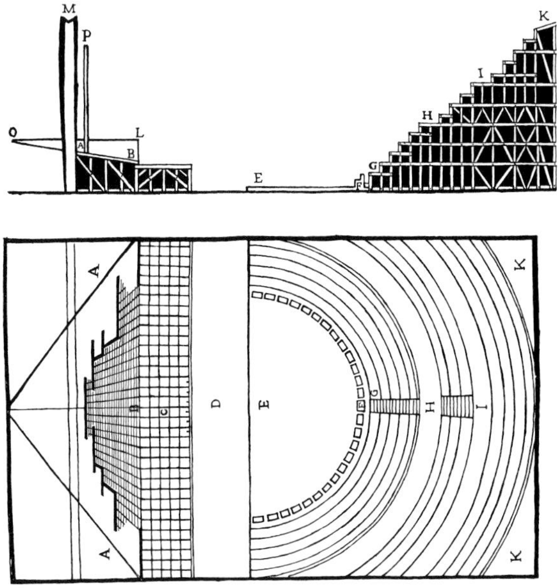
M
P
K
I
H
O
L
A
B
G
E
A
D
E
G
H
I
K

81 (*right*) Serlio's temporary Court theatre

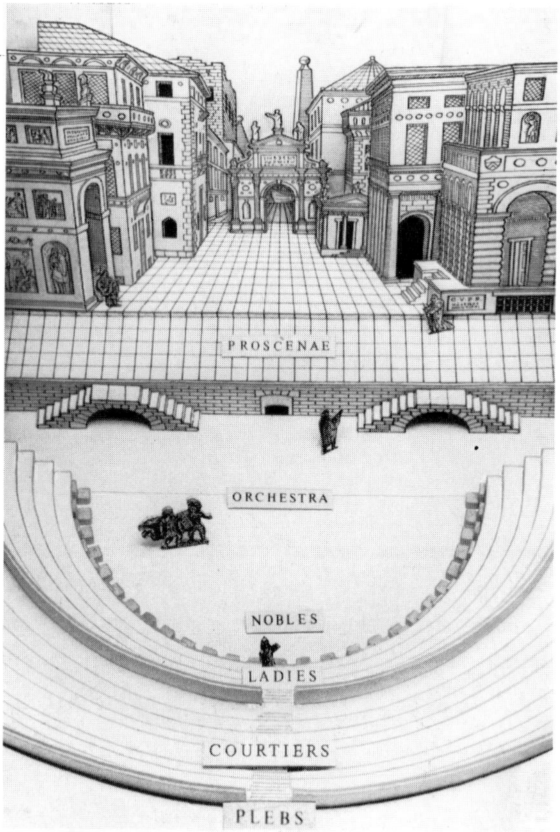
PROSCENAE
ORCHESTRA
NOBLES
LADIES
COURTIERS
PLEBS

82

Serlio's designs for:
82 *Tragic Scene*
83 *Comic Scene*
84 *Satyric Scene*

The theatres of the early Renaissance were not permanent buildings, each being erected for a particular occasion in the great hall or court of a palace. Serlio illustrated just such a temporary stage [81] Within a rectangular space he shows timber scaffolding arranged concentrically around a slightly raised semicircular *orchestra*, with individual seats for the nobles of the Court around the circumference, as in the *prohedriai* of the Ancient Greeks. Behind these are the steps or *gradines* for the ladies, separated by a gangway from the *gradines* allocated to the courtiers; beyond, on the uppermost portion of the scaffolding, are the plebs.

Adjoining the *orchestra* is a flat, rectangular space beyond which is a flat stage or *proscenae* raised to the level of a man's eyes. Beyond this the stage is built on an incline with a backscene set at a sufficient distance from the rear wall of the hall to permit people to move behind it, and flanked by two flat wings in front of which are three further sets of wings, each having a return face on their inner (or on-stage) ends. These are painted and built to conform to the tragic, the comic, or the satyric scenes, [82–84] while the front wings are decorated in scale with an actor on the *proscenae*.

It will be realized that the perspective scene limits the use of the scenic area by actors – since they cannot decrease their size to conform to the diminishing size of the perspective buildings! Serlio limits this diminution by placing his vanishing point beyond the rear wall of the hall, but he still suggests that the actors may be replaced by cut-out figures if movement is required within the perspective scene.

83

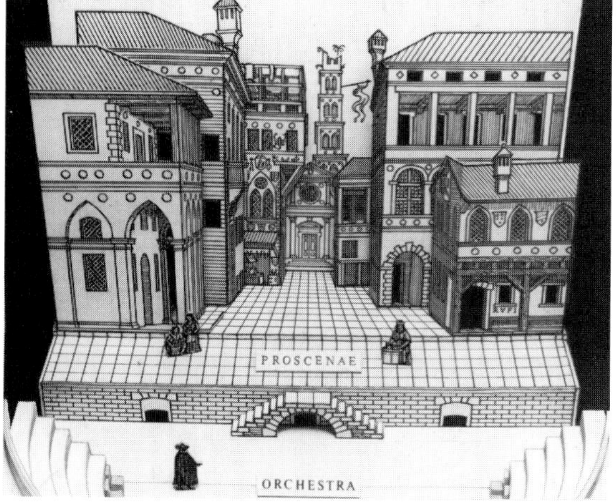
PROSCENAE
ORCHESTRA

84

LADIES
PROSCENAE
ORCHESTRA
NOBLES
COURTIERS
PLEBS

In early examples of the attempted return to classical conditions, the mansions of the Terentian stage permitted a continuance of the medieval relationship between the practical mansions and the 'place' around which they were situated, while the introduction of the new perspective scene reduced the practicability of the houses to (at most) the first pair of screens. It would seem that we are now facing a major change in the relationship of scenic items to actor.

After 1511, editions of Vitruvius were published with illustrations especially prepared for them, including in 1556 an Italian translation with illustrations by Daniello Barbaro, who had researched classical architecture with the Vicenzian architect, Andrea Palladio. Like the Roman Academy, the Olympic Academy of Vicenza founded in 1555, had from time to time built temporary theatres for their productions of classical plays, and in 1580 a permanent theatre, the Teatro Olimpico, [85] was erected to Palladio's designs.

This differed from the Roman prototype in being roofed and, because of the exigencies of the site, in having an elliptical auditorium in place of the Roman semicircle. [86] A raised stage is backed by a richly decorated *frons scaenae*, with a central arched opening flanked by four minor openings, with windows over in the side walls. The ceiling over the stage is coffered to represent

85 Teatro Olimpico, Vincenza, Italy, 1580–4

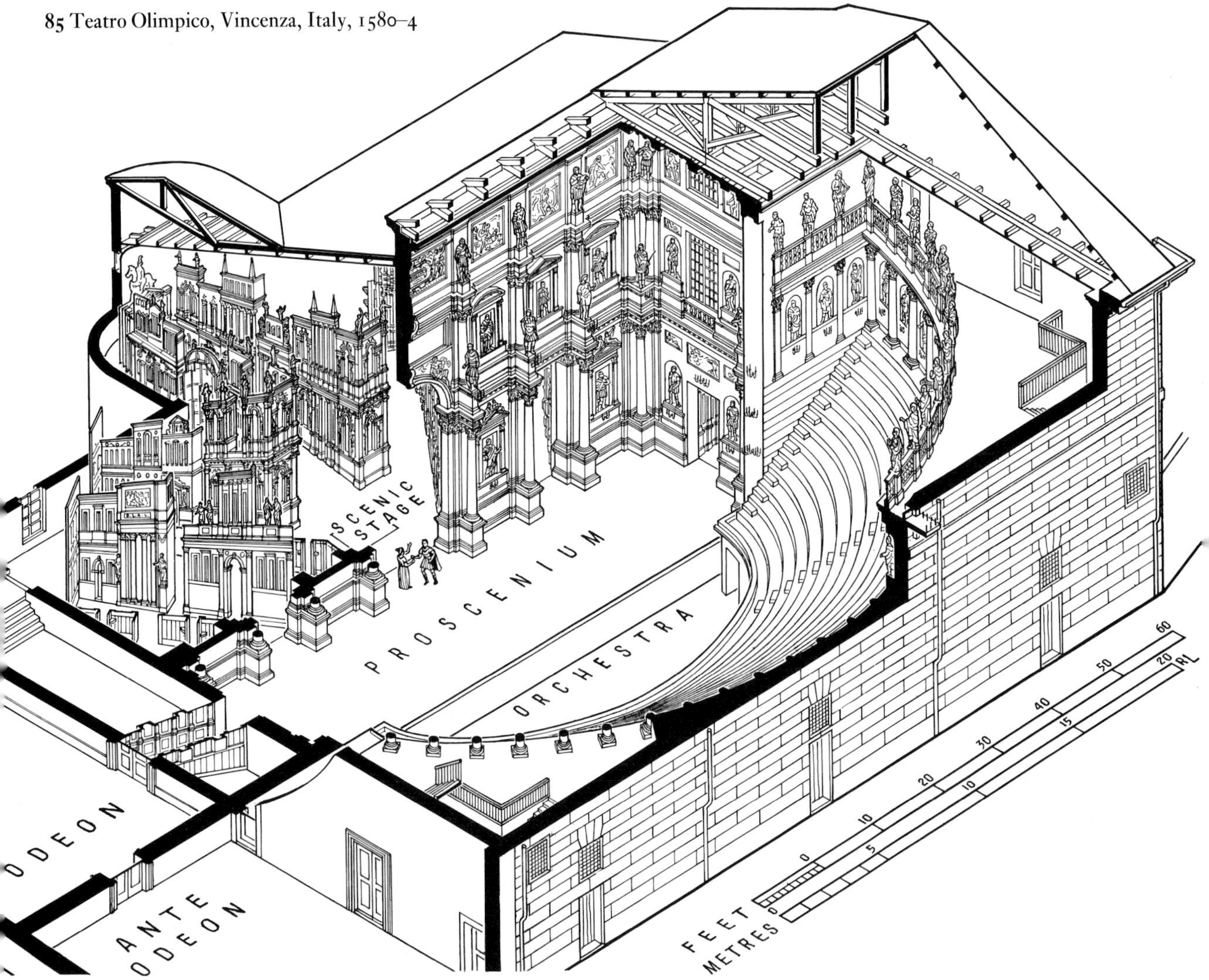
SCENIC STAGE
PROSCENIUM
ORCHESTRA
ODEON
ANTE ODEON
FEET
METRES
0
10
20
30
40
50
60
5
15
20
RL

Teatro Olimpico, Vicenza
86, 87 rear of scene to the right of
88 central vista

89 Teatro Olimpico, Sabbioneta, Italy
90 Strolling players with platform stage

86

87

88

a timber roof, while that to the auditorium is thought to have been painted to represent a *velarium*. Behind the *frons scaenae* is a further stage area with a sloping floor, and a domed plaster ceiling painted as the sky.

Palladio died before the building was finished, and it was completed by his son, Silla, and Vincenzo Scamozzi. Behind each opening Scamozzi developed a street of houses built solidly in perspective, so that at

89

90

least one street was visible to each member of the audience. [88] The houses were built of timber and plaster with three-dimensional statues, columns, and mouldings, and with pierced windows and doors lit from behind by small glass oil-lamps. [87] Each street ends in a painted panel extending the vista into the distance. As in the Roman theatre, the *orchestra* could be used either by the actors or for additional seating. Both theatre and scenery still stand, and are used for dramatic festivals. The actors perform on the proscenium, or raised stage, approached through the five openings.

While the Teatro Olimpico, Vicenza, represents the contemporary academic theatre, the court theatre illustrated by Serlio can be seen built in permanent form by Scamozzi at Sabbioneta in 1588. [89] Serlio's temporary staging here takes the form of five stepped *gradines*, arranged in a semicircle around a slightly sloping orchestral area which flows into and is unified with a rectangular floor area. Adjoining this is a raised stage or *proscene*, backed by a sloping scenic stage on which is arranged a single perspective vista of houses. A contemporary drawing (on which our reconstruction is based) shows such a setting consisting of Serlian angled screens, while the *proscene* is flanked by perspective houses with practical doors and windows.

The orchestral area was probably approached from the stage by steps similar to those indicated on Serlio's scenic drawings. [82–4] Mural paintings on the side walls continue a free-standing colonnade with giant columns flanking an arched opening, and the manner in which the painted entablature stops on the line of the sloping stage suggests that it was continued at this point across the hall by a painted cornice. Such a cornice could have concealed the various machines which provided for the movement of gods and painted clouds, as described by Nicola Sabbattini in his book *The Practice of Building Scenes and Machines*, published in the first third of the seventeenth century.

Although there was much argument and discussion regarding the form and nature of the classical Roman theatre, there was one form of presentation which had survived through the centuries. The art of pantomime – not always silent, but always with a strong emphasis on mimetic expression and gesture – had been sustained by troupes of itinerant players, who performed on simple platform stages which they set up in the open air, [90] or in any suitable hall. Now in the fourteenth and fifteenth centuries, the Italian Comedy developed as the Commedia dell'Arte, and Commedia players (who, unlike the 'erudita' or 'serious' players, were of both sexes) and their stages are illustrated in the engravings of Giacomo Callot. [91].

91 Commedia dell'Arte platform stage

The stages are shown as being high, rectangular platforms, hung about with cloths and with a curtained room behind. Entrance to the stage was through openings in the plain or painted curtains, or from ground level by means of ladders. With the new interest in classical drama, the more important companies were accepted by both princes and learned academics, so it is not surprising to find them performing in the Teatro Olimpico at Vicenza, and at the courts of Mantua [92] and Ferrara, using the new perspective scenes.

92 Serlian-style vista

7 French tennis courts, parterres, and amphitheatres

The Confrèrie de la Passion and the Hôtel de Bourgogne. Parterres, loges, and amphitheatres. Tennis-court theatres. Mahelot and the Comédiens du Roi. The Théâtre du Marais.

Italian Renaissance theatrical ideas spread across Europe in the sixteenth century, and French scholars performed in the Renaissance manner as part of their education. In 1548 the Confrèrie de la Passion, an organization of Parisian craftsmen and citizens who had been licensed to perform Mystery plays in 1402, built themselves a roofed, rectangular theatre on the site of the Hôtel de Bourgogne. [94a]

The stage was raised about 6 feet (1.82m) above a level *parterre*, where a large part of the audience stood to watch the performance. To either side of this flat 'pit', and raised above head-height on timber posts, were a number of boxes or *loges* approached by narrow passages adjoining the outer walls. Above was a railed space known as the *paradis*. Facing the stage at the level of the boxes was a steeply raked *amphitheatre* (similar to that noted at Lucerne), beneath which, at *parterre* level, 'the widow Dellin' sold refreshments. While the Confrèrie were presenting their Mysteries, they used a simultaneous setting of mansions arranged across the back and down the sides of the stage.

In November 1548, the Confrèrie were forbidden to perform further Mysteries as the content of their productions had become too secular. They assumed, however, that they had been given a monopoly of acting in Paris, and charged companies of strolling players a fee to set up temporary theatres in covered tennis courts (constructed for the original, or 'royal' indoor game) which fell vacant within the city. [93] These courts were long, narrow, rectangular halls, a full-size court house

93 Royal Tennis Court

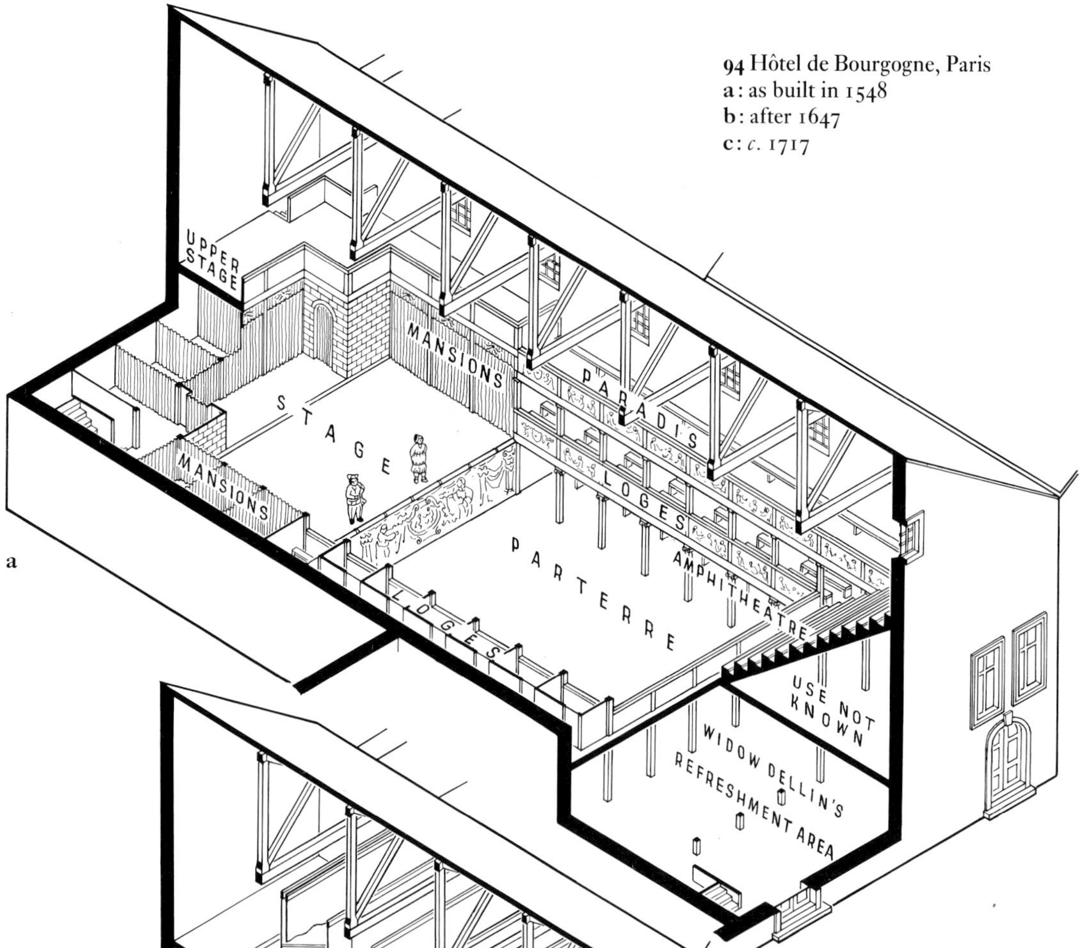
UPPER STAGE
MANSIONS
STAGE
MANSIONS
PARADIS
LOGES
PARTERRE
AMPHITHEATRE
LOGES
USE NOT KNOWN
WIDOW DELLIN'S REFRESHMENT AREA

a

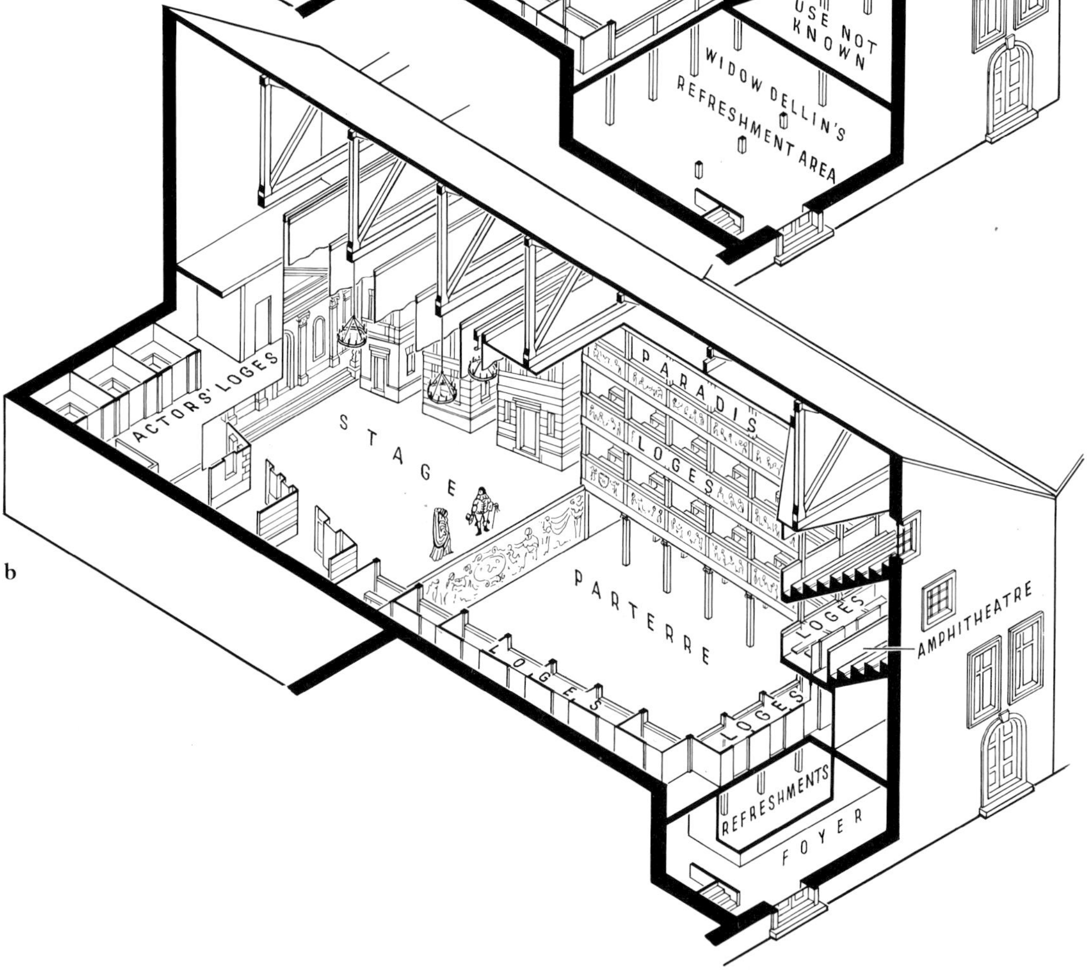
ACTORS' LOGES
STAGE
PARADIS
LOGES
PARTERRE
LOGES
AMPHITHEATRE
LOGES
LOGES
REFRESHMENTS
FOYER

b

94 Hôtel de Bourgogne, Paris
a: as built in 1548
b: after 1647
c: *c.* 1717

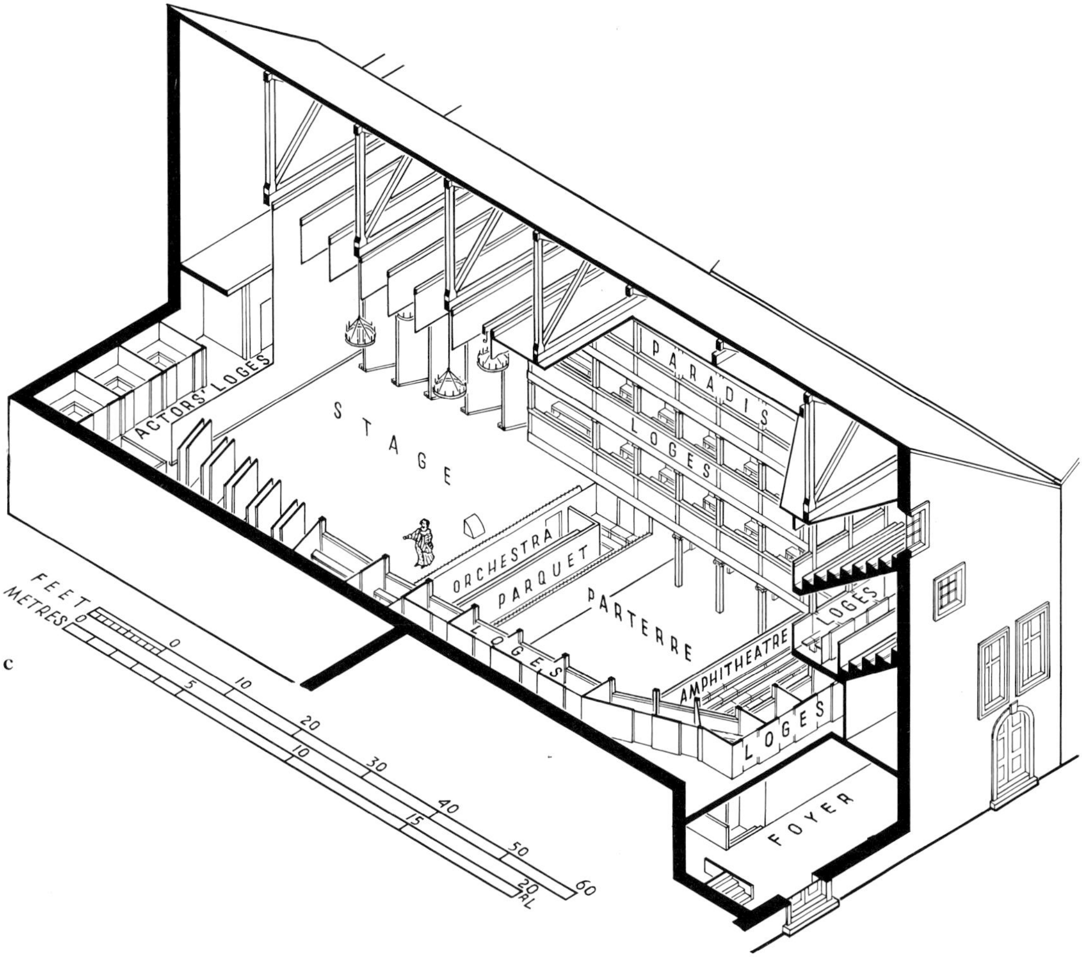
ACTORS' LOGES
STAGE
PARADIS
LOGES
ORCHESTRA
PARQUET
PARTERRE
LOGES
AMPHITHEATRE
LOGES
LOGES
FOYER
FEET
METRES
0
0
5
10
10
20
30
15
40
50
20
60
RL

c

being 110 feet (33.53m) long by 31 feet 8 inches (9.65m) wide. Internally the hall had a corridor with a sloping roof, or penthouse, along one side and across the ends, this being separated from the court proper by a waist-high partition. At one end within the penthouse was a gallery, and around the top of the walls was an open or glazed space to light the hall.

When adapted for use as a theatre the layout was similar to that described for the Hôtel de Bourgogne. [94] This similarity had come about, as will be noted in many further cases of adaptation described in this book, because the players had to accept limitations imposed by the existing structures, these then creating conventions of acting patterns and actor-audience relationships which of necessity had to be incorporated when purpose-built theatres were erected.

By 1578 the Hôtel de Bourgogne was being leased to other companies, among them the Italian Comedians. By 1629 the resident company had become the Comédiens du Roi, and the settings designed by Mahelot in the 1630s depict combinations of medieval mansions and Serlian screens arranged for simultaneous use within a single vista. The Comédiens are also to be seen on a stage arranged in the manner of a classical *frons scaenae*. [95]

In 1644 the Théâtre du Marais, opened as an adapted tennis court some ten years earlier, was rebuilt after a fire with two levels of nine boxes each on either side of the hall and a *paradis* above; further ranges each of four boxes faced the stage. The contract for the rebuilding suggests that the upper four boxes were backed by an amphitheatre; but by 1663 it would appear that an amphitheatre was contained within the boxes, being separated from the *parterre* by 'a partition seven *pieds* high'.

Que ce Theatre est magnifique !
Que ces Acteurs sont inuentifs !
Et qu'ils ont de preseruatifs
Contre l'humeur melancolique !
Icy d'vne posture drolle
Ils nazardent le mauuais temps ;
Et charment tous les Escoutans,
Auec vne seule parolle
Icy l'ingenieux Guillaume
Contrefaisant l'homme de Cour,
Se plaist à gourmander l'Amour,
Troussé comme vn joueur de paume
Icy d'vne façon hagarde
Turlupin veut faire l'Escroq ;
Et l'Espagnol de peur du choq,
Fuit le François qui le regarde.
Mais le vray Gautier les surpasse,
Et malgré la rigueur du sort,
Il nous fait rire apres sa mort,
Au souuenir de sa grimasse

95 Hôtel de Bourgogne

In 1647 [94b] the Hôtel de Bourgogne was altered to conform to the Marais, with a similar arrangement of boxes and presumably a rear amphitheatre and perhaps an upper gallery at *paradis* level. It is possible that the line of the side boxes was now inclined slightly inwards, as shown on a plan of the theatre published by Dumont in 1773, in an attempt to improve sight-lines. The stage was extended into the *parterre*, and the boxes on the stage were removed.

At first musicians were seated at the sides of the stage, but later they were moved to the adjoining boxes. By 1717, [94c] when Sir James Thornhill drew a rough plan of the theatre, an orchestra pit had been installed, together with a seated area, the *parquet*, partitioned off from the *parterre*. Thornhill also indicates that the more remote side boxes had been angled inwards to enclose an amphitheatre like that described at the Marais in 1663. Side boxes appear to have been built on the stage similar to those which had by then been introduced by d'Orbay at the Comédie Française [113], and oblique side wings set in grooves, in the manner described by Andrea Pozzo in 1692, had replaced the earlier Serlian screens.

8 Bulls, bears, and actors: the Elizabethan stage

James Burbage and The Theatre. Bull- and bear-baiting yards. De Witt and the Swan. 'My lord's room.' The Globe, the Fortune, and the Hope. The second Globe. Doors, windows, and discovery spaces. Indoor theatres and the Blackfriars.

In England the new Serlian productions were also introduced in the schools and universities, but the strolling players continued to use the medieval styles of production in the halls of manor houses and inns, and in the adapted environments of existing bull- and bear-baiting yards. In 1576, following the licensing of professional performers by the Master of the Revels, James Burbage built a permanent home for his players, The Theatre, in Finsbury Fields, the first of a number of such 'public' or open-air theatres to be constructed in the Elizabethan and Jacobean period. Although there are several illustrations of such theatres, few are reliable, in that the same building may be shown in one instance as circular and in another as multi-sided. All, however, confirm the close resemblance between the built playhouses and the baiting yards – a resemblance which is not surprising when it is realized that some of the buildings were of a multi-purpose nature, being used both as gaming houses and for plays.

tectum
porticus
sedilia
orchestra
mimorum aedes
ingressus
proscænium
planities sive arena

96 The Swan, after de Witt

The one theatre for which we have reliable visual evidence is the Swan. Built between 1594 and 1596 by Frances Langley, it was sketched by a Dutch visitor, de Witt, who sent the drawing [96] to his friend von Buchel, together with a description of the building, which he claimed could seat 3,000 persons. He further described it as being built of a 'concrete of flint stones' and supported by 'wooden pillars painted to imitate marble', and suggested that it showed traces 'of the Roman style', as indicated on the copy of his drawing made by von Buchel.

This drawing confirms various written comments regarding such public theatres as The Theatre, the

97

98

Curtain, and the Rose in which mention is made of three galleries, a yard, a tiring house or 'place where the players make them ready', 'my lord's room', and a 'room over the tiring house'. All these features, with the exception of my lord's room, are seen in the sketch. A raised, rectangular stage [97] is set within an open, circular yard where the groundlings stood, surrounded by three galleries, [98] the uppermost being designated by de Witt as a Roman *porticus*.

According to another visitor, Thomas Platter of Basle, the galleries provided additional, more comfortable standing room, but it was also possible to sit. The visitor paid a penny to enter the yard,

but if he wants to sit, he is let in at a further door, and there he gives another penny. If he desires to sit on a cushion in the most comfortable place of all, where he not only sees everything well, but can also be seen, then he gives yet another English penny at another door.

This was no doubt my lord's room, which would have been available when 'my lord' – the member of the nobility required to legitimize a company by his patronage – was not visiting his players.

The various companies of players not only performed in these playhouses, but also toured the country, where they appeared before the screens in the great halls of guilds and also in private houses. It is not unexpected, therefore, that the *mimorum ades* depicted by de Witt should have two doors at stage level and an open gallery above, similar to the hall screens.

99

The Swan: 97 general view
98 view after de Witt
99 aerial view

If this analogy is carried further it may be assumed that 'my lord's room' would occupy a similar position to that of the lord of the manor seated at the high table directly opposite the screens. One is indeed tempted to feel that de Witt, having spent his three English pennies, was seated in my lord's room when he made his original sketch.

The rear portion of the stage is sheltered by a roof which was almost certainly ceiled below with a flat, painted 'Heavens' through which ascents and descents, an essential part of medieval performances, could be made, together with Ben Jonson's 'creaking throne' – accompanied no doubt by clouds. Above the roof the tiring house was carried up to form a room containing the machinery needed for the various scenic devices mentioned above. [99]

In 1599 The Theatre was pulled down and its timbers were used to build the Globe on the South Bank, and in 1600 came the Fortune [307], which differed from the other playhouses in being square rather than circular. The circular Hope, however, built in 1613, was designed as a multi-purpose structure to be used both for plays and games. To this end the stage was removable, and since the Heavens could thus not be supported by columns they had instead to be cantilevered at roof level.

Contracts exist for both these theatres, and are of value in providing dimensions for the main measurements of the theatres, and for details of their construction. The contract for the Fortune states that the stage should project to the centre of the yard, and be 43 feet (13.11m) wide set in a yard 55 feet (16.76m) square. The stage should also be designed in accordance with a plan originally attached to the contract, which suggests that it was not the simple rectangle seen in the Swan.

The Globe was destroyed by fire on 29 June 1613, to be rebuilt the following year. Both the Hope and the second Globe are shown on Hollar's *Long View* [100], where the latter can be seen to have a dual-pitched roof to the machine room, which occupies half the yard space and spans its full width. In the Swan drawing the width of the machine room conforms to the width of the stage, and we may perhaps assume that the stage of the second Globe also conformed to the width of its machine room and occupied the full width of the yard. The stage of the Swan, with its two doors of entry, followed the medieval pattern with its stage or 'plain' surrounded most probably by practical scenic mansions [101] such as are listed in Henslowe's inventory for the Rose: a tomb, Hell's Mouth, a tomb of Dido, trees, mossy banks, and a wooden canopy.

In Italy we noted that such features were being replaced by doors, arranged either in the Terentian manner or in the correct classical way within a *frons scaenae* like that at Vicenza, and it may be assumed that these classical features were now being introduced in England into the theatres of educational establishments and into the

100 The second Globe (*left*) and the Hope (*right*)

indoor or 'private' theatres. Stage directions in contemporary plays call for windows and upper galleries, and a discovery space behind a curtain of sufficient size to accommodate at least twelve people or such furnishings as a table, a bed, and a cupboard. In the indoor theatres this space probably occupied a central position into which most of the audience could see, flanked by doors on either side of the stage, or in the Phoenix (converted by Beeston from a cockpit in Drury Lane), set in the oblique walls like those in the later Cockpit in Court. [110]

The Swan represents clearly the general architectural reaction to the Italian Renaissance in Britain in that, with few exceptions, throughout the greater part of the sixteenth century classsical features were

101 The Swan, with medieval style mansions

integrated with traditional building techniques, and it was not until the early seventeenth century that Renaissance theories were fully understood and implemented. In 1614, when the second Globe [102] was built, it would have been surprising if the tiring house had not conformed more closely to the classical *frons scaenae* than had been the case in the earlier Swan.

In 1596 James Burbage adapted premises in the Blackfriars, on the western edge of the City of London, which, from 1608, were used by the King's Company in conjunction with the Globe. Little is known regarding this roofed playhouse, but mention is made of side galleries and a gallery facing the stage, but the audiences in the equivalent area to the open yard of the unroofed theatres, unlike their French colleagues in the *parterre* of the Hôtel de Bourgogne, are known to have been seated on benches in what was now called the pit.

Stage directions from contemporary plays mention doors as being 'opposite', suggesting that the doors, probably with windows or balconies above, were set in the side walls of the stage. Such doors, windows, and discovery space could take on any character which the play demanded. As these conventions became accepted, and with an audience confined by the rectangular shape of the hall to a more polarized relationship to the stage, it is reasonable to think that if plays were to be successfully transferred from the Blackfriars to the Globe, then the architectural arrangements of the latter must have begun to conform more closely to the patterns dictated by the roofed playhouse, except in their respective sizes.

Our reconstruction of the second Globe has a tiring house arranged as a classical *frons scaenae* with a central, curtained opening for use as a discovery space, flanked by two openings with double doors. Two further doors are set in the first oblique facets of the main frame of the theatre. At first gallery level the five openings are reflected by open galleries or windows, and above these are further openings with a central room for musicians – a feature also provided in one way or another in the roofed playhouses.

The increase in the number of doorways from the two of the Swan to the five proposed here was made possible by the increased width of the stage, which permitted greater flexibility of movement on the stage and in the use of the upper galleries. Ascents and descents to and from Heaven were still possible, and traps permitted movement through the stage floor. The

102a The second Globe Theatre, 1614

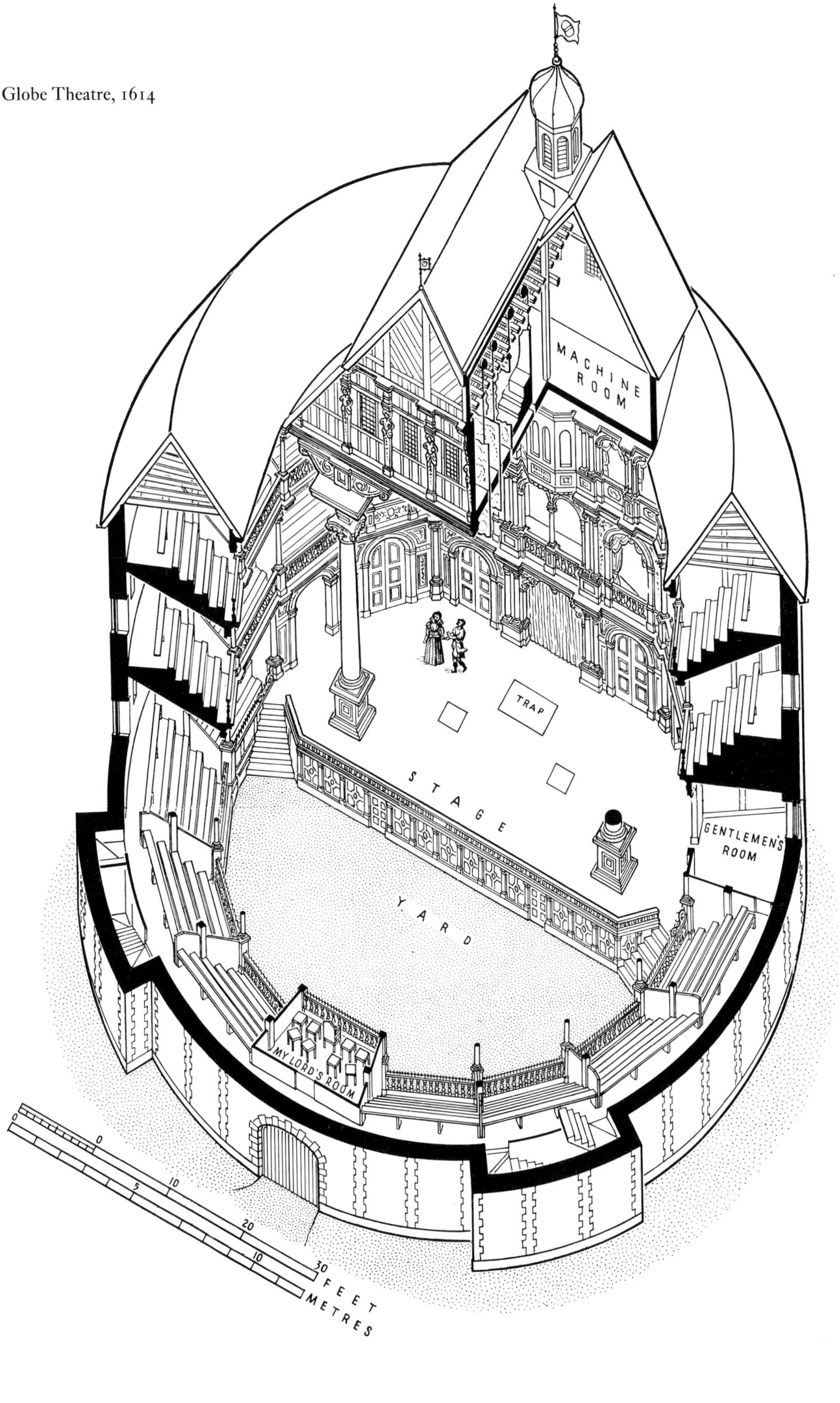
MACHINE ROOM
TRAP
STAGE
GENTLEMEN'S ROOM
YARD
MY LORD'S ROOM
0
0
10
5
20
10
30
FEET
METRES

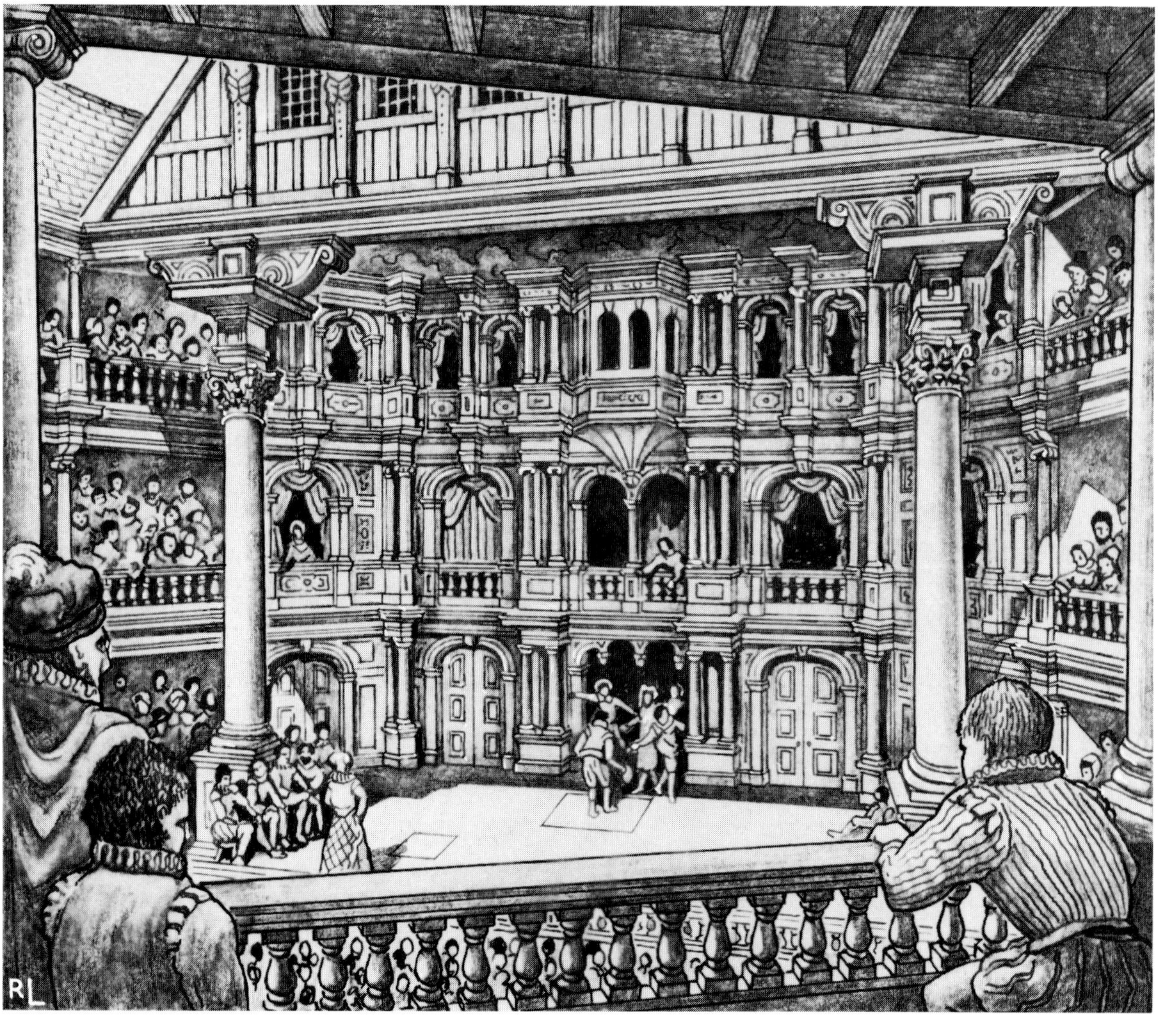

102b The second Globe Theatre

under-stage space was also approached by doorways directly from the yard, which was now connected to the stage by permanent steps, replacing the ladders of earlier periods. In addition to 'my lord's room', gentlemen's rooms were now included adjoining the stage, to which they gave access, so that the gentlemen could sit on the stage – a habit presumably introduced in the more restricted space of the indoor theatres.

The increase in the size of the stage and its related areas meant a corresponding decrease in the areas occupied by the audience, which can now be seen to be more axially related to the tiring house than had been the case in the Swan; so each facet of the frame could be separated from its neighbour by partitions to form separate boxes. The provision of benches in the pit at the Blackfriars meant that this area now catered for a higher social class, and the groundlings were banished to an upper gallery facing the stage, where they eventually became the 'gods'. But in the second Globe the groundlings still occupied the reduced space in the yard, although some had doubtless moved to standing spaces at the rear of the seating in the galleries.

9 Changeable scenes and court masques

Scene changes. Wings and shutters. Aleotti and the Teatro Farnese. Machines and wing carriages. Inigo Jones and grooves. Florimène. An unknown theatre. The Cockpit-in-Court. The revived frons scaenae and the doors of entry.

In Italy the perspective scene as described by Serlio had largely remained as a permanent background to the actors throughout a performance, but it was not long before the possibilities inherent in a change of scene were realized, and methods were gradually introduced which enabled the various pieces of a scene to be replaced by units making up a new vista. On the Serlian stage the scenery was so arranged as to contain the view of the audience within the vista, leaving areas on either side where actors could congregate. Above the vista the view could be enclosed by the arch of the sky, which had to be carefully designed to permit the passage of clouds and gods and yet contain the view.

The introduction of elaborate machinery around the visual area complicated the problem of concealment, and it was necessary to provide screens and a cornice which could frame in the perspective scene. By 1561 Bartolemmeo Neroni had used a grand frontispiece to a Serlian vista, and in 1585 Buontalenti built a theatre in the Uffizi Palace, Florence, for which he designed an everchanging series of scenes including a perspective view of the city, a cloud machine complete with actors, a cavern spouting flames and smoke, landscapes which changed from spring to autumn, and a seascape.

To make this possible, some means of changing the wings and backscene had to be contrived. The Serlian angled wing was difficult to change, and, although ways were suggested by which this could be done, the angle wings were replaced by flat wings, set either parallel with or obliquely to the front of the stage. These could be slid on- or offstage in a series of grooves to reveal a further set of wings behind. Triangular *periaktoi* could also be used, both singly as wings or in a line to form a backscene, but their use was limited as they could only depict three scenes.

A backscene could, however, be made in two halves which slid apart. These sliding wings and shutters permitted a multiplicity of scenes, as it was always possible to remove a used scene and replace the wings and shutters by a fresh set which could be pushed on stage when required. This method of scene changing was used by Aleotti at the Academic Theatre at Ferrara in 1606.

In Serlio's theatre the perspective scene was intended only as a backing to the actors on the raised stage, the rapidly reducing scale of the perspective panels making it ridiculous for the actors to venture beyond the first pair of wings. The desire to enliven the vistas had led to the introduction of cut-out figures and children dressed as adults, but such devices were never really satisfactory, and ways and means of introducing the performers within the perspective scene must have been examined from an early date, not least because the use of cloud machines and similar effects was intended to introduce the performers *within* the perspective scene.

One way of overcoming this problem was to increase the number of side wings, thus increasing the practical depth of the scenic vista. This meant that the section of perspective vista painted on each screen did not reduce as sharply as it had done on the Serlian screen, and the difference in scale between the performer and the painted side wing was not so great. Consequently the actors could now venture further into the scene without appearing out of scale, especially when the wings depicted non-architectural features such as clouds, rocks, or trees.

Aleotti was commissioned to built a theatre on the first floor of the Farnese Palace at Parma in 1618. [103] His stage was only 30 feet (9.14m) short of the overall length of the auditorium, a size made necessary by the inclusion of a deep scenic vista consisting of some nine sets of side wings and a set of backscenes. It is not clear if contemporary plans indicate the original settings or a later variation, but it is interesting to note that one early plan indicates the stage as ending on the second cross wall: it may be that it was extended when even deeper vistas became the order of the day.

While it is clear that Aleotti designed the stage with sufficient depth to permit the use of the new-style vista, it is not known with any certainty how the wings were originally moved. Aleotti may have used his flat wings

103 Teatro Farnese, Parma, Italy, 1618–20

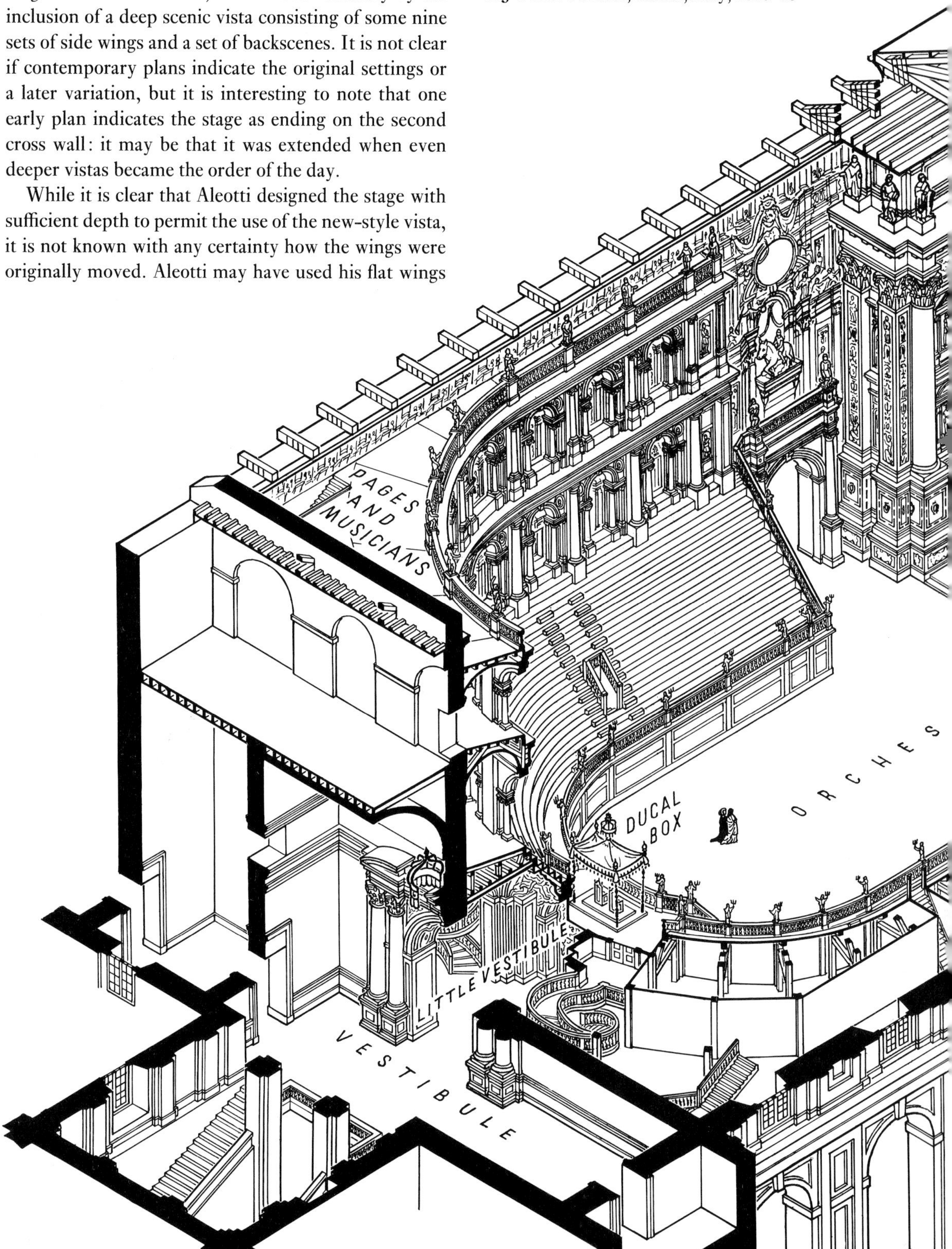
PAGES AND MUSICIANS
DUCAL BOX
ORCHES
LITTLE VESTIBULE
VESTIBULE

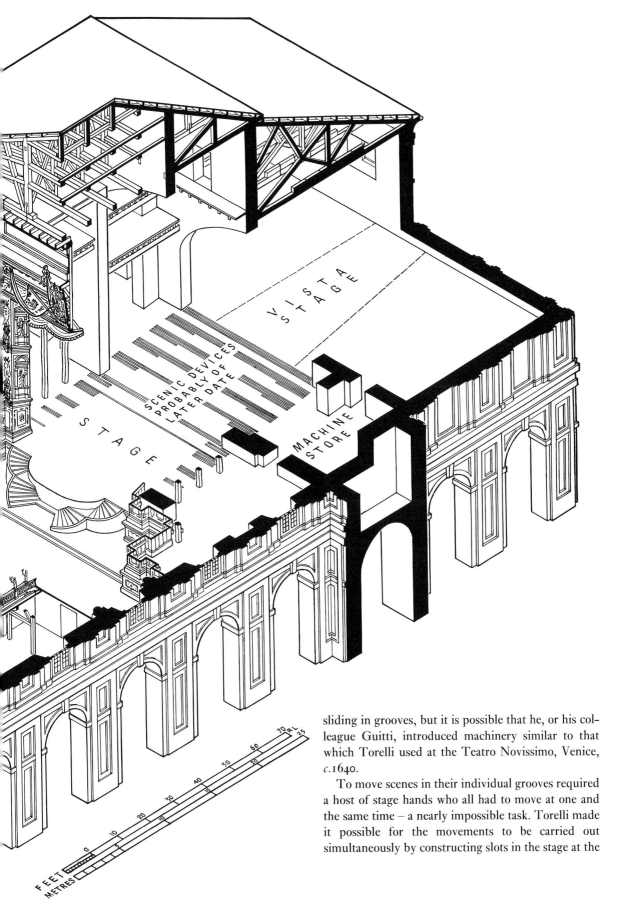

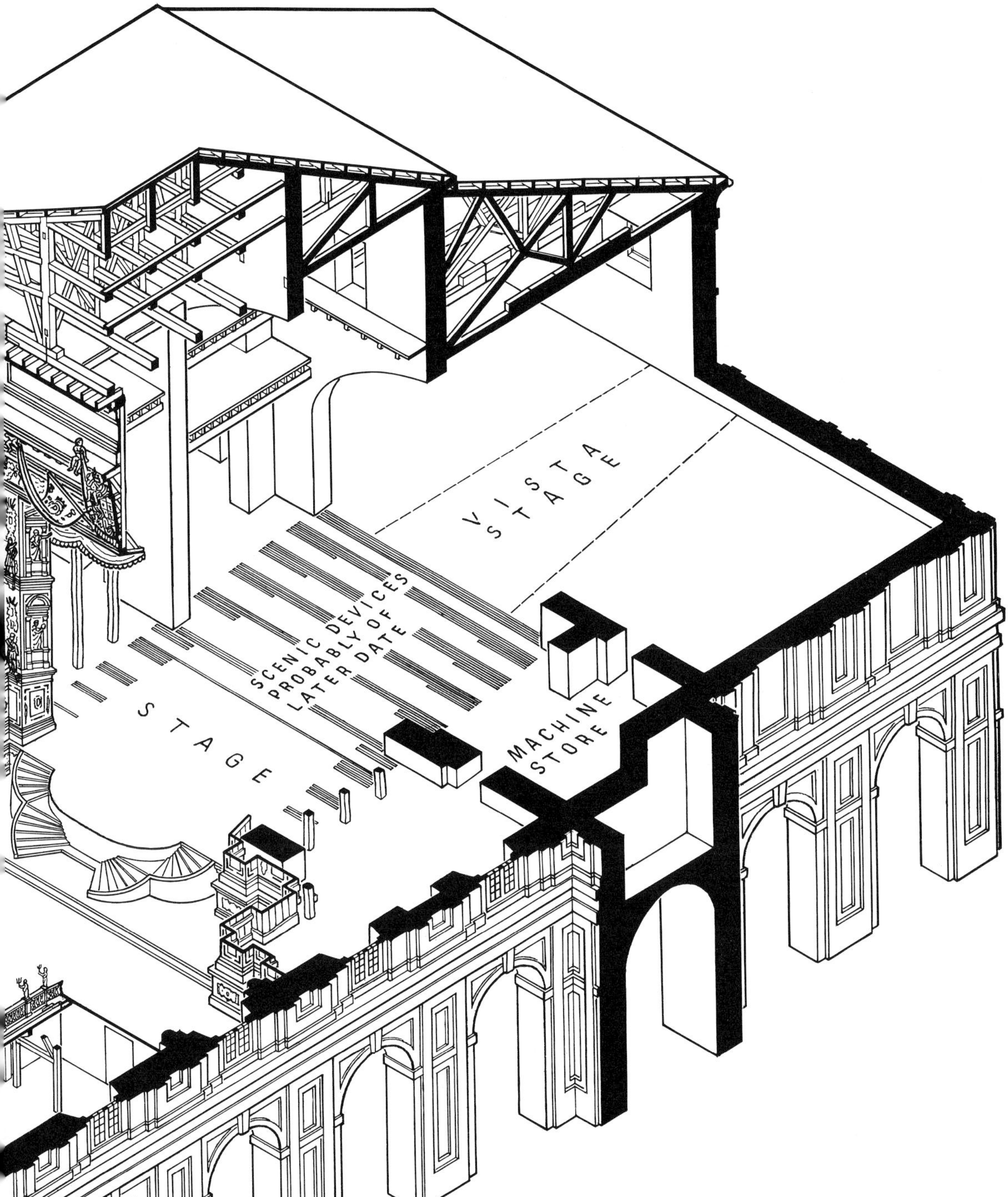
VISTA
STAGE
SCENIC DEVICES
PROBABLY OF
LATER DATE
STAGE
MACHINE
STORE

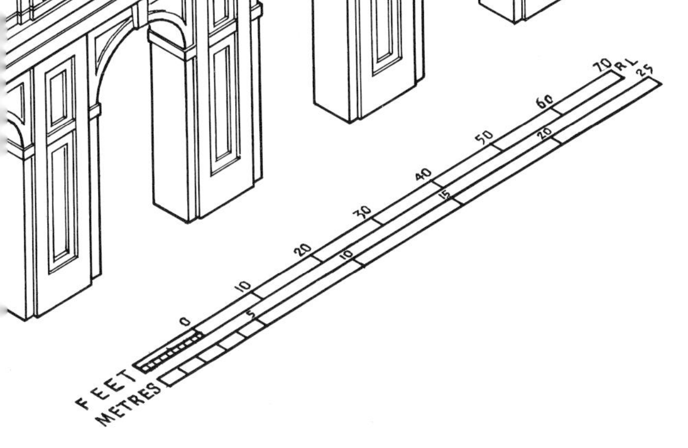
FEET
METRES
0 10 20 30 40 50 60 70
5 10 15 20 25

sliding in grooves, but it is possible that he, or his colleague Guitti, introduced machinery similar to that which Torelli used at the Teatro Novissimo, Venice, *c.*1640.

To move scenes in their individual grooves required a host of stage hands who all had to move at one and the same time – a nearly impossible task. Torelli made it possible for the movements to be carried out simultaneously by constructing slots in the stage at the

Teatro Farnese; **104a, 104b, 105**

104a

104b

wing positions, and fastening the wings to a series of carriages which projected through the stage and ran on rails beneath. Each carriage was connected by ropes to a central drum beneath the stage, so that, when the drum was turned by hand or by counterweights, all the carriages were drawn on or off stage in concert. In this manner it was possible to withdraw all the wings of one setting at the same time, while replacing them with a second set.

The stage [104a] was separated from the main hall by a wall decorated as a Roman *frons scaenae*, but with a single great opening framing [105] the scenic vista. Immediately adjoining the stage was a flat orchestral area, similar to that at Sabbioneta, approached by an archway in the side wall. [104b] Unlike Sabbioneta, however, where the *gradines* enclosed a semicircular extension of the *orchestra*, the raised seating here enclosed an extended U-shaped space, from which it was separated by a wall topped by a balustrade. A royal box was placed directly above the entry-way at the correct viewing-point for the perspective vista.

105

The open floor was still used by the performers in the manner of the earlier court festivals, but in place of the small perspective vista seen at the Petit Bourbon [74] we now have the additional space set aside for the scenes and machinery in what appears to be an adjoining room, viewed through an opening in the separating wall.

Masques and *intermezzi* with singers and dancers, in which the personages of the court often took part, were performed with theatrical extravagance. The scenic devices provided a spectacular background from which the royal performers could descend on their cloud thrones and make their way by steps to the orchestral area, where they led the dancing. Pageant cars, monsters, and similar features were also introduced.

The opening performance was a mixture of drama, opera, tournament, and marine spectacle. Visiting princes rode up into the theatre, while the bridal couple sat in the seats of honour. Gods and goddesses flew through the air, while the orchestral area, having been sheathed with lead, was flooded, and monsters and warriors on islands floated into the hall where they fought. Finally the flood subsided and the gods ascended into heaven.

The whole auditorium was ceiled with light fir planks, an improvement on the use of canvas on stretchers, which appears to have been the accepted method in earlier theatres. All the interior structure, including the *gradines*, colonnade, and *frons scaenae*, was of timber, the two latter being faced with plaster, providing resonant acoustic qualities on which an eighteenth-century English visitor, Joseph Addison, commented favourably.

The new scenic ideas were introduced into England by Inigo Jones in his designs for masques at the court of Whitehall, and these show the developing pattern of the changeable scene. In 1604 he staged a masque in the medieval way with scenery set around the open floor of the hall. By the end of the year, however, he was concealing the scene by a great painted curtain, which fell to reveal a seascape with moving waves, effected by the use of barley-sugar columns laid flat and turned by stagehands (in this instance the side wings were probably the Serlian angled type, which did not move). At Oxford in 1605 Jones staged a tragedy for which he used *periaktoi* for both the side wings and the backscene, thus giving himself three changes of setting; he also made use of descending clouds behind which a scene change took place, and by 1631 five changes were being achieved.

Plans and drawings of Jones's designs for *Florimène* in 1635 show how the Tudor Hall in Whitehall [106] was adapted for theatrical performances. [107] The audience was accommodated on three sides of the hall on *gradines*, or degrees, which enclosed both the dancing area and the royal State. The State was set at such a height and position that the seated king's eyes were level with the horizon of the scenic vista. On the stage, erected in front of the hall screens which were hidden by a sky cloth, was a setting composed of angled wings and back shutters, all enclosed behind a frontispiece. Above, between the shutters and the sky cloth, was a gallery with steps, which could be used by performers who appeared seated on thrones amid clouds, or by musicians.

The Tudor Hall, Whitehall, adapted for *Florimène*
106 (*above*), **107** (*below*)

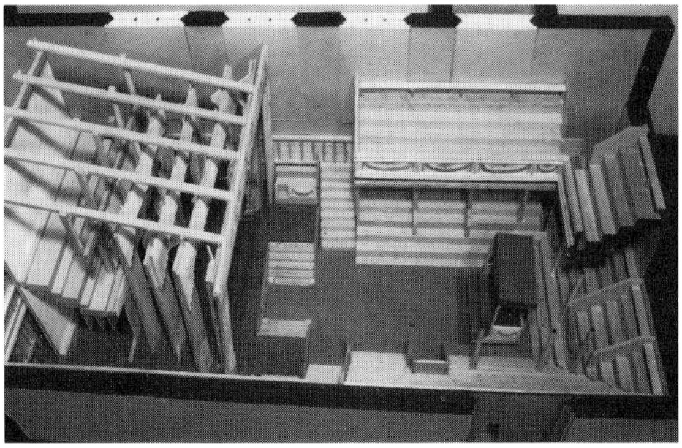

For *Salmacida Spolia* in 1640, Jones introduced grooves for the side wings, so that these too could be drawn off to the sides. A plan shows that provision was made for four wings at each position and three sets of backshutters. If further scenes were required, it would have been necessary to withdraw the used wings and replace them by new pieces, but it will be appreciated that additional space would be required in the 'wings' or sides of the stage to permit this manoeuvre to be accomplished. Space is limited in the *Salmacida Spolia* plan, and it is unlikely that this was tried, but it is interesting to note that the design for an unknown hall, which may have been specifically conceived by Jones (maybe for Somerset House), has a T-shaped plan providing additional space for stage wings.

This off-stage movement of scenery was concealed from the audience by the frontispiece, so that the hall was effectively divided into two parts – the stage and the auditorium. The performers, however, made their appearances both on the stage and in the body of the hall where they danced before the State.

The advent of perspective scenery meant that the audience could no longer enter the hall through the doors of the screens without viewing all the secrets of the scenes and machines. It would seem that Jones appreciated that the arrangement of the audience in the Tudor Hall followed closely the old medieval pattern, as seen at Penshurst, [75] and that while they had a good view of the performers on the floor of the hall their view of the perspective scene was severely limited. One way of overcoming this problem can be seen in the plan of the unknown hall, where Jones included eight additional degrees at the rear of the hall, so that the greater part of the audience were now seated in a more favourable position to view the scenic delights.

A theatre designed by Inigo Jones [108] could represent an updating of Shakespearian stage arrangements to suit the new classical theme. While the Tudor Hall illustrates the introduction of the perspective vista, this unknown theatre introduces us to a second Renaissance feature – the revival of the classical Roman theatre. Following a visit to Vicenza and Palladio's Teatro Olimpico, Jones was able to put his interest in the classical theatre into practice when he and John Webb converted the Cockpit-in-Court into a small theatre, [109] with a raised stage occupying half the

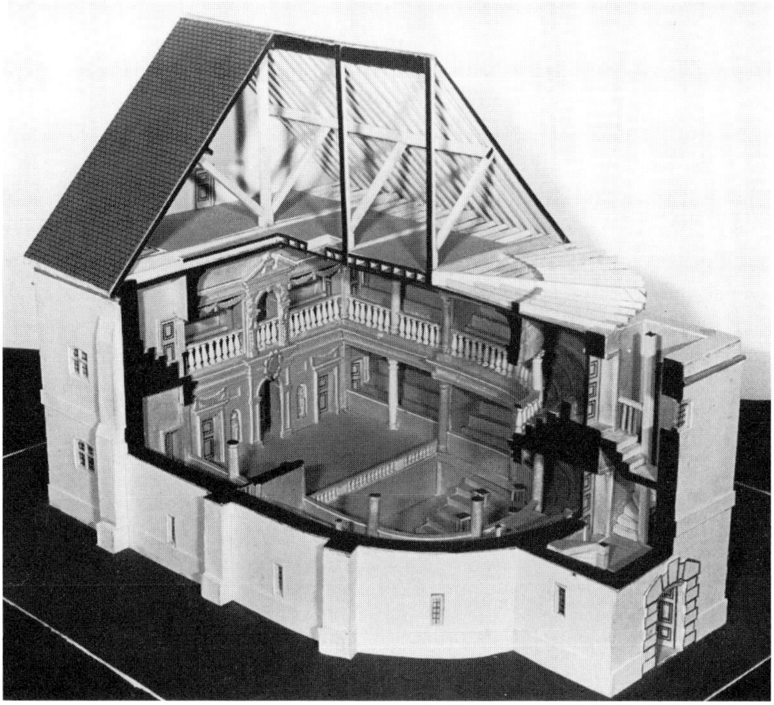

108 Unknown theatre by Inigo Jones

109 Cockpit in Court, Whitehall

auditorium space and backed by a semi-circular *frons scaenae* of two storeys. [110]

A central arched opening, framing a small changeable perspective scene, was flanked by two doors on either side, with a centrally placed opening at the upper level. On the central axis, facing the stage, was the royal State, with two benched galleries filling the remainder of the hall. The pit was fitted out with degrees for an audience presumably seated on stools or fixed benches, the angle of the degrees on plan ensuring that no one sat with their back to the King. No trap is indicated on a stage plan, but there may have been at least one. The ceiling of the hall is known to have been covered with calico and stars of silver foil, and was made to open for the passage of a throne worked by machinery in the roof space.

The introduction into Britain of the Roman *frons scaenae*, as seen in these two theatres, with its numerous doorways and balconies over, set the seal of approval on the continued use of such doors of entry as had earlier been provided in the medieval screens. [75]

110 Cockpit in Court, Whitehall

10 Public theatres and opera houses

Italian opera houses. SS. Giovanni e Paolo. Scenic devices. Torelli and Vigarani in Paris. Deep vista stages. Salle des Machines. D'Orbay's Comédie Française.

The courtly performances were a mixture of plays, music, and dancing, and in Italy these presentations developed during the early seventeenth century into what we would recognize today as opera. In 1637 a public opera house was opened in San Cassiano in Venice, and followed in 1639 by the theatre of SS. Giovanni e Paolo. [111] This had a U-shaped auditorium similar to that of the Teatro Farnese, but the seating enclosing the open floor was separated into individual loges or boxes, arranged on five tiers. These could be rented on an annual basis, while the *parterre* remained open for a standing audience who paid an entry fee for each performance.

Sabbattini had earlier suggested that a partition be erected to separate the milling audience from the stage. The intervening space could be used for different purposes, but was not least useful in providing some light for the understage mechanics. At SS. Giovanni e Paolo an additional barrier was installed to provide space for an orchestra. Numerous such public theatres

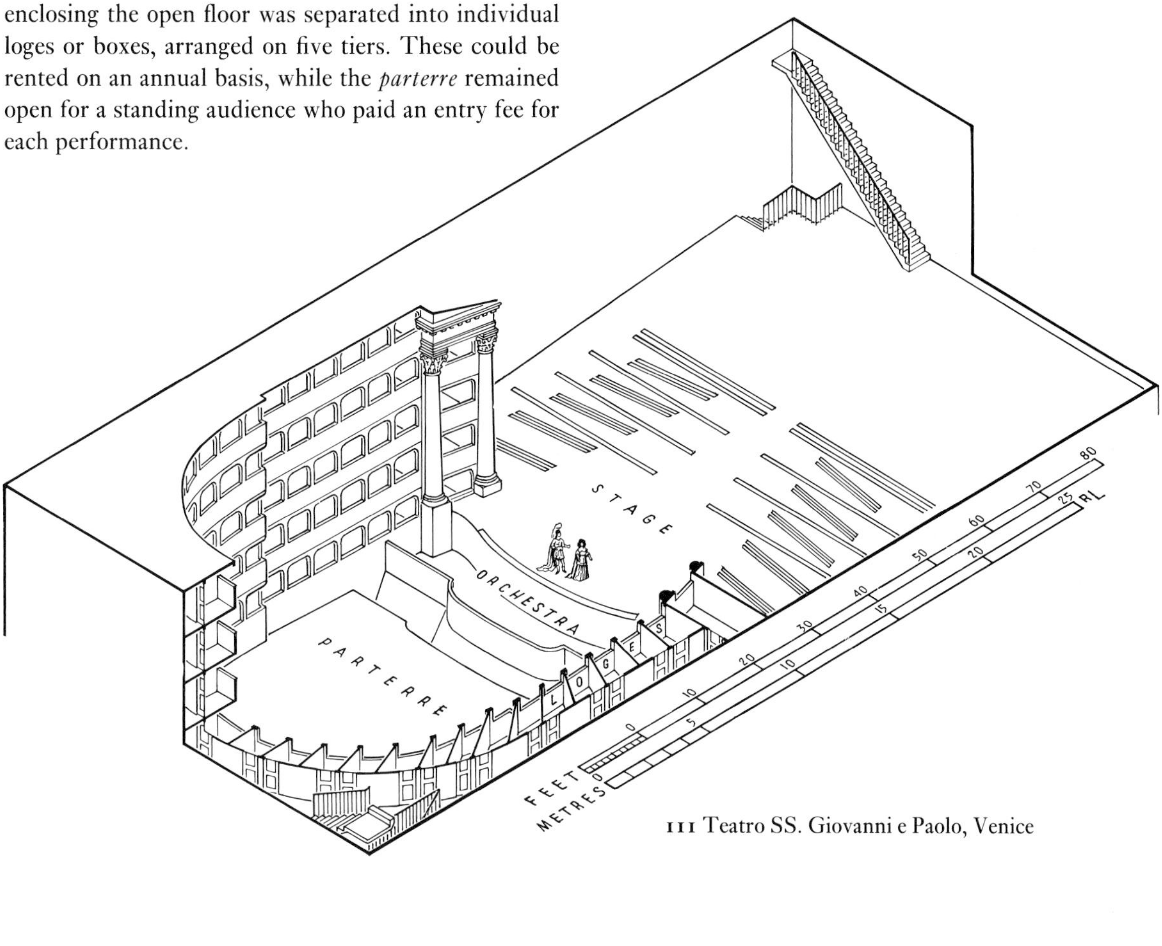
STAGE
ORCHESTRA
PARTERRE
LOGES
FEET
METRES
0
10
20
30
40
50
60
70
80
5
10
15
20
25
RL

111 Teatro SS. Giovanni e Paolo, Venice

were built in Italy: for acoustic reasons the auditoria assumed various shapes, but that most commonly used was an ellipse, with the partitions between the boxes centered on the stage.

These public theatres used the new scenic devices which Torelli had introduced at the Teatro Novissimo. In 1645 he was sent to Paris, where he introduced his ideas at the Théâtre du Petit Bourbon, and in 1647 he presented *Orphée* at the newly adapted Palais Royal. At this time it would seem that this hall was rectangular with a flat *parterre* and open galleries along the sides. Beyond the *parterre* were a series of flat *gradines* facing the raised stage, which was separated from the hall by a single large flat-arched opening, beyond which Torelli set his vistas.

Torelli was replaced by another Italian machinist, Vigarani, who in 1662 was instrumental in advising on the design of a theatre which came to be known as the Salle des Machines, [112] named after the very deep vista stage which occupied some 140 feet (42.67m) of the 226 feet (68.88m) depth of the theatre. The auditorium consisted of a series of *gradines* facing the stage within a U-shaped, two-storeyed colonnade, behind which were further elliptical *gradines*.

Although this theatre was criticized for its poor acoustics, the arrangement of the seating, unlike that of the new Italian auditoria, permitted a large proportion of the audience to have a good view of the important and elaborate scenes – an approach which may have accounted for the introduction of the enclosed amphitheatre adjoining the *parterre* in the Marais theatre of 1663, where the use of machinery was also important.

In the Comédie Française, [113] designed in 1689 by d'Orbay on the site of an existing tennis court, two tiers, each of 23 boxes, were arranged in the Italian U-shape manner, but opening out at the stage end to provide better sight-lines for the side boxes. Above was

112 Salle des Machines, Paris

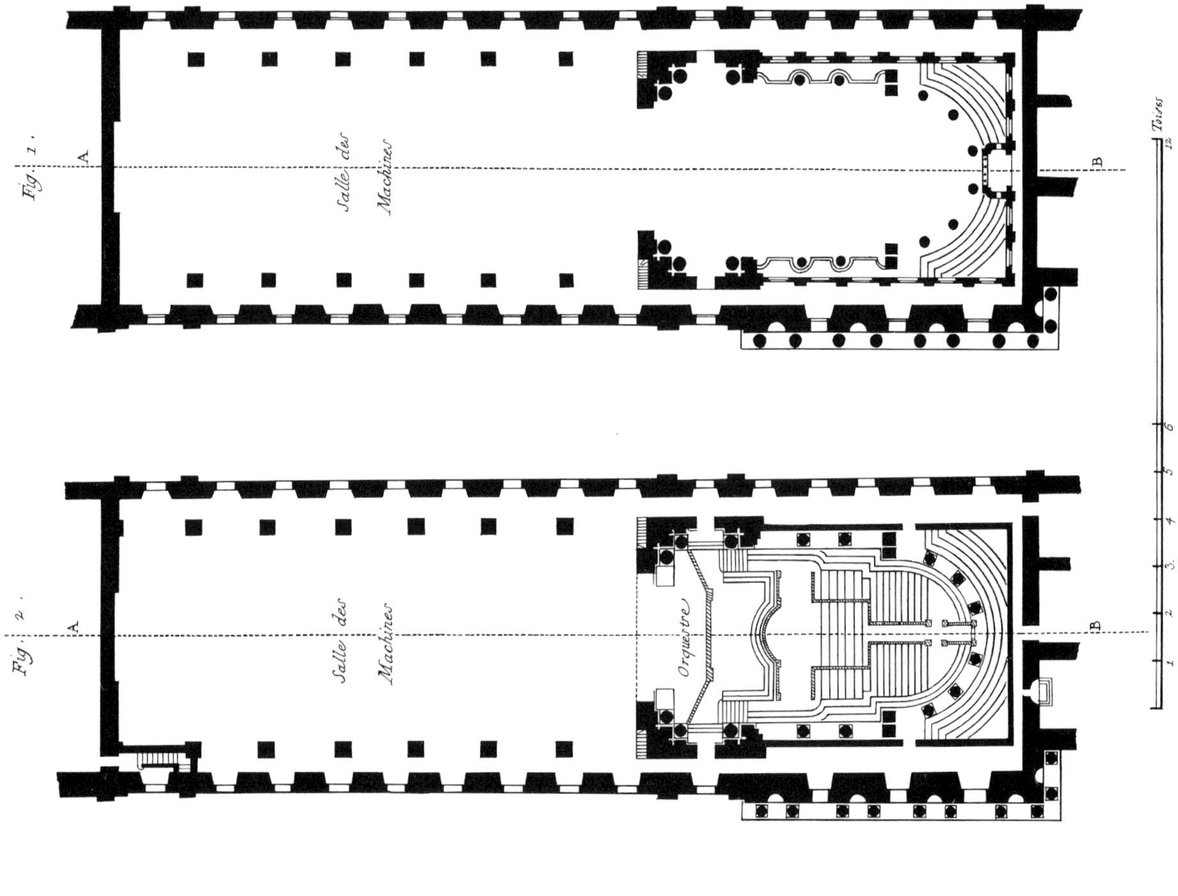
Fig. 1.
A
Salle des Machines
B
Toises
Fig. 2.
A
Salle des Machines
Orquestre
B

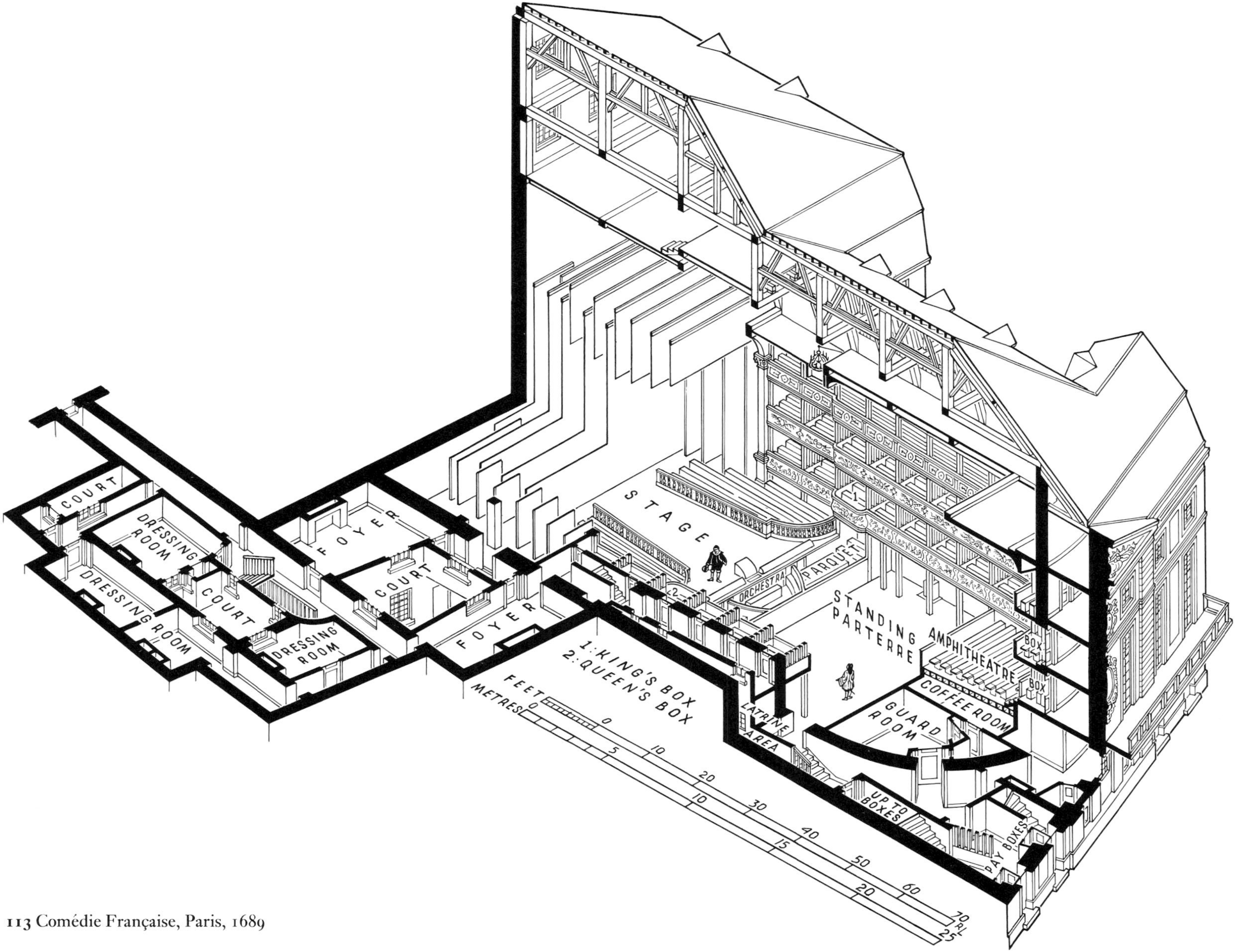
STAGE
ORCHESTRA
PARQUET
STANDING PARTERRE
AMPHITHEATRE
BOX
BOX
COFFEE ROOM
GUARD ROOM
LATRINE
AREA
UP TO BOXES
PAY BOXES
1: KING'S BOX
2: QUEEN'S BOX
FEET
METRES
FOYER
FOYER
COURT
COURT
COURT
DRESSING ROOM
DRESSING ROOM
DRESSING ROOM

113 Comédie Française, Paris, 1689

the usual open gallery or *paradis*. Unlike the Salle des Machines, which had a royal dais set at the viewpoint of the perspective scene, no such provision was made in this public theatre: instead, a box on either side of the stage was set aside when required for royal use, the box on the right-hand side being called the King's Box, and that directly opposite the Queen's Box.

Adjoining the stage was the by-now usual orchestra pit, but only the central semicircular portion was used by the musicians, the two side areas being fitted as a *parquet* with backless benches for some 40 to 50 spectators. A sloping *parterre* for the standing patrons extended beneath the side boxes, and beyond was an amphitheatre, which was now contained within the range of boxes, being entered at the rear through the centre box.

Unlike the contemporary Italian houses, the partitions of the boxes were still set at right angles to the box fronts. The need to crowd a larger paying audience into this commercial theatre resulted in the provision of partitioned areas, each containing five benches on either side of the stage, where they were backed by two additional boxes. By 1772, when Diderot illustrated the theatre, the *parquet* had been extended to include the orchestral space, and a new orchestra pit had been made by reducing the depth of the stage – an arrangement made possible by the removal of the on-stage seating, in the manner noted below. (See p. 75.)

This public theatre, unlike the Salle des Machines, had only a small scenic stage, with six pairs of wing positions, backshutters, and additional interspersed shutters. Obviously the deep vista scenes were proving too costly both in scenery and land space (in Inigo Jones's masques the depth of stage had been limited by the size of the existing hall). Presumably audiences were now accepting the actors within the scene, which they looked upon as mere decoration – for scenes viewed from any but the correct viewing point tend to lose their perspective continuity.

Each pair of wings had a horizontal border which could be raised or lowered to match the movement of the wings, by the rotation of a barrel. The roof over the stage was raised to provide space for this machinery, and for a room to accommodate the carpenters and scene painters. There was a shallow basement beneath the stage for the movement of the wing carriages. Foyers and dressing rooms were in adjoining premises, and a large room in the roof space over the auditorium had openings in the floor through which the chandeliers lighting the auditorium could be raised.

11 The Restoration playhouse and the fan-shaped auditorium

Restoration playhouses. Davenant and Killigrew. Tennis-court theatres. Lincoln's Inn Fields. First Theatre Royal, Drury Lane. Wren's Drury Lane. Alterations by Garrick and Adam. Fan-shaped auditoria. Shepherd's Covent Garden.

In England the Civil War brought a halt to theatre building, and all theatres were closed in 1642. With the Restoration in 1660, Sir William Davenant and Thomas Killigrew were given a monopoly on the presentation of dramatic performances. At first both made use of theatres that had survived the Interregnum, but then, like the French, they adapted existing tennis courts. During the war Davenant had managed to stage performances at his own home, Rutland House, of the opera *The Siege of Rhodes*, with perspective scenes by John Webb. It is not surprising, then, to find him adapting Lisle's Tennis Court, in Lincoln's Inn Fields, [114] to make provision for the new perspective scenes.

114 Lincoln's Inn Fields, 1661

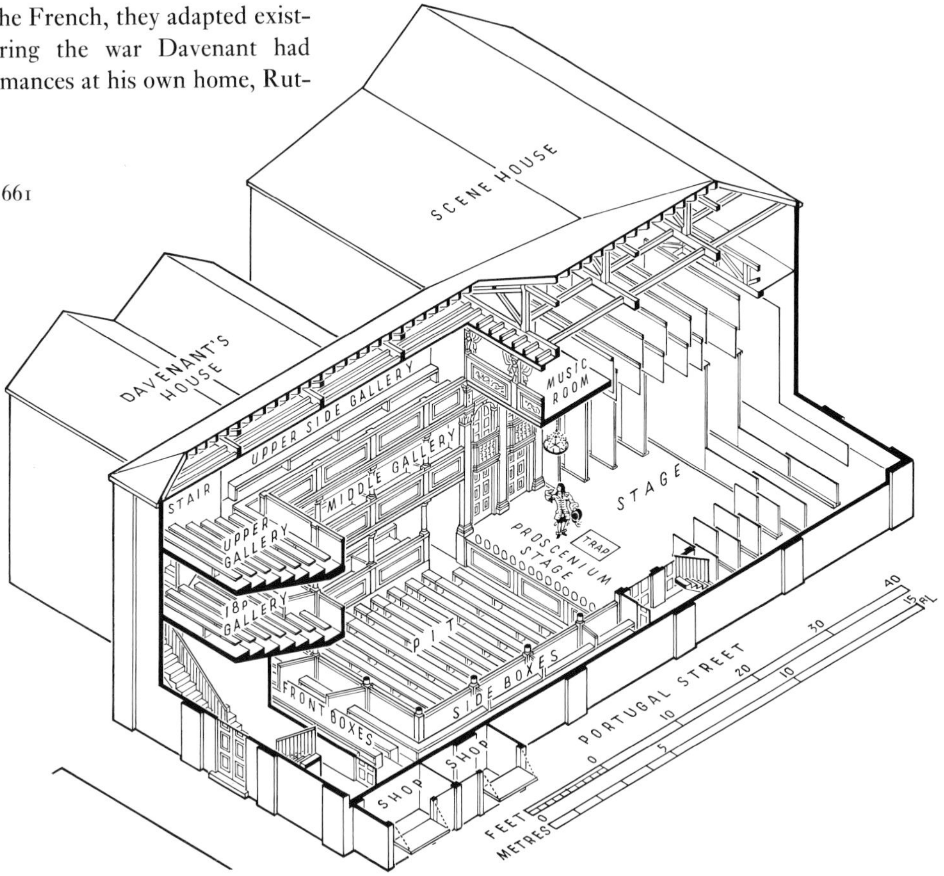
SCENE HOUSE
DAVENANT'S HOUSE
UPPER SIDE GALLERY
MIDDLE GALLERY
MUSIC ROOM
STAIR
UPPER GALLERY
18P GALLERY
STAGE
PROSCENIUM STAGE
TRAP
PIT
FRONT BOXES
SIDE BOXES
SHOP
SHOP
SHOP
PORTUGAL STREET
FEET
METRES
0
10
20
30
40
0
5
10
15
RL

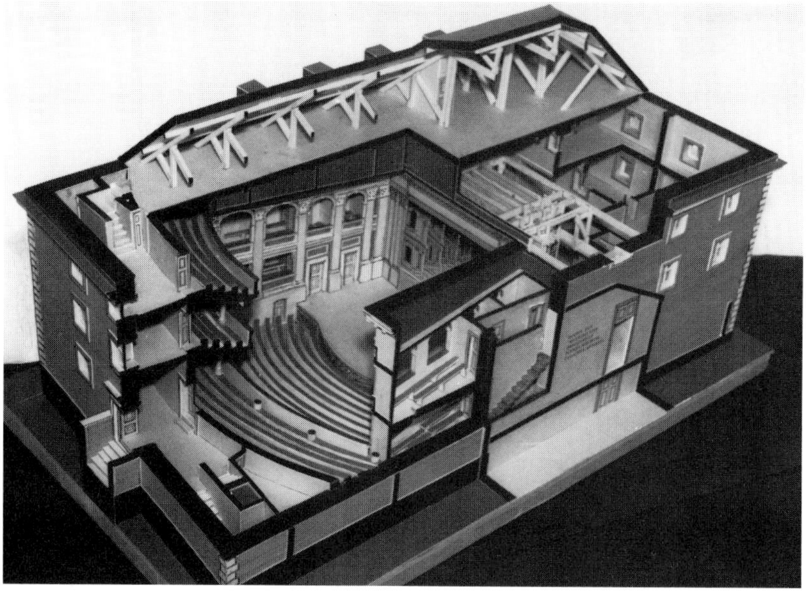

Theatre Royal, Drury Lane, 1674
115, 116, 117

116

As in France the long, narrow shape of these tennis courts imposed restrictions on the layout of the playhouses. Old ways die hard, and actors who had worked before the Civil War would have been used to the conventions associated with the use of doors with windows and balconies over. But if full value was to be given to the perspective scene then the scenic stage needed to be as wide as possible, and so it is reasonable to assume that the doors would have been set in the side walls of the stage. It is known that there were at least two doors on each side in this theatre, and the auditorium had boxes, pit, an upper gallery, and an 'eighteen pence gallery'. Pepys speaks of a 'side balcone over against the musique-room', from which he 'did hear, but not see, a new play'.

The success of Davenant's spectacular productions led Killigrew to build a new theatre, the first Theatre Royal in Drury Lane, which opened on 28 June 1661. It would seem that some attempt was made here to break away from the patterns imposed by the tennis courts, and to design an auditorium conforming more closely to classical traditions. The auditorium was 'nearly of a circular form, surrounded, in the inside by boxes separated from each other, and divided into several rows of seats'. A further description mentions benches in the pit 'rising one behind the other like an amphitheatre and covered with green cloth'. Pepys writes of a 'cupola at the top' and there is also mention of a middle and an upper gallery.

In 1672 the Theatre Royal was burnt down, to be replaced in 1674 by the second Drury Lane, designed by Sir Christopher Wren. Our revised reconstruction [115, 116] provides us with a picture of a Restoration playhouse in which a large proportion of the audience were seated in ideal positions for viewing the perspective scene, with the remainder, however, not being so well disposed in side boxes.

The side walls of the auditorium [117] sloped inwards towards the stage as a continuation of the perspective vista, particularly when viewed from the central position of the royal box. The side boxes, on two levels, were separated by giant Corinthian pilasters, which reduced in size towards the stage in conformity with the diminishing perspective. Although not well placed to view the scene, the audience in the side boxes were well related to the actors on their proscenium stage within the auditorium, and since attendance at the theatre was for many only an occasion for social intercourse, they were well situated both to see and be seen.

Half the depth of the auditorium was taken up by the actors' stage, approached by two doors on either side, set between the pilasters. The central portion of the stage front was slightly curved, concentric with the backless benches filling the gently rising pit, which was entered by doors at the front, leading from passages beneath the side boxes.

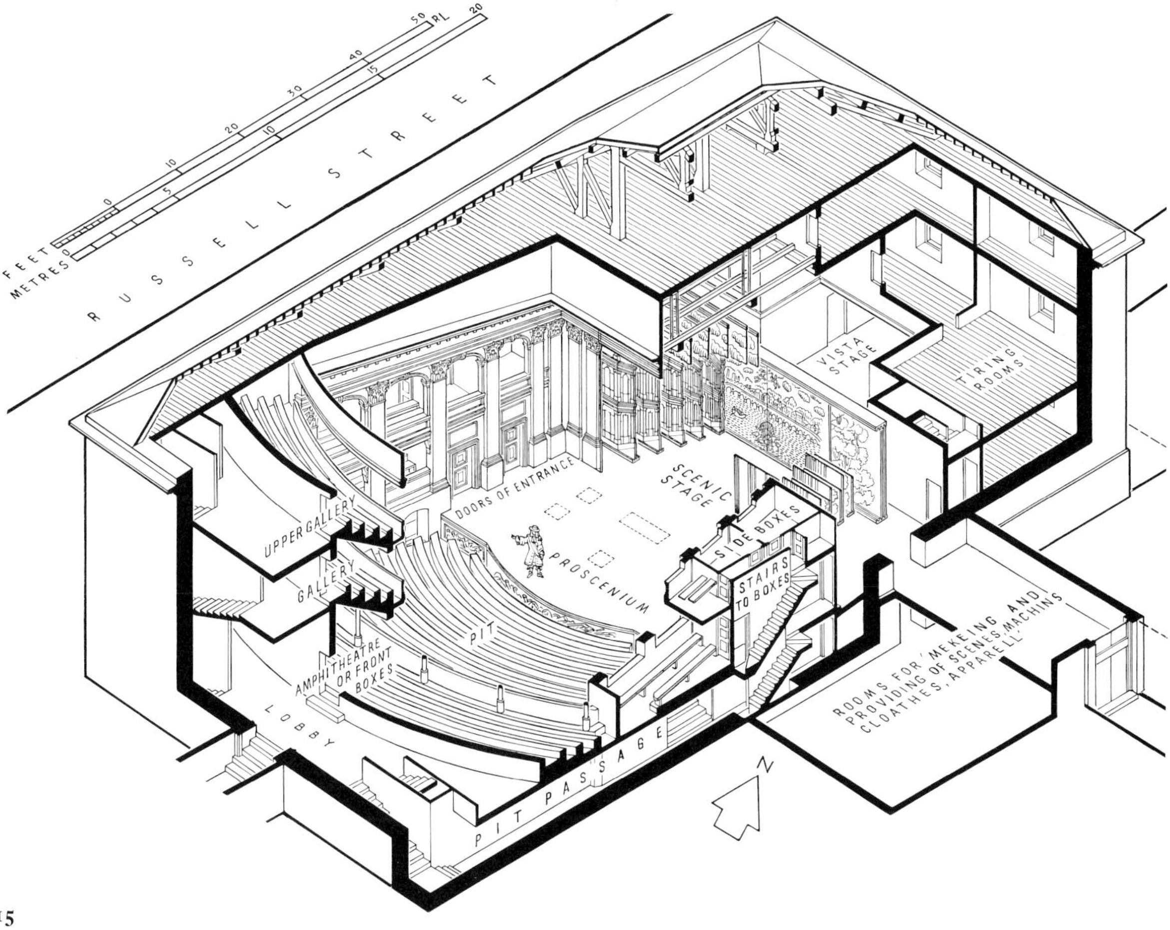
FEET
0
10
20
30
40
50
METRES
0
5
10
15
20
RL
RUSSELL STREET
VISTA STAGE
TIRING ROOMS
SCENIC STAGE
DOORS OF ENTRANCE
SIDE BOXES
STAIRS TO BOXES
UPPER GALLERY
GALLERY
PROSCENIUM
PIT
AMPHITHEATRE OR FRONT BOXES
LOBBY
PIT PASSAGE
ROOMS FOR 'MEKEING AND PROVIDING OF SCENES, MACHINS CLOATHES, APPARELL'
N

115

117

118

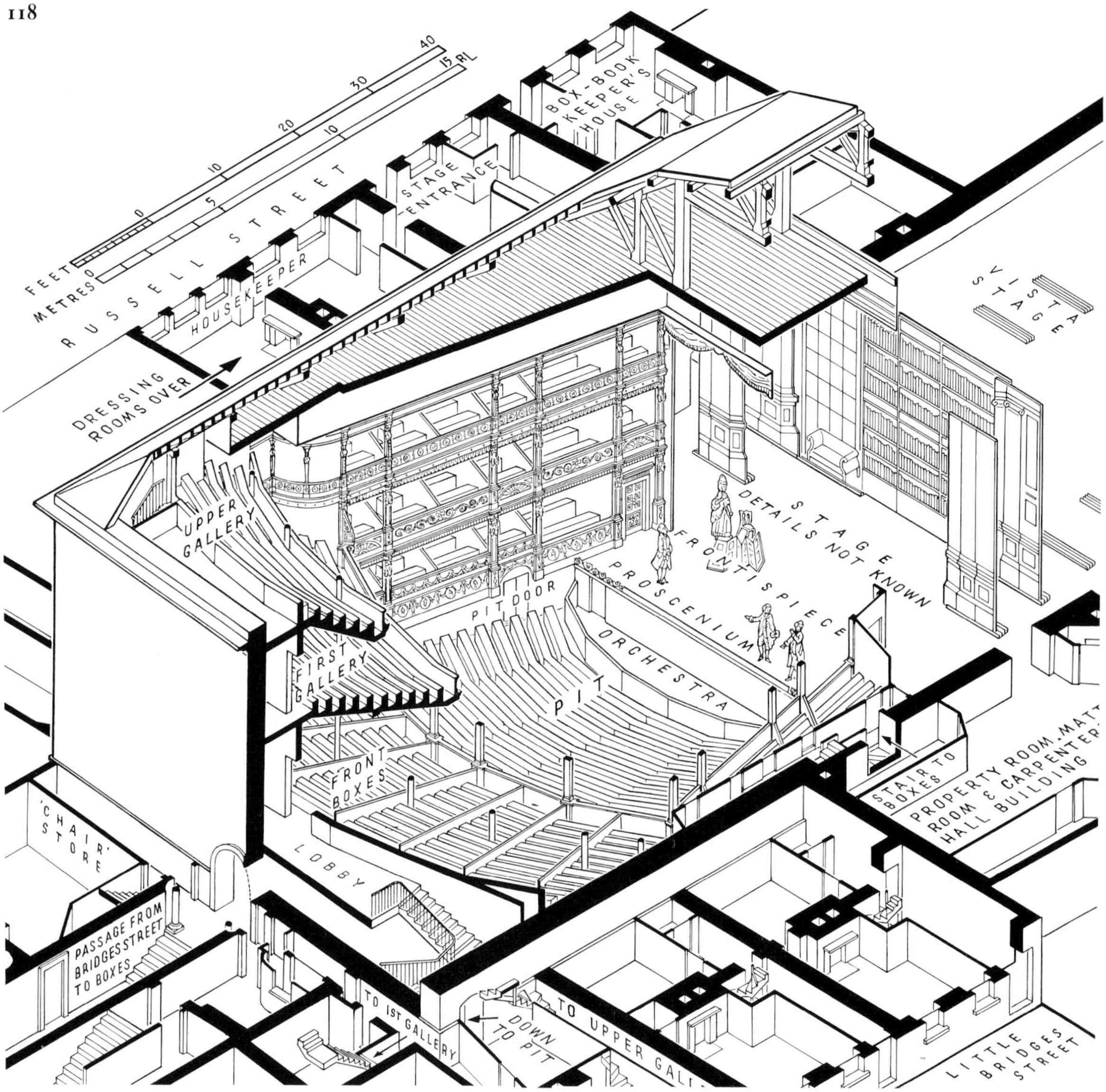
FEET
METRES
0
5
10
20
30
40
0
10
15
RUSSELL STREET
HOUSEKEEPER
STAGE ENTRANCE
BOX-BOOK KEEPER'S HOUSE
DRESSING ROOMS OVER
VISTA STAGE
UPPER GALLERY
FIRST GALLERY
FRONT BOXES
PIT DOOR
PIT
ORCHESTRA
PROSCENIUM
FRONTISPIECE
STAGE DETAILS NOT KNOWN
STAIR TO BOXES
PROPERTY ROOM. MATT ROOM & CARPENTER HALL BUILDING
'CHAIR' STORE
LOBBY
PASSAGE FROM BRIDGES STREET TO BOXES
TO 1ST GALLERY
DOWN TO PIT
TO UPPER GALL
LITTLE BRIDGES STREET

Theatre Royal, Drury Lane, 1775
118, 119

No orchestra pit separated the audience from the stage, and the musicians must have been housed in one or other of the side boxes. Facing the stage and concentric with the pit benches were three levels of stepped benches: the lowest of these formed the front boxes, with a gallery and an upper gallery above. The whole stage sloped up until it reached an inner, flat vista stage set between dressing rooms, which also bridged this area at two levels. As in the Comédie Française, the audience continued to sit on the sides of the stage, enclosed behind low partitions. By 1696 some 4 feet (1.22m) had been cut off the front of the stage to provide additional space for the audience, or perhaps for musicians, and the lower 'doors of entry' had been replaced by boxes, further doors being positioned on the scenic

119

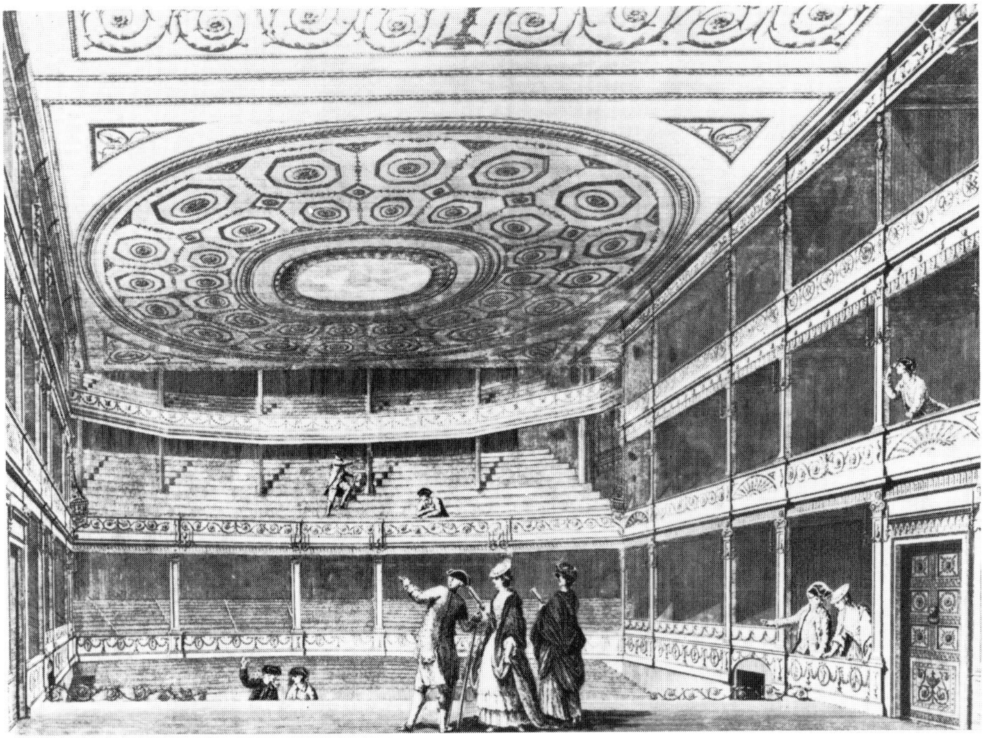

stage. Stage and auditorium were continuously lit by hoops of candles.

Although the presence of members of the audience on stage interfered with the stage picture and the movement of the players, the custom was commercially acceptable to the management – and also to the actors on the occasion of their benefit nights. In Paris spectators were banned from the stage of the Comédie Française in 1759, and the actors' financial loss was offset by a subsidy, and David Garrick, wishing to remove the inconvenience from Drury Lane, had had to offset the monetary loss by providing further accommodation in the auditorium. He called in Robert Adam, who carried out a thorough restoration of the building in 1775, contriving three tiers of boxes within the same height as Wren's two tiers, and gaining additional seating by replacing Wren's heavy Corinthian pilasters by narrow, glass-fronted pilasters and thermes. [118, 119]

Unfortunately this resulted in many more members of the audience being badly placed in the side boxes of the fan-shaped auditorium in relation to the stage, which had already been cut back once. Now Adam moved his frontispiece further upstage, and reduced the proscenium stage from Wren's 21 feet (6.40m) to approximately 11 feet (3.35m), leaving space for an orchestra pit and additional benches in both pit and front boxes, increasing the latter from four to eleven rows.

Wren's fan-shaped auditorium had set the pattern for new theatres, including Covent Garden as designed by Edward Shepherd in 1731–2, but when this fan-shaped auditorium was enlarged in 1782 the fronts of the side boxes were made more nearly parallel in an attempt to improve the sight-lines. At Drury Lane the increased size of the front boxes, and of the first and upper galleries, meant that the majority of the audience had an excellent view of the stage.

There was now only one pair of proscenium doors, but the opportunity was taken to extend the rear of the stage to provide extra depth for scenic vistas and spectacular processions. Additional rooms were becoming essential to a theatre, and dressing rooms (for actresses as well as actors since 1660), green rooms, scene rooms, and management offices were now provided in adjoining premises. At Covent Garden, and possibly at Drury Lane, the roof space over both stage and auditorium was used to provide carpenters' workshops and paint rooms.

12 Scenic spectacle and civic pride

Scenes and theatres of the Bibiena family. Teatro Scientifico, Mantua. Margravine's Opera House, Bayreuth. The Manoel Theatre, Malta. La Scala, Milan. Private boxes and the Old Price Riots. Queen's Theatre and Holland's Covent Garden. Drottningholm and scenic machines.

In Italy the opera flourished both in the court and the commercial theatres – and with it scenic spectacle, particularly in the hands of the Bibiena family. Andrea Pozzo had developed a technique of continuing the appearance of a single architectural feature from one piece of scenery to another, and the Bibienas developed the use of multiple vistas in a single scene by the use of cut-out scenes and scenic units placed on the stage additional to the side wings. [120]

It was natural that they should also design theatres to set off their spectacles, and in 1769 Antonio Bibiena designed the Teatro Scientifico in Mantua. [121] Here

120 Stage design by Giuseppe Bibiena, 1719

the *loges* are arranged with a central concave curve flowing into convex wings, behind a facade reminiscent of the Roman theatre of Marcellus, [59] the stage, in this instance, having a permanent architectural surround. The Margravine's Opera House, Bayreuth, [122] has a similar plan, but in contrast to the severely classical treatment of the former, it has a magnificent royal box, lavishly decorated in keeping with the remainder of the

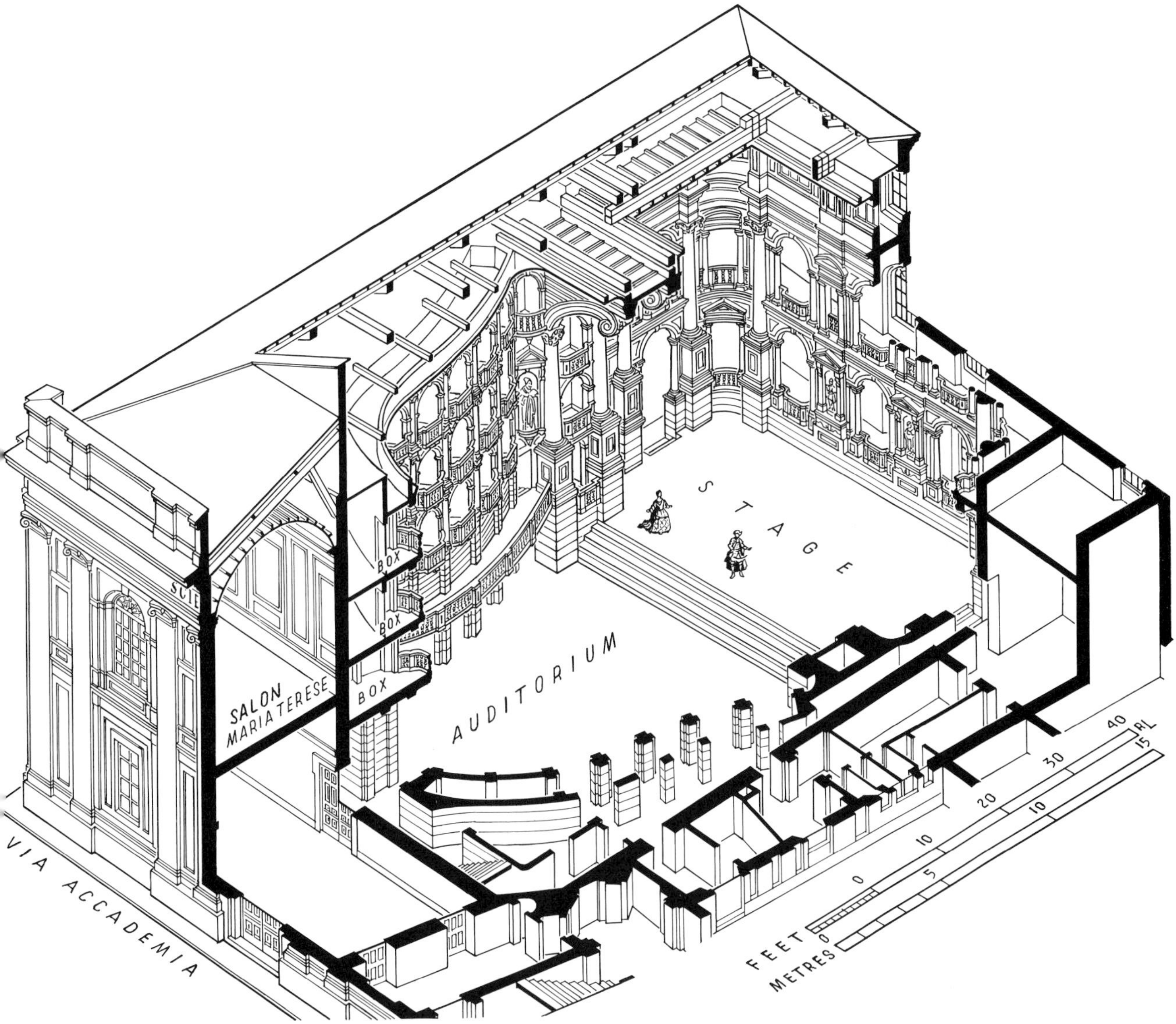
STAGE
AUDITORIUM
BOX
BOX
BOX
SALON MARIA TERESE
VIA ACCADEMIA
FEET
METRES
0
10
20
30
40
0
5
10
15
RL

121 Teatro Scientifico, Mantua, Italy, 1769

122

The Margravine's
Opera House,
Bayreuth

123

124

125

Manoel Theatre, Valetta, Malta
124, 125, 126

126

auditorium, with all the flamboyance and richness of the Baroque period, which was now in full force. [123]

The Manoel Theatre, Valetta, [125] Malta (1731), had a more normal U-shaped auditorium, with three tiers of *loges* and an upper tier with five central *loges* facing the stage, and open galleries on either side. The front of the stage and the orchestra-well were flanked by further boxes between two giant Corinthian pilasters, [124, 126] supporting a lower arched ceiling serving as a sounding board. A small stage had seven positions for wing chariots, while two fly galleries followed the lines of the diminishing scenic vista, connected by a rear gallery for use with sky machinery.

80 : Scenic spectacle and civic pride

An outstanding example of the standard Italian arrangement for an opera house is La Scala, Milan, opened in 1778. [127] Designed as a free-standing architectural unit, it had foyers, saloons, and offices at the front, together with a *porte cochère* which enabled patrons to leave their carriages under cover. The auditorium was designed as a horseshoe with five tiers of individual *loges* and an open gallery above, while the open ground floor, equivalent to the English pit, was entered at the back beneath the ducal box.

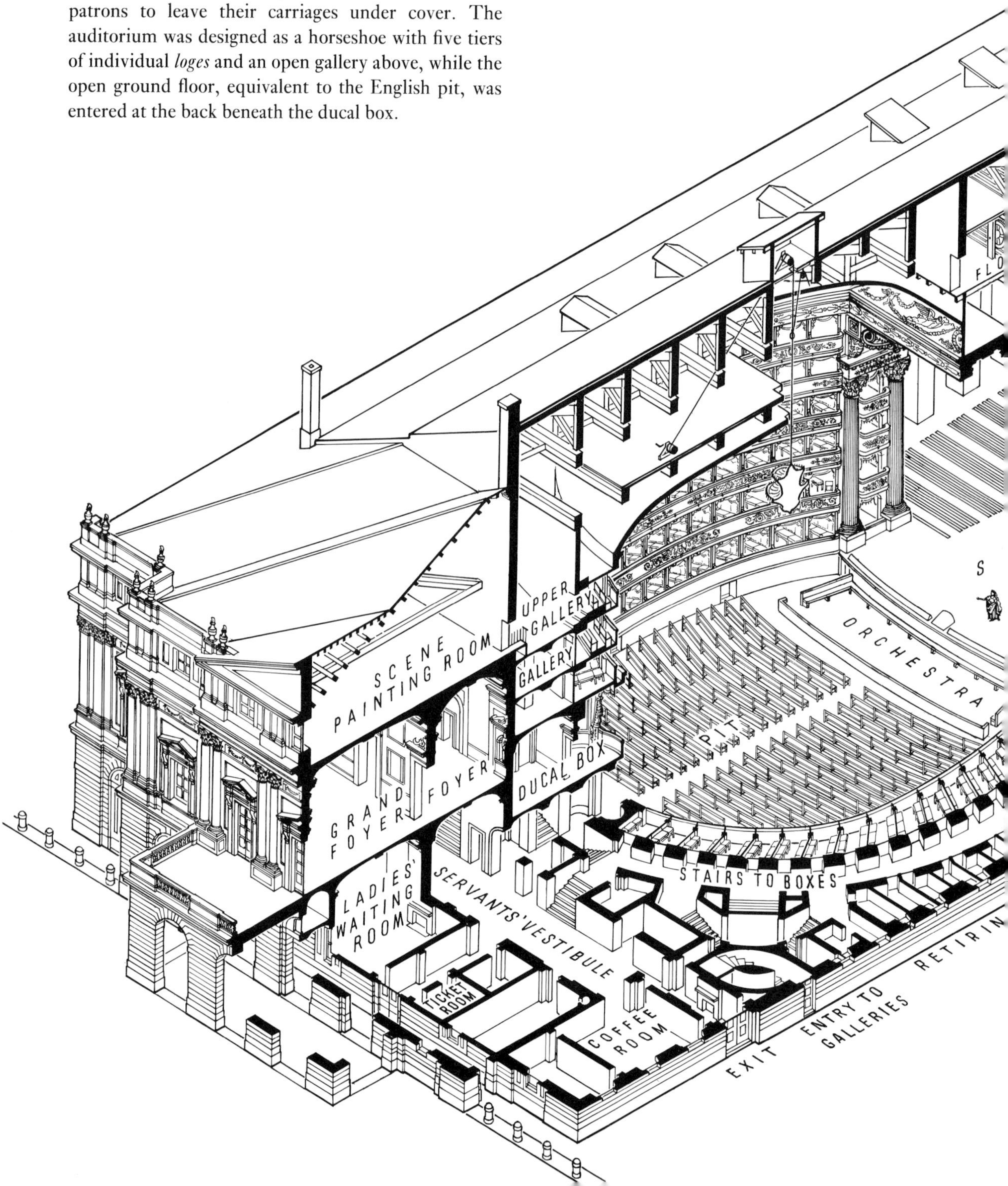
SCENE PAINTING ROOM
UPPER GALLERY
GALLERY
DUCAL BOX
GRAND FOYER
FOYER
LADIES' WAITING ROOM
SERVANTS' VESTIBULE
TICKET ROOM
COFFEE ROOM
STAIRS TO BOXES
PIT
ORCHESTRA
EXIT
ENTRY TO GALLERIES

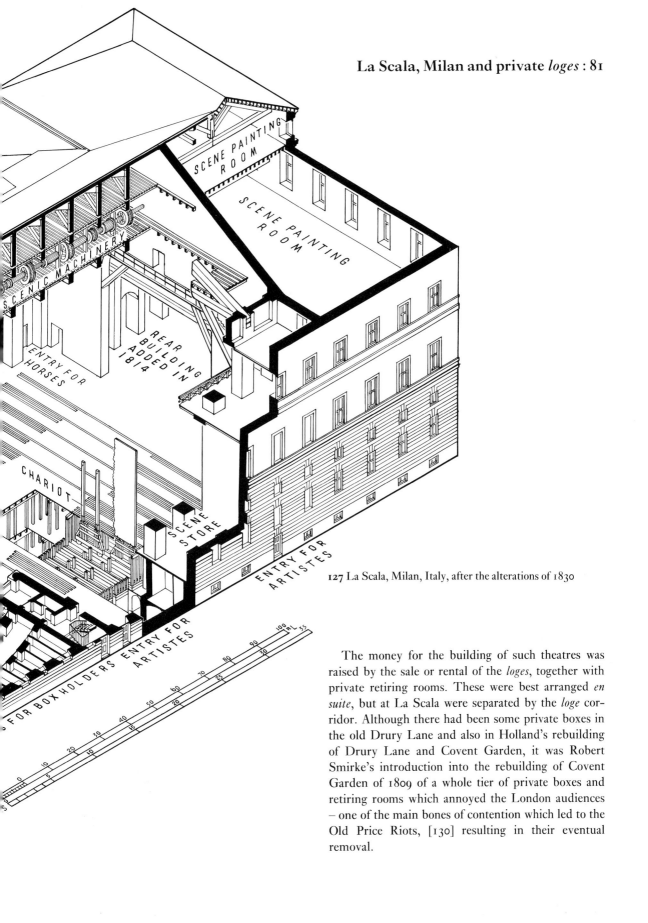

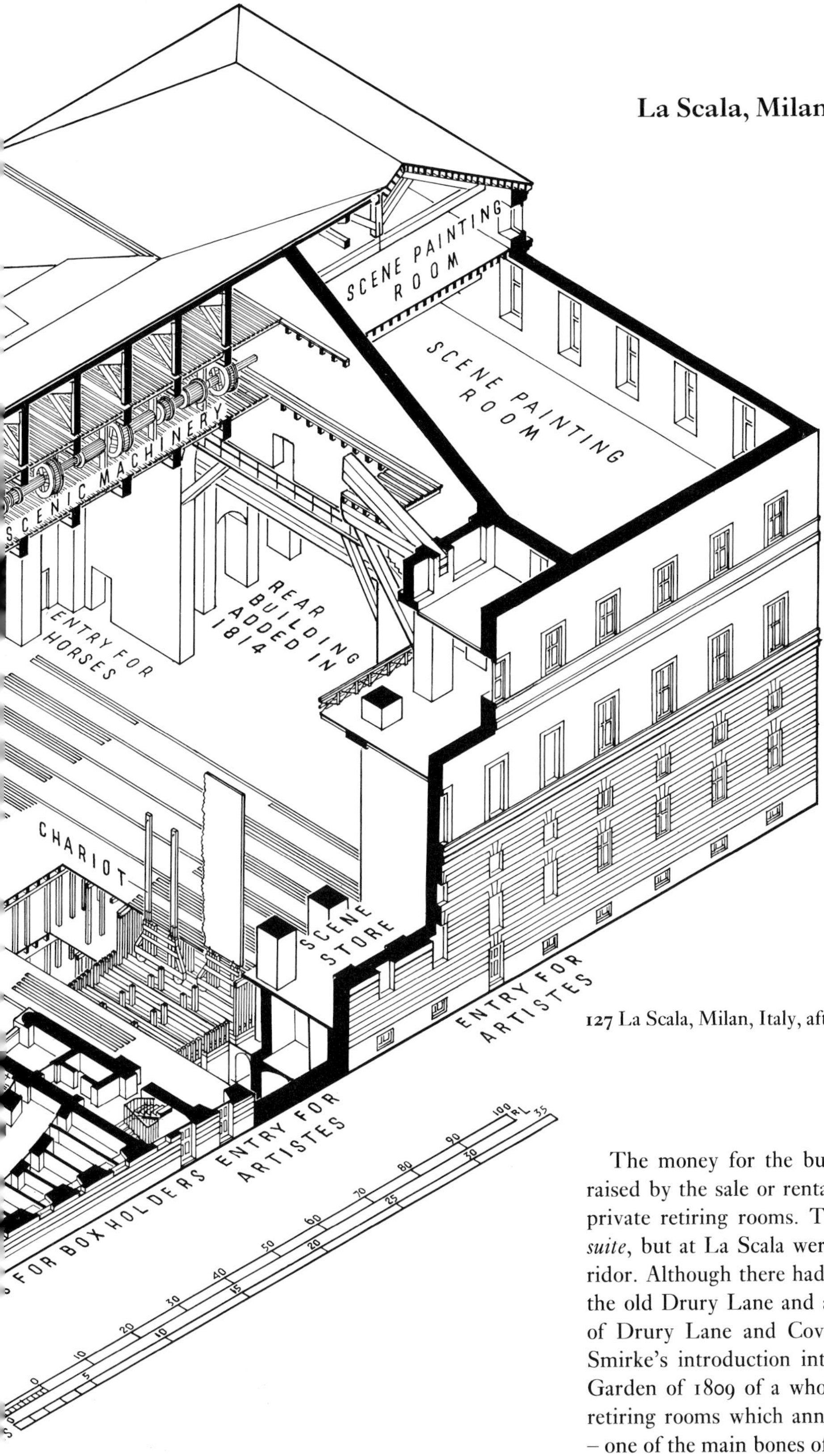
SCENE PAINTING ROOM
SCENE PAINTING ROOM
SCENIC MACHINERY
REAR BUILDING ADDED IN 1814
ENTRY FOR HORSES
CHARIOT
SCENE STORE
ENTRY FOR ARTISTES
ENTRY FOR ARTISTES
FOR BOX HOLDERS

127 La Scala, Milan, Italy, after the alterations of 1830

The money for the building of such theatres was raised by the sale or rental of the *loges*, together with private retiring rooms. These were best arranged *en suite*, but at La Scala were separated by the *loge* corridor. Although there had been some private boxes in the old Drury Lane and also in Holland's rebuilding of Drury Lane and Covent Garden, it was Robert Smirke's introduction into the rebuilding of Covent Garden of 1809 of a whole tier of private boxes and retiring rooms which annoyed the London audiences – one of the main bones of contention which led to the Old Price Riots, [130] resulting in their eventual removal.

The pit at La Scala had eighteen rows of benches with a central gangway, and was separated from the proscenium stage by a railed space for an orchestra. It was not until 1906–7 that this area was rebuilt in the manner of the orchestra well in the Teatro Regio, Turin (1740), [128] where the wooden floor of the orchestra pit was built over a concave channel which served to increase the resonance of the music. On either side of the proscenium stage were *loges* flanked by giant Corinthian columns supporting consoles and a low ceiling.

The scenic stage had ten sets of wing positions, and an aisle on each side divided into bays for use as scene stores and staircases. There were fly floors on either side above the aisles, and the roof space over both stage and auditorium was a single open area, partly separated above the proscenium opening by a masonry wall with arched openings. Minimum space was provided beneath the stage, sufficient only for the movement of the scene carriages and machinery.

In 1782 Michael Novosielski proposed that the Queen's Theatre in London be altered so that it should have 'the lines of an Italian Opera house' with a horseshoe arrangement of boxes; and, when fire destroyed the original building in 1789, his design for a new theatre included an auditorium arranged in this manner, with five tiers of boxes each enclosed by curtains in 'the fashion of the Neapolitan theatres and furnished with six chairs'.

A similar arrangement was used by Henry Holland when he adapted Covent Garden in 1791, [129] but instead of separate boxes the four tiers were designed as open galleries separated only by low partitions, the two uppermost tiers opening out into central, English-style galleries, each having fourteen rows of benches. Behind the front boxes in the lowest tier, and beyond a cross-passage, was a further amphitheatre of seven benches, subdivided into seven deep boxes known as 'basket boxes'. The pit, with twenty benches, was separated from the stage by a full-width orchestra pit, built in the continental manner over an inverted arch 'to assist the general sound'.

The scenic arrangements included in the continental, as in some British theatres are well illustrated by the scenes and machines which are still in use in the Court Theatre at Drottningholm, Sweden, which dates from 1766. [131a] The King and Queen sat on armchairs at the front of a T-shaped auditorium, flanked on either side by the royal family, while the courtiers sat on benches filling the tail of the T, on a single stepped slope. Small screened boxes in the side walls were used as

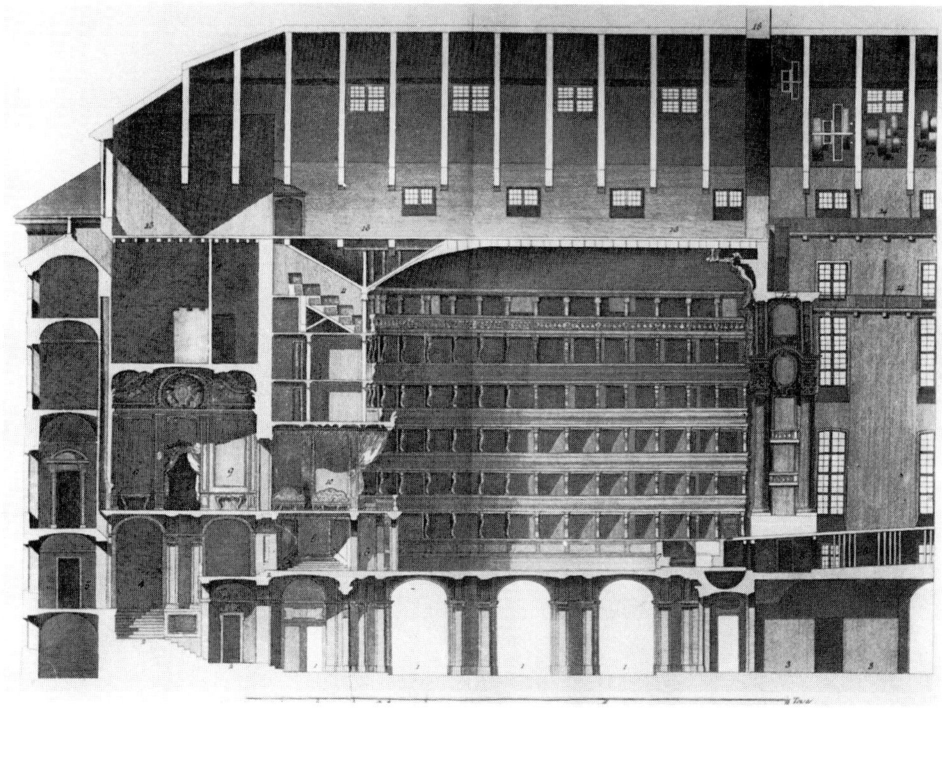

128 Teatro Regio, Turin, Italy

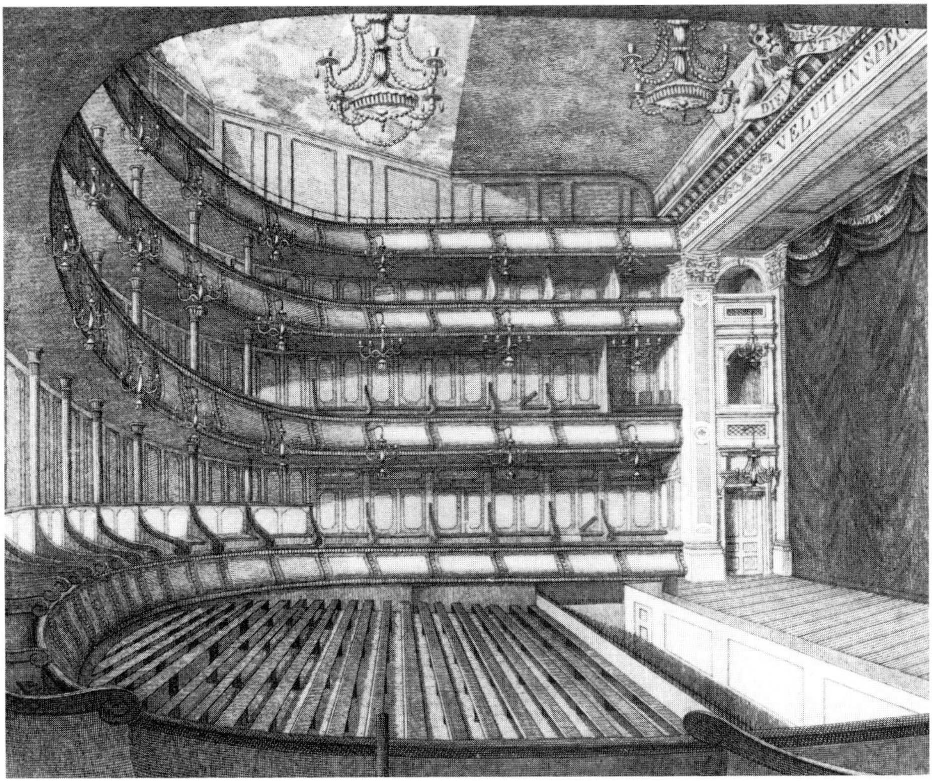

129 Theatre Royal, Covent Garden, in 1794

130 Theatre Royal, Covent Garden. Old Price Riots of 1809

John Bull
against
Kemble
Remember
Dublin
Twn Man
OLD PRICES
OLD PRICES
No Italian
Boxes
NO PIGEON
HOLES
NO PRIVATE
BOXES
PRICES
Fire Office 80.000
Old Material 25.000
185.000
New Theatre 150.000
RL

retiring rooms for the royal couple.

Space for an orchestra is railed off from the seating and separates it from a small proscenium stage, beyond which is the main stage equipped with six sets of wing positions, the first four sets each having four pairs of chariots, with three in the fifth position and two in the sixth. In addition there are four traps in the raking stage. Beneath the stage, [131c] a cellar houses the wing chariots running on timber rails, which can be moved on and off stage as required by a large capstan. Lights on vertical shafts behind each set of wings can be turned to lighten or darken the stage, and further mechanism raises or lowers the footlights. Additional drums work the traps in the rear of the stage.

In the roof space over the stage [131b] a centrally placed barrel or roller runs the full depth of the scenic vista, and to this are attached the lines moving the sets of horizontal borders related to each set of wings. The roller is operated by a windlass in the cellar. At the sides there are further, smaller shafts and drums controlling the sections of cloud scenery, which can descend to stage level in conjunction with the ascent or descent of actors seated on one or other of the two chariots. Further drums operate these and the individual drop scenes, and another works the front curtain. Above the ceiling to the proscenium stage is a machine for creating the effect of thunder. At stage level various scenic devices can be introduced in the form of rostra and stairs, and a set of five 'barley-sugar' columns simulate the effect of waves, on which cut-out ships can move.

131 Court Theatre, Drottningholm, Sweden, 1766
a: Stage and auditorium
b: Machinery above and
c: below stage

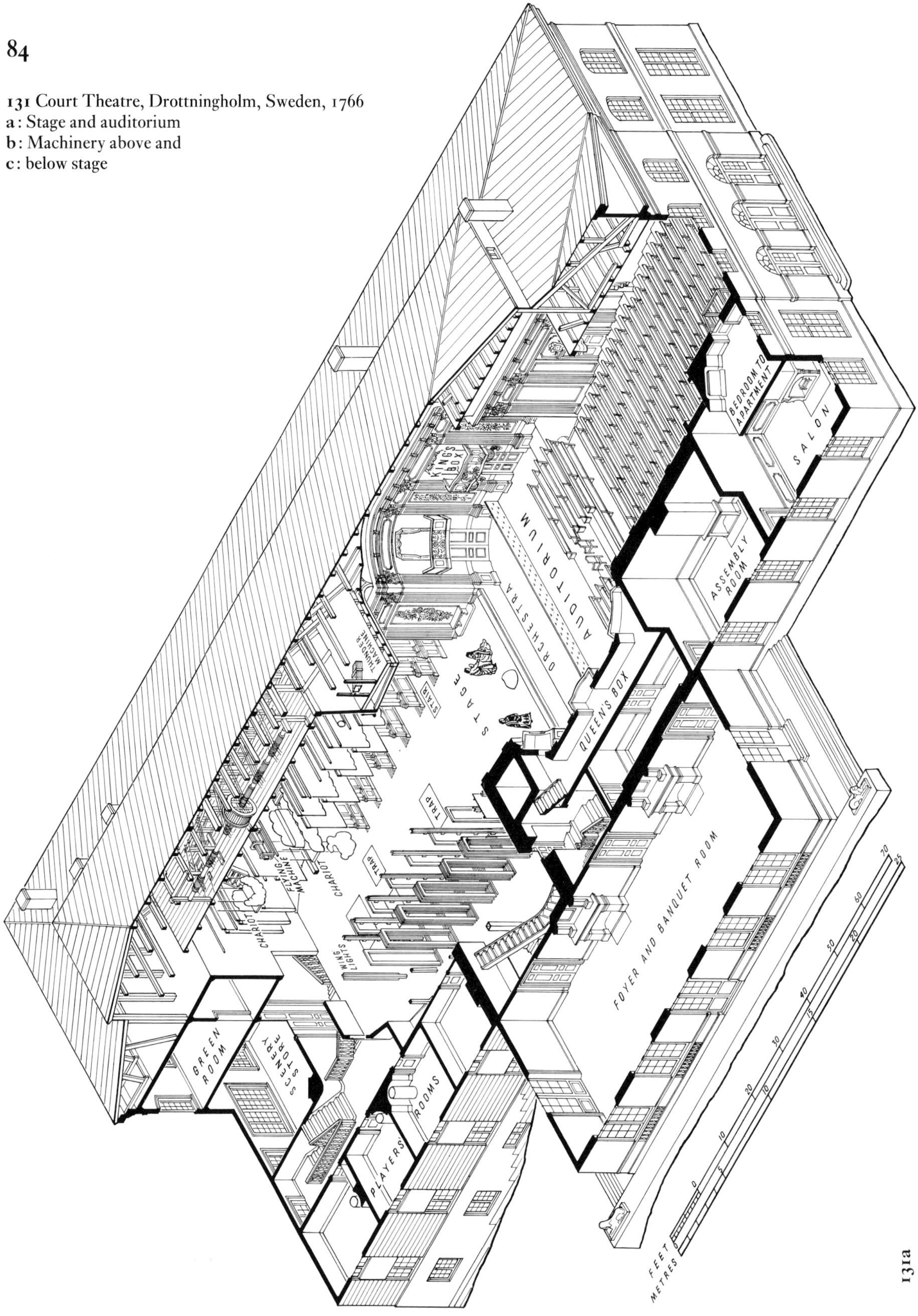
BEDROOM TO APARTMENT
SALON
ASSEMBLY ROOM
KING'S BOX
AUDITORIUM
ORCHESTRA
QUEEN'S BOX
THUNDER MACHINE
STAIR
STAGE
TRAP
TRAP
CHARIOT
FLYING MACHINE
CHARIOT
WING LIGHTS
FOYER AND BANQUET ROOM
GREEN ROOM
SCENERY STORE
PLAYERS' ROOMS
FEET
METRES
0 10 20 30 40 50 60 70
0 5 10 15 20 25

131a

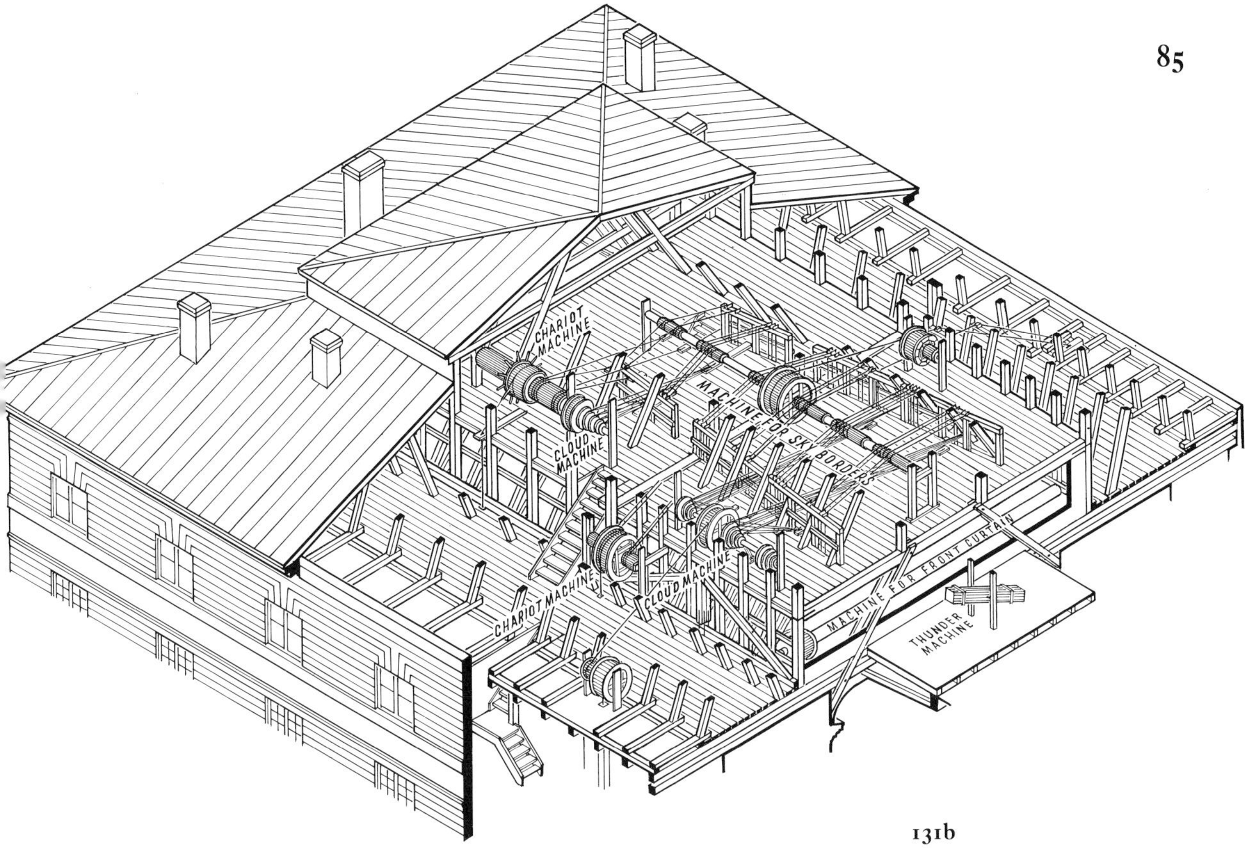
CHARIOT MACHINE
CLOUD MACHINE
MACHINE FOR SKY BORDERS
CHARIOT MACHINE
CLOUD MACHINE
MACHINE FOR FRONT CURTAIN
THUNDER MACHINE

131b

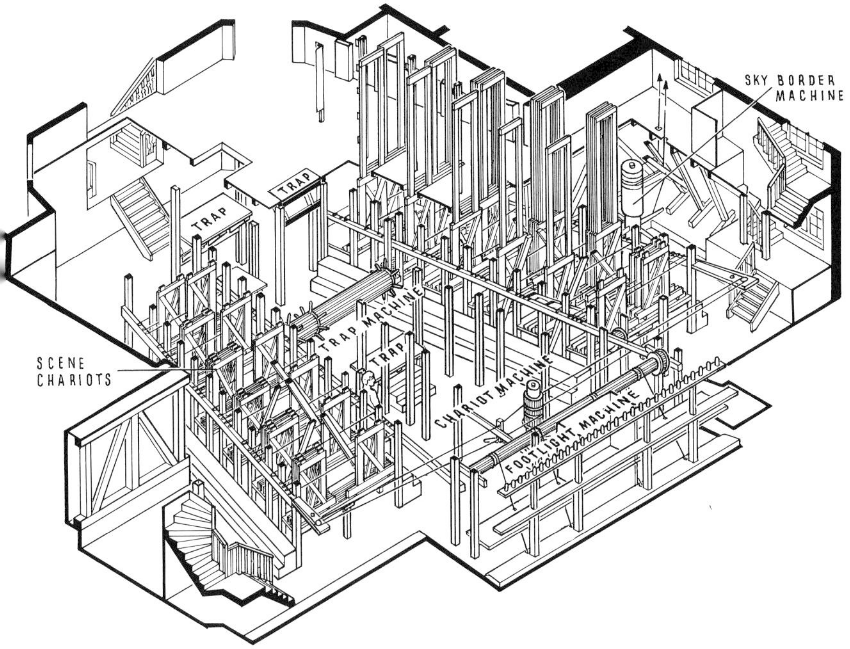
SKY BORDER MACHINE
TRAP
TRAP
TRAP MACHINE
TRAP
SCENE CHARIOTS
CHARIOT MACHINE
FOOTLIGHT MACHINE

131c

13 Safety and acoustics

Eighteenth-century problems of safety and acoustics. Soufflot's theatre at Lyons. Victor Louis' Grand Theatre, Bordeaux. Saunders's Treatise on Theatres. Ledoux's theatre at Besançon. Holland's Theatre Royal, Drury Lane. Spectacle and declamation.

By the mid-eighteenth century, greater attention was being given to problems of safety and acoustics. In 1762 Count Algarotti suggested that theatre buildings should be fireproof, and therefore constructed of brick or stone, but retaining the use of timber in the auditorium for acoustic purposes. He favoured the classical circle for the auditorium, but accepted the more normal elliptical shape. Charles Nicholas Cochin developed a project for a theatre in which the ellipse was set with its main axis parallel to the stage front. Whilst this placed a greater proportion of the audience in a good viewing position relative to the stage, and improved the acoustics by bringing the spectators closer to the actors, it required a very much wider stage, a problem which Cochin resolved by providing three proscenium openings, each with its own scenic vista. Such a scheme was utilized by Cosimo Morelli in the theatre at Imola in 1779, [132] although here the auditorium reverted to a partly truncated longitudinal ellipse.

An important move towards the protection of theatres and their audiences was the erection of free-standing buildings on island sites. One of the earliest of such 'detached' theatres was built at Lyons in 1754 by Soufflot. [133] It retained the elliptical auditorium, with the ground floor subdivided into orchestra, *parquet*, standing *parterre*, and benched amphitheatre,

132 Theatre at Imola, Italy. Section and plan

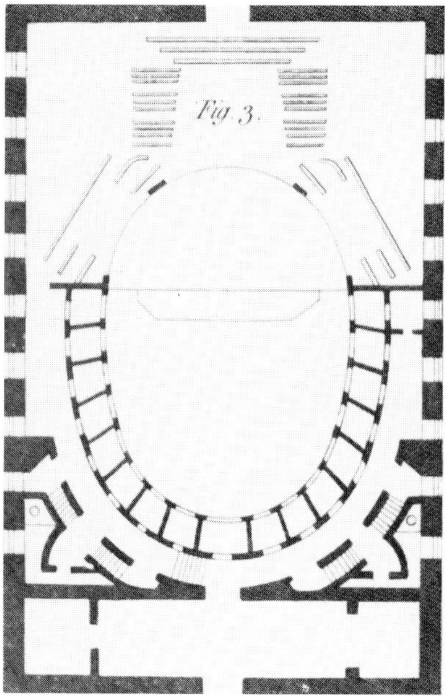
Fig. 3.

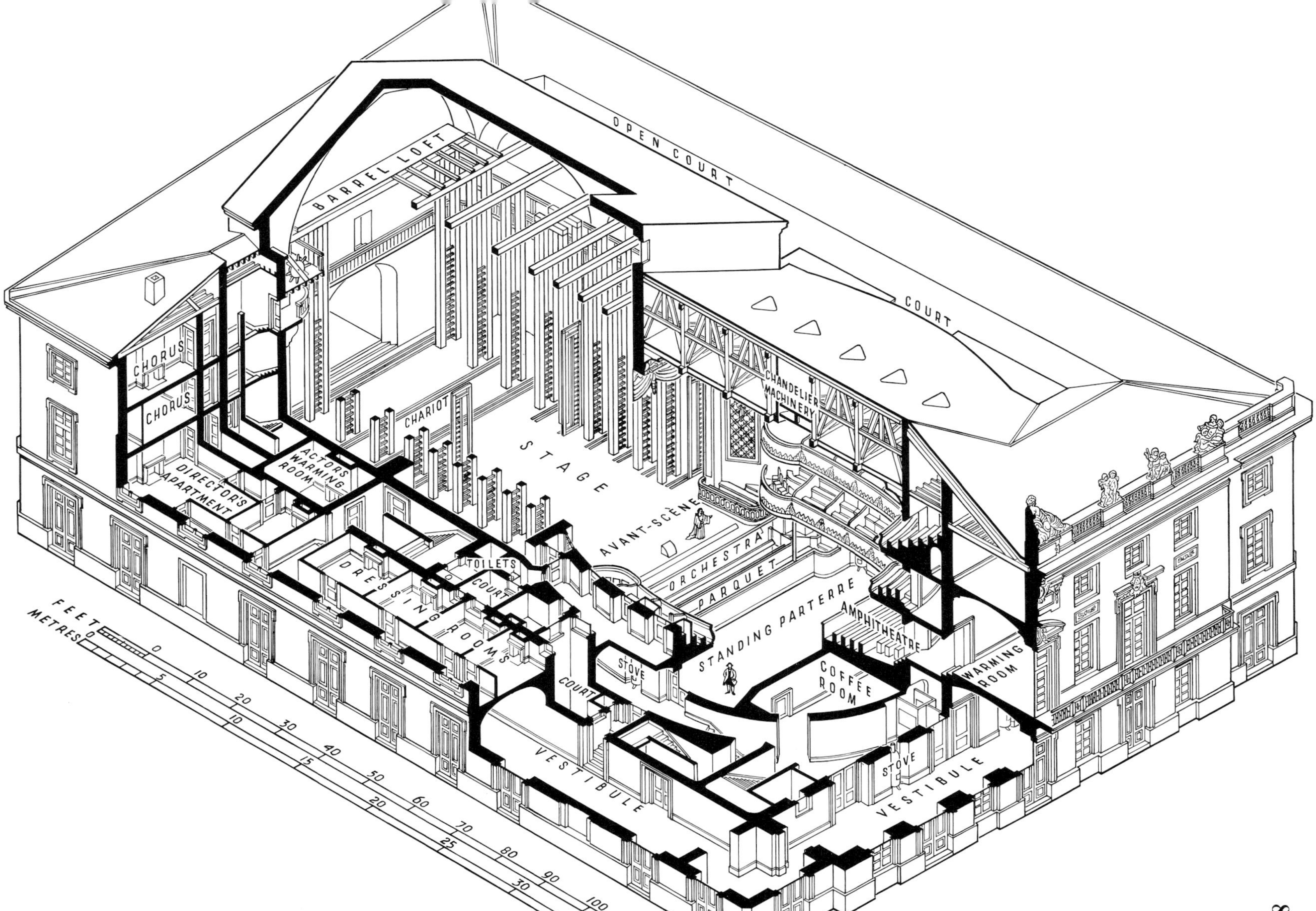
OPEN COURT
COURT
BARREL LOFT
CHORUS
CHORUS
DIRECTOR'S APARTMENT
ACTORS WARMING ROOM
CHARIOT
STAGE
CHANDELIER MACHINERY
AVANT-SCÈNE
ORCHESTRA
PARQUET
STANDING PARTERRE
AMPHITHEATRE
WARMING ROOM
COFFEE ROOM
TOILETS
COURT
DRESSING ROOMS
STOVE
COURT
VESTIBULE
STOVE
VESTIBULE
FEET
METRES

133 Theatre at Lyons, France, 1754

134 The Grand Theatre, Bordeaux, France, 1773–80

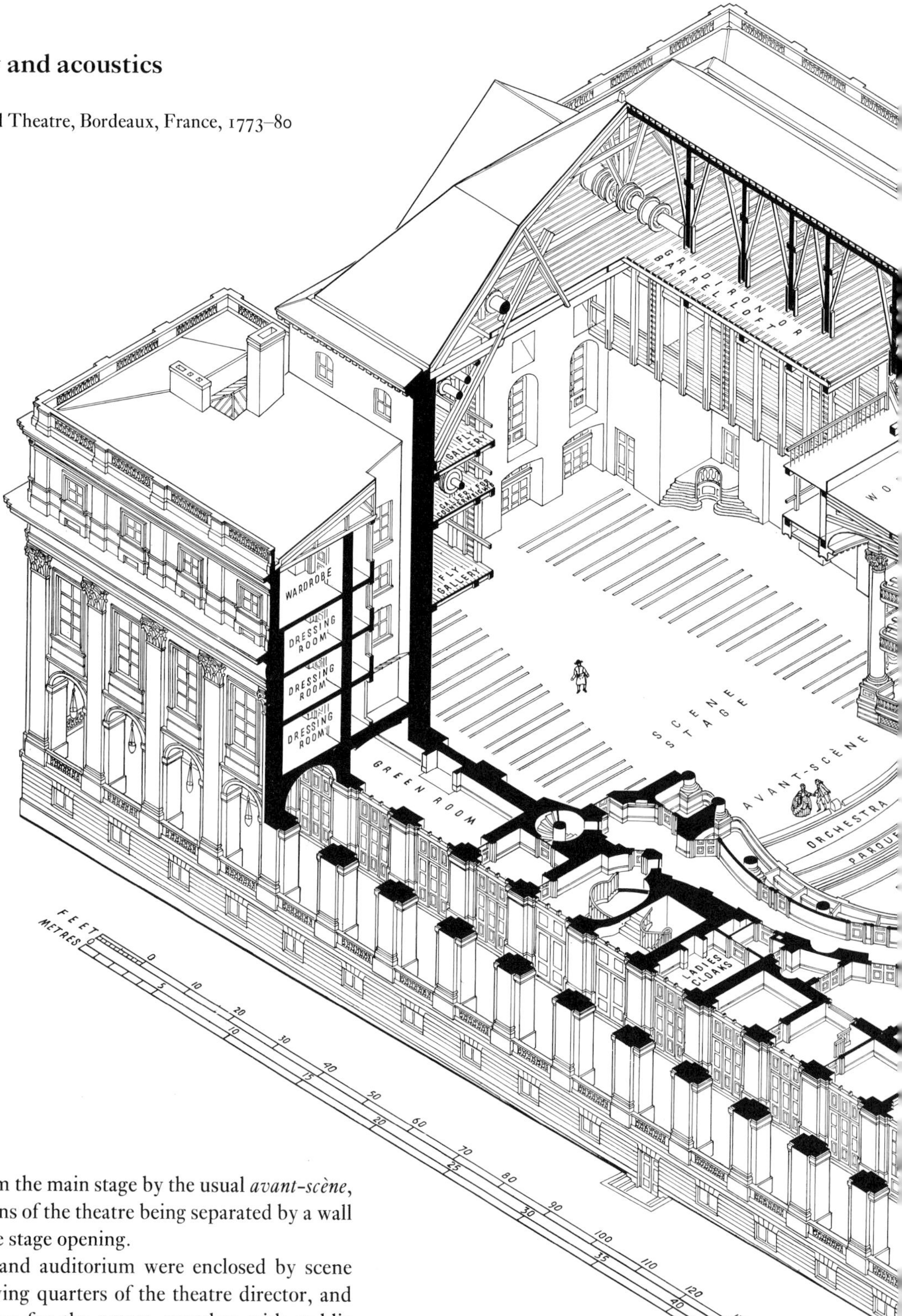
GRIDIRON OR BARREL LOFT
FLY GALLERY
GALLERY FOR COUNTERWEIGHTS
FLY GALLERY
WARDROBE
DRESSING ROOM
DRESSING ROOM
DRESSING ROOM
GREEN ROOM
SCENE STAGE
AVANT-SCÈNE
ORCHESTRA
LADIES CLOAKS
FEET
METRES

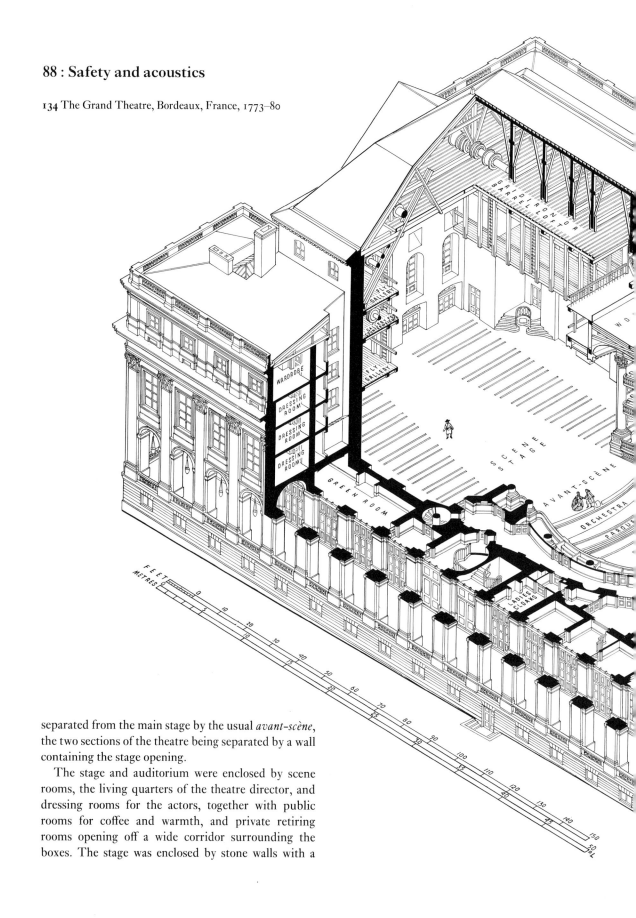

separated from the main stage by the usual *avant-scène*, the two sections of the theatre being separated by a wall containing the stage opening.

The stage and auditorium were enclosed by scene rooms, the living quarters of the theatre director, and dressing rooms for the actors, together with public rooms for coffee and warmth, and private retiring rooms opening off a wide corridor surrounding the boxes. The stage was enclosed by stone walls with a minimum of openings, flanked by open courts and stair wells, and roofed with stone vaulting. It was surrounded at the upper level by an internal stone gallery, equipped with leather pipes and taps through which water for fire-fighting could be supplied from two reservoirs.

One of the finest and most influential of such theatres was the Grand Theatre built by Victor Louis in 1773–80 at Bordeaux. [134] For his auditorium Louis used a circular plan with four tiers of boxes, each projecting forward between giant columns, two of which formed the front pair of the normal proscenium arrangement supporting a low ceiling. The opposing pair at the rear of the auditorium supported flat arches matching the

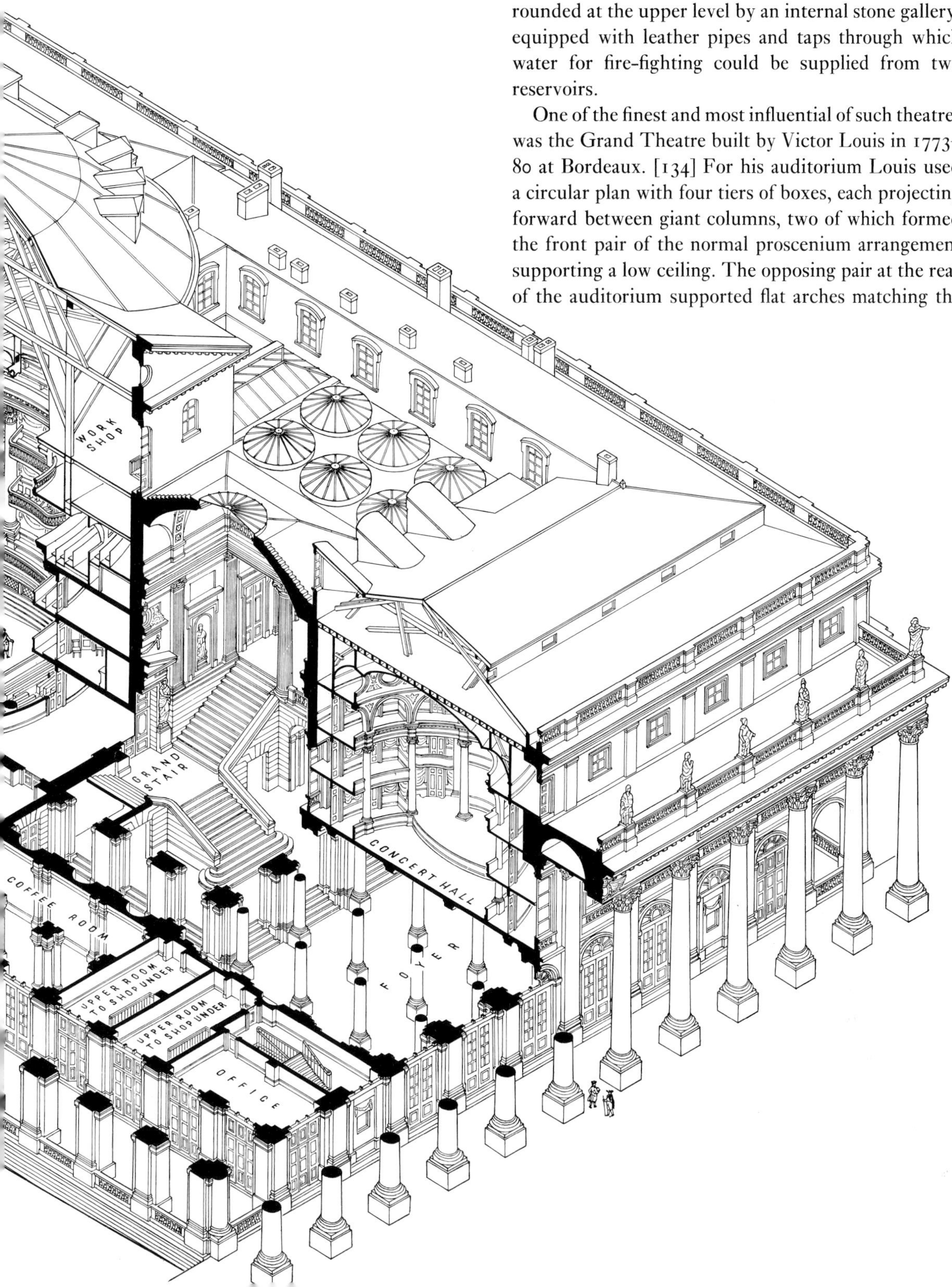
WORK SHOP
GRAND STAIR
CONCERT HALL
COFFEE ROOM
FOYER
UPPER ROOM TO SHOP UNDER
UPPER ROOM TO SHOP UNDER
OFFICE

135 The Grand Theatre, Bordeaux.
Present day auditorium

proscenium opening which, together with two similar side arches, carried a circular dome over the auditorium. [135]

At the upper level within the three arches were open galleries, while the ground floor was subdivided in a similar manner to that at Lyons. At the front of the theatre an open colonnade formed a *porte cochère*, giving access under cover to a large foyer which in turn connected with a grand staircase leading to the various levels of the auditorium. The large stage had twelve positions for wing carriages. As originally designed, a concert hall occupied the space over the main entrance foyer, but this has since been removed.

In England George Saunders wrote in 1790 a *Treatise on Theatres*, in which he declared:

all persons acquainted with the theatre at Bourdeaux, are unanimous in their decision in its favour. They all agree that the voice of the actor spreads more equally in this than in any other theatre.

As a result, Saunders suggested that auditoria should be circular, and that no member of the audience should be more than 70 feet (21.33m) from the actors. His own ideal auditorium had an upper gallery of five benches, a first gallery of nine benches, and a lower tier of boxes, subdivided only by low partitions, behind an open balcony of benches. As was now usual in the English theatre, the pit was filled with benches.

Saunders proposed that the auditorium, like those of the French theatres, should be surrounded by a thick wall, and that the stage and auditorium be separated by a similar wall, which should be supported above the proscenium opening by an arch, to the full height of the roof, through which it should be carried.

The passages communicating with the boxes should all be arched, and have an easy access to spacious stone staircases, that would in case of fire enable the audience to depart without the least hazard.

There should be side aisles to the stage for the storage of scenes, while the wardrobe, green room, and dressing rooms should be placed beyond the stage, from which they were to be separated by a solid wall with minimal openings. Saloons, coffee rooms, and rooms where the audience could await their carriages were to be provided at the front of the building.

The neoclassical approach to architecture, epitomizing a rational analysis of (and a return to) classical first principles, was represented in France by Claude-Nicolas Ledoux among others, and resulted in his returning to the classical theatre for the basis of his auditorium design. In his small but significant theatre at Besançon, built in 1778, [136, 137] Ledoux did away with the standing *parterre* and filled the whole of the ground floor with a stepped and benched *parquet*. This he surrounded with a balcony for the town officials, and by two tiers of boxes, beyond which was an amphitheatre of benches where he seated the former inhabitants of the *parterre*.

His tiers of boxes were, however, not arranged in the normal manner, one above the other; instead they followed a classical section, so that the balcony was separated from the *parquet* by a balustrade, and the two tiers of boxes by a decorative frieze. The rear of the new 'parterre' was enclosed by a colonnade in the manner of a Roman *porticus*, with additional seats

136 The Theatre, Besançon, France, 1778
137 after the alterations
of 1836, 1857

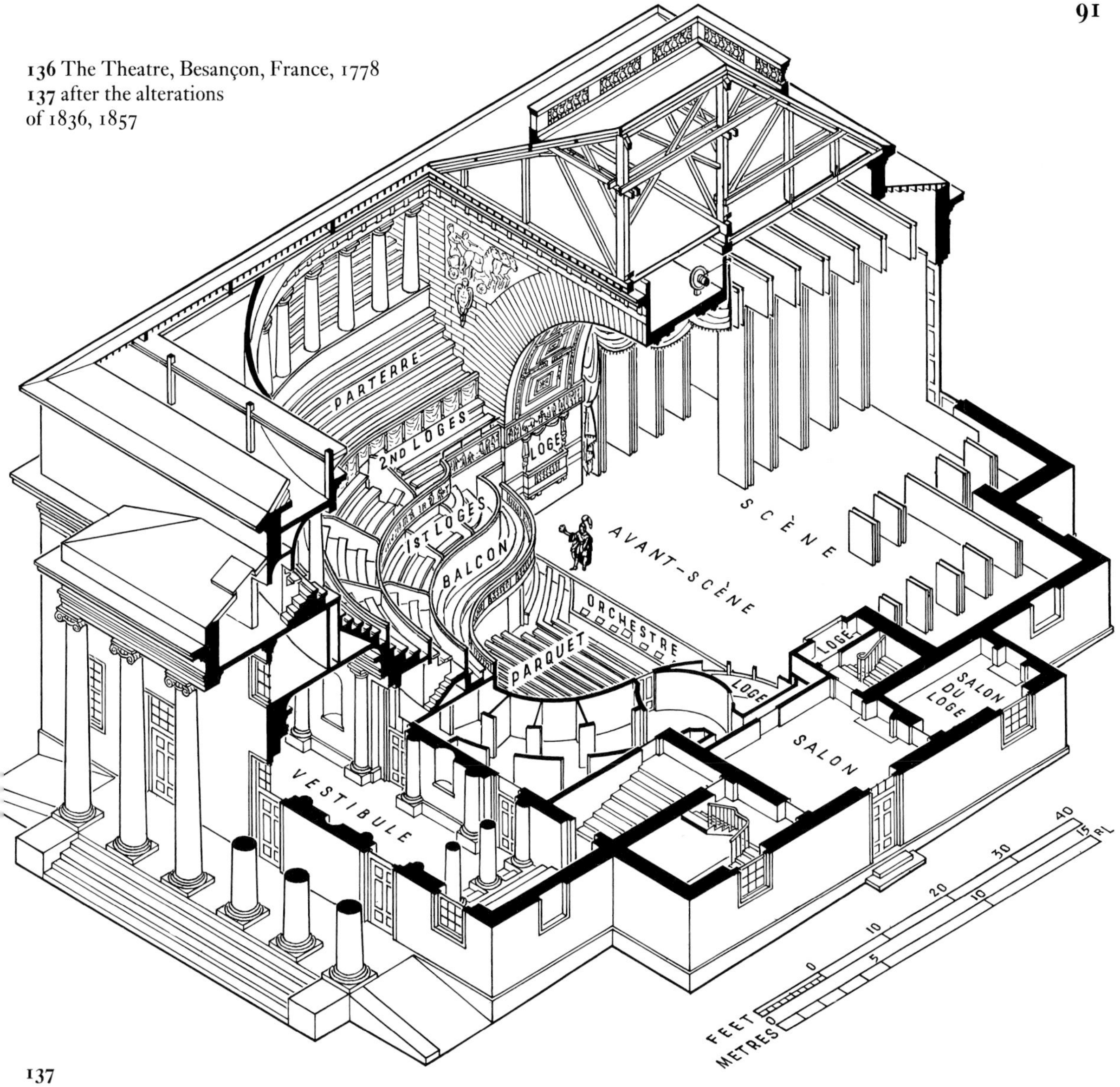
PARTERRE
2ND LOGES
LOGE
1ST LOGES
BALCON
SCÈNE
AVANT-SCÈNE
ORCHESTRE
PARQUET
LOGE
LOGE
SALON DU LOGE
SALON
VESTIBULE
FEET
METRES
0
10
20
30
40
5
10
15
RL

137

beyond for the poorest members of the audience. In attempting to combine a classical-type *cavea* with a proscenium stage, Ledoux ran headlong into the problem of sight-lines which we noted on a smaller scale at Epidaurus, the ends of the *parterre* and most of the side seating behind the colonnade having little, if any, view of the stage.

Although Saunders was suggesting that the proscenium stage was no longer of any use, Ledoux looked upon his *avant-scène* as an essential link between the auditorium and the main stage. This, contrary to normal practice, he reduced in depth, including within its increased width three perspective vistas. Within his great proscenium arch he included two boxes for the Intendant, the Governor of the Province, and important visitors, and there were two further boxes for use by the actors at *parquet* level.

Ledoux's use of the single-slope auditorium was intended to create a feeling of social integration among the townspeople, whilst still reflecting the existing social strata. Thus he set the pattern for such later theatres as those at Worms and Bayreuth (his orchestra, set partly beneath the stage with a curved reflecting rear wall, was also taken up by Wagner in the latter theatre). However, prior to the opening of Ledoux's theatre the town authorities took fright at his design, and requested that two front benches be used as *parquet* or stalls seating, with the normal standing *parterre* behind; but they were dissuaded from this by Bertrand, the architect in charge. Ledoux developed and improved on this Besançon scheme when he designed the theatre at Marseilles.

In England, the Theatre Royal, Drury Lane, was finally demolished to make way for a new building designed by Henry Holland. Tate Wilkinson, writing in 1790, had drawn attention to the well-designed theatres of France, which were not only 'noble and spacious' but also free-standing, with 'good open road for carriages round'. Holland was well acquainted with the Parisian theatres, and so it is not surprising to find that his design for the new Theatre Royal, opened in 1794, covered the whole site formerly occupied by the theatre and the surrounding buildings, containing offices, dressing rooms, public stairs, and foyers.

This area was to have been isolated by a new road to the east of the site, which, however, never materialized. The design, unlike the continental examples, included, in addition to the theatre, a coffee house, a tavern, shops, and living quarters for the performers, but these, like the road, had not been built by 1809, when the theatre was burnt down.

As with his design for Covent Garden, Holland made use of a horseshoe auditorium, with four tiers of open boxes. The first (or dress) circle was extended at the centre-back by a further eleven 'basket boxes' facing the stage, and the second tier, with three rows of benches at the sides, was likewise increased in depth at the centre to contain six rows. The third and fourth tiers of boxes flanked a two-shilling and a one-shilling gallery respectively, with fifteen and seven rows of benches, all directly facing the stage.

Unlike the previous Drury Lane, the benched pit was entered from the rear, the sides being flanked by 'slips boxes'. An orchestra well separated the pit from a proscenium stage, which had four tiers of boxes on either side and a low, sounding-board ceiling above. As originally designed the proscenium doors were omitted, but in 1797 it was found necessary to include one on either side on the main stage. [138–139] Outside the main shell of the building were two wings containing public rooms, with separate staircases leading to the different parts of the auditorium, and dressing and green rooms adjoining the stage.

Stage and auditorium were separated by a wall, but this was carried up no higher than the auditorium ceiling, the whole of the roof space being occupied by carpenters', painters', and property stores. The proscenium opening could be closed by an iron curtain, while, as at Lyons, four cisterns in the roof space held water, for use in case of fire. The stage was equipped with seven sets of wing positions, with two pairs of carriages in each position. In addition, sets of upper grooves supported the tops of the 30 feet (9.14m) high wings, while the carriages ran on rails in the basement. There were two fly galleries on either side of the stage, and barrels for working the cloths and borders were situated in a loft above. Apertures in the stage allowed for raising and lowering the footlights and for the passage of scenery and performers.

By comparison with the previous Theatre Royal, this building was enormous, with a capacity for some 3,611 as compared with the 2,000 which the previous building is supposed to have held in its final form, the greatest distance between the actor and the most remote member of the audience being increased from some 60 feet (18.29m) to 100 feet (30.48m).

The increase in the size of both stage and auditorium made for profound changes in the nature of the productions: the costs of providing scenery rose sharply and the nature of the actors' performances also had to alter. The intimate actor-audience relationship of 'Old Drury' had permitted Garrick's 'moving brow and penetrating eye' to be appreciated by all his audience: as his 'passions shifted, and were by turns reflected from the mirror of his expressive countenance, nothing was lost', but 'upon the scale of modern Drury many of the finest touches of his act would of necessity fall short'.

To make himself heard in the furthest recesses of

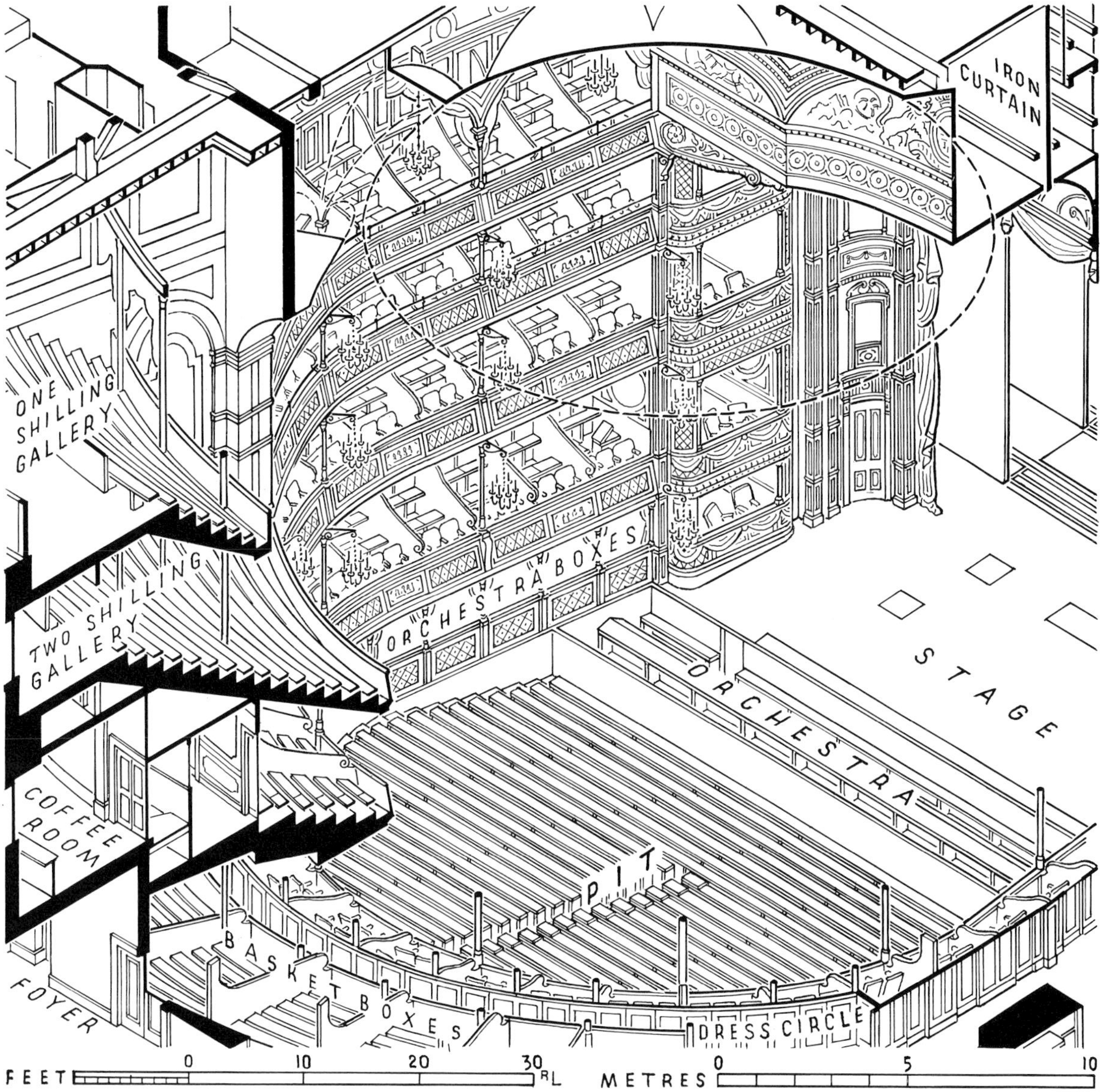
IRON CURTAIN
ONE SHILLING GALLERY
TWO SHILLING GALLERY
ORCHESTRA BOXES
STAGE
ORCHESTRA
COFFEE ROOM
PIT
BASKET BOXES
FOYER
DRESS CIRCLE
FEET 0 10 20 30
METRES 0 5 10

138 Theatre Royal, Drury Lane, after the alterations of 1797

Holland's theatre, Kemble is recorded as answering an outcry from the gallery with the comment, 'I will *raise* my voice, and the GALLERIES shall *hear* me', which led inevitably to a broader style of declamation than had been necessary in the intimate confines of Garrick's theatre. The vast scale of the theatre also encouraged the increasing vogue for scenic spectacle which accompanied the growth of melodrama.

139 Theatre Royal, Drury Lane, after 1797

14 The provincial theatre

Circuit theatres. The Georgian Theatre, Richmond, Yorks. Loughborough. Wisbech and North Walsham. From rectangular to U-shaped auditoria. Development of the Theatre Royal, Ipswich. The Theatre Royal, Bristol.

140

The Georgian Theatre,
Richmond, Yorks
140, 141, 142

141

Throughout the provinces, theatres were built in the late eighteenth and early nineteenth centuries and run by managers whose companies made a regular touring circuit of towns and villages. In the larger towns they built 'proper theatres', but in smaller localities they made do with halls and barns. The theatre in Richmond, Yorkshire (1788) is some 28 feet (8.53m) wide by 61 feet (18.59m) long, and therefore presents a great contrast to the vast house of Drury Lane. [140–2] It shows little continental influence, the arrangement of boxes and pit reflecting the earlier Restoration tennis-court theatres rather than sophisticated contemporary models from the Metropolis.

142

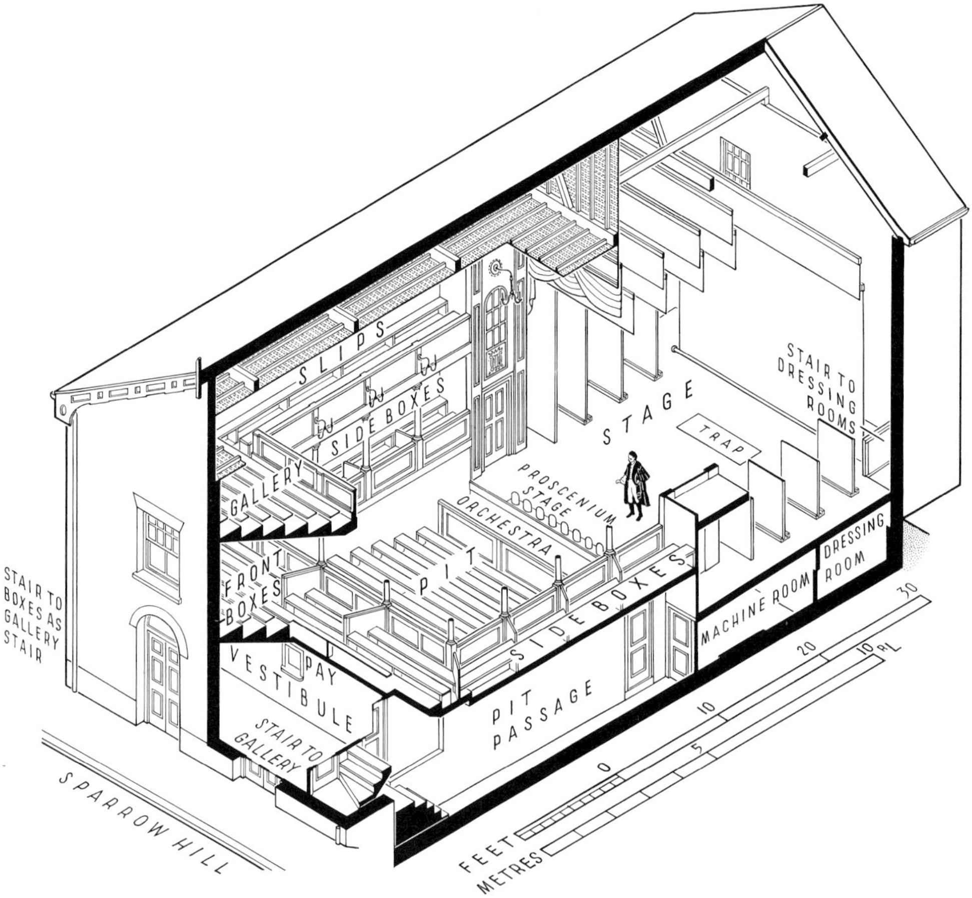
SLIPS
SIDE BOXES
GALLERY
STAGE
TRAP
STAIR TO DRESSING ROOMS
PROSCENIUM STAGE
ORCHESTRA
FRONT BOXES
PIT
SIDE BOXES
DRESSING ROOM
MACHINE ROOM
STAIR TO BOXES AS GALLERY STAIR
PAY
VESTIBULE
PIT PASSAGE
STAIR TO GALLERY
SPARROW HILL
FEET
METRES
0
5
10
20
30

143

Sparrow Hill Theatre, Loughborough, Leics.; 143, 144

144

AUCTION
MART
ADKINSON & FRECKELTON

The circuit managers built their theatres so that as far as possible the scenery and productions could be moved from one comparable venue to another with ease. As late as 1822 the theatre at Loughborough, Leicestershire, was almost identical in size and layout to that at Richmond, except that the front boxes facing the stage may well have been deeper. [143, 144] Similar small theatres were found on the Continent, like that at Vadstena in Sweden, built in 1826. [145, 146]

The interior of the Richmond theatre is almost equally divided into stage and auditorium, the two overlapping in a small proscenium stage flanked by stage doors with balconies above. Two dressing rooms fit beneath the rear half of the stage, with a machine room in front, equipped with two corner traps, a central

The Theatre, Vadstena, Sweden, 145, 146

145

146

grave trap, and a mechanism for raising and lowering the footlights. [190]

The stepped and benched pit was approached by a passage beneath the side boxes, from which an adjoining door gave access to a small orchestra pit. Side and front boxes, separated only by small Doric columns and low partitions, were both approached from a small lobby beyond a curving rear wall. Above the lobby and front boxes was an open gallery with five rows of benches facing the stage, flanked by open slips above the side boxes. A single pay-box ingeniously controlled the entrance to all parts of the house, providing a most satisfactory solution to the need for economy in the use of staff.

147 The Theatre, Wisbech, Cambs, 1793

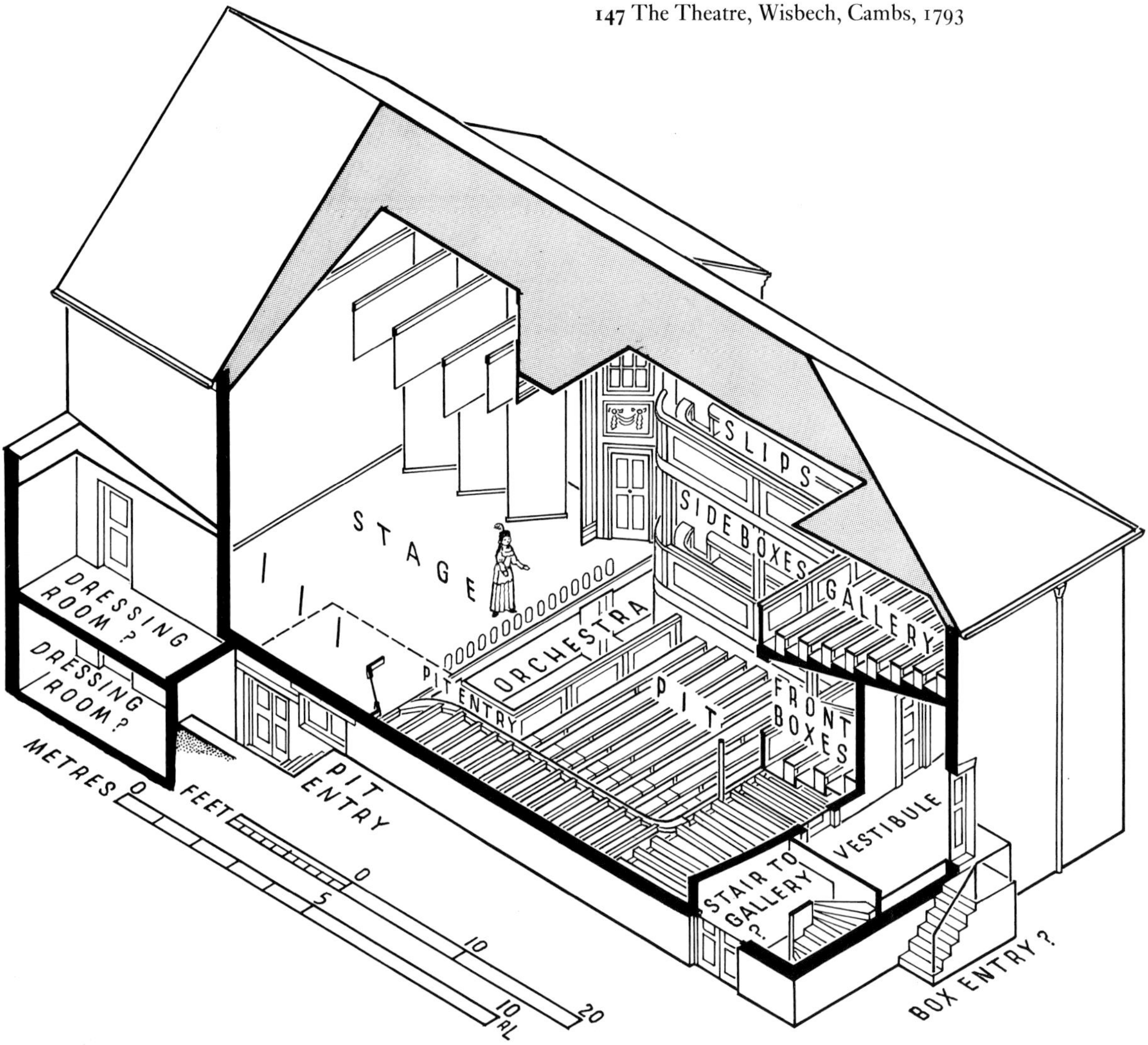
SLIPS
SIDE BOXES
GALLERY
STAGE
ORCHESTRA
PIT
PIT ENTRY
FRONT BOXES
VESTIBULE
STAIR TO GALLERY ?
BOX ENTRY ?
DRESSING ROOM ?
DRESSING ROOM ?
PIT ENTRY
METRES 0
5
10
FEET 0
10
20

The influences of the Metropolis, however, began to spread, and the theatre at Wisbech, Cambridgeshire (1793), shows signs of change. [147] Curved timbers in the corners between the front and side boxes, and at the stage end of the side boxes, indicate first moves towards a U-shaped auditorium, which, although composed of a series of straight facets, can be seen in contemporary views of the North Walsham, Norfolk, theatre [148-50] which was rebuilt in 1827. The introduction of the curved ends to the side boxes made it possible to extend the proscenium stage to the full width of the building: but this meant that if the stage doors were to be usable they had to be set obliquely, in which position they gave access to the backstage areas and were at the same time brought into the view of most of the audience.

Fisher's Theatre, North Walsham, Norfolk, 1827
148, 149

148

150 The great bespeak for Miss Snevellicci

149

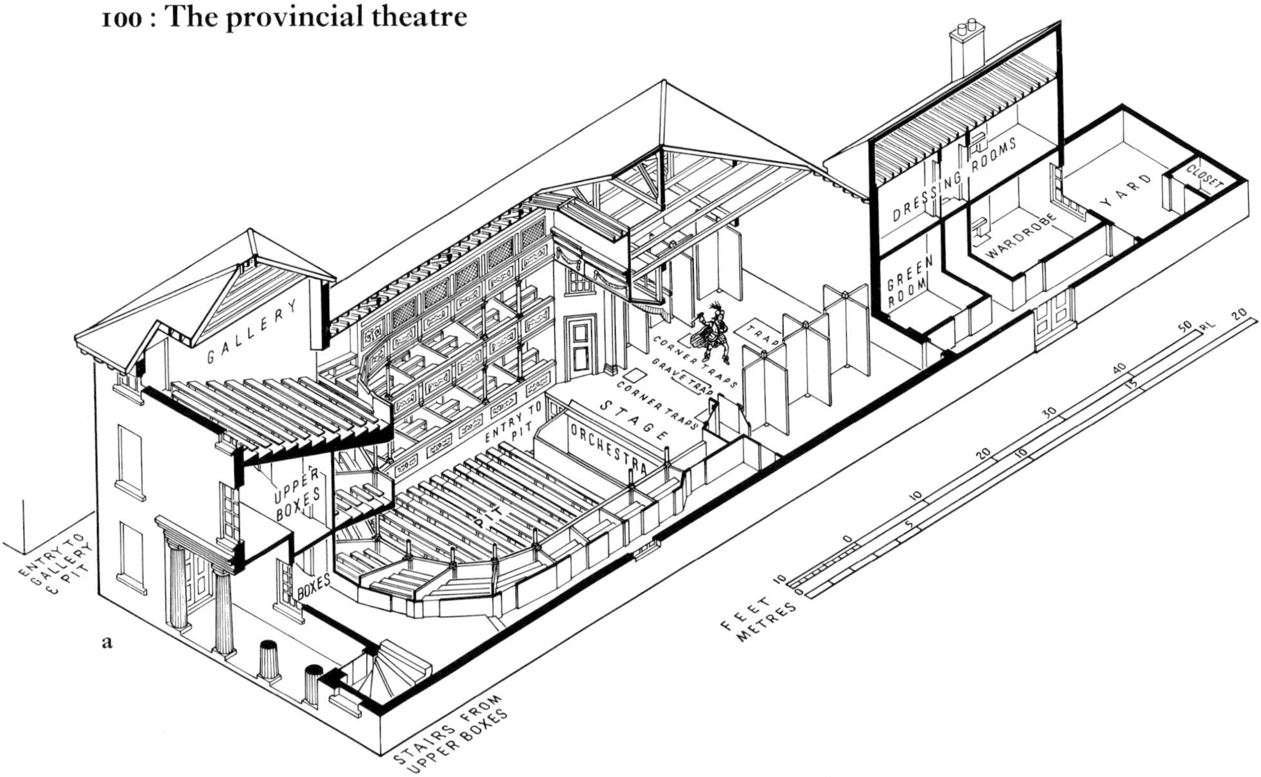
GALLERY
DRESSING ROOMS
YARD
CLOSET
WARDROBE
GREEN ROOM
TRAP
CORNER TRAPS
GRAVE TRAP
CORNER TRAPS
STAGE
ENTRY TO PIT
ORCHESTRA
UPPER BOXES
PIT
BOXES
ENTRY TO GALLERY & PIT
STAIRS FROM UPPER BOXES
FEET
METRES

a

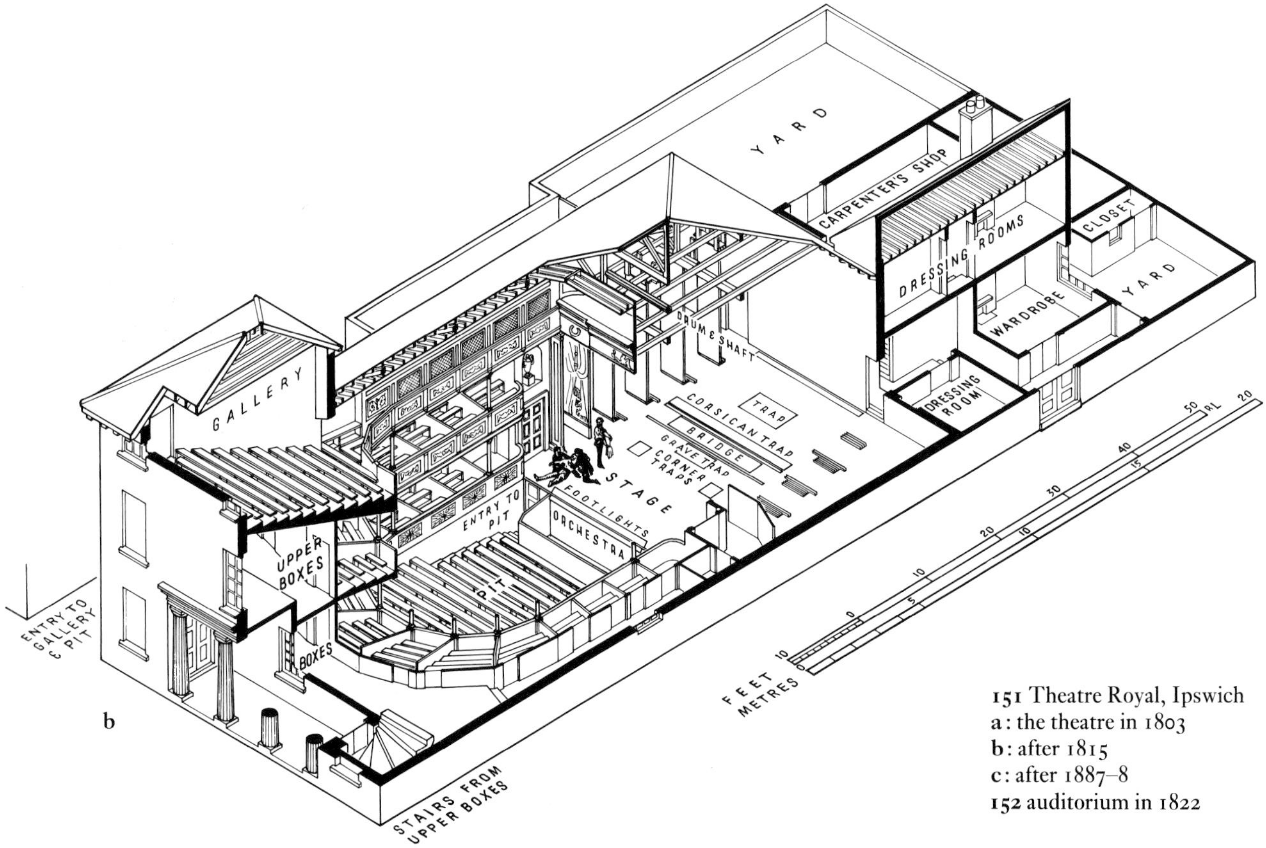
YARD
CARPENTER'S SHOP
DRESSING ROOMS
CLOSET
YARD
WARDROBE
DRESSING ROOM
GALLERY
DRUM & SHAFT
TRAP
CORSICAN TRAP
BRIDGE
GRAVE TRAP
CORNER TRAPS
STAGE
FOOTLIGHTS
ENTRY TO PIT
ORCHESTRA
UPPER BOXES
PIT
BOXES
ENTRY TO GALLERY & PIT
STAIRS FROM UPPER BOXES
FEET
METRES

b

151 Theatre Royal, Ipswich
a: the theatre in 1803
b: after 1815
c: after 1887–8
152 auditorium in 1822

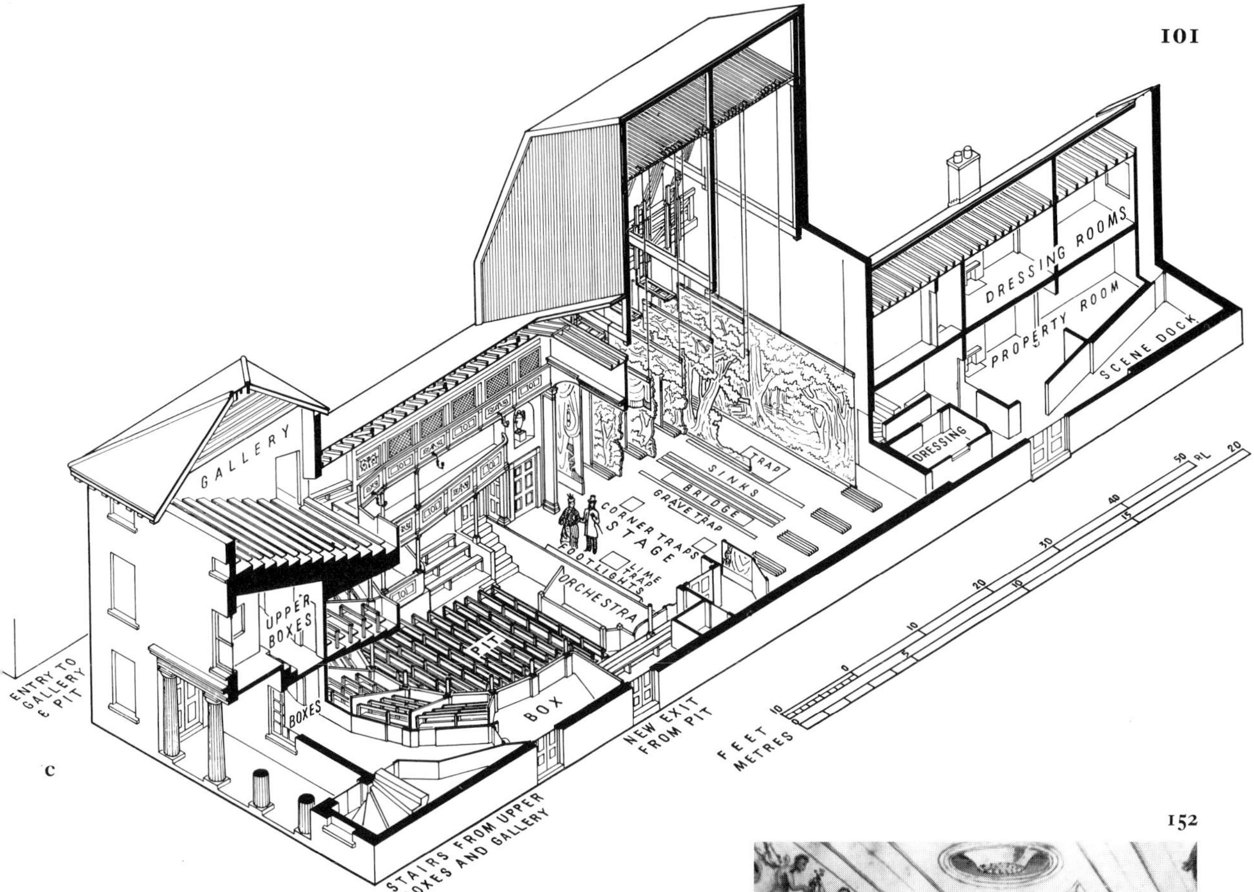
GALLERY
UPPER BOXES
BOXES
PIT
BOX
ORCHESTRA
FOOTLIGHTS
LIME TRAP
STAGE
CORNER TRAPS
GRAVE TRAP
BRIDGE
SINKS
TRAP
DRESSING ROOMS
PROPERTY ROOM
SCENE DOCK
DRESSING
ENTRY TO GALLERY & PIT
STAIRS FROM UPPER BOXES AND GALLERY
NEW EXIT FROM PIT
FEET
METRES

c

152

Theatres are living organisms being altered and adapted throughout their existence to conform with changing and developing ideas and patterns. The Theatre Royal at Ipswich, [151a] originally opened in 1803, had a U-shaped auditorium which occupied some two-thirds of the total theatre space, but by 1815 [151b, 152] the development of scenic spectacle led to an increase in the depth of the stage at the expense of the seating. At the same time the width of the proscenium was increased by the introduction of curved ends to the side boxes, though in this instance there was still enough room offstage for the existing, obliquely-placed stage doors to be replaced by doors set at right angles to the stage front. From plans, sections, and many details compiled by H. R. Eyre, the manager, it has been possible to prepare the comparative reconstructions showing the theatre at these stages of its development, and also following the further alterations of 1887–8. [151c]

The oldest provincial theatre still in use today, but very much modernised, is the Theatre Royal, Bristol, [153–4] built by Thomas Paty, and opened in 1766 as a house where the London companies could perform during the summer, when the theatres in the capital were closed. In its size and shape it is based on a plan and section supplied by 'Mr. Saunders Carpenter of Drury Lane Play House', but unlike Old Drury the Bristol auditorium is U-shaped beyond the first, splayed bay decorated with giant Corinthian pilasters.

Theatre Royal, Bristol 153

153, 154

154

15 Sound, vision, economics, and the picture frame

Wyatt's Drury Lane. The Theatre Royal, Bury St. Edmunds. The circular auditorium and picture frames. Rising costs and 'Orchestral Stalls'. Social problems of theatre design. The Theatre Royal, Leicester.

In February 1809, Holland's Drury Lane was burnt down, to be replaced in 1811–12 by a new theatre designed by Benjamin Wyatt, following a competition in which one of the unsuccessful architects was William Wilkins, who was later to design the Theatre Royal, Bury St. Edmunds (1819), as part of his family's circuit. [155, 156] The auditorium in this latter theatre, as in Wyatt's Drury Lane, was influenced by Saunders's Ideal Theatre, being circular in form. [157]

155 Theatre Royal, Bury St. Edmunds, 1819

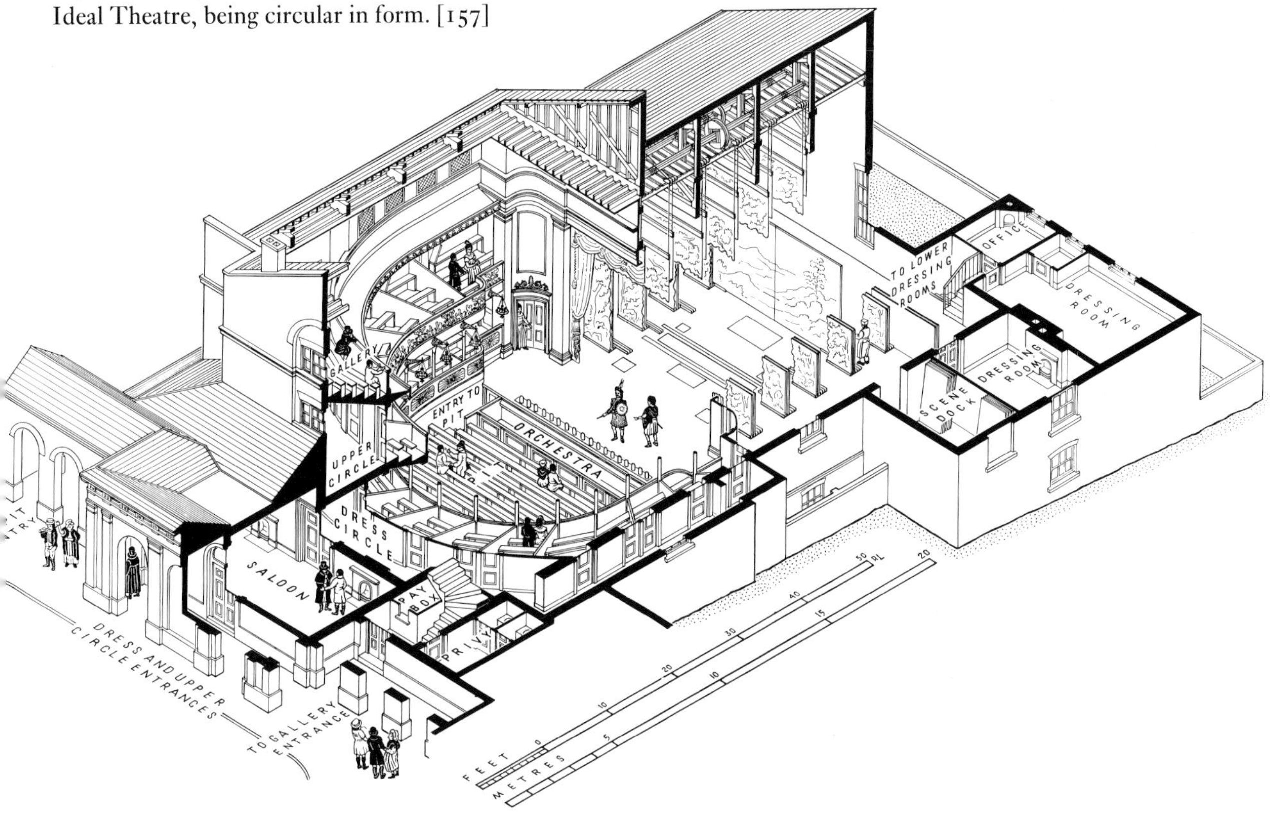
GALLERY
ENTRY TO PIT
ORCHESTRA
UPPER CIRCLE
DRESS CIRCLE
SALOON
PAY BOX
PRIVY
TO LOWER DRESSING ROOMS
OFFICE
DRESSING ROOM
DRESSING ROOM
SCENE DOCK
DRESS AND UPPER CIRCLE ENTRANCES
TO GALLERY ENTRANCE
FEET
METRES

156

Wyatt's Drury Lane [158] had four circles of open boxes, and two galleries facing the stage. Four private boxes were included in the proscenium sides and fourteen more surrounded the pit directly below the dress circle of boxes. To reduce the acoustic problems encountered in Holland's Drury Lane, with its 74 feet (22.56m) distance from stage front to the rear wall of the boxes, Wyatt made this dimension some 53 feet 9 inches (16.38m), which he based on Saunders's (and his own) observations of sound as noted in the open air. He used the circular plan in the belief that this provided the best sight-lines for the majority of the audience.

Wyatt designed his auditorium to hold as large an audience as possible – a total of some 3,200 persons – in order to raise sufficient income to make the theatre profitable. He nevertheless realized that, with every extra foot of width given to the proscenium opening, the amount of material needed for constructing and painting scenery and the number of 'extras' required for crowd scenes would be increased. Unlike Wilkins, whose provincial company still used the proscenium doors, Wyatt dispensed with these as he looked upon

157

EXIT

Theatre Royal, Bury St. Edmunds **156** timber-framed proscenium (compare fig. 105); **157** auditorium of 1965

158 Theatre Royal, Drury Lane, 1812

the proscenium as a 'Frame to the Scenic Picture', and although he included a large area of stage within the auditorium, the actors (including Old Dowton from our Preface) were forbidden to step out of the picture; but by 1818 the proscenium had been altered to include stage doors.

In addition to considering the problems of sound and vision, Wyatt was concerned with the safety of the audience, to the extent of making adequate provision for entrances and exits from the various parts of the house. The circles of boxes were reached from the main entrance *via* a rotunda and principal staircase, while the gallery had its own separate stairs, one on either side of the building; the pit, too, was entered from either side. In 1858 the building was praised for its multiplicity of exits, but a critic pointed out that not all were in use, as the duplication of entrances and exits required a duplication of staff to man them. A system of perforated water pipes was installed, subdivided into sections so that the whole, or parts, of the building could be protected from fire.

Although Wyatt did not separate the stage from the auditorium, he separated both from the surrounding foyers, offices, dressing rooms, and workshops. The whole of the roof space over the main building was used as a carpenters' shop, with further rooms for use by carpenters and property men in the basement, below two scene rooms built at the back of the stage, which were equipped with movable paint frames. The scenery was operated in the continental manner, with six sets of wing places each having two pairs of chariots and matching sets of sloat cuts [161, 176] for the vertical movement of scenery.

James Boaden, writing in 1825, had commented on the rising costs of production and the increasing salaries of the performers, and noted that theatre managements not only needed to increase the size of their audiences but the price of seats as well. Ways and means of charging higher prices led managements to adapt the front rows of the pit to form 'Orchestral Stalls', and even the front rows of the galleries were renamed gallery stalls.

His Majesty's Theatre was furnished in this way in 1815, and by 1840 John Nash had altered the Haymarket by removing the actors' stage within the auditorium, replacing it by orchestral stalls. By 1880 Wyatt's idea of a picture frame had resulted in the installation of a gilded frame encircling the proscenium opening at the Haymarket, [159] and there was no longer any need to forbid the actors to step out of the frame, as there was now no stage for them to step on to.

The introduction of stalls created new problems for theatre architects, as their occupants were regarded as coming from a different class of society from the folk who inhabited the pit. They had to have their own entrances, foyers, and saloons, although they might share these with the occupants of the dress circle. In the Theatre Royal, Leicester, built in 1836, [160] the problem was dealt with by requiring the stalls patrons to ascend to the dress circle, pass around this, and descend a stair adjoining the proscenium, in order to reach their seats. This theatre also illustrates a further move in auditorium design, in that pit and stalls are no longer enclosed by boxes, but, like the earlier French *parterre*, extend the full width of the auditorium beneath a horseshoe-shaped dress circle, above which was a gallery and side slips.

159 Haymarket Theatre, London, 1880

160

Theatre Royal, Leicester
160 auditorium
161 stage after 1888
162 upper grooves

16 Machines and fly towers

The English wooden stage at Leicester. Machinery at Bath. Fly towers and fire curtains. Counterweight flying systems. Paris Opera House. Scene stores. Dresden Opera House and Vienna Court Theatre.

The Leicester stage [161] conformed to the pattern described by E. O. Sachs as the 'English wooden stage'. In addition to the square corner traps for individual actors and a rectangular, centrally-placed 'grave trap', the stage was divided into a series of openings reflecting the wing positions. Sections of stage could slide apart, leaving 'cuts' in the floor to the full width of the proscenium. Narrow 'sloat cuts' permitted the raising of horizontal 'ground-rows' matching the side wings. Between these, wider openings made it possible to raise groups of actors, or units of built scenery, to stage level.

Although the larger London theatres did use wing carriages, the smaller theatres continued to move the scenes by sliding them in grooves laid on the stage and hung from fly galleries. The upper scene grooves [162] normally supported a set of wings, but when a hinged

161

162

portion was lowered they could be used to guide a pair of shutters on stage until these met in the middle. The bottom grooves were laid on the stage, and extension pieces could be added when it was necessary to run a back or intermediate pair of shutters onto the stage. Shutters, however, were now being replaced by cloths, hung from an open floor or grid above the stage. These were raised or lowered by the use of a roller attached to the bottom of the cloth. [163] The upper areas of the stage were still masked by cloth borders related to the wings, and moved by barrels [164] or rollers, [165] like those photographed in the fly gallery of the Theatre Royal, Bath.

By the 1880s, stage roofs were being raised to permit cloths to be 'flown', or lifted vertically out of sight above the proscenium opening, so that J. G. Buckle, writing in 1888, required that the height of a stage should be 'twice that of the proscenium opening'. Until 1888 the Theatre Royal, Leicester, had a continuous roof from front to rear, covering both stage and auditorium, the roof space being used as a carpenter's shop, but in that year the stage roof was raised to enable 'the scenes to "hang" without being rolled up or folded'. The resulting architectural feature [166] was to be the character-

163 Normansfield Hospital Theatre.
Roller cloth (*top left*)
and upper grooves (*top right*)
Theatre Royal, Bath
164 scene barrels
165 prompt side fly gallery
with rollers and hemp lines

164

165

166 Theatre Royal, Leicester, with fly tower of 1888

istic fly tower of contemporary theatres. Its effect on small provincial theatres may be seen in the third reconstruction [151c] of the Ipswich theatre.

At Leicester there were now two fly galleries on either side of the stage, which was spanned by catwalks at both levels, with an open grid at roof-truss level supporting sets of pulleys, each having three hemp lines. [167] These were taken back to a head-block above the prompt-side fly gallery from which they descended to be tied-off to cleats on the upper fly rail, the spare rope being stored on the lower gallery. The barrels which had previously operated sets of borders were now dispensed with, each set of lines being worked independently by one or more flymen.

By 1891, when D'Oyly Carte's New English Opera House was built, hemp lines were being replaced by wires [168] attached to counterweights, which ran in tracks supported on the side walls. [169] The weights could be adjusted to balance the scenic item, which was attached to a bar fastened to the on-stage end of the wires, thus enabling the scenes to be 'manipulated with great facility and steadiness'. If necessary it was still

167 Hemp line flying system

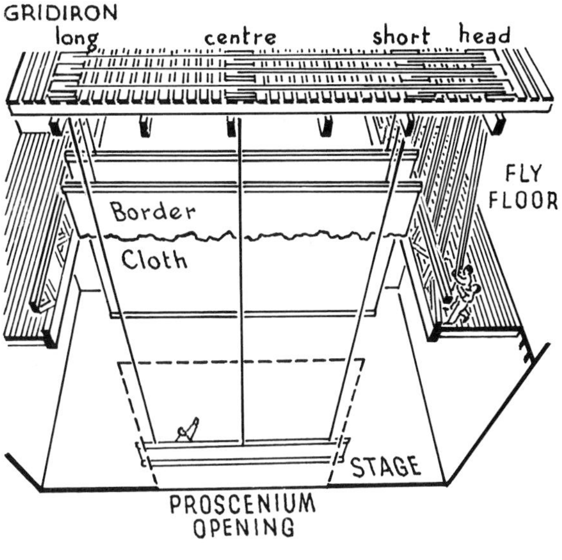
GRIDIRON
long
centre
short
head
FLY FLOOR
Border
Cloth
STAGE
PROSCENIUM OPENING

168 Her Majesty's Theatre, London. Grid with timber roller and wire lines

possible to link a series of counterweighted lines together, so that they could be moved simultaneously or used to raise a whole set scene. The raised fly tower made it easier to introduce a fire-resisting curtain to the proscenium opening, and by 1896 the London County Council was in a position to require such an installation in new theatres.

On the Continent, stage machinery had always been more complicated and ambitious, the presentation of opera in particular requiring the use of elaborate scenery, while the size of the choruses and *corps de ballet* necessitated larger stages, and correspondingly increased accommodation both for performers and stage staff. When the great state-subsidized National Opera House in Paris, designed by Charles Garnier, opened on 5 January 1875, one requirement of the clients was that in size, design, and elaboration it should outshine the new Vienna Opera House as conceived in 1860.

Both houses were built as much for their use for state occasions as for opera, and, in each, stage and auditorium alike were designed on an enormous scale. Nevertheless, these areas are almost lost in the mass of surrounding corridors, foyers, saloons, loggias, and similar accommodation, provided on a grand and luxurious scale. Both theatres continued the practice set by the Italian opera houses, of having a horseshoe-shaped auditorium surrounded by tiers of individual *loges*.

169 Palace Theatre, London (formerly New English Opera House of 1891)

Although the stage of the Paris Opera House is large, it included few new features which were not already in use in the standard timber stages of the French theatre, including the use of drums and shafts in both flies [170] and mezzanines. [171, 172] Wood was used, but iron replaced it in minor details, and in those parts of the main construction where the unusually large dimensions of the theatre made the adoption of metal essential. The stage was not deep, but the rear of the vista area opened into a corridor where heavy pieces of built-up scenery were placed. On either side of the stage, counterweight boxes were arranged with spaces between, through which scenery in use in the current production could be moved into a series of scene docks.

Sachs tells us that in England, Germany, and Austria, the backstage vista area was the place more normally used for the immediate storage of scenes. Scene stores for items not in current use were generally provided at some distance from the opera house – a practice encouraged by the authorities, who recognized the greater fire risk involved when scenery was stored in the theatre building. The Paris scene store was burnt down in 1894.

By English standards, many of the continental theatres were large. In the Flemish Theatre, built in Brussels in 1887, there were two gridiron floors and three sets of fly galleries, but only one mezzanine floor for the chariots beneath the stage. Semper's Opera

170

The Opera House, Paris, 1875;
170 fly gallery;
171 stage cellar;
172 mezzanine floors and cellar

171

172

House in Dresden (1878) had only one gridiron, but it had five sets of fly galleries and two mezzanine floors, and the Vienna Court Theatre (1888) had a single gridiron, five sets of fly galleries, three mezzanine floors, and a cellar. [173–175]

These continental stages not only had the equivalent of the English bridge and sloat cuts, but they also had the narrow openings through which frames and poles supported on chariots at mezzanine level could project. [176] These openings were normally only at the wing positions, but in some theatres and in some positions they ran right across the stage opening. Chariots varied in size: some had a single pole on which a small piece of scenery, such as a cut-out tree, could be supported, while larger ones were capable of carrying the full side wings.

173

175

176

Court Theatre, Vienna, 1888
173 flying bars above stage 174 gridiron
175 under-stage machinery

174

176 Backstage at a continental theatre

17 A return to the fan-shaped auditorium

Bayreuth Opera House. Continental seating. Peoples' Theatre, Worms. Community spirit. Forestages.

In 1872–6 Richard Wagner and Otto Bruckwald designed an Opera House in Bayreuth for the express purpose of presenting Wagnerian operas. [177] This theatre differed in a number of fundamental points from those discussed above, in that the tendency noted at Besançon [136] for a return to a classical section for the auditorium was more fully implemented. The auditorium [178] was designed as a fan-shape seating 1,345 on a single slope, with rows of seating extending the full width of the auditorium, and with exits at each end through a series of architectural wings to adjoining lounges and escape stairs. This arrangement, with the seats set far enough apart from back to back to permit the space between the rows to be used as a gangway, came to be called 'continental seating'.

Additional entry points led directly into the midst of the rear seats, in the manner of Roman *vomitoria*. The rear wall of the auditorium contained a royal box, flanked by boxes for distinguished strangers, each fitted with loose chairs and seating a total of 300. Above was a small gallery. A large orchestra well separated the audience from the stage, but this was partly sunk beneath the stage so that the musicians would not distract attention from the performance.

There was a double proscenium which, unlit, effectively separated the real world of the auditorium from

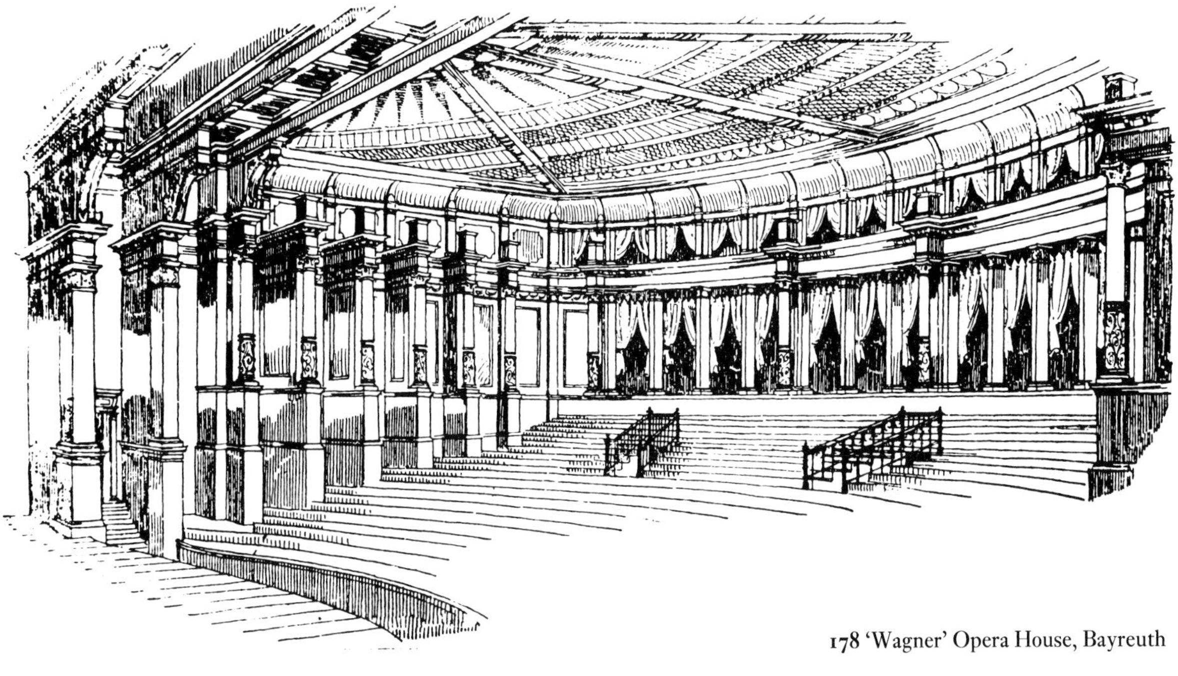

178 'Wagner' Opera House, Bayreuth

114 : A return to the fan-shaped auditorium

177 'Wagner' Opera House, Bayreuth, 1876

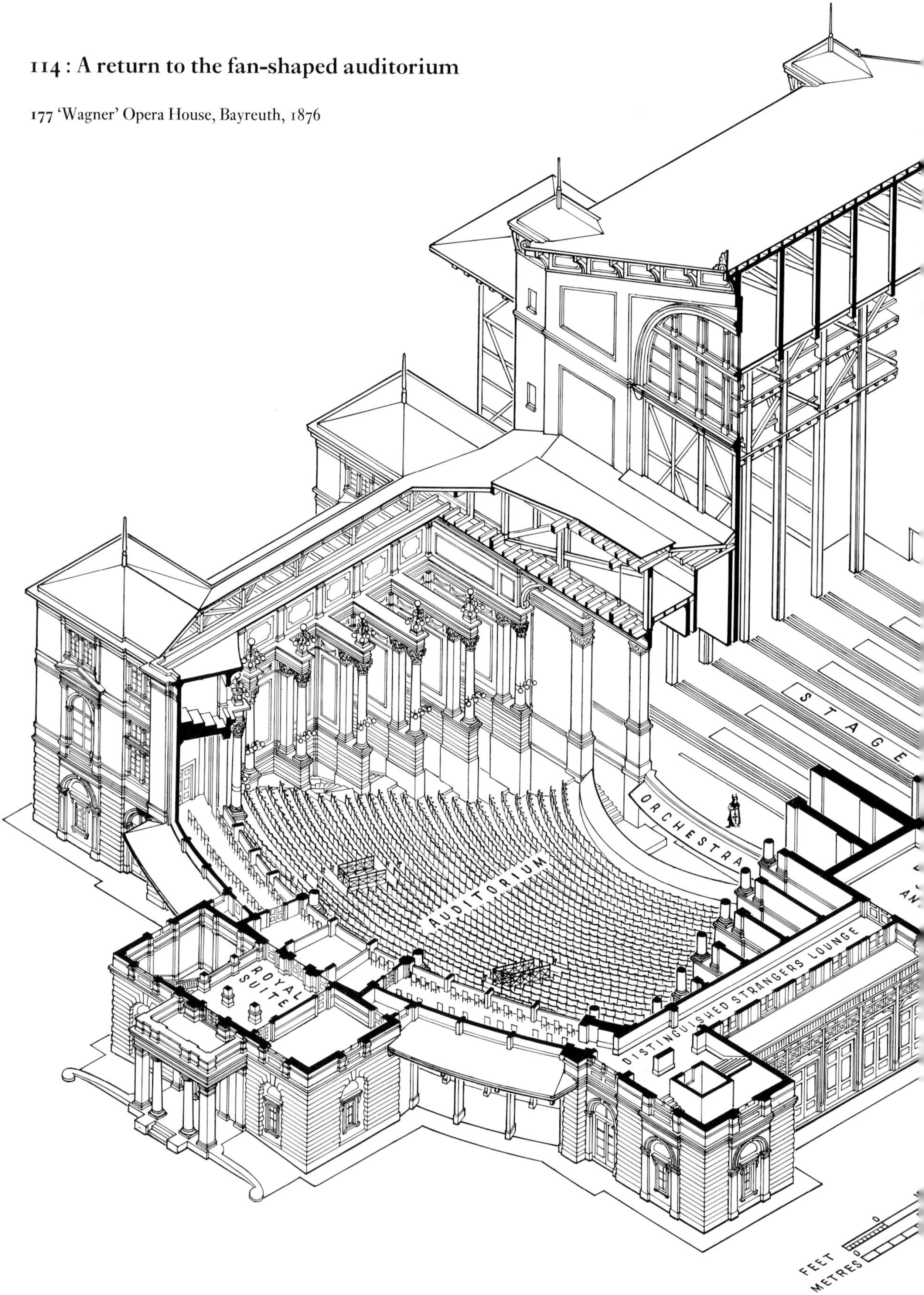
STAGE
ORCHESTRA
AUDITORIUM
ROYAL SUITE
DISTINGUISHED STRANGERS LOUNGE
0
FEET
0
METRES

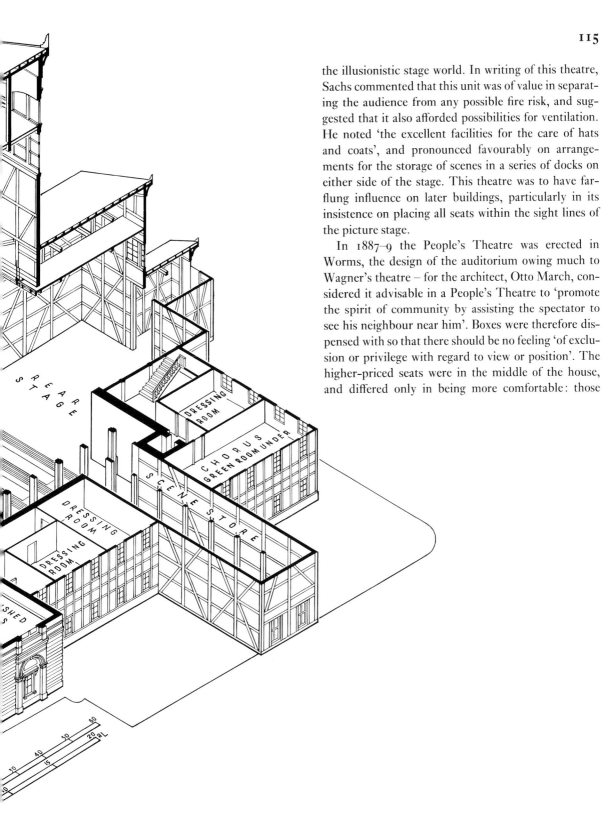

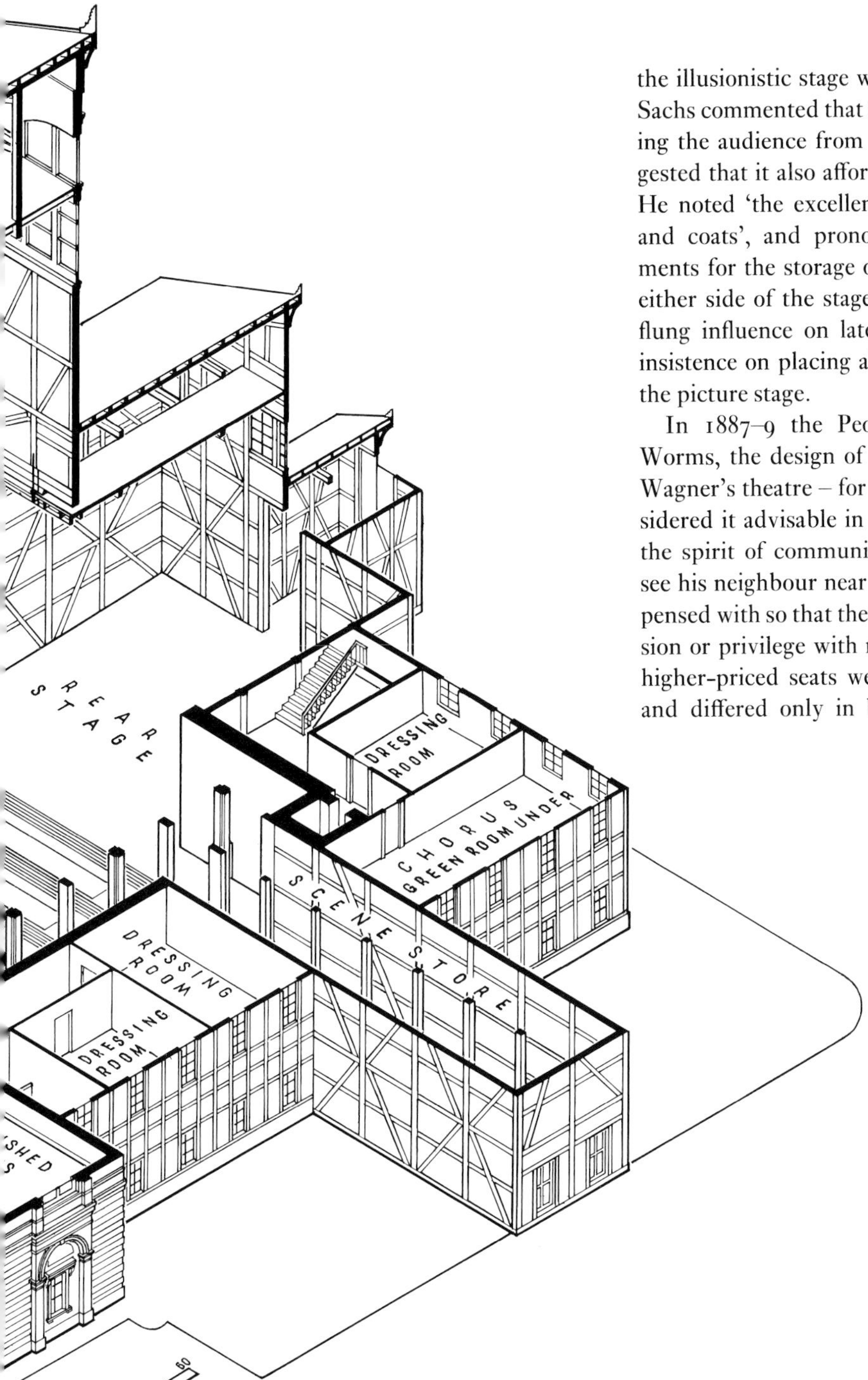
REAR STAGE
DRESSING ROOM
CHORUS GREEN ROOM UNDER
SCENE STORE
DRESSING ROOM
DRESSING ROOM

the illusionistic stage world. In writing of this theatre, Sachs commented that this unit was of value in separating the audience from any possible fire risk, and suggested that it also afforded possibilities for ventilation. He noted 'the excellent facilities for the care of hats and coats', and pronounced favourably on arrangements for the storage of scenes in a series of docks on either side of the stage. This theatre was to have far-flung influence on later buildings, particularly in its insistence on placing all seats within the sight lines of the picture stage.

In 1887–9 the People's Theatre was erected in Worms, the design of the auditorium owing much to Wagner's theatre – for the architect, Otto March, considered it advisable in a People's Theatre to 'promote the spirit of community by assisting the spectator to see his neighbour near him'. Boxes were therefore dispensed with so that there should be no feeling 'of exclusion or privilege with regard to view or position'. The higher-priced seats were in the middle of the house, and differed only in being more comfortable: those members of the audience who occupied them were nevertheless still sitting in the midst of their fellow townsmen. There were, however, some fourteen boxes forming the rear wall of the auditorium, with a narrow gallery of seats situated all round the walls at an upper level. [179]

In addition to an orchestra well, space for an organ and choir was provided centrally at the rear of the auditorium. A circular skylight lit the auditorium by day, with artificial lights above for night use. There was a normal proscenium opening, but a return was made here to earlier principles by covering the orchestra to provide a forestage approached from recesses on either side. [180]

The forestage, backed by curtains, was used for recitations, dialogues, and for such plays as could dispense with scenic effects, for which the main stage could also be used, enclosed by monochrome drapes. The possibility of presenting plays without the use of elaborate scenic devices was, however, largely for the future. For the present the emphasis was on the development of machinery to make possible the rapid replacement of one elaborately realistic scene by another.

179

The People's Theatre, Worms.
Auditorium with
179 orchestra and
180 forestage

180

18 Realism and stage mechanics

Iron and mechanical power. The Asphaleia stage. Buda-Pest Opera House. The Auditorium Building, Chicago. Limitations of machinery. Drury Lane bridges. Scenic realism and box settings. Revolving stages in Munich. Brandt's Reform Stage.

The gradual change from timber to iron in stage consctruction was reflected in a slower change from manual to mechanical power. Steam power was originally incorporated in the Vienna Opera House, but the power most widely used was hydraulic. This was exploited by the 'Asphaleia' syndicate, who designed a system in which the stage floor was divided into a series of 'bridges', each subdivided into three parts, resting on hydraulically operated plungers. [181] These could be raised or lowered, singly or in combination, and they could also be rotated at an angle or set at a slope to the stage floor. The sloat system of raising scenes from beneath the stage was continued, but with the addition of a similar slide running from front to back on each side of the stage, through which wings could be raised.

The system also incorporated a panoramic sky-cloth enclosing the scenic area. Such a cloth would obviously impede the lateral movement of scenery at stage level, and when an Asphaleia stage was installed in the Buda-Pest Opera House in 1875–84, a 50 feet (15.24m) high cloth was hung from the grid in such a manner that it could be raised some 25 feet (7.62m) above the stage to permit movement beneath. A single large skycloth made the use of wings, borders, and cloths obsolete as a means of concealing the backstage areas, but they continued to be used for those productions, such as opera and ballet, where they had become traditional.

The gridiron at Buda-Pest was set some 90 feet (27.43m) above the stage, and carried 104 sets of three wires each, connected to 36 small hydraulic rams worked from switchboards in a small gallery on the front part of the stage, from which position the resident engineer found difficulty in controlling the movement

181 Asphaleia Stage

of individual cloths. Such mechanization was intended not only to simplify scenic movement and permit relatively easy handling of heavier and more cumbersome pieces, but to make for economy by replacing the numerous stage hands with a single engineer. It was, however, pointed out that the trained operatives were paid more than the stage hands, and that anyway the latter were still required for the original setting of scenes, numerous hands being needed when large pieces of scenery had to be tied-off to the permanent battens.

The Auditorium Building in Chicago, designed by Sullivan in 1886, made use of similar equipment. [182] Here the Asphaleia stage was divided into sections which could be moved jointly or separately from below to some 12 to 15 feet (3.66-4.57m) above stage level. It was, however, quickly realized that these improvements had inbred limitations, Herr Rudolph of the Vienna Opera House pointing out that any such system of traps in the stage required the stage manager 'to arrange the scenes according to the stage, rather than the stage according to the scene', a problem which applies not only to the equipment of the stage but to its architectural form as well (p. 216).

Continental theatres and opera houses ran on a repertoire basis, presenting a different production each evening, and so a rapid means of changing the scenes, particularly in the variation of stage levels, was desirable. The contemporary London stage, however, operated a system of long runs of single productions, and so it was argued that the introduction of such complicated and expensive equipment was scarcely viable. Nevertheless, two hydraulic lifts were installed in the Theatre Royal, Drury Lane, in 1896, [183, 184] and in 1898 two electrically operated bridges were added. [185] All four are still *in situ*, but are now covered over, suggesting that Herr Rudolph's comments were indeed valid. In 1899 Sachs altered the stage at Covent Garden to include five bridges, the front two being each subdivided into eight sections which could be operated separately.

182

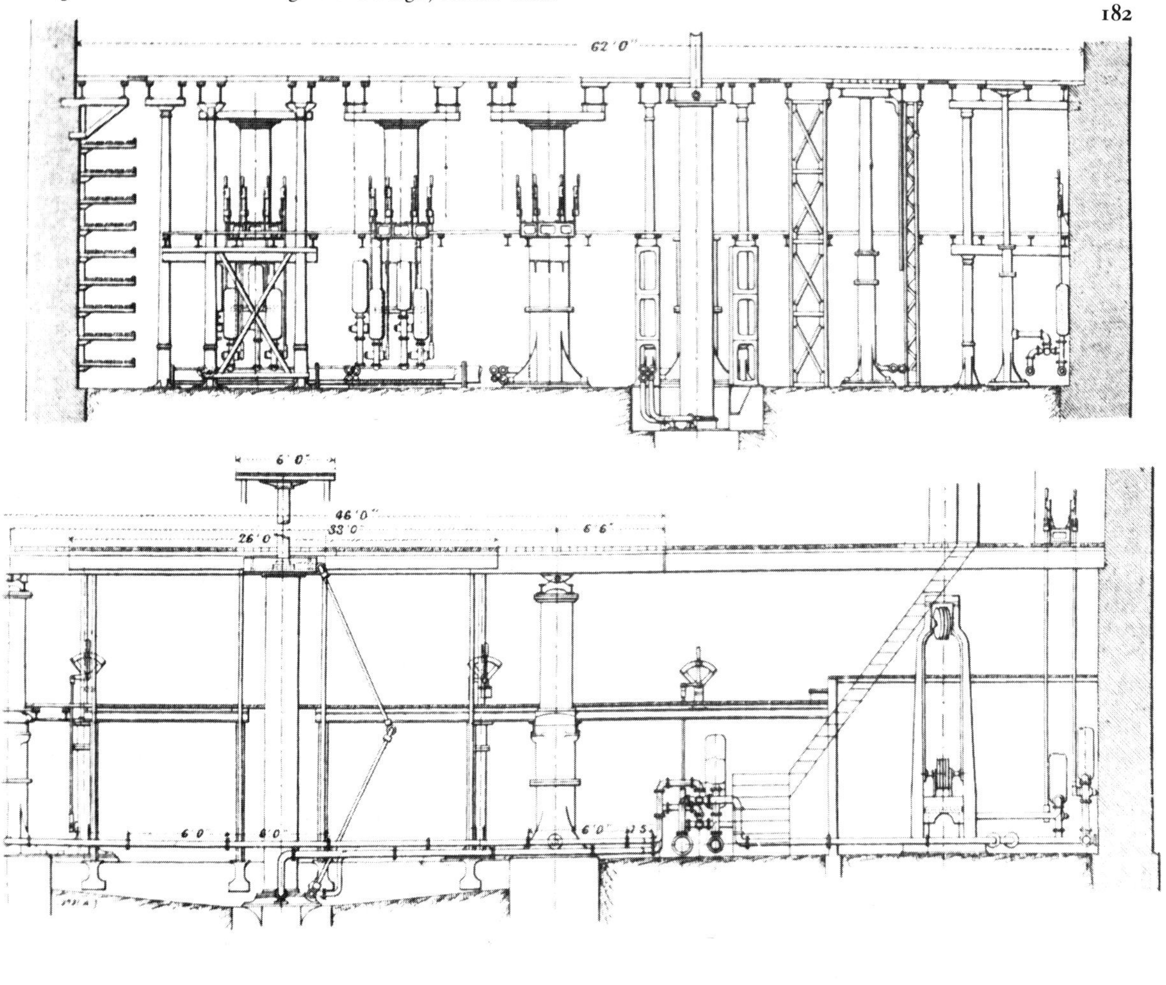
62' 0"
6' 0"
46' 0"
33' 0"
26' 0"
6' 6"

183

Theatre Royal, Drury Lane:
183–4 hydraulic bridges of 1896;
185 electric bridges of 1898

184

182 Auditorium Building,
Chicago. Asphaleia Stage

185

From the 1860s, greater realism in plays was reflected in the scenery, and wing and border setting [186a] began to be replaced by box settings [186b] representing 'real' rooms with side walls and ceilings. But, since stages still retained their 'perspective' rake, this created difficulties: It was not until 1897 that a flat stage was first used by C. J. Phipps at Her Majesty's Theatre. The more realistic the scene, moreover, the longer it took to change. The equipment therefore slowly began to reflect the need to make changes more rapidly, but the bridges and sloats of the wing and border setting were by now such an ingrained feature of stage design that they tended to inhibit new ideas.

Many variations were tried out on the Continent and in the United States, including such complicated arrangements as that introduced by Steele MacKaye in 1879 in the Madison Square Theatre in New York, where two stages were arranged, one above the other, so that each in turn could be raised or lowered into position behind the proscenium opening.

In 1896 Karl Lautenschlaeger introduced a revolving stage at the Residenztheater in Munich, and then prepared a project for a fuller installation in the Munich Court Opera House. [187] Here a large part of the stage and the first and second mezzanines were designed as a great turntable with a diameter of some 78 feet (23.77m), to provide for the many and rapid changes of scene needed in Wagnerian operas. Two, three, or more scenes were to be set on the single stage, and moved into position behind the proscenium opening, the scenes, when finished with, being removed and replaced by further settings.

Even this idea, however, did not make a full break with the past, as the turntable was equipped with all the standard features of the older theatres: bridges, sloats, and traps, as well as chariots. The bridges could be raised some 6 feet 6 inches (1.98m) above stage level, or dropped some 14 feet (4.27m) below, on a central piston which could be detached from the bridge and lowered below the second mezzanine level, so that the turntable could be rotated on rollers running on tramlines: these were laid on sleeper walls which enclosed the cellar.

Eighty-eight iron bars were supported above the stage by wire cables running over pulleys on the gridiron, and each of these bars could be worked independently, or coupled together up to forty. A further innovation was the use of electric motors to provide motive power for all the machinery both above and below stage level. Electricity was also used for the nine lighting battens suspended above the stage. The turntable was to be used in conjunction with a panorama or 'horizon', which could be moved forwards or backwards or flown sufficiently high to permit the movement of actors and stage staff beneath it, but not high enough to permit a scene set on the turntable to be cleared.

Further moves to provide for rapid scene changes were made by Herr Brandt of the Berlin Court Theatre, who designed his Reform Stage [188] with three movable platforms. Two of these could be drawn off into a recess on either side of the front part of the stage, the third being withdrawn into the rear stage area, in which positions the scenes could be changed and the platforms returned on-stage behind the proscenium opening.

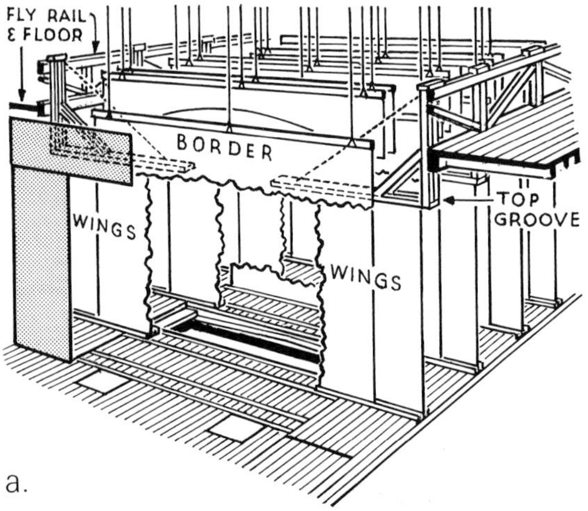
FLY RAIL & FLOOR
BORDER
WINGS
TOP GROOVE
WINGS

a.

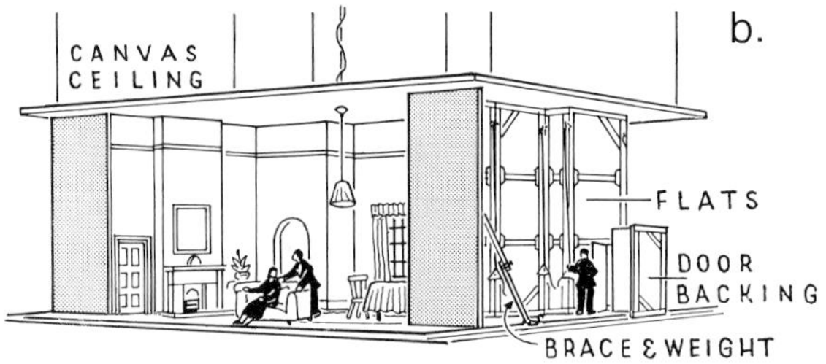
CANVAS CEILING
FLATS
DOOR
BACKING
BRACE & WEIGHT

b.

186a wing and border setting **b** box setting

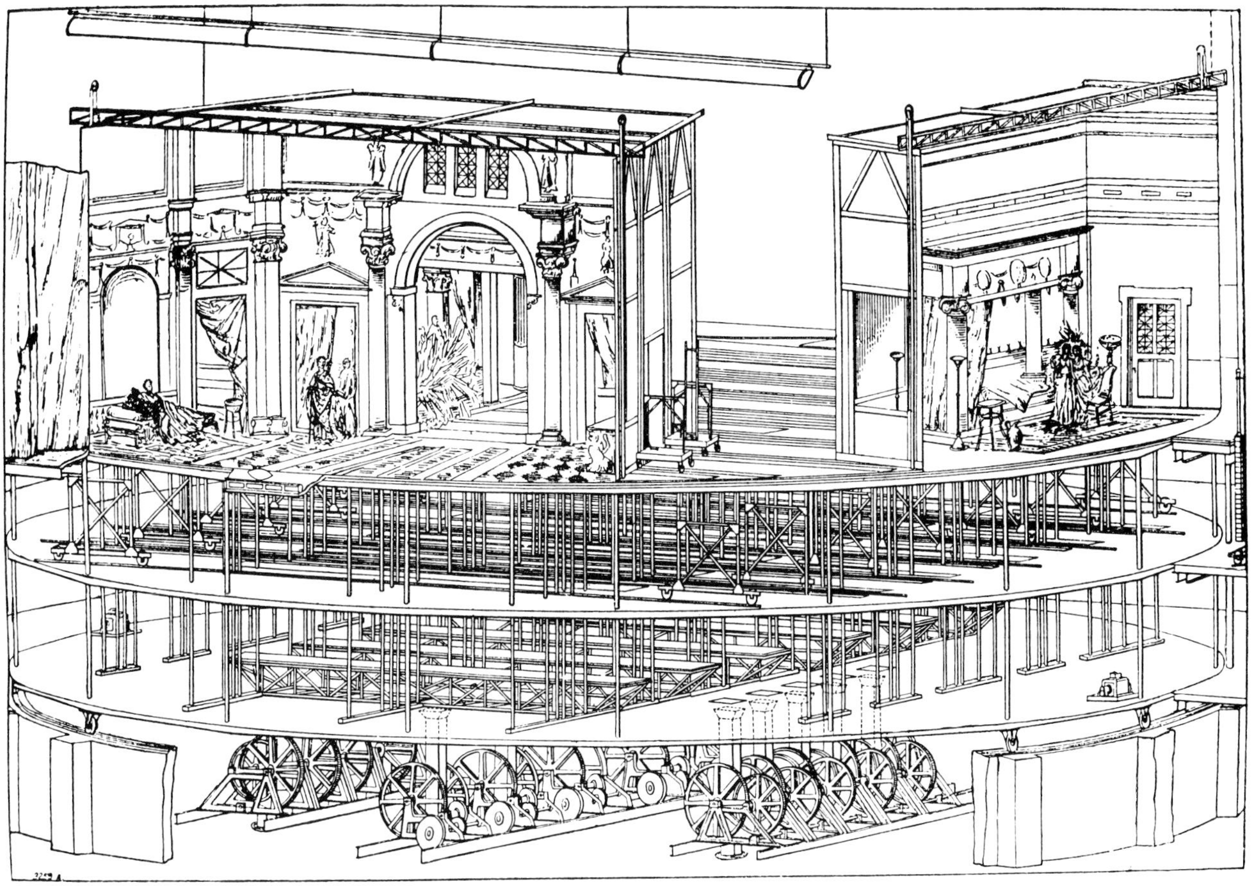

187 Project for a revolving stage

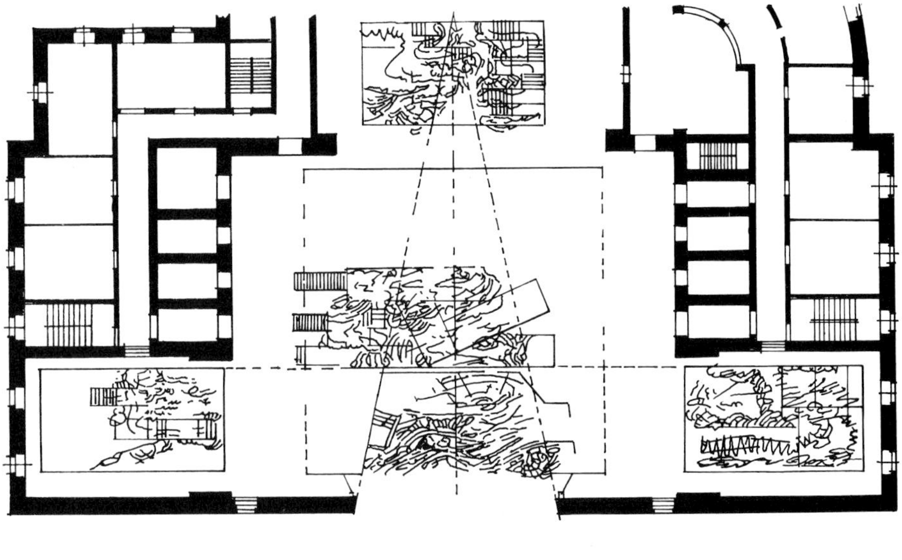

188 Brandt's 'Reform Stage'

19 Lighting and sky-domes

Oil, gas, and electric lighting. Adolph Appia and Mario Fortuny. Skycloths and cycloramas. The Schauspielhaus, Dresden. Mobile stages. Direct and diffused light. Plastic setting and revolving stages. Mobile platforms. Ziegfeld Theatre, New York. Limitations of mechanical devices. Front scenes and forestages.

Until the beginning of the nineteenth century, stages and auditoria had been lit by candles and later by oil lamps, and ingenious devices were invented which made it possible to lighten or darken the stage. [189, 190] Although each candle or lamp could be masked or snuffed out, this was obviously a slow and laborious process, but when numbers of lights were mounted together the whole fitting could be raised or lowered through a slot in the stage, or, when mounted vertically behind each wing, they could be turned away or shuttered in a single movement [131a]. It was not easy to darken the auditorium, although this was partially achieved in some instances by withdrawing the candelabra or chandeliers through the ceiling, as was done at the Comédie Française [113] and La Scala. [127]

The advent of gas meant that whole sections of lighting could be controlled by the turn of a tap, and varying degrees of brilliance could readily be achieved. [191] To the hazards of fire, which had been inseparable from the earlier methods, were now added the dangers of explosion from leaking joints, especially when portable units with flexible hosing were plugged-in to permanent outlets.

The use of electricity for lighting both stage and auditorium became widespread in the 1880s, and the high degree of control which this offered by comparison

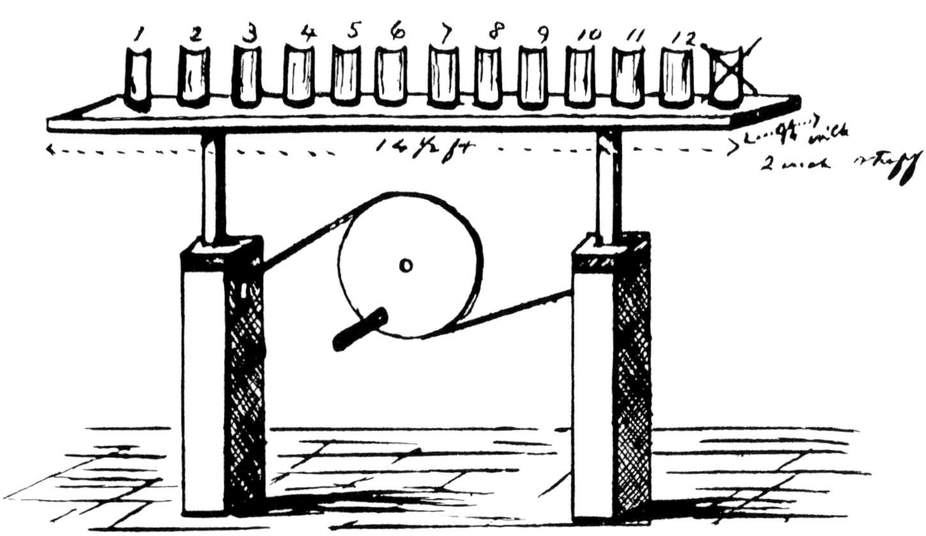
1 2 3 4 5 6 7 8 9 10 11 12
14½ ft

189 Movable footlights

190 'Lighting the footlights'

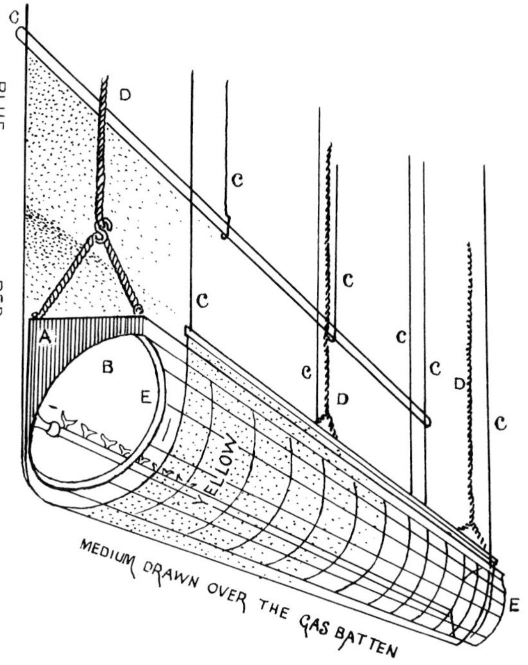
C
D
BLUE
RED
A
B
E
C
D
YELLOW
MEDIUM DRAWN OVER THE GAS BATTEN
E

191 Gas batten with three colour medium

with previous methods led to consideration of the wider theatrical effects that could be obtained by its use. By 1899 Adolph Appia had published his ideas on how electric lighting could be used for the staging of the opera *Tristan and Isolde*: he saw it as a means of presenting the visual appearance of the inner spiritual drama, and asked,

What method of stage setting should be adhered to in a drama where the physical setting, the outer world it embodies, is so essentially unimportant? Unquestionably, the utmost simplification of all of its decorative and pictorial elements.

Much of his scheme depended on contrasting the vast area of sky with carefully lit scenic items and varying stage levels, with the result that scene painting was reduced to a minimum.

In his later designs, Appia placed the actor first and foremost, and believed that the audience should not be distracted by over-elaborate painted scenery. He disliked the contrast between the reality of the actor and the flatness of the scenery, and tried to surround the three-dimensional actor with equally three-dimensional scenery, achieving his effects of distance by the use of light on a skycloth rather than by painted perspective.

Appia's ideas of stage lighting married well with the inventions of Mario Fortuny. His system, put into operation around 1902, obtained the effects of daylight by projecting white light onto bands of coloured silk, which acted as reflectors diffusing light over the whole scene. [192] The effect of unlimited sky was obtained by the use of a half-dome, originally made of silk [193] but later constructed of plaster. The use of such a half-dome made it possible to remove the sky borders and the side wings, as it could completely enclose the sight-lines from the audience.

This total enclosure of the acting area was obviously ideal for its purpose, but it introduced difficulties of access to the stage area for actors, technicians, and scenic items alike. The use of mobile sky-domes, [194] capable of running up and down stage, allowed the introduction of new scenery from the sides, brought on either manually or on mobile wagons or sliding stages; nevertheless, vertical movement into the flies was restricted, except when the dome was in its furthest upstage position, where it performed its enclosing function less successfully. Although at first sight the need to use cloths and other items of flying scenery would appear to have been done away with, their use persisted and required a compromise solution permitting the simultaneous use of both forms of scenic device.

192 Fortuny lighting system

193 Fortuny sky dome

194 Mobile sky dome

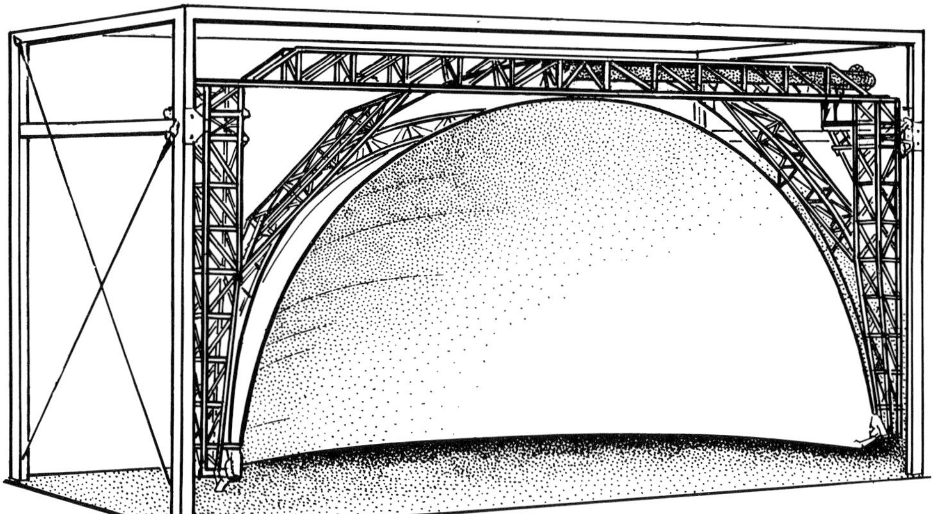

Adolph Linnebach, as technical director at the Schauspielhaus, Dresden (1913–14), [195] had a sky-dome incorporated as a structural feature, but in place of Fortuny's perfect semi-dome Linnebach compromised to the extent that his dome was elliptical on plan, with two straight sides, enclosing almost the total depth of the stage. On section the dome curved forward and stopped at approximately the mid-point of the stage at a height of some 70 feet (21.34m).

The almost total enclosure of the stage on plan made the horizontal movement of scenery at stage level impossible, so the stage was divided into three sections which could be raised or lowered on hydraulic plungers. The front two sections each had two trapped areas built into them, and could sink to the level of the basement floor. Here there were four mobile platforms, ready set with scenery, which would in turn be rolled onto the stage sections and raised up to stage level, where they could leave the supporting sections and run up and down stage like great bridges spanning the open space. Each section could be raised to 8 feet (2.44m) above stage level, to provide a variety of acting levels.

To increase the width of settings, smaller wagons were moved into place on either side of the main stage sections, where parts of the stage could sink so that the floor of these wagons was at stage level. The mobile wagons were driven by a built-in electric motor, controlled from a central position through a trailing wire and guided by hand. Scenery wagons arriving at the theatre were driven from the street on to a large elevator, and lowered to the level of the scene docks.

An inner, flexible proscenium opening could vary in size from 46 feet (14.00m) wide by 33 feet (10.00m) high to 26 feet (8.00m) by 13 feet (4.00m) to suit small scenes which, because they might look lost against the vast expanse of the main cyclorama, could be enclosed by a smaller, mobile cyclorama; or the scene could make use of a normal backcloth, since a full flying system was included, an upper portion of the cyclorama being hinged to permit the use of upstage lines.

Three lighting bridges spanned the stage, equipped with specially designed arc lights capable of providing direct light to the cyclorama and diffused light to the stage. To serve as spotlight perches and for lighting maintenance, there were six electrically-operated open cabin elevators, which the occupant could move both vertically and across the stage, each cabin containing two powerful spotlights. The cyclorama was also lit from a sunken pit at its base. So great was the height of the stage that an elevator for stage personnel was located alongside the proscenium opening. In contrast to this modern stage equipment, the auditorium was arranged with circle, gallery, and side boxes in a traditional pattern.

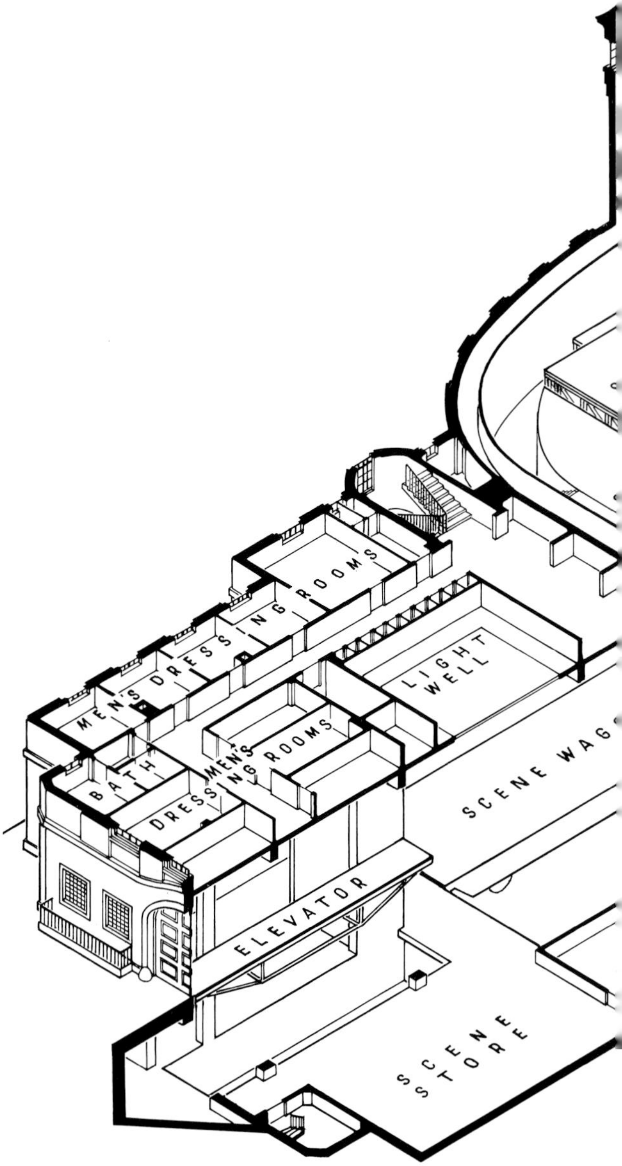
MENS DRESSING ROOMS
LIGHT WELL
MENS DRESSING ROOMS
BATH
SCENE WAG
ELEVATOR
SCENE STORE

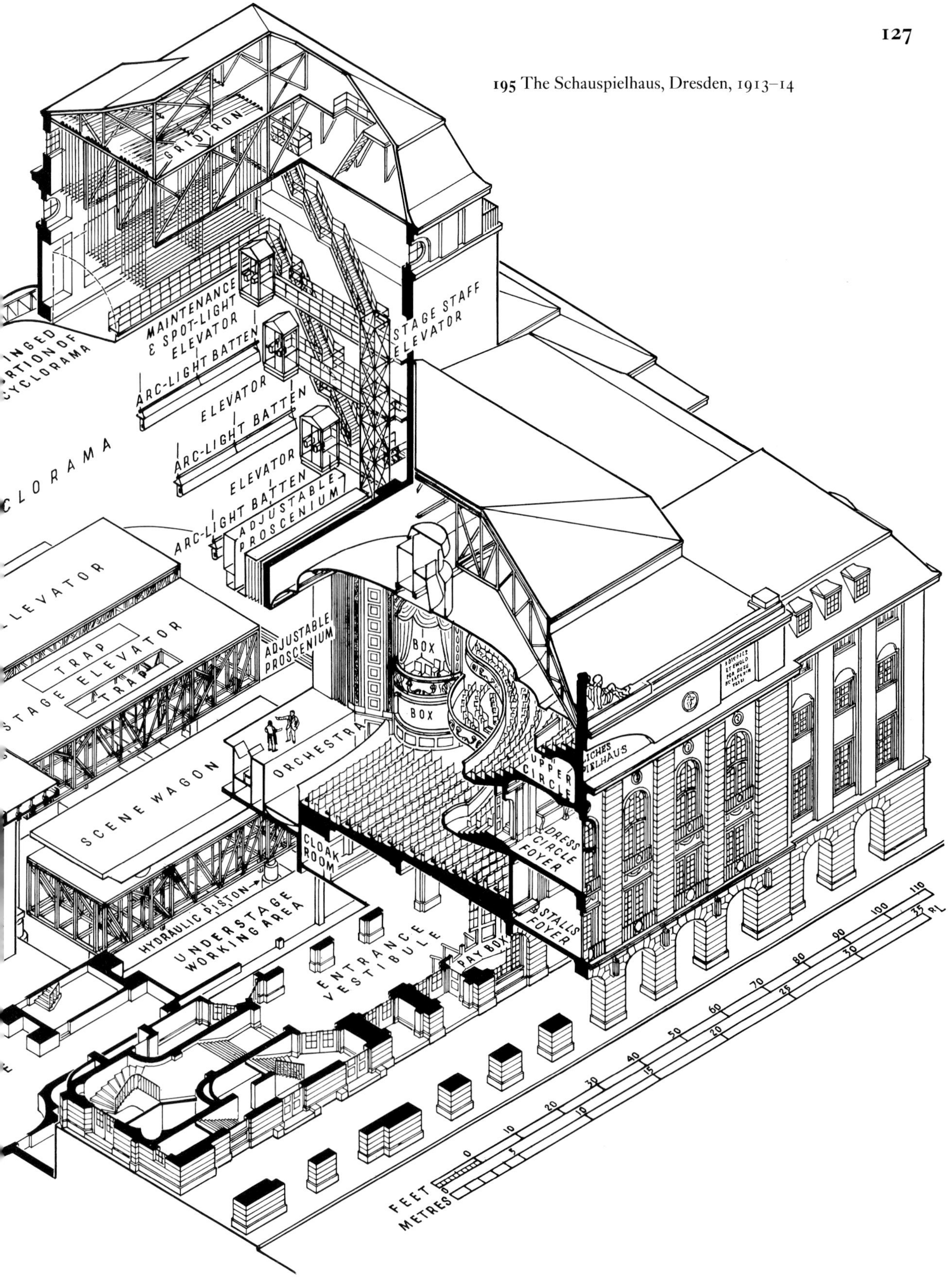
GRIDIRON
MAINTENANCE & SPOT-LIGHT ELEVATOR
STAGE STAFF ELEVATOR
ARC-LIGHT BATTEN
ELEVATOR
ARC-LIGHT BATTEN
ELEVATOR
ARC-LIGHT BATTEN
ADJUSTABLE PROSCENIUM
ADJUSTABLE PROSCENIUM
ELEVATOR
TRAP
STAGE ELEVATOR
TRAP
BOX
BOX
ORCHESTRA
SCENE WAGON
UPPER CIRCLE
DRESS CIRCLE FOYER
CLOAK ROOM
STALLS FOYER
HYDRAULIC PISTON
UNDERSTAGE WORKING AREA
ENTRANCE VESTIBULE
PAY BOX
FEET
METRES

195 The Schauspielhaus, Dresden, 1913–14

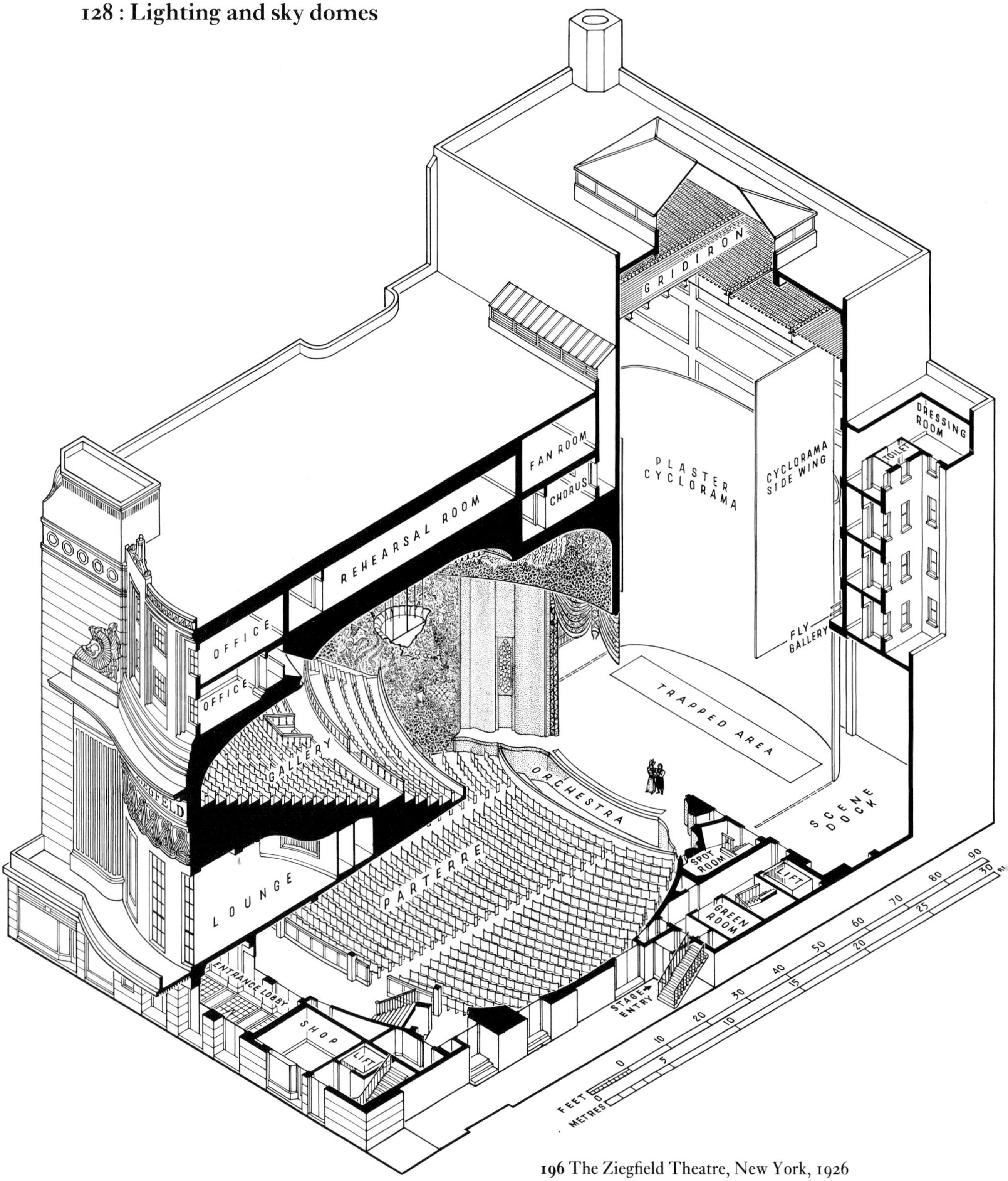
GRIDIRON
DRESSING ROOM
FAN ROOM
CHORUS
REHEARSAL ROOM
PLASTER CYCLORAMA
CYCLORAMA SIDE WING
TOILET
OFFICE
OFFICE
FLY GALLERY
TRAPPED AREA
GALLERY
ZIEGFELD
ORCHESTRA
SCENE DOCK
SPOT ROOM
LIFT
PARTERRE
LOUNGE
GREEN ROOM
ENTRANCE LOBBY
STAGE ENTRY
SHOP
LIFT
FEET
METRES

196 The Ziegfield Theatre, New York, 1926

The subsequent arrangement generally found in theatres incorporated wagons or sliding floor sections at stage level, with the cyclorama confined to the rear. The revolving stage was, however, a useful alternative. When first used it was found to be somewhat limiting, as the tendency was to try to fit together on the one turntable scenes which were designed as standard box sets or outdoor scenes, arranged in such a way that when one scene was no longer needed it could be struck and replaced by another set.

While still useful for this purpose, the gradual movement away from the painted to the plastic scene permitted scenery to be built on the turntable in a more sculptural, three-dimensional form, presenting changing aspects when revolved or seen under different arrangements of lighting. Indeed, with the much greater control now possible with electric light, specific portions of the plastic setting could be lit for a particular scene, and the movement of the turntable itself used in the action of the performance – as, for example, when actors were seen walking from one portion of a setting to another while the stage revolved.

With the productions of Max Reinhardt, the revolving stage came into its own. His trees, bushes, and undulations of ground forming the forest for his production of *A Midsummer Night's Dream* were set before the star-studded sky of the enclosing cyclorama which J. Bab here describes:

soon we had no longer individual pictures in the various segments of the revolving stage passing before our eyes but an entire structure, shown through the rotations of the stage from all possible angles.

On stages not equipped with mechanical devices, other means had to be found for moving the scenery. The simplest was the use of small wagons, which could be juggled into a series of combinations to provide a variety of scenes. In 1914 the American production of Elmer Rice's *On Trial* used two narrow platforms, pivoted on either side of the proscenium opening, so that each in turn was swung into position before the audience, the other meanwhile being situated in the appropriate stage wing.

In contrast to the highly mechanized stages, Joseph Urban's Ziegfeld Theatre, New York (1926), was designed for spectacular productions, [196] but even so it was considered that the use of expensive machinery on or under the stage was impracticable, and that it was wiser to keep the stage 'elastic for the different uses of each production'. As a result it was equipped only with a cyclorama dome of wire and plaster with movable side wings, an electrically-operated counterweight system, a means of providing traps in the rear portion of the stage, and a first-class electric lighting system. This idea of introducing temporary devices on a flat stage has much to commend it, since permanent features favoured by one director or designer seldom find favour with a different team. It should also be realized that the tempo of a production can be severely prescribed by the time it takes for an inherent mechanical system to complete its appropriate function; but, as noted above, it must still be possible to form openings in the stage as and when required.

Urban's proscenium opening was enclosed by two curved surfaces with a door on either side giving access to a forestage, 'which seems to bring the individual actor into the closest communication with the audience'. It was suggested that 'Front Scenes' might be played on the forestage while large scenic changes were being made behind the curtain, a device developed during the latter part of the nineteenth century by which complicated scenes could be changed prior to the development of the mechanical equipment discussed above.

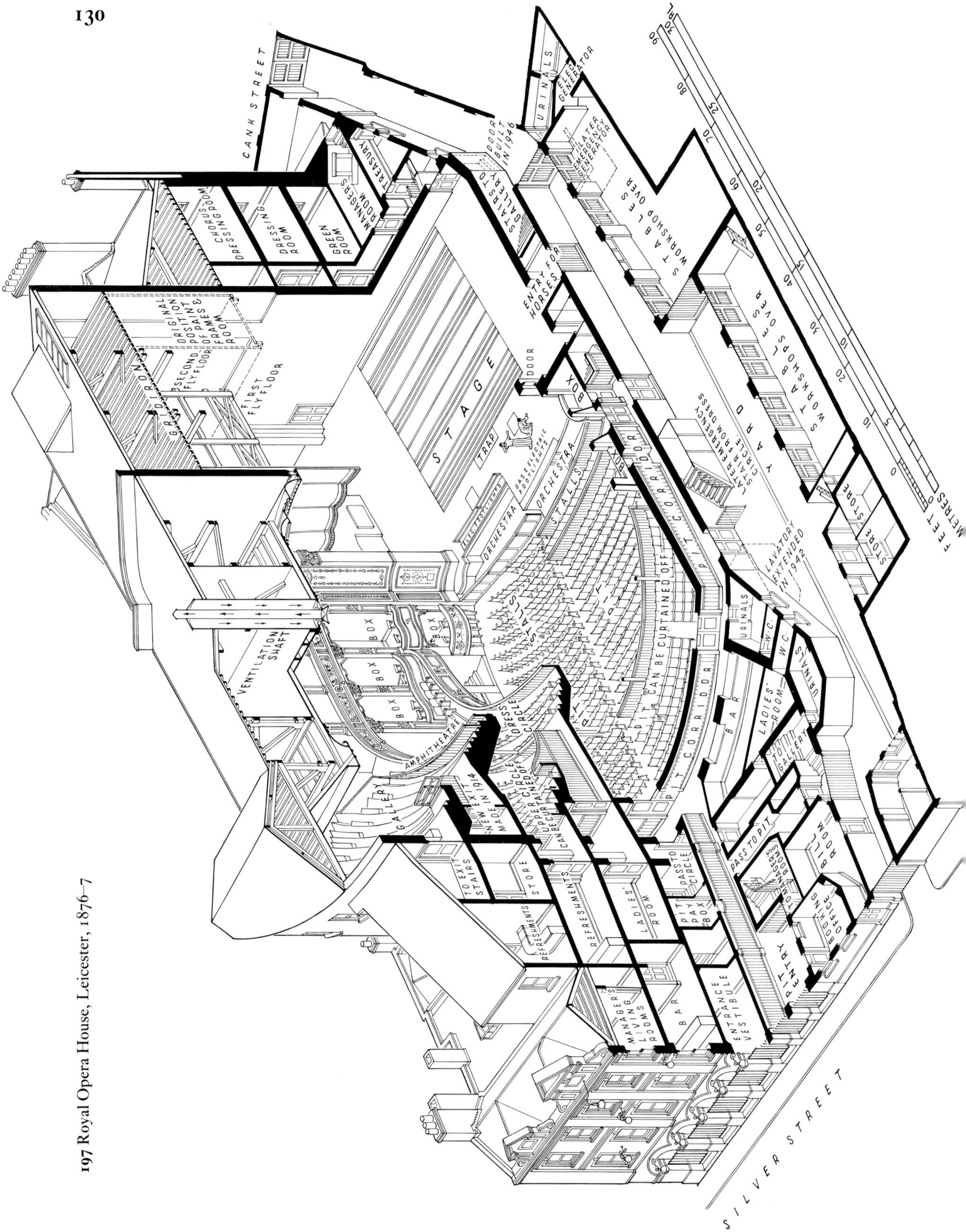
CANK STREET
SILVER STREET
STAGE
TRAP
GRIDIRON
SECOND FLYFLOOR
FIRST FLYFLOOR
CHORUS DRESSING ROOM
DRESSING ROOM
GREEN ROOM
MANAGER'S ROOM
TREASURY
URINALS
ELEC. GENERATOR
DOOR BUILT IN 1946
STAIRS TO GALLERY
ENTRY FOR HORSES
DOOR
STABLES WORKSHOP OVER
YARD
VENTILATION SHAFT
BOX
ORCHESTRA
STALLS
PIT
PIT CORRIDOR
CAN BE CURTAINED OFF
DRESS CIRCLE
AMPHITHEATRE
GALLERY
NEW EXIT MADE IN 1914
TO EXIT STAIRS
STORE
REFRESHMENTS
LADIES' ROOM
PIT PAY BOX
PASS TO CIRCLE
PASS TO PIT
BAR
URINALS
W.C.
LAVATORY EXTENDED IN 1942
TO GALLERY
BILLIARD ROOM
BOOKING OFFICE
PIT ENTRY
ENTRANCE VESTIBULE
MANAGER'S LIVING ROOMS
FEET
METRES

197 Royal Opera House, Leicester, 1876–7

20 Adaptable auditoria

Multi-purpose buildings. Mobile pit floors, walls and ceiling units. Covent Garden and Leicester Opera House. Adaptable audience capacities. The Chicago Auditorium.

As early as 1613 the Hope theatre [100] was designed as a multi-purpose building, and theatres have been made adaptable for other purposes on numerous occasions. The introduction of machinery which made it possible to raise the sloping pit floor level with the stage – as, for example, in the Altes Residenztheater in Munich in 1750–3, and in Barry's Theatre Royal, Covent Garden of 1858 – meant that the whole area could be used for masquerades, public dinners, and similar functions. It was also possible to change the size and shape of the auditorium to suit different forms of production.

The Royal Opera House, Leicester, designed by C. J. Phipps in 1876, [197] was arranged so that the rear portion of the pit and the upper circle could both be curtained off to adjust the accommodation to suit the needs of the occasion, which varied from morning concerts to flower shows and promenade concerts. To make the latter possible the pit floor could be raised level with the stage to provide a large floor area suitable for balls and circuses – the ring being partly in the pit and partly on stage for equestrian and similar displays.

Stabling for horses was beneath the carpenters' and property workshops, which were here built as a separate unit, instead of being in the more usual position in the roof over the auditorium. Water tanks and a water sprinkler system added further fire precautions, but it was not until 1906 that the stage and auditorium were separated by a brick wall, carried above roof level and equipped with a fire curtain.

The idea of cutting off portions of the auditorium by the use of curtains or screens was developed at Malmo, Sweden, in 1944 [265], and in the Eugenia Van Wezel Auditorium, Sarasota, Florida, in 1970. In the 1886 Chicago Auditorium [198] it was possible to close off the upper and lower balconies by the movement of hinged ceiling units, and the grand tier could be reduced by twelve rows by the use of a curtain hanging from the lower balcony, the total capacity thus varying from 2,500 to 4,200. The size of the proscenium could also be altered from a mere 47 feet (14.33m) width for drama, opera, or concert to 75 feet (22.86m) for use with massed choirs,or for conventions or balls.

198 Auditorium Building, Chicago

Numerous such adaptable auditoria have since been built in the United States, such as the Civic Theatres of El Paso, Texas (1974), and Roanoke, Virginia (1971), where the seating capacities are reduced by lowering the ceiling to cut off balcony seating, a device also incorporated in the Theatre Royal, Plymouth, in 1982.

21 Shakespearian revivals and the intimate theatre

Early Shakespearian reconstructions: Düsseldorf, Munich, William Poel, Max Krüger, and Nugent Monck. The Shakespearean Festival Theatre, Ashland, Oregon. The Arts Theatre, Munich, and the Relief Stage. Gordon Craig. The amateur movement and 'little theatres'. The Little Theatre, New York. The Little Theatre, London.

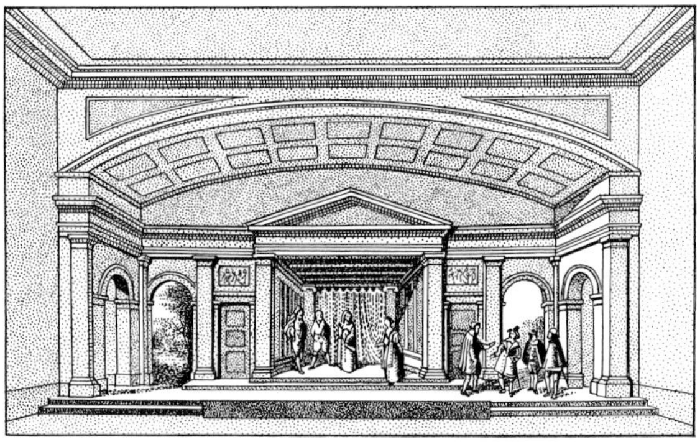

199 Karl Immermann's *Twelfth Night*

As early as the mid-nineteenth century, some theatre workers were stressing that dramatic content was more important than spectacle, and numerous attempts were being made to design theatres permitting a more direct actor–audience relationship, comparable to that which Garrick had enjoyed, and at the same time to do away with any need for the actors to declaim their lines. Early experiments were mainly concerned with the presentation of Shakespeare's plays, which had in many cases been rewritten to conform to the 'Front Scene' patterns noted above. It was felt that these problems could be overcome by a return to what were considered to be Shakespearian production methods, on what were thought to be reconstructions of Elizabethan stages.

In Düsseldorf, 1840, Karl Immermann designed such a stage [199], which had a distinct classical flavour. In 1889 the Munich Court Theatre staged Shakespearian plays in a setting with a central, curtained rectangular opening with curtained doors and arched openings above on either side. [200] The 'inner stage' had flanking walls and a ceiling, with further doors and arched openings acting as a form of false proscenium to naturalistic settings beyond, which could be changed behind the curtains while the play proceeded on the front stage.

200 Perfall's *King Lear*

In 1888, von Buchel's copy of De Witt's drawing of the Swan was discovered, and as a result future experimenters had some basis on which to formulate their ideas. In 1879, William Poel, dissatisfied with the commercialism of the English theatre, had started a movement towards the simplification of Shakespearian

201

201 William Poel's *Measure for Measure*, Royalty Theatre, London, 1893

202 Max Krüger's reconstruction of the Swan

203 The Maddermarket Theatre, Norwich

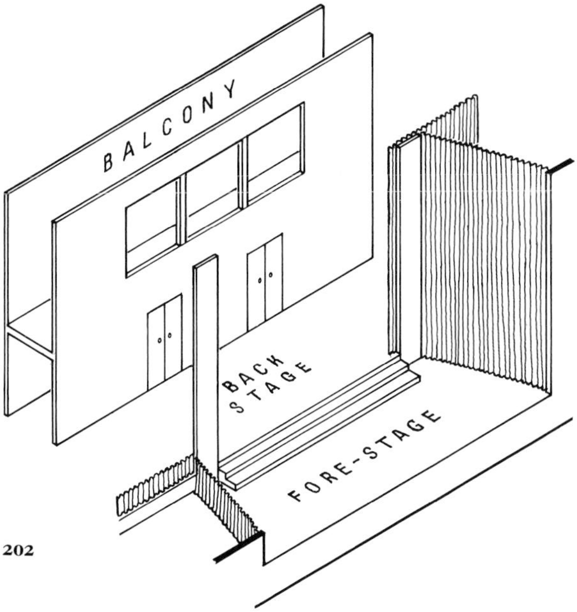
BALCONY
BACK STAGE
FORE-STAGE

202

203

productions, and turned from the acting editions of the plays then in use to the original versions.

In 1881 Poel staged *Hamlet* on a bare, draped platform with no scenery or interval. Twelve years later he built a replica of his idea of the Fortune Theatre on the stage of the Royalty Theatre. [201] He followed this in 1895 by performances before the screens in the Hall of Gray's Inn, and later by a presentation of *Twelfth Night* in the Hall of the Middle Temple, for which he built a stage based on de Witt's drawing.

At much the same time, Max Krüger in Germany prepared a basic reconstruction of the Swan, with a forestage flanked by curtains and separated from a rear stage by three steps and a pair of wings enclosing the rear area. [202] Curtains at this point could separate the two stages. At the rear, a flat wall contained two double doors with an open gallery above. Then, in 1921, the Maddermarket Theatre was built in Norwich by a disciple of Poel's, Nugent Monck, who converted a small existing hall into a semblance of an Elizabethan theatre. [203]

At this time Shakespearian stages were reconstructed as black and white half-timbered buildings, rather than with colourful Renaissance decorations. Such playhouses as the Shakespearean Festival Theatre, Ashland, Oregon, built in 1959, [204] permitted an understanding of the use of basic permanent architectural surrounds and levels, as contrasted with the flamboyant picture-stages of the period. The earlier examples, catering for limited audiences, were small, but they nevertheless drew attention to the more direct relationship possible between an actor and his audience no longer separated by the picture frame or the proscenium wall.

204 The Festival Theatre, Ashland, Oregon

205 The Greek Theatre, Bradfield College

207

Many of these Shakespearian theatres had a limited theatrical use of a scholarly nature, a limitation shared by the reconstructions of classical theatres which were conditioned by the need to study Greek in a practical manner, such as that still in use at Bradfield College near Reading. [205] This break-away from the picture stage was eventually to lead to the development of a number of variations on the standard actor-audience relationship, but the picture stage was too well-established for them to have much immediate impact on the general run of productions.

One very early reaction had been seen in the small Arts, or Künstler, Theatre [206] built in Munich in 1907–8 to the ideas of Georg Fuchs and Max Littmann, who were influenced by the Wagner Opera House in Bayreuth, but here modified the fan-shaped auditorium [207] to a rectangle to improve the sight-lines. This auditorium was arranged in a single slope of continental seating, backed by five boxes, holding in all some 642. Exits in the side walls led to spacious foyers at the sides and front of the auditorium.

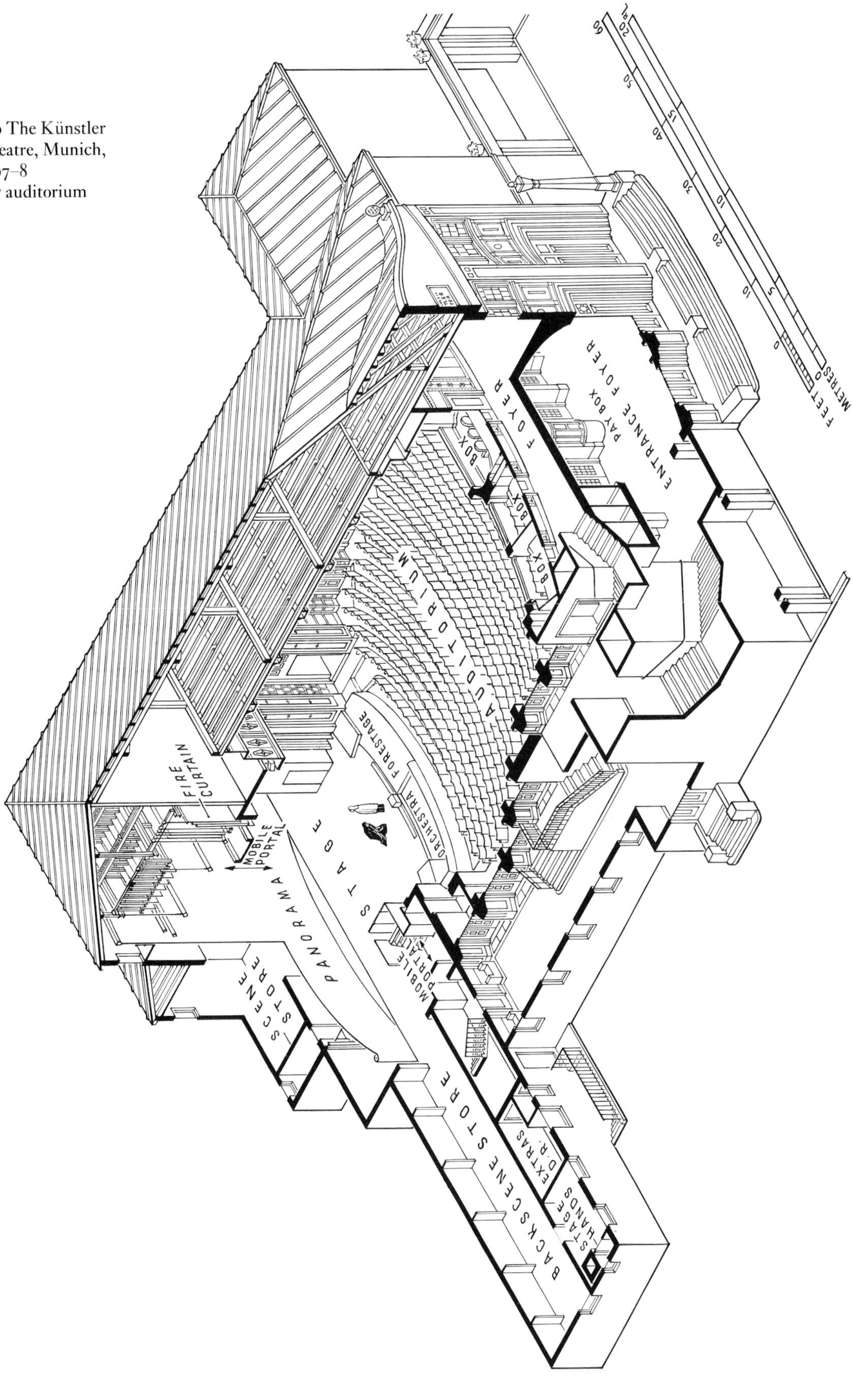
FIRE CURTAIN
MOBILE PORTAL
PANORAMA
STAGE
FORESTAGE
ORCHESTRA
AUDITORIUM
BOX
BOX
BOX
FOYER
ENTRANCE FOYER
PAY BOX
SCENE STORE
BACKSCENE STORE
EXTRAS
D.R.
STAGE HANDS
FEET
METRES

206 The Künstler Theatre, Munich, 1907–8
207 auditorium

208 The Künstler Theatre, Munich

A sunken orchestra separated the audience from the main stage. This could be covered to form a forestage, approached from either side through doors, so that this area, together with a low ceiling, formed a proscenium unit similar to those of the Restoration and Georgian theatres. [208] Beyond was an area of stage flanked by two walls painted a neutral grey, each with a door and opening over, and joined above by a lighting bridge, forming a ceiling which could be raised or lowered. As these side walls could be moved on and off stage, the whole unit formed a kind of mobile portal or flexible inner proscenium, which provided an architectural surround to the front 8 feet (2.43m) of the stage, and could be used in a similar manner to the architectural surrounds of the Shakespearian stages, as an interior or an exterior scene.

The remainder of the stage, some 10 feet (3.04m) deep, was backed by a pit, in which stood a panorama fixed to two rollers. The size of the portal was related to that of the panorama in such a way that all sight-lines were contained by it without the need for wings or borders. Unlike the standard theatre of the period, in which curtains and cloths were flown vertically above the stage, their movement here was horizontal, the cloths running on tracks direct from the adjoining scene store. A space between the proscenium unit and the lighting bridge permitted the movement of front curtains and of a three-part safety curtain.

The scenery was built solidly with three-dimensional modelling, and the whole was normally painted in monochrome, effects of light, shade, and colour being obtained solely by the use of diffused and direct lighting, mainly thrown from above to simulate natural lighting. To avoid what was considered to be the unfavourable effect of footlights, Schwabe tunnel lights with shutters were housed in a space built into the proscenium soffit, but a section of indirect footlights still had to be included to counteract the shadows resulting from the overhead lighting.

Ideas developed in the 1870s and 1880s by Duke George II of Saxe-Meiningen in his court theatre were used in the arrangement of scenery. The Duke had achieved the suggestion of great crowds and armies by allowing a part only to be visible. It was this last aspect of his staging that was used in Munich, as noted by Huntley Carter:

If a castle wall, or a terrace, or a bridge is thrown across the middle-distance, it goes out of the scene left and right; while the castle itself, the columns of the banqueting-hall, . . . are carried right up out of sight, thus leaving something to the imagination.

The theory behind the 'relief stage' was that on a shallow stage the actor would stand out against the background like a figure in bas-relief, thereby increasing his importance. The shallowness of the stage virtually ruled out movement up and down, and replaced it by lateral movement through the doors or behind the mobile portal. The limited physical depth of the stage was offset by the impression of unlimited space obtained by the use of the evenly-lit panorama. However, such an impression can only be obtained from a panorama or cyclorama so long as the eye cannot focus on any part of the cloth or plaster surface: the effect can therefore be defeated if a crease or stain appears on it.

In 1905 Gordon Craig published *The Art of the Theatre*, but as early as 1902 he had presented Laurence Housman's *Bethlehem* as a relief-stage production, setting his hessian-clad actors and sheep among hurdles, all picked out from the surrounding darkness by controlled areas of light. Craig largely removed the footlights and the wings and borders, placing his lights in positions where they could play an individual part in the illumination of the actor and the scene. He set his three-dimensional actors in a 'three-dimensional place', achieving his spatial effects by the use of the cyclorama, and of plain and geometric surfaces which spread out into the wings and disappeared aloft into darkness. Craig also experimented with the use of screens which could change and unfold before the spectators' eyes, and across which lights, changing in intensity and colour, could play, so that the scene itself took on a dramatic value of its own.

Among those few of Craig's designs actually to be realized on the stage was a *Hamlet* at the Moscow Art Theatre with Stanislavsky in 1912, and a production of Ibsen's *The Pretenders* at the Royal State Theatre, Copenhagen, in 1926, when Craig used his screens, banners, rostra, and steps in conjunction with the effects of projected scenery. Although Craig prepared one 'Design for a Theatre, open to the air, the sun and moon', which he illustrated as the frontispiece to *The Theatre Advancing*, and a project for the performance of Bach's *St. Matthew Passion*, his main influence was on scenic design, his ideas being expressed generally within the standard proscenium stage.

The Künstler Theatre, which Huntley Carter described in 1912 as a 'theatre of artists' – 'this small, beautiful, practical, and complete theatre', which he would like to see 'repeated in every town and city of the United Kingdom' – was to have a profound effect on theatrical ideas, and led to the development of an amateur movement building its own theatres.

The Little Theatre movement was founded by amateurs who loved the theatre and wished to participate in all its many facets, rather than just be spectators. These societies raised money to build their own premises, and presented a number of productions each year which were often experimental in artistic outlook and staging. As theatres established themselves some found it possible to employ professional assistance; it also became policy in some instances, as at Bradford Civic Playhouse, Yorkshire, to provide training classes for members who hoped to join the professional theatre. Both the Maddermarket, Norwich, [203] and the Questors Theatre, Ealing, [291] developed from these beginnings. In the United States, the Little Theatres gave all members of the community the opportunity of participation, and the theatre, used not only for dramatic and musical productions but for all types of activities, is a central feature of life in the area, as noted at Midland, Texas. [318]

In 1917 the American architect Edward Kinsila had written: 'The most important innovations have been made in the little theatres created throughout the country for the presentation of advanced plays', and he noted that 'A more ambitious step towards advanced theatre construction has been made by Winthrop Ames in New York'. Ames had built the Little Theatre [209] in 1912 to provide, as a critic in *Architecture* said, 'a more intimate relation between the drama enacted on

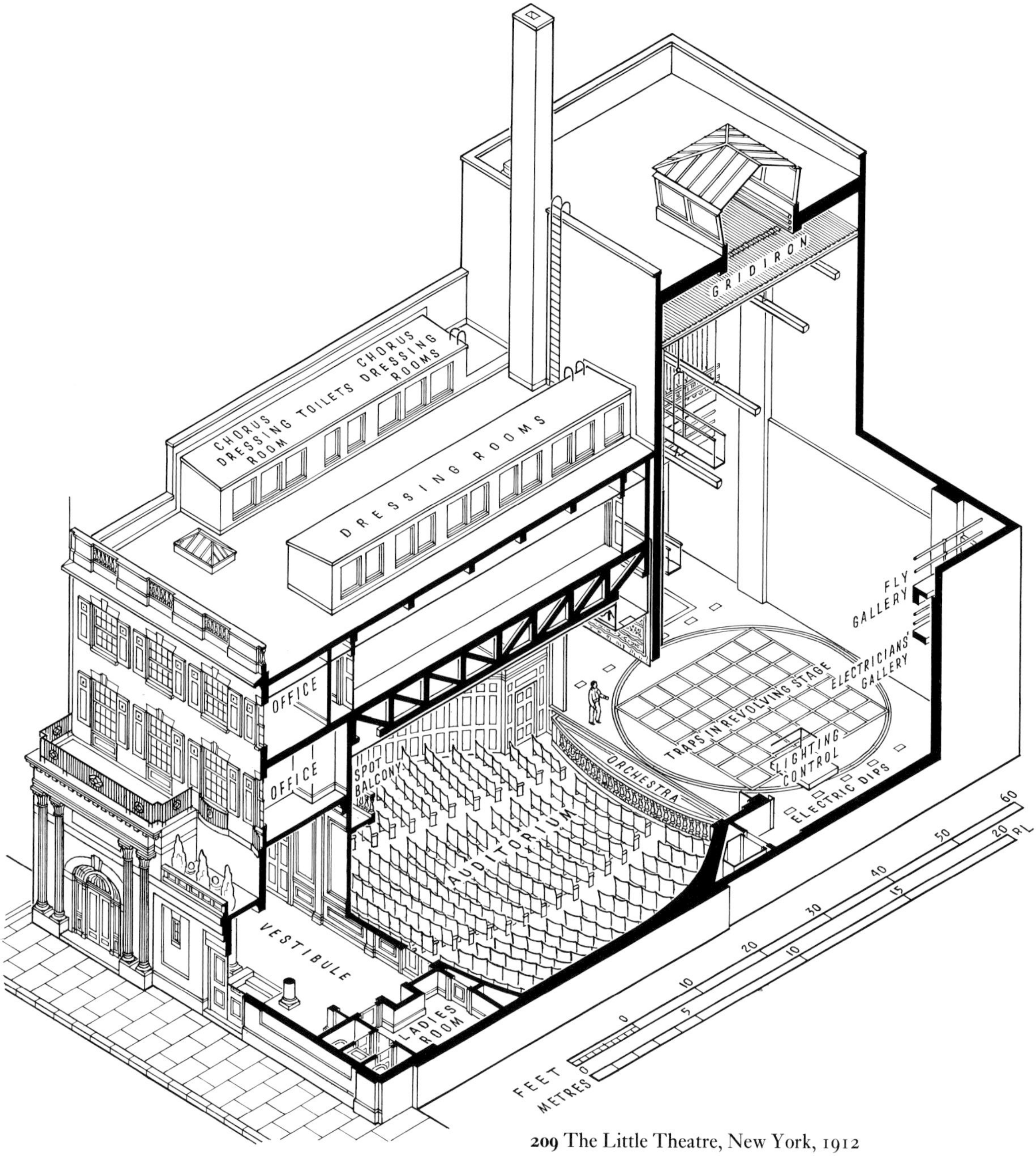

CHORUS DRESSING ROOM
TOILETS
CHORUS DRESSING ROOMS
DRESSING ROOMS
GRIDIRON
FLY GALLERY
ELECTRICIANS' GALLERY
OFFICE
OFFICE
SPOT BALCONY
TRAPS IN REVOLVING STAGE
LIGHTING CONTROL
ORCHESTRA
ELECTRIC DIPS
AUDITORIUM
VESTIBULE
LADIES ROOM
FEET
METRES

209 The Little Theatre, New York, 1912

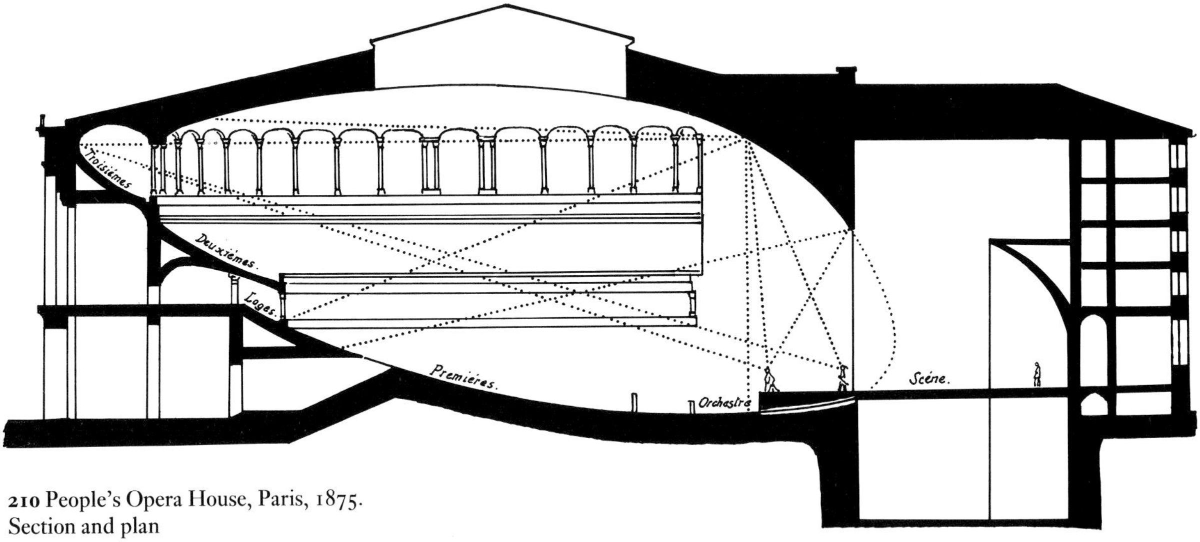
Troisièmes
Deuxièmes.
Loges.
Premières.
Orchestre
Scène.

210 People's Opera House, Paris, 1875.
Section and plan

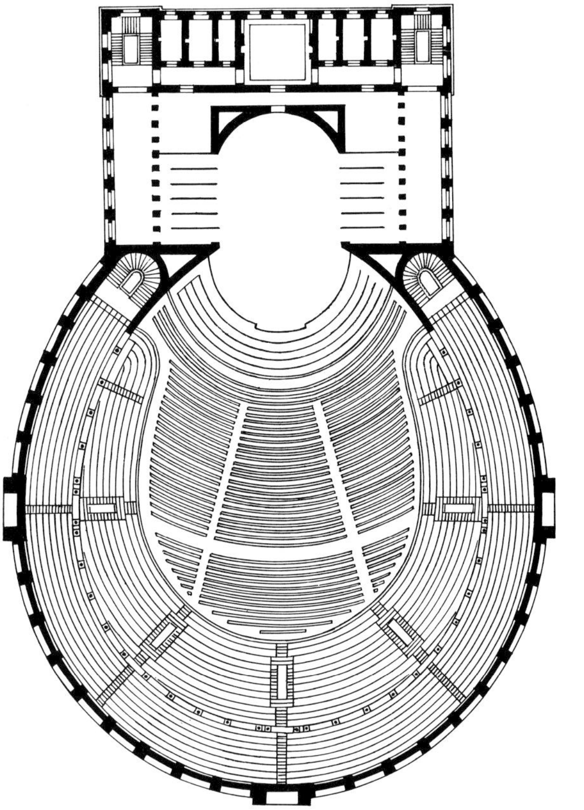

the stage, and the audience . . . so that the piece might proceed much as it would in real life without the over-emphasis either of voice, gesture, costuming or makeup necessary to "carry" in a big house'.

The auditorium had a single slope of seats accommodating some 299 persons – the capacity being kept below 300 since above this figure the fire regulations would have required more of the already restricted site to be given over to escape alleyways. Unlike the Künstler Theatre, where the floor was stepped, the floor here was designed on a developing curve which progressively raised the seating as sight-line problems increased with the distance from the stage – a design feature used as early as 1875 in a project by Davioud and Bourdais for a People's Opera House in Paris. [210]

The auditorium of the Little, with its curved and panelled walls flanking a recessed proscenium opening and its rear wall concentric with the curved seating, was designed under the guidance of Professor Wallace C. Sabine, the acoustics expert. The stage had a manually-operated revolve with 35 traps, to which an electric motor was fitted in 1916. Portions of the auditorium ceiling could be lowered so that spotlights might be directed to the stage at an angle of 45 degrees.

By 1917, David Belasco was supplementing such overhead lighting by the use of concealed spotlights set in the balcony front, and by 1925 Irving Pichel was commenting that many new theatres were now making use of such front-of-house lighting.

A theatre which had set a precedent for Winthrop Ames was Miss Gertrude Kingston's Little Theatre in John Adam Street, London. [211] This had been constructed in 1910 in premises formerly occupied by Messrs. Coutts the bankers, their banking hall being converted into an auditorium whose rectangular shape was no doubt dictated by the existing structure. This had a single slope of seating, backed by seven boxes, accommodating some 300 persons in all. Above the boxes was a kinematograph projection room. The stage was connected to the auditorium by what may be described as a 'hole in the wall': it was backed by a plaster cyclorama, with a normal gridiron above the front portion of the stage. Although the wing space was wider on the prompt side, there was little room for the storage of scenery.

Both here and in the Little Theatre, New York, the need to accommodate a cheaper class of seating eventually necessitated the introduction of a balcony in both theatres. The London theatre was reconstructed in 1912 to include a balcony seating 88, with four boxes below, while the New York theatre was similarly enlarged in 1919 to a new capacity of 532.

211 The Little Theatre, John Adam Street, London, 1910

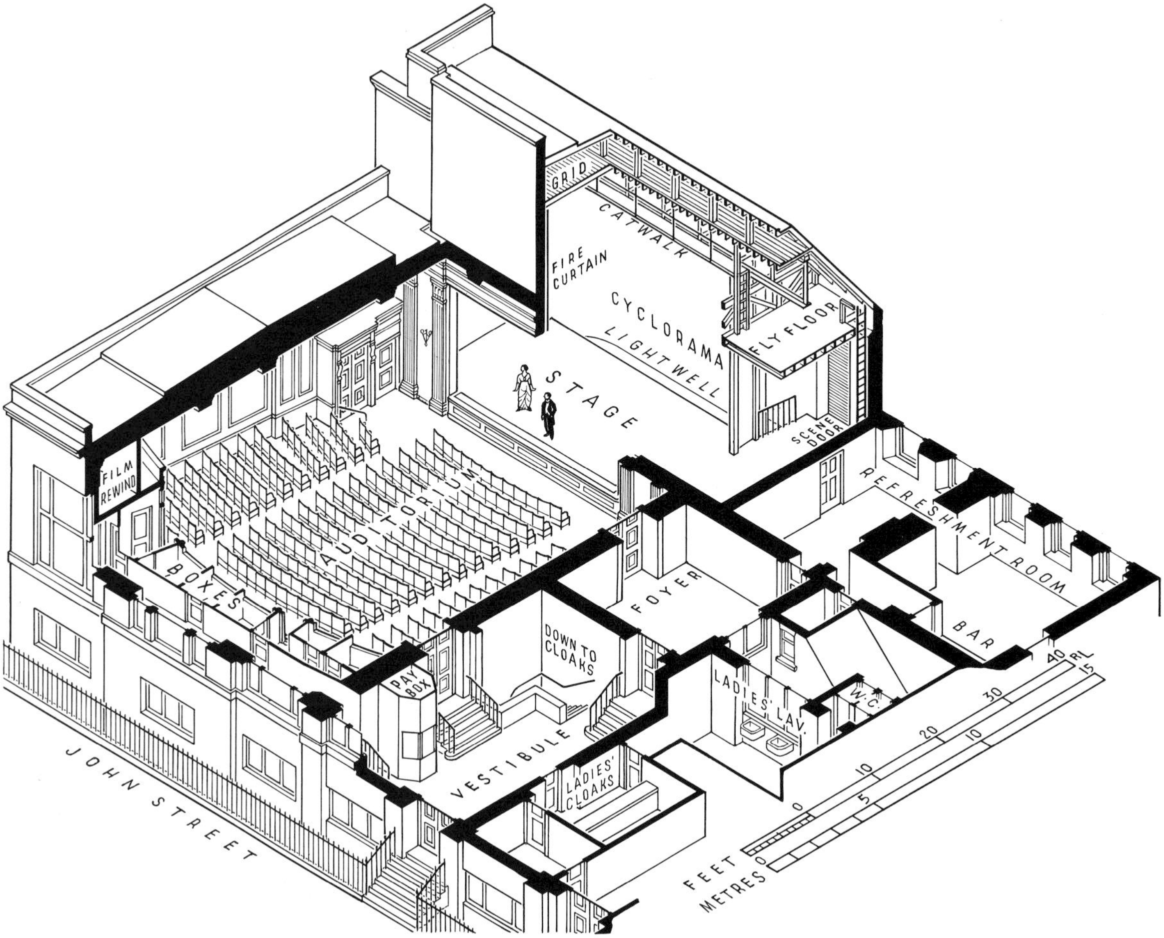
GRID
CATWALK
FIRE CURTAIN
CYCLORAMA
LIGHTWELL
FLY FLOOR
STAGE
SCENE DOOR
FILM REWIND
AUDITORIUM
BOXES
REFRESHMENT ROOM
FOYER
BAR
DOWN TO CLOAKS
PAY BOX
LADIES' LAV.
W.C.
VESTIBULE
LADIES' CLOAKS
JOHN STREET
FEET
METRES
0
10
20
30
40
0
5
10
15
FT
M

22 Actor and audience in a single space

Reinhardt's Grosses Schauspielhaus. Spiritual unity of actors and audience. Norman Bel Geddes and 'Theatre No. 6'. Terence Gray and the Festival Theatre, Cambridge. Settings of mood rather than realism.

In complete contrast to these 'little theatres' was Reinhardt's vast Grosses Schauspielhaus. In 1910 he had used the Schumann Circus in Vienna for a production of *Oedipus Rex*, building a reconstruction of a Greek temple at one end of the circus, connected by steps to an orchestra in the circus ring, partly occupied by the audience grouped around a central wedge-shaped acting area. The following year saw Reinhardt's London production of the *Miracle* in Olympia, which he transformed into a cathedral encompassing both actors and audience in one great 'spiritual unity'.

Reinhardt's wish to build a 'theatre of five thousand' which would do full justice to his great spectacular productions was based on a return to the Teatro Farnese style, combining picture-stage and orchestra within the auditorium. This communion of actors and audience in a single space was the basis for the design of the Grosses Schauspielhaus in Berlin, adapted by Hans Poelzig from the existing Circus Renz in 1919–20. [212]

The theatre had a fully equipped scenic stage almost entirely enclosed by an elliptical cyclorama, cut back at the top to permit scenery to be flown over the front half of the stage. A revolve occupied the greater part of the main stage, the front portion of which could be separated. Both portions could be raised as a whole or independently, together with flanking stairways which led up or down to the side wings of the stage.

In front and within the auditorium was a forestage, built in six sections which could again be raised or lowered independently. The three sections nearest to the main stage were flanked by steps leading from vomitoria, and could rise and fall to match the forestage: in their lowest position they could serve as an orchestra well. Beyond was a U-shaped orchestra with a vomitory stair at its far end. [214]

There was no proscenium as such, but the scenic stage could be separated from the auditorium by a curtain or by sliding panels – noted on drawings as a fire curtain – decorated to conform with the architecture of the auditorium. When the panels were drawn, the six-part forestage and orchestra became what we would recognize today as a thrust stage.

The seating, for approximately 3,500, enclosed this thrust stage in what was virtually a single slope, subdivided by horizontal gangways. At the front and sides were boxes, with loose seats which could face either stage. The main body of the auditorium was crowned by the dome of the original circus, disguised by stucco 'stalactites' concealing a lighting gallery. The relationship of actor and audience was ideal for Reinhardt's love of mass relationships between these participants, and when the stages were filled with dancers, crowds of Roman citizens, or revolutionary mobs mingling with the audience, [213] the building achieved its purpose; but the lone actor set in a spotlight delivering a soliloquy was lost in the vast scale.

213 Reinhardt's *Danton's Death*

142 : Actor and audience in a single space

Grosses Schauspielhaus, Berlin, 1919–20, **212, 214**

212

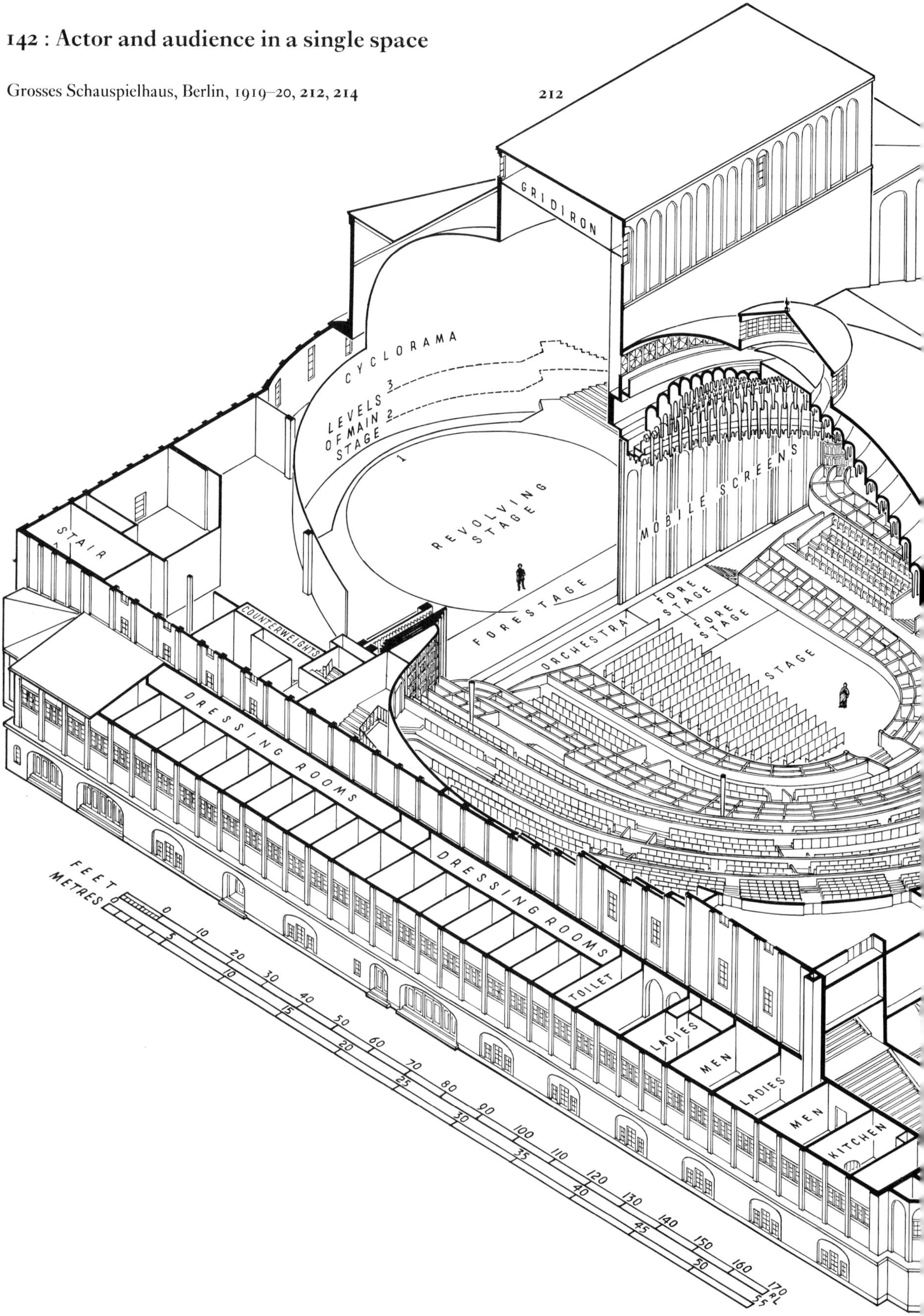
GRIDIRON
CYCLORAMA
LEVELS OF MAIN STAGE
3
2
1
REVOLVING STAGE
MOBILE SCREENS
STAIR
COUNTERWEIGHTS
FORESTAGE
ORCHESTRA
FORE STAGE
FORE STAGE
STAGE
DRESSING ROOMS
DRESSING ROOMS
TOILET
LADIES
MEN
LADIES
MEN
KITCHEN
FEET
METRES

214

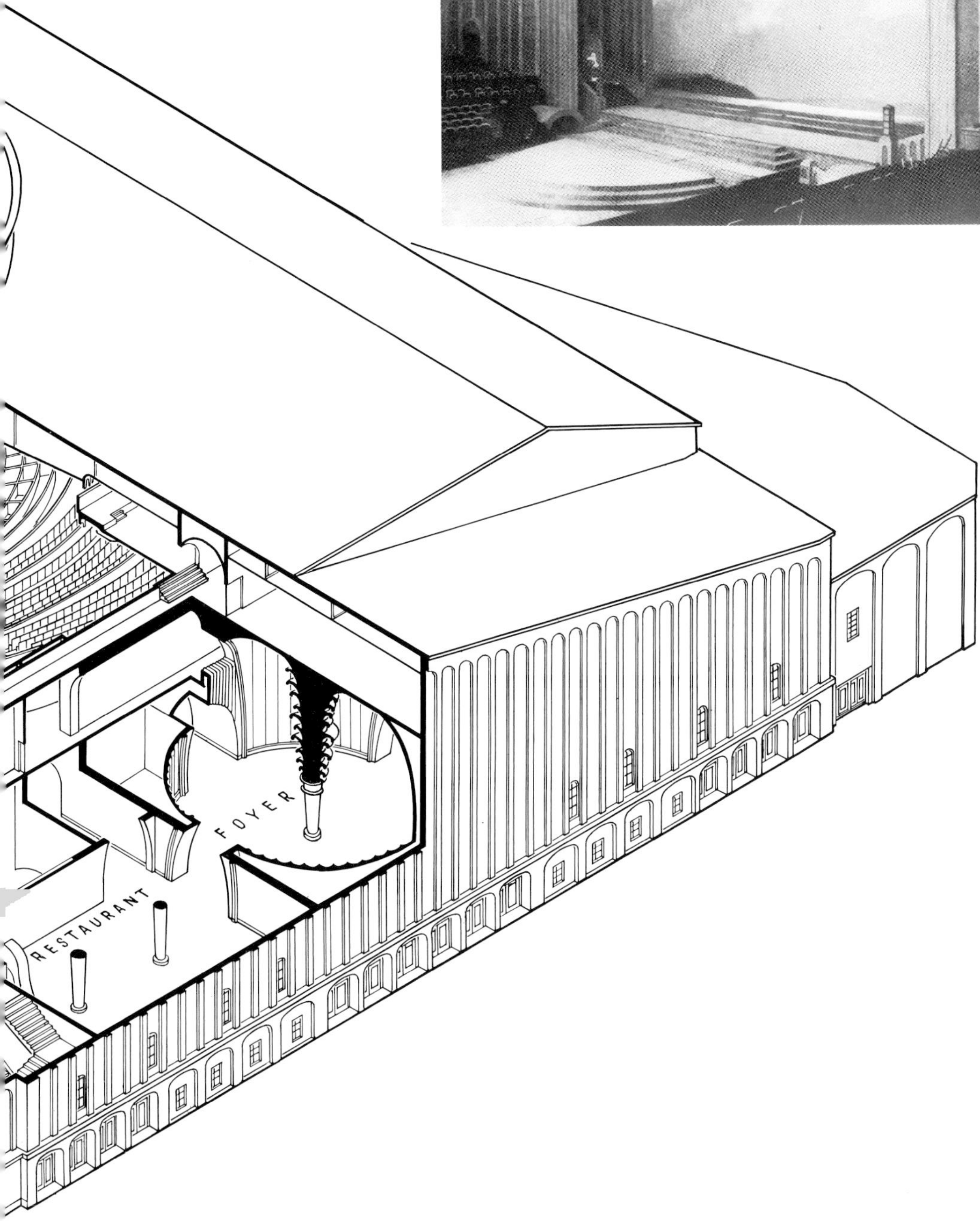
FOYER
RESTAURANT

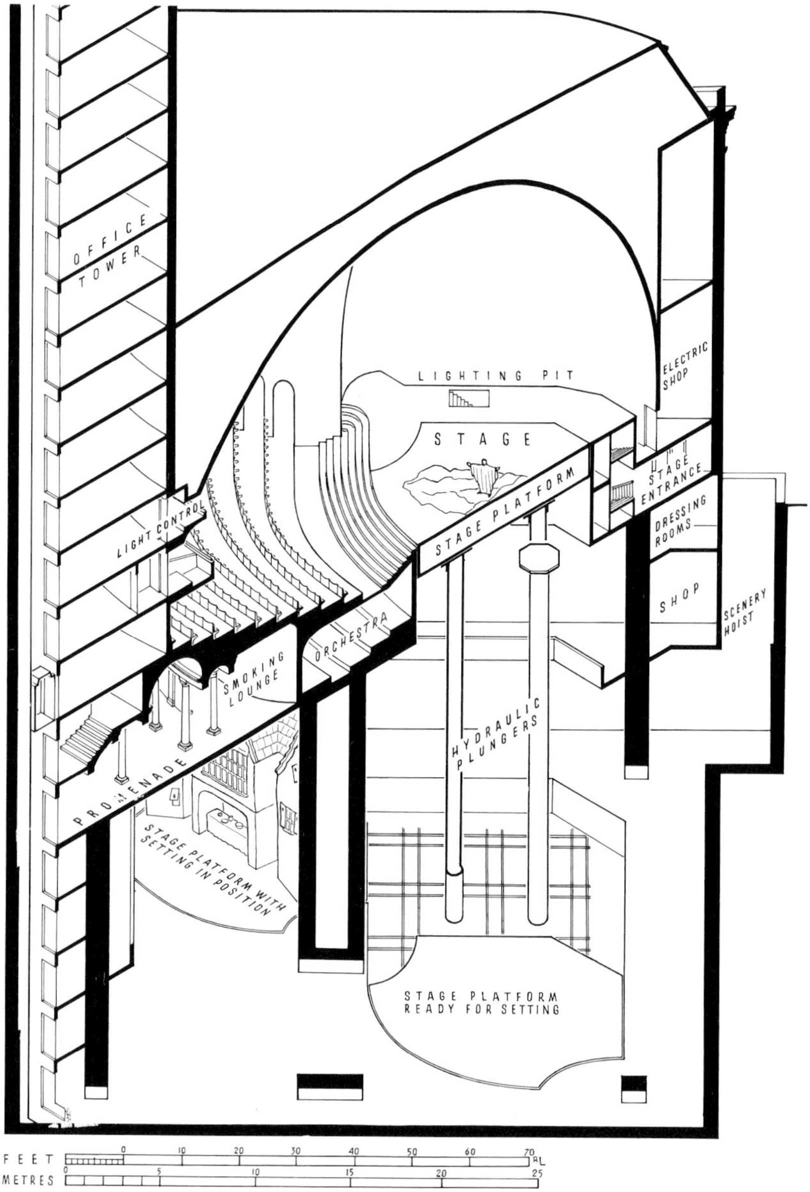
OFFICE TOWER
LIGHTING PIT
STAGE
ELECTRIC SHOP
STAGE ENTRANCE
DRESSING ROOMS
LIGHT CONTROL
STAGE PLATFORM
SHOP
SCENERY HOIST
ORCHESTRA
SMOKING LOUNGE
HYDRAULIC PLUNGERS
PROMENADE
STAGE PLATFORM WITH SETTING IN POSITION
STAGE PLATFORM READY FOR SETTING
FEET
METRES

215 Norman Bel Geddes, Theatre No. 6, 1922

Reinhardt's problems of communication were not helped by the difficult acoustics. As a result, the building was never really successful, and within less than two years he had moved on. In the theatre's later days the orchestra was filled with seats and the picture-stage was used on its own, but the majority of seats were not well placed for this use. It must be remembered that the furthest seats were some 88 feet (26.82m) from the orchestra, 131 feet (39.93m) from the forestage, and some 151 feet (46.02m) from the revolve.

In America, Norman Bel Geddes had designed as early as 1914 a theatre with stage and auditorium within the same space. Enclosed by a cyclorama, the stage, with a curved front and flight of steps, was set in the

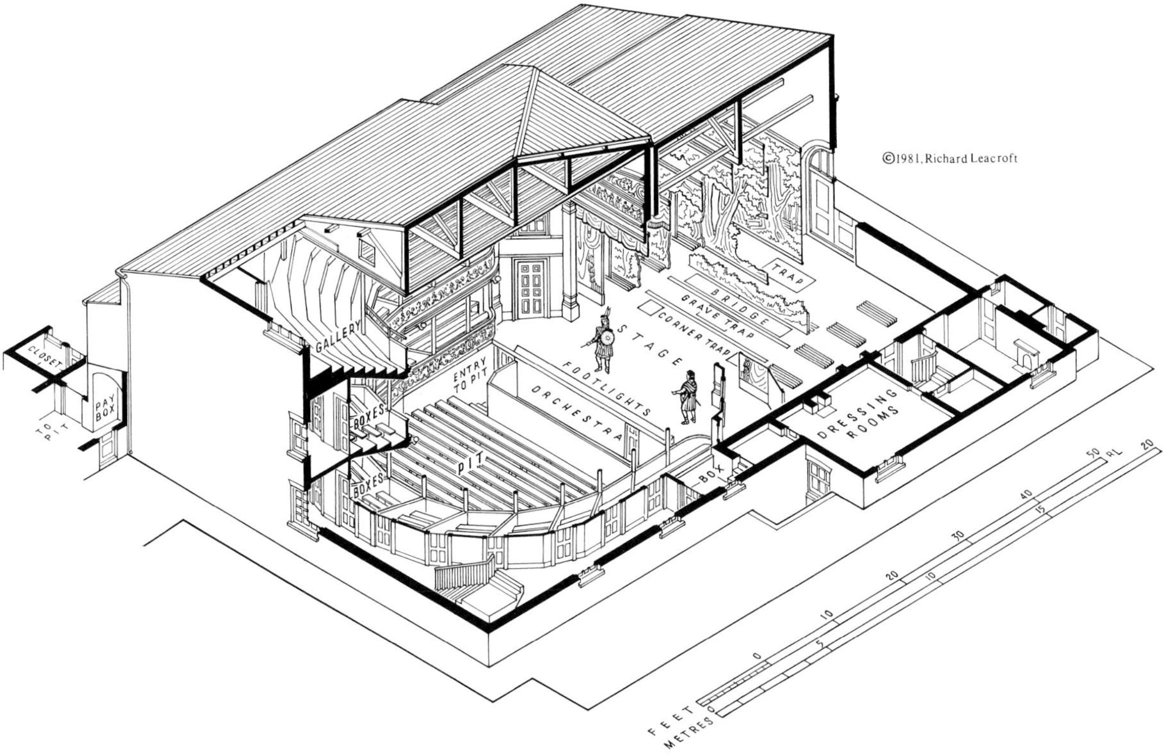
©1981, Richard Leacroft
TRAP
BRIDGE
GRAVE TRAP
CORNER TRAP
STAGE
FOOTLIGHTS
ORCHESTRA
ENTRY TO PIT
GALLERY
BOXES
PIT
BOXES
BOX
CLOSET
PAY BOX
TO PIT
DRESSING ROOMS
FEET
METRES

216 The Barnwell Theatre, Cambridge, *c.* 1816

corner of a square building. Concentric rows of seats were divided by gangways radiating from the centre of the stage. The scheme was redesigned in 1922 as 'Theatre Number 6', when the basic pattern was retained but much simplified. [215] The auditorium was designed with continental seating for 866, each row discharging at either end through arched openings into passageways leading to a promenade on the floor below, opening directly to the street. Charles Bragdon tells us:

The stage is undivided from the auditorium . . . the same great dome spans actor and spectator; there is no visible orchestra pit, no footlights, no proscenium arch, nor even a curtain between the two.

The cyclorama was lit from a pit at the back of the stage, and the electrician had a booth above nine boxes set in the rear wall of the auditorium, from which he could have a clear view of the light and colour effects. But Bragdon was perhaps making somewhat optimistic claims for

the new uses to which light is put and the extraordinary functions it is made to perform. . . . By the use of lenses light can be so concentrated and controlled that 'masking' of the old-fashioned sort – concealing by means of curtains, flats, borders – is no longer necessary; darkness can be made to obliterate and light to reveal whatever is desired.

These Bel Geddes stages remained, however, as projects, the ideas which they envisaged finding only occasional expression – as in such experiments as Terence Gray's adaptation of the early nineteenth-century Barnwell Theatre in Cambridge, [216] which he opened as the Festival Theatre in 1926. [217]

Gray removed the nineteenth-century proscenium

217

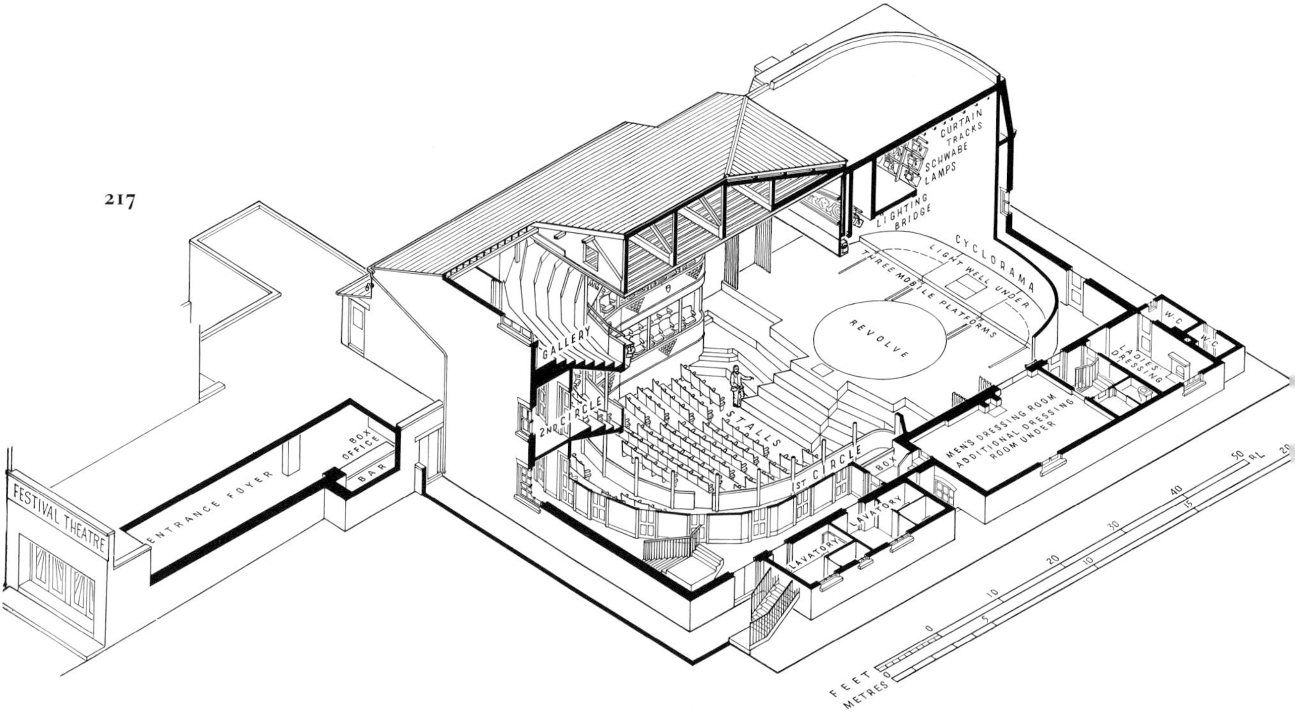
CURTAIN TRACKS
SCHWABE LAMPS
LIGHTING BRIDGE
CYCLORAMA
LIGHT WELL UNDER
THREE MOBILE PLATFORMS
REVOLVE
GALLERY
2ND CIRCLE
STALLS
1ST CIRCLE
BOX
W.C
W.C
LADIES' DRESSING
MEN'S DRESSING ROOM
ADDITIONAL DRESSING ROOM UNDER
LAVATORY
LAVATORY
BOX OFFICE
BAR
ENTRANCE FOYER
FESTIVAL THEATRE
FEET
METRES

Festival Theatre, Cambridge, 1926; **217**; **218**; **219**, setting for *Salomé*

with its stage doors, retaining only a portion of the wall between stage and auditorium. The original stage was replaced by a series of stepped platforms, which connected the main stage with the lowest level of the stepped pit. Entries were provided through the original stage boxes, redecorated in contemporary style, and down gangways through the new pit seating, together with an entrance with steps to the pit through the OP (or right-hand) side wall of the stage. [218]

The main stage had a revolve, beyond which was a rostrum that could move forward on rails to open up a space through which actors could ascend to stage level. Two traps, one in front of the revolve and the other in the mobile rostrum, provided further points of entry. The rear stage was enclosed by a permanent, plastered cyclorama, behind which the actors could pass.

Gray built his scenes of platforms, steps, ramps, and varying two- or three-dimensional shapes to provide the necessary acting levels, and to create a mood rather than a realistic setting for a play. [219] This approach to theatre was an example of the reaction breaking out all over the Continent against the over-realistic interpretation of nature on contemporary picture-frame stages. In contrast to the normal view, this new theory required that the audience was never permitted to forget that they were attending a theatrical performance. In 1932 Gray wrote:

218

As for this new Theatre, which many of us will live to see in its youth; men such as Mr Norman Bel-Geddes have shown us its architectural form, and early attempts at the actual construction of such theatres have been made; such attempts have been premature and still-born, and the artists were not at hand with the necessary technique for their use. In these theatres stage and auditorium will be a unity, the audience will once more view the stage from diverse angles so that actors will really be seen in the round; make-believe reality will be unwanted and impossible, scenery will no longer seek to reproduce the external appearance of the place of action.

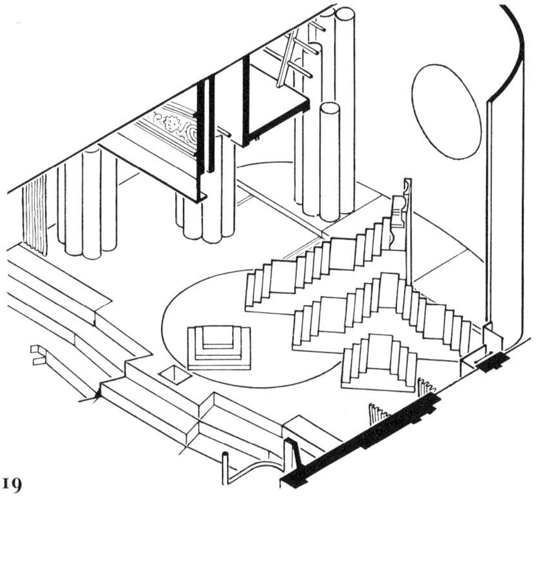

219

To this end, for one production at least, Gray removed any form of masking, so that the audience could see the stage hands and waiting actors in the wings. Actors performed in and made their entrances through the auditorium, in a similar manner to that used by Reinhardt for his production of *Danton's Death*. [213]

In 1917 Kinsila was writing that

the extra high scene loft, which has ever been a troublesome architectural feature, may be eliminated . . . as hanging room for scenery. The old style painted scenery with its 'flats', 'wings', and ugly 'sky borders' is . . . gradually giving way to modern plastic scenery.

The use by Gray of three-dimensional solid units of scenery, reflecting the solidity of the actors, made just such a radical change to the theatre structure as was inherent in Bel Geddes's designs: there was no fly-tower at Cambridge, or even flying space as such. Curtain tracks were attached to the stage ceiling so that varying effects of enclosure could be obtained, in contrast to the spacious effects obtainable with the cyclorama. Black wings or curtain legs and drapes were used to create further effects of space against which the coloured cross-lighting could paint the shapes with colours indicative of the mood required.

As lighting played such an important part in the scenic conventions, a lighting bridge spanned the front part of the stage, and housed a battery of lighting units used in conjunction with the cyclorama, which was also lit from an open pit at its base. The vestigial remains of the proscenium wall concealed a spot batten for use with the main stage, and 'focus lamps' were fixed to the ends of the second circle and to the central balustrade of the gallery.

221 Palace Theatre of Varieties, Leicester

23 The picture-frame theatre of the 'thirties

Frank Matcham's Palace of Varieties, Leicester. Reconstruction of the 1930 Adelphi Theatre. The Oxford Playhouse. Forestages and the London Theatre Studio. The Shakespeare Memorial Theatre. Fan-shaped auditoria, balconies, and forestages.

That the Festival Theatre differed from the average contemporary theatre may be seen by comparing it with Frank Matcham's Palace of Varieties, Leicester (1901) [220] which, although built primarily for use as a music hall, is nevertheless a representative theatre of its period, with its circles, boxes, and gallery decorated in a lavish oriental style. [221]

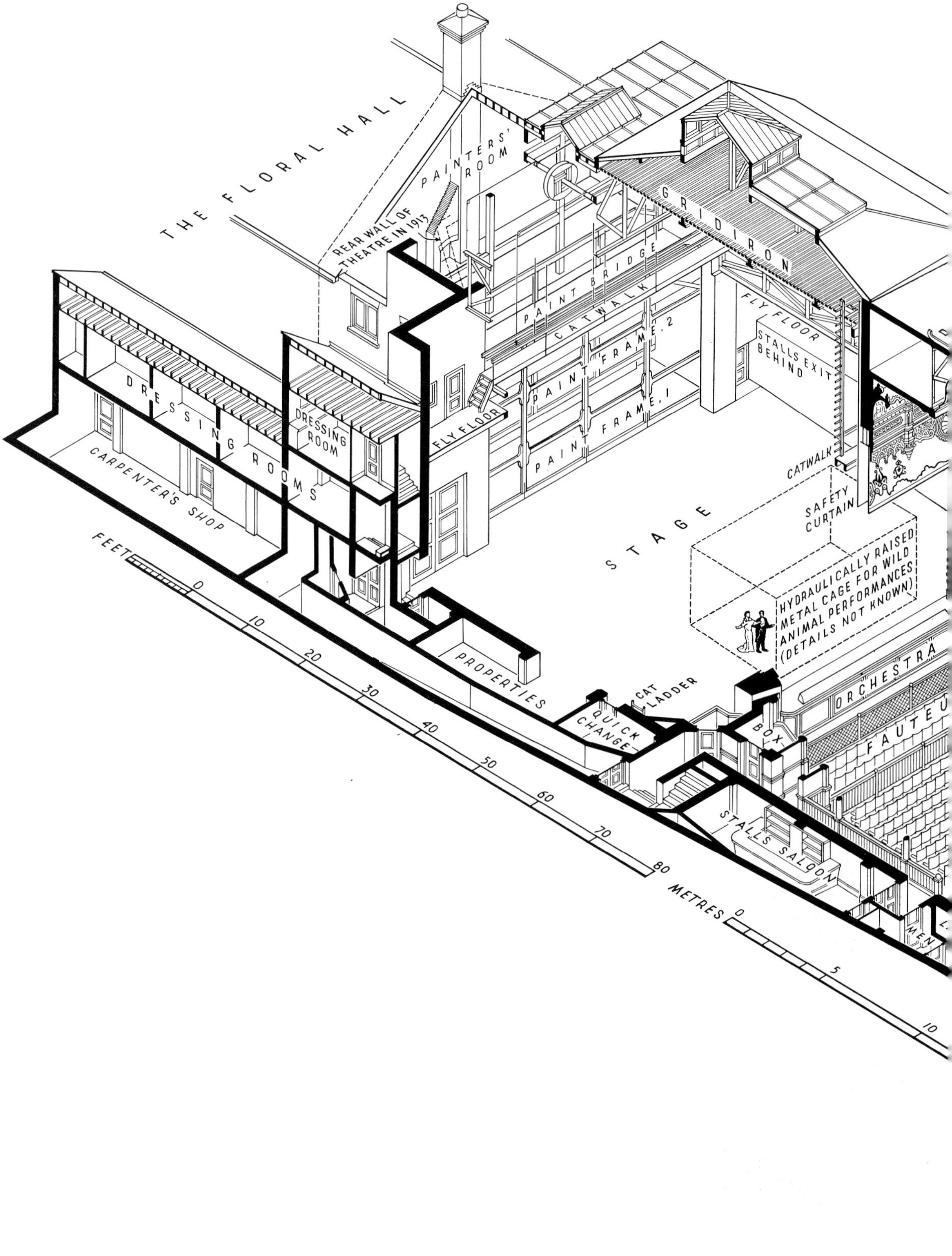
THE FLORAL HALL
PAINTERS' ROOM
REAR WALL OF THEATRE IN 1913
GRIDIRON
PAINT BRIDGE
CATWALK
FLY FLOOR
STALLS EXIT BEHIND
PAINT FRAME. 2
PAINT FRAME. 1
FLY FLOOR
DRESSING ROOMS
DRESSING ROOM
CARPENTER'S SHOP
CATWALK
SAFETY CURTAIN
STAGE
HYDRAULICALLY RAISED METAL CAGE FOR WILD ANIMAL PERFORMANCES (DETAILS NOT KNOWN)
FEET
0
10
20
30
40
50
60
70
80
PROPERTIES
CAT LADDER
QUICK CHANGE
BOX
ORCHESTRA
STALLS SALOON
METRES
0
5
10

220 Palace Theatre of Varieties, Leicester, 1901

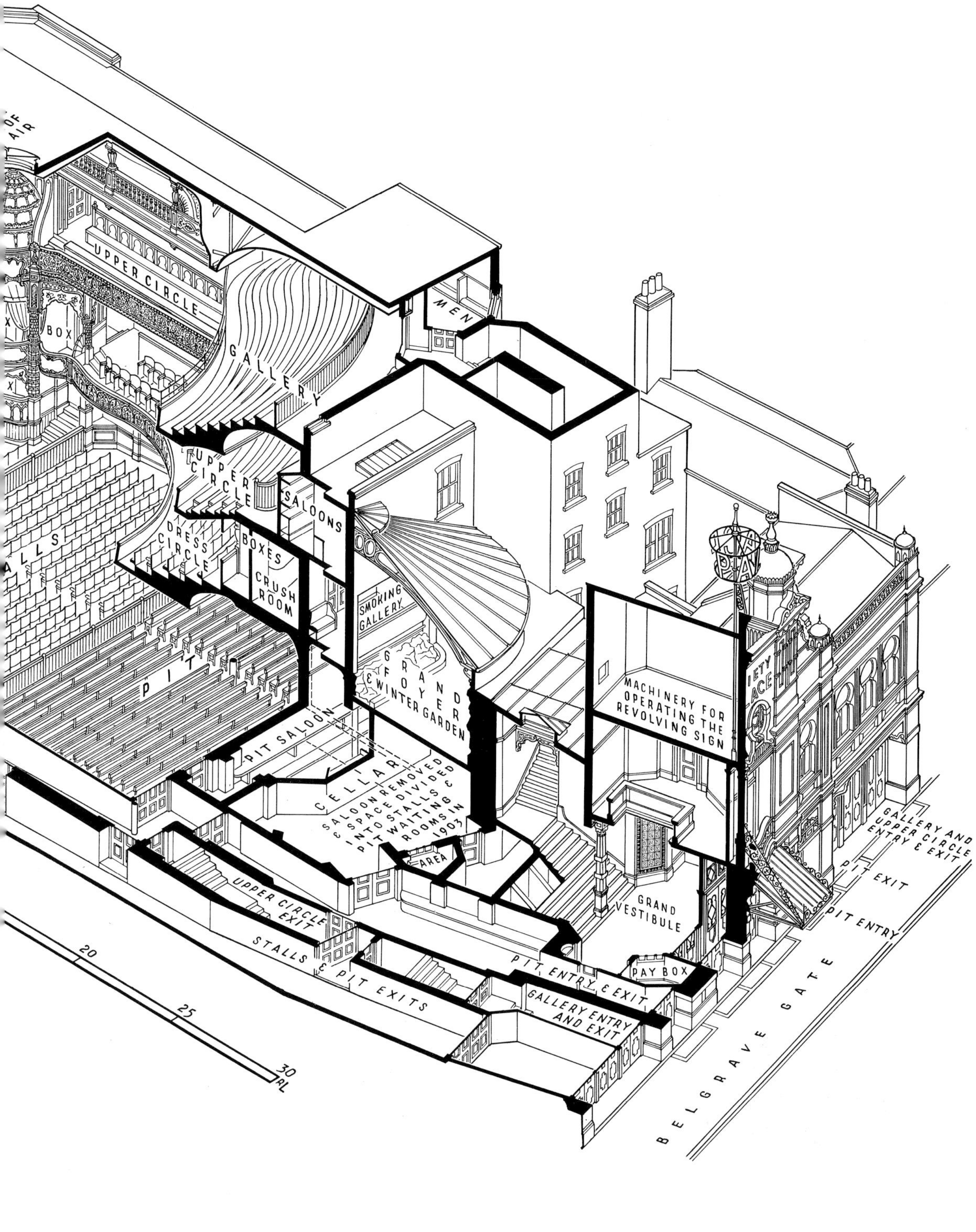
OF
AIR
UPPER CIRCLE
BOX
GALLERY
MEN
UPPER CIRCLE
SALOONS
ALLS
DRESS CIRCLE
BOXES
CRUSH ROOM
SMOKING GALLERY
GRAND FOYER & WINTER GARDEN
PIT
MACHINERY FOR OPERATING THE REVOLVING SIGN
PIT SALOON
CELLAR
SALOON REMOVED & SPACE DIVIDED INTO STALLS & PIT WAITING ROOMS IN 1903
AREA
GRAND VESTIBULE
UPPER CIRCLE EXIT
STALLS & PIT EXITS
PIT ENTRY & EXIT
PAY BOX
GALLERY ENTRY AND EXIT
GALLERY AND UPPER CIRCLE ENTRY & EXIT
PIT EXIT
PIT ENTRY
BELGRAVE GATE
20
25
30
RL

222 Royal Adelphi Theatre, London, 1858

223 Century (Adelphi) Theatre, London, 1901

Theatres of the 1930s are well illustrated by the reconstruction of the Adelphi Theatre, London. [222–223] The theatre prior to the alterations of 1930 [224] had eleven rows of stalls and eleven pit benches. The pit had its own pay box and entrance, while the stalls were approached by a private corridor leading from a 'Grand Vestibule', which also gave access to the proscenium boxes, two on either side at stalls, dress circle, and upper circle levels. Eight further boxes formed the rear wall of the dress circle directly facing the stage. Both upper circle and gallery had their own separate pay-boxes and enclosed staircases. The stage opened at the rear into a large scene dock, above and to the side of which were dressing rooms, separated from the stage as a fire precaution by solid walls. There was no fly-tower, the roof over the stage continuing that over the auditorium.

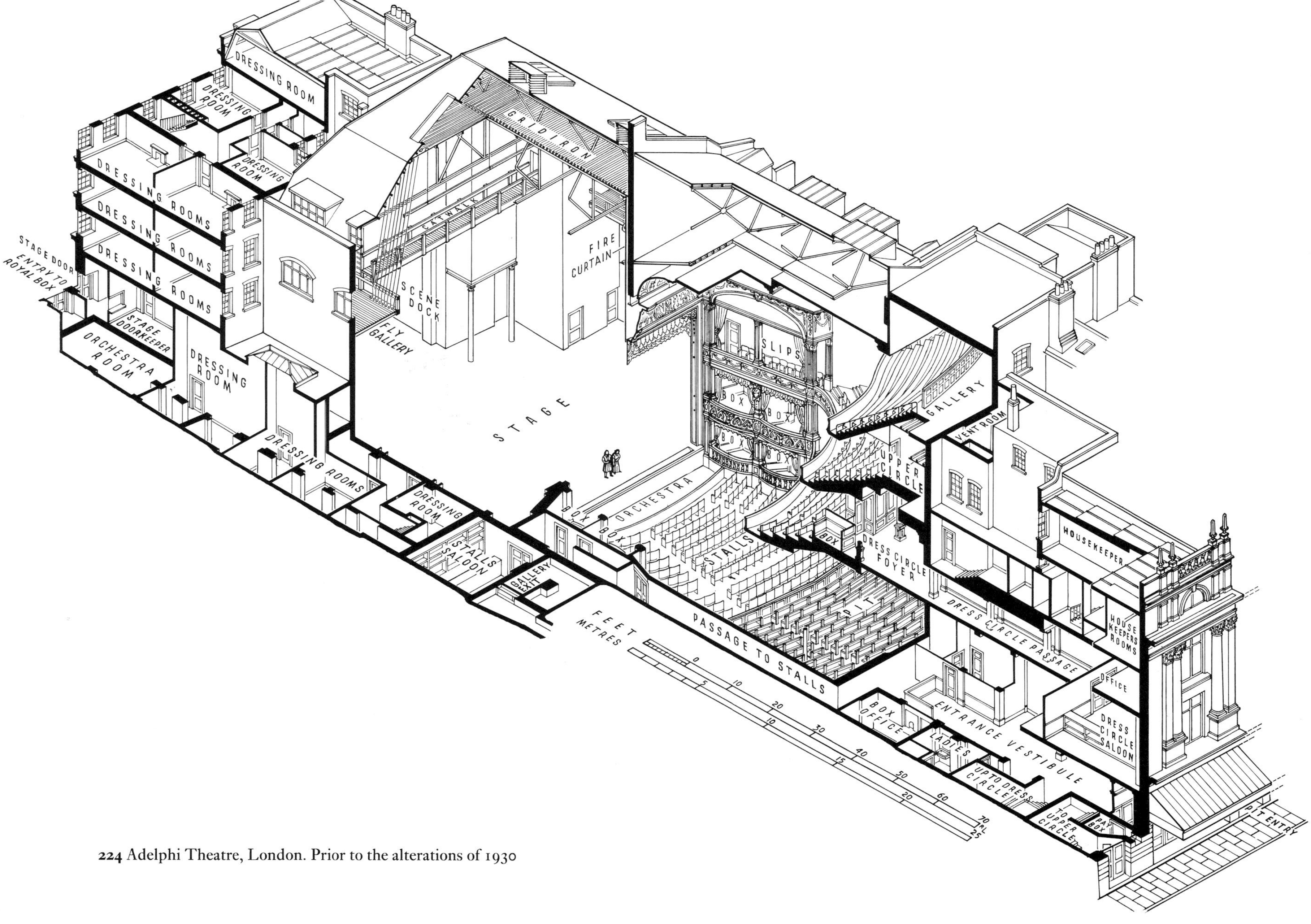
DRESSING ROOM
DRESSING ROOM
DRESSING ROOM
DRESSING ROOMS
DRESSING ROOMS
DRESSING ROOMS
STAGE DOOR
ENTRY TO ROYAL BOX
STAGE DOORKEEPER
ORCHESTRA ROOM
DRESSING ROOM
DRESSING ROOMS
DRESSING ROOM
GRIDIRON
CATWALK
SCENE DOCK
FLY GALLERY
FIRE CURTAIN
STAGE
SLIPS
BOX
BOX
BOX
BOX
GALLERY
VENT ROOM
UPPER CIRCLE
ORCHESTRA
BOX
BOX
STALLS
BOX
DRESS CIRCLE FOYER
HOUSEKEEPER
HOUSE KEEPERS ROOMS
STALLS SALOON
GALLERY EXIT
PIT
DRESS CIRCLE PASSAGE
OFFICE
FEET
METRES
PASSAGE TO STALLS
BOX OFFICE
ENTRANCE VESTIBULE
DRESS CIRCLE SALOON
LADIES
UP TO DRESS CIRCLE
TO UPPER CIRCLE
PAY BOX
PIT ENTRY

224 Adelphi Theatre, London. Prior to the alterations of 1930

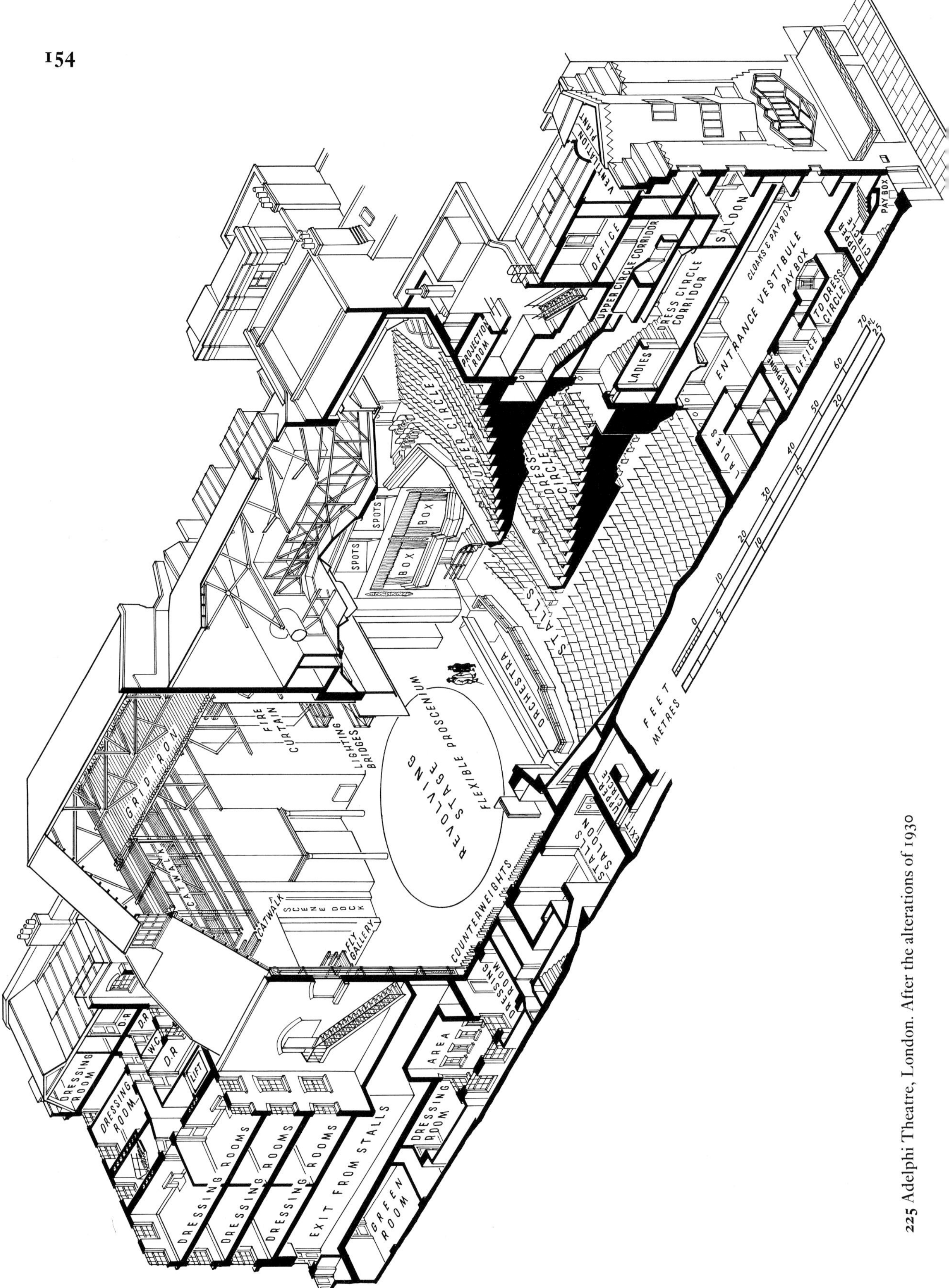
VENTILATION PLANT
PAY BOX
TO UPPER CIRCLE
SALOON
CLOAKS & PAY BOX
ENTRANCE VESTIBULE
PAY BOX
TO DRESS CIRCLE
OFFICE
UPPER CIRCLE CORRIDOR
DRESS CIRCLE CORRIDOR
LADIES
TELEPHONE
OFFICE
LADIES
PROJECTION ROOM
UPPER CIRCLE
DRESS CIRCLE
STALLS
SPOTS
SPOTS
BOX
BOX
ORCHESTRA
FLEXIBLE PROSCENIUM
REVOLVING STAGING
FIRE CURTAIN
LIGHTING BRIDGES
GRIDIRON
CATWALK
CATWALK
SCENE DOCK
FLY GALLERY
COUNTERWEIGHTS
FEET
METRES
0 10 20 30 40 50 60 70
0 5 10 15 20 25
FT
M
UPPER CIRCLE
EXIT
STALLS SALOON
DRESSING ROOMS
AREA
DRESSING ROOM
GREEN ROOM
EXIT FROM STALLS
DRESSING ROOMS
DRESSING ROOMS
DRESSING ROOMS
DRESSING ROOM
DRESSING ROOM
D.R
W.C
D.R
LIFT

225 Adelphi Theatre, London. After the alterations of 1930

The reconstruction [225] increased the seating capacity from 1,100 to 1,500, in spite of a reduction in the overall height of the auditorium and the replacement of the original three tiers of circles and gallery by two flatter but deeper, wedge-shaped balconies. [226] All but four of the boxes were removed, those at stalls level permitting a widening of the auditorium, while those at upper circle level were replaced by front-of-house lighting positions, for which provision was also made above the new auditorium ceiling. Each portion of the auditorium was approached by its own single entrance to simplify control, but each had four exits.

Backstage, the original timber construction of flies and grid was replaced by steel, and the roof over the stage was equipped with a new fire lantern operated by fusible links – a safety device intended to draw any stage fire away from the auditorium. The original hemp-line flying system gave way to modern counterweights, and the stage was rebuilt to include an electrically-operated revolve.

226 Adelphi Theatre, 1930

SAFETY CURTAIN
EXIT
EXIT

227 The Playhouse, Oxford, 1938

228 London Theatre Studio, 1937

On a smaller scale, a typical theatre of the period was the Playhouse, Oxford (1938), which owed much in its plan and form to Miss Kingston's 1910 Little Theatre. A rectangular auditorium, with twenty straight rows of seats and a small, rear balcony with four rows, was separated from the stage by a wall pierced by a rectangular opening equipped with a fire resisting curtain. [227] The theatre was decorated in a plain and clinically-severe manner, with little attempt at creating a theatrical atmosphere. The auditorium has since been reconstructed with a forestage, and lighting louvres to walls and ceiling.

Numerous attempts were being made, however, to break out of the picture frame, and theatres were adapted by the introduction of forestages built over the orchestra pit; but such improvisations were seldom suitable in the existing theatres, with their sight-lines from the many circles directed to the main stage. Nevertheless, theatres with forestages and Georgian-style entry doors were built, an important example being the small theatre designed for Michel St. Denis's drama school, the London Theatre Studio in Islington (1937), which had a narrow forestage flanked on either side by doors, with balconies over. [228]

229 Shakespeare Memorial Theatre, Stratford upon Avon, 1932

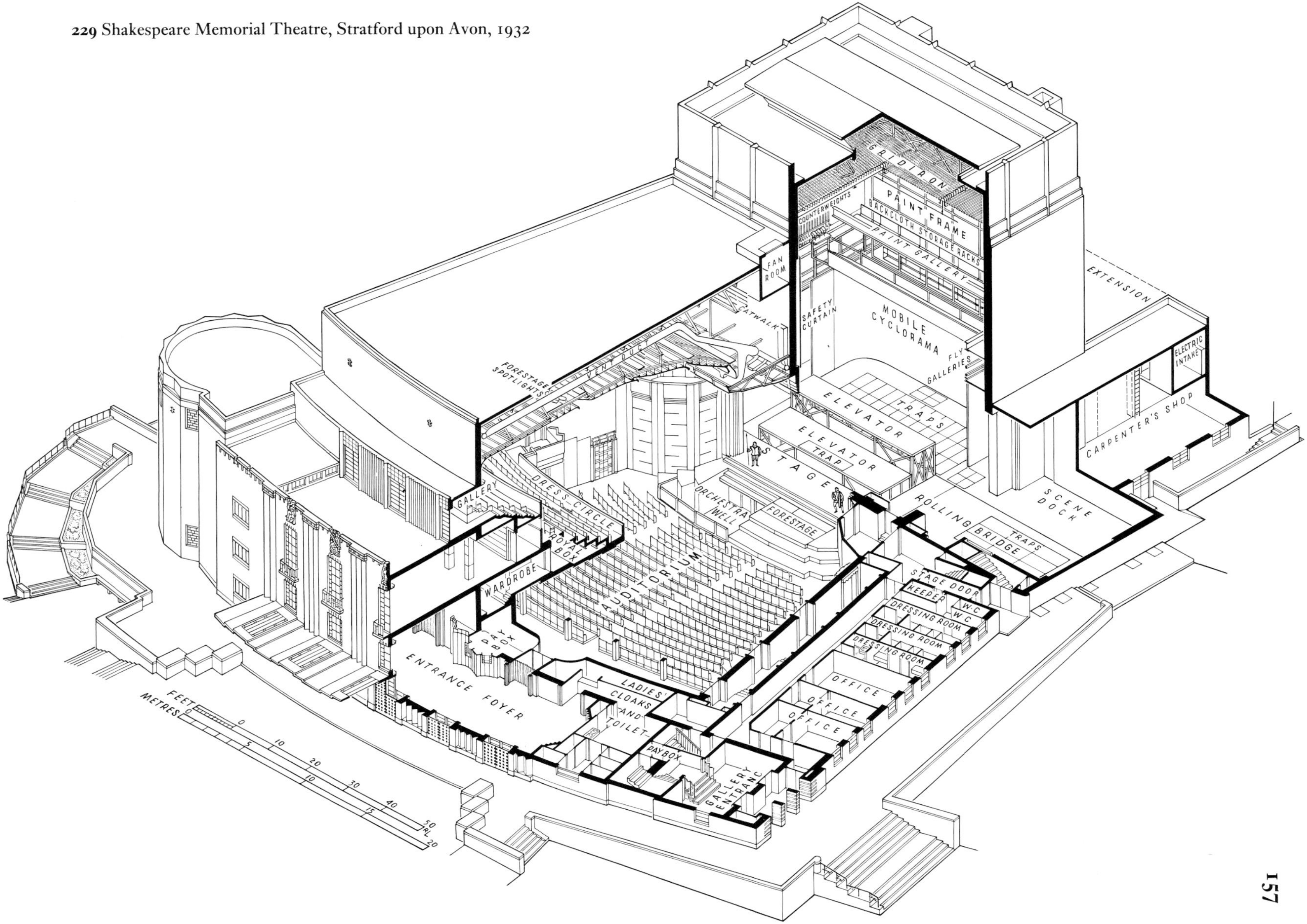

GRIDIRON
PAINT FRAME
BACKCLOTH STORAGE RACKS
PAINT GALLERY
COUNTERWEIGHTS
FAN ROOM
EXTENSION
CATWALK
SAFETY CURTAIN
MOBILE CYCLORAMA
FLY GALLERIES
ELECTRIC INTAKE
CARPENTER'S SHOP
FORESTAGE SPOTLIGHTS
ELEVATOR
TRAPS
ELEVATOR TRAP
STAGE
SCENE DOCK
ROLLING BRIDGE
TRAPS
GALLERY
DRESS CIRCLE
ORCHESTRA WELL
FORESTAGE
ROYAL BOX
AUDITORIUM
WARDROBE
STAGE DOOR KEEPER
W.C.
W.C.
DRESSING ROOM
DRESSING ROOM
DRESSING ROOM
PAY BOX
ENTRANCE FOYER
LADIES' CLOAKS AND TOILET
OFFICE
OFFICE
OFFICE
PAYBOX
GALLERY ENTRANC
FEET 0 10 20 30 40 50
METRES 0 5 10 15 20

230

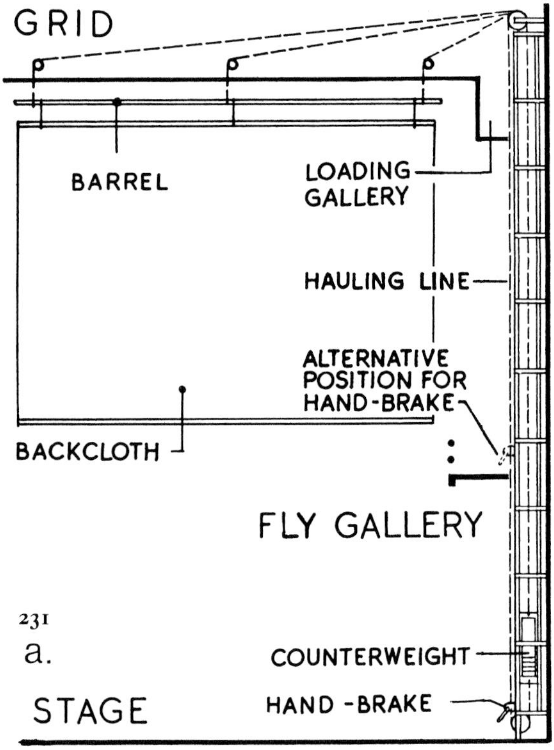
GRID
BARREL
LOADING GALLERY
HAULING LINE
ALTERNATIVE POSITION FOR HAND-BRAKE
BACKCLOTH
FLY GALLERY
COUNTERWEIGHT
HAND -BRAKE
STAGE

231
a.

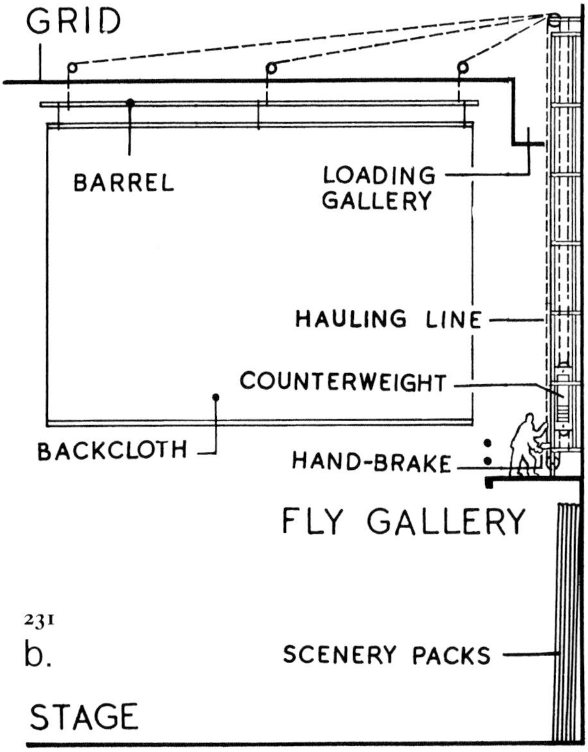
GRID
BARREL
LOADING GALLERY
HAULING LINE
COUNTERWEIGHT
BACKCLOTH
HAND-BRAKE
FLY GALLERY
SCENERY PACKS
STAGE

231
b.

In 1932, when the Shakespeare Memorial Theatre was built in Stratford, it took the form of a standard picture-frame theatre with a cyclorama. [229] Occupying the front part of the stage were rolling bridges, with traps, which slid off into the wings when a scene change was needed. When the rolling bridges were removed, two bridges could be brought into use, these being built with two levels so that it was possible to create an inner stage and an upper gallery.

A fly tower with a double-purchase counterweight system [231] covered the main stage area, and a stepped forestage projected into the auditorium, flanked by two large bastions with doors and balconies over. The forestage was removable to reveal an orchestra pit for use in operatic performances, and the cyclorama could be moved downstage to act as a sound reflector for concerts. Sixteen rows of seats set on a raked and stepped floor formed the stalls, and the dress circle had seven rows, above and beyond which was a gallery with six rows of padded benches. The whole auditorium was fan-shaped to provide what were considered to be the best conditions for both sight and sound.

While narrow forestages proved reasonably successful, the wider forestage here simply acted as a barrier or no man's land between the nearest seat and the actual scene in which the action of necessity took place. If a simple Elizabethan tiring-house facade had been erected directly within the proscenium opening, then the forestage would have been the main acting area and a Shakespearian intimacy could have resulted. But the very nature of the equipment provided on the picture stage inevitably led to the use of full scenic productions built on the mobile stages, so removing the action some 30 feet (9.14m) or more from the nearest seat.

Conforming to its period, the decor of the auditorium, [230] with the exception of the proscenium area, tended to plainness, with large areas of plaster on the side walls, the effect of which (particularly to those seated in the gallery) was to make the actors seem even more remote than they actually were.

230 Shakespeare Memorial Theatre, 1932

231 Counterweight flying systems
a: single purchase
b: double purchase

24 The non-existent proscenium opening

The Belgrade, Coventry. Reintroduction of side and rear boxes. The Forum, Billingham. Eden Court and the Barbican. Design changes reflected in the Shakespeare Memorial Theatre.

The division between actors and their audiences continued into the second half of the twentieth century, and was largely conditioned by the need to separate the scenic fire risk from the auditorium. But attempts were made to break away from a situation in which the actors were seen through a 'hole in the wall' (so vividly illustrated by the Oxford Playhouse) to one in which the actual separation between the participants was no more than the ending of the side walls and ceiling of the auditorium – a 'non-existent' proscenium opening, [232] which omitted Wyatt's picture frame but still permitted the essential separation provided by the fire curtain.

The Belgrade Theatre, Coventry (1958), was designed in this way. [233] Here the scenic stage projected into the auditorium as a narrow forestage with

RL49

232 A 'non-existent' proscenium opening

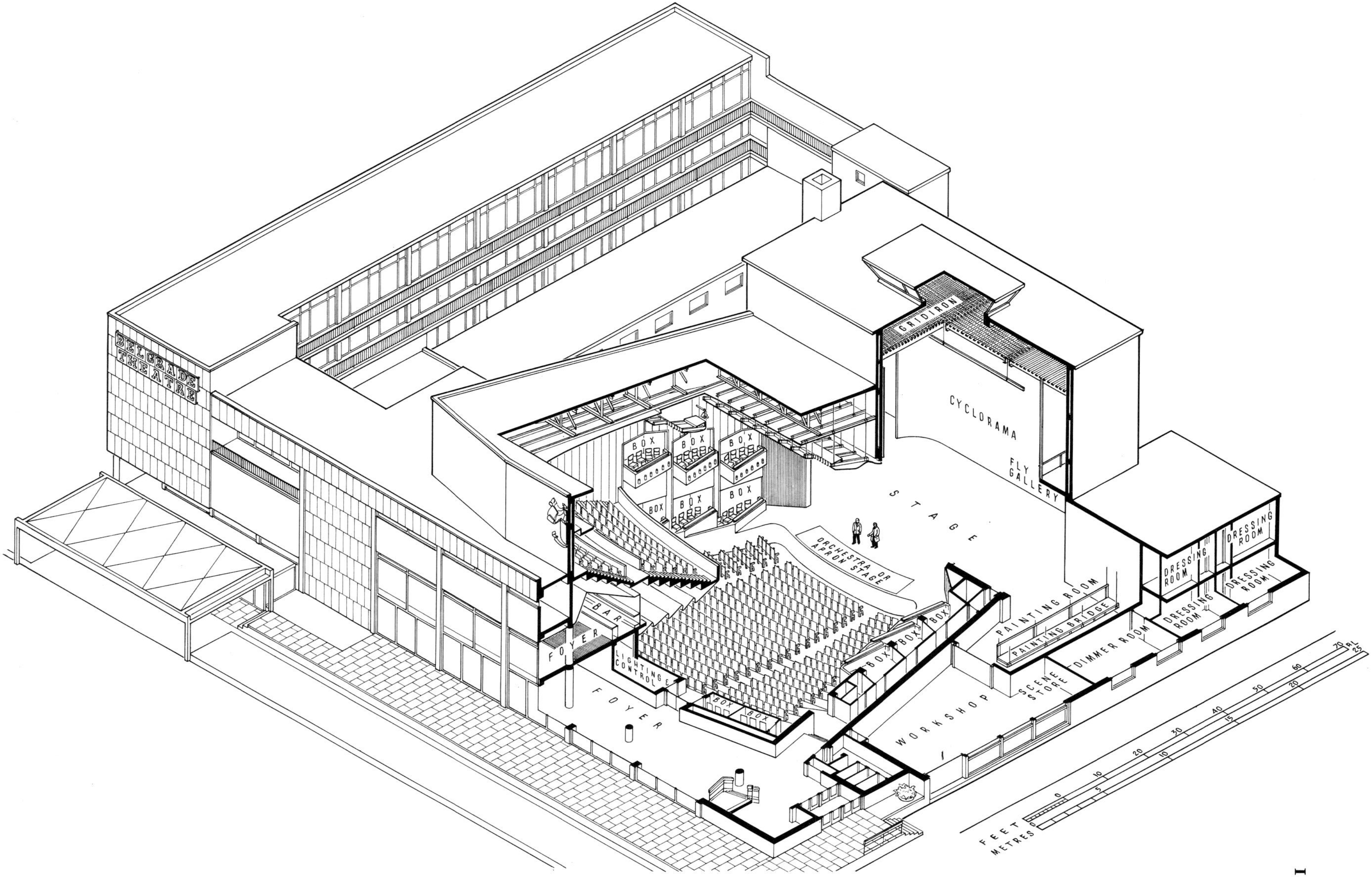
BELGRADE THEATRE
GRIDIRON
CYCLORAMA
FLY GALLERY
STAGE
ORCHESTRA OR APRON STAGE
BOX
BAR
FOYER
LIGHTING CONTROL
PAINTING ROOM
PAINTING BRIDGE
DIMMER ROOM
DRESSING ROOM
SCENE STORE
WORKSHOP
FEET
METRES

233 Belgrade Theatre, Coventry, 1958.

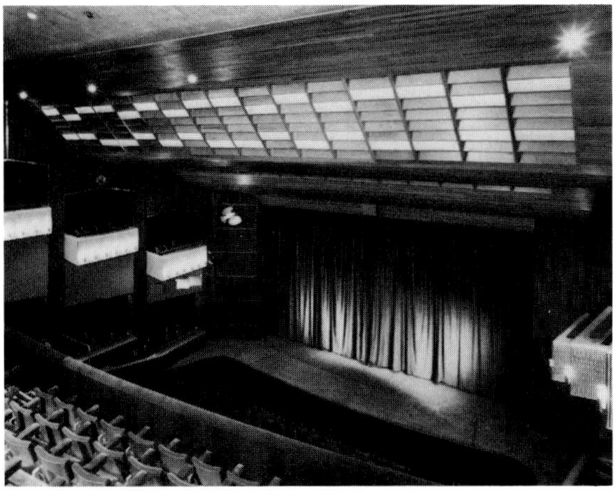

Belgrade Theatre, Coventry: 234; 235

234

side wings, in an attempt to relate the actor more closely to the audience. [234] In the Memorial Theatre, the circle and gallery seemed remote from the forestage, and in the Adelphi the stalls, circle, and gallery were all separate entities cut off from one another and from the stage: it was now suggested that such problems might be overcome by linking the upper levels to the stage by the introduction of boxes, projecting from the side walls and stepping down to stage level. [236] This arrangement was used in the Belgrade auditorium, where seating for 910 was provided on two levels with boxes linking the actor to his circle audience. [235]

An electrician's control room was included at the rear of the auditorium in the manner suggested by Bel Geddes, so that the stage picture could be more readily viewed and controlled than had been possible when the switchboard was situated in the prompt corner of the stage, behind the proscenium wall.

235

236 Circle with side boxes

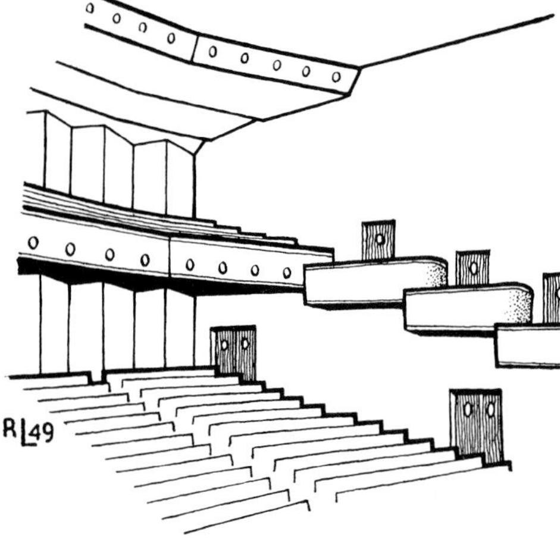
RL49

These last examples concentrated on placing the audience in the best viewing position relative to the stage picture (using, indeed, a similar arrangement to that introduced by Wren at Drury Lane), but it may be noted, particularly with regard to the Adelphi, that they indicate a tendency to reduce the number of circles – a move which made it necessary to increase their depth if the same or, as in that particular example, increased numbers were to be accommodated.

However, if the desired intimacy between the actor and audience was to be achieved, then every means of reducing the distance between the actor and the most remote member of his audience had to be investigated. One suggestion was the re-introduction of boxes as 'family units', arranged one above the other in tiers to form the rear wall of the auditorium, so placing the audience closer to the stage and at the same time reducing the apparent depth of the house – the use of side boxes once again serving to link these upper areas to the stage. [237]

The Forum Theatre, Billingham (1968), [238] used variations on this theme with three narrow, box-like circles forming the rear wall of an elliptical auditorium,

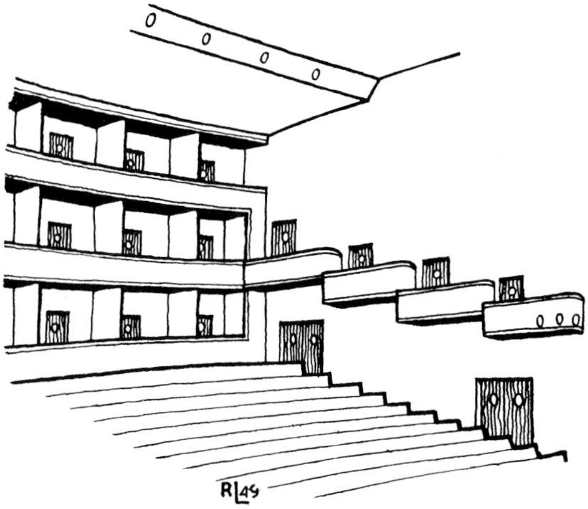

237 Rear wall boxes and side boxes

238 The Forum Theatre, Billingham, 1968

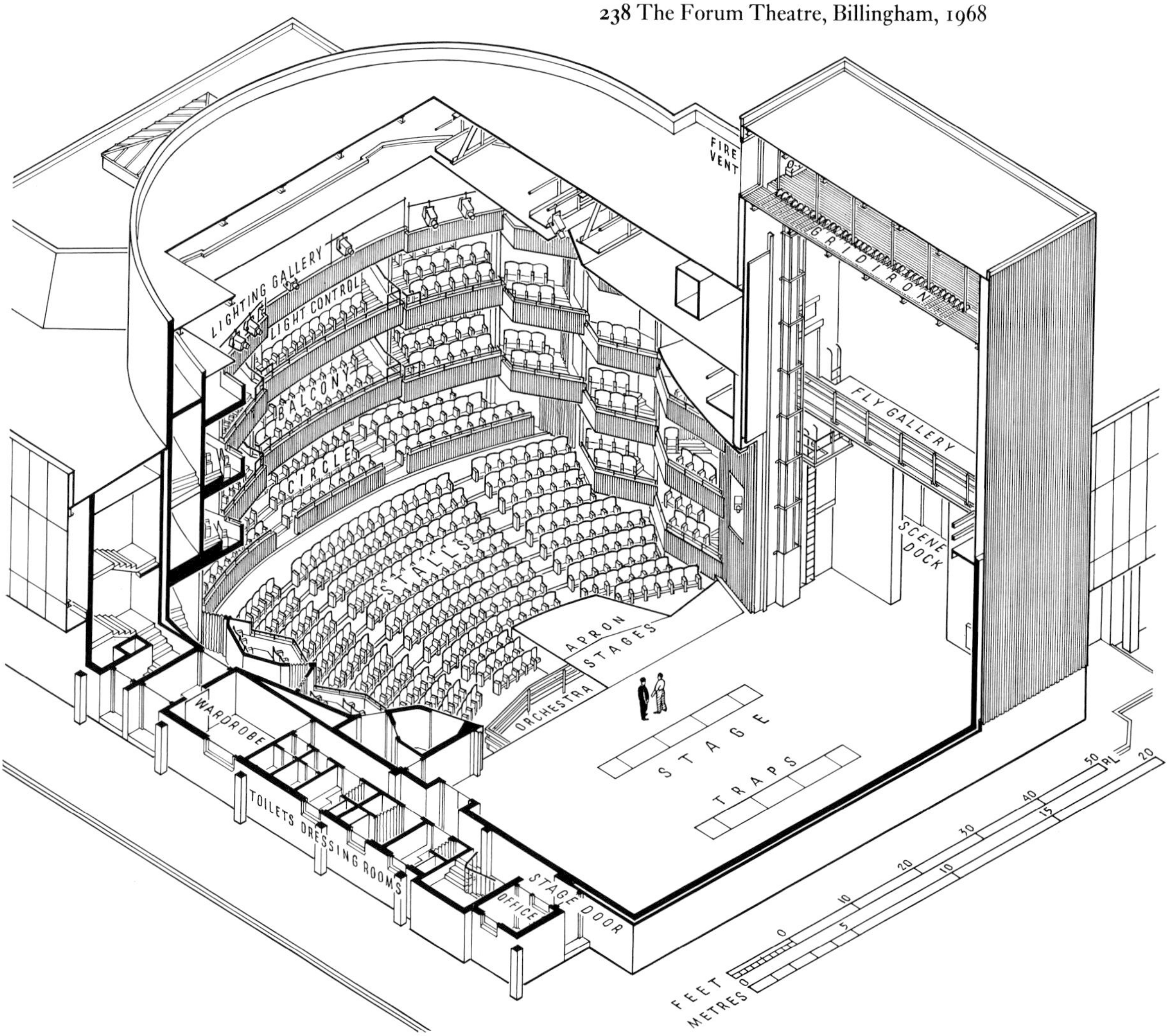
FIRE VENT
LIGHTING GALLERY
LIGHT CONTROL
BALCONY
CIRCLE
STALLS
GRIDIRON
FLY GALLERY
SCENE DOCK
APRON STAGES
ORCHESTRA
STAGE
STAGE TRAPS
WARDROBE
TOILETS DRESSING ROOMS
OFFICE
STAGE DOOR
FEET
METRES
PL

164 : The non-existent proscenium opening

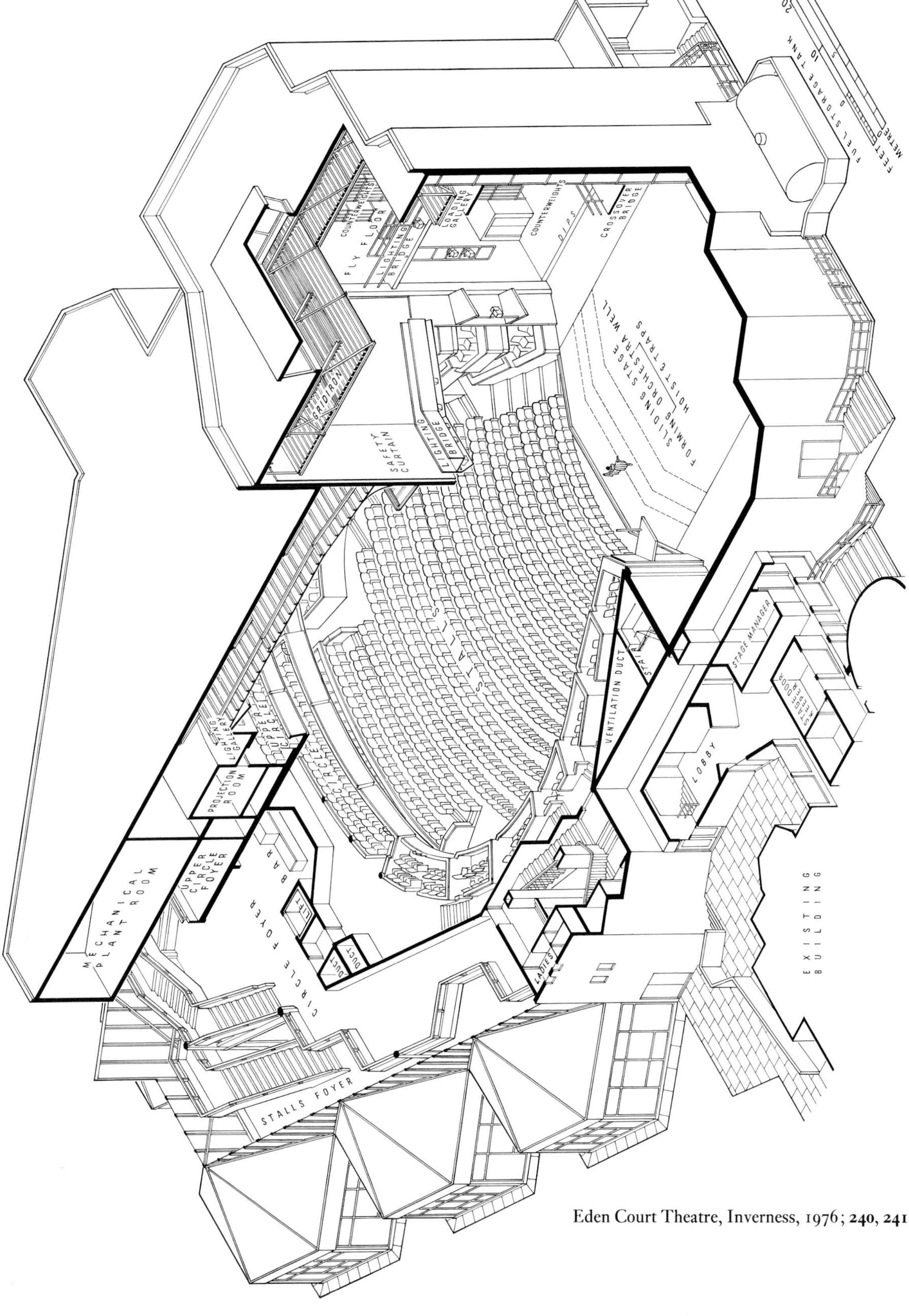
FEET
METRE
FUEL STORAGE TANK
COUNTERWEIGHTS
FLY FLOOR
LIGHTING BRIDGE
LOADING GALLERY
COUNTERWEIGHTS
DIPS
CROSSOVER BRIDGE
GRIDIRON
SAFETY CURTAIN
LIGHTING BRIDGE
HOIST TRAPS
FORMING ORCHESTRA WELL
SLIDING STAGE
FORMING
STALLS
VENTILATION DUCT
STAIR
STAGE MANAGER
STAGE DOOR
LOBBY
LIGHTING GALLERY
UPPER CIRCLE
PROJECTION ROOM
CIRCLE
MECHANICAL PLANT ROOM
UPPER CIRCLE FOYER
BAR
LIFT
DUCT
DUCT
CIRCLE FOYER
LADIES
STALLS FOYER
EXISTING BUILDING

Eden Court Theatre, Inverness, 1976; **240, 241**

239a, b The Forum Theatre, Billingham

linked to the stage by four levels of projecting boxes on either side. [239a, b] A similar scheme was used in the Eden Court Theatre, Inverness (1976), [240] but in this instance the lowest of the three levels of box-circles continued the line of and was only separated from the main slope of the seating by a low partition. [241] The most recent example of this theme is the main theatre in the Barbican Arts Centre, London (1982), where a series of narrow circles, each with two rows of seats, step forward progressively towards the stage to which they are linked by boxes stepping down the side walls. [242]

241

242 The Barbican Theatre, London

243

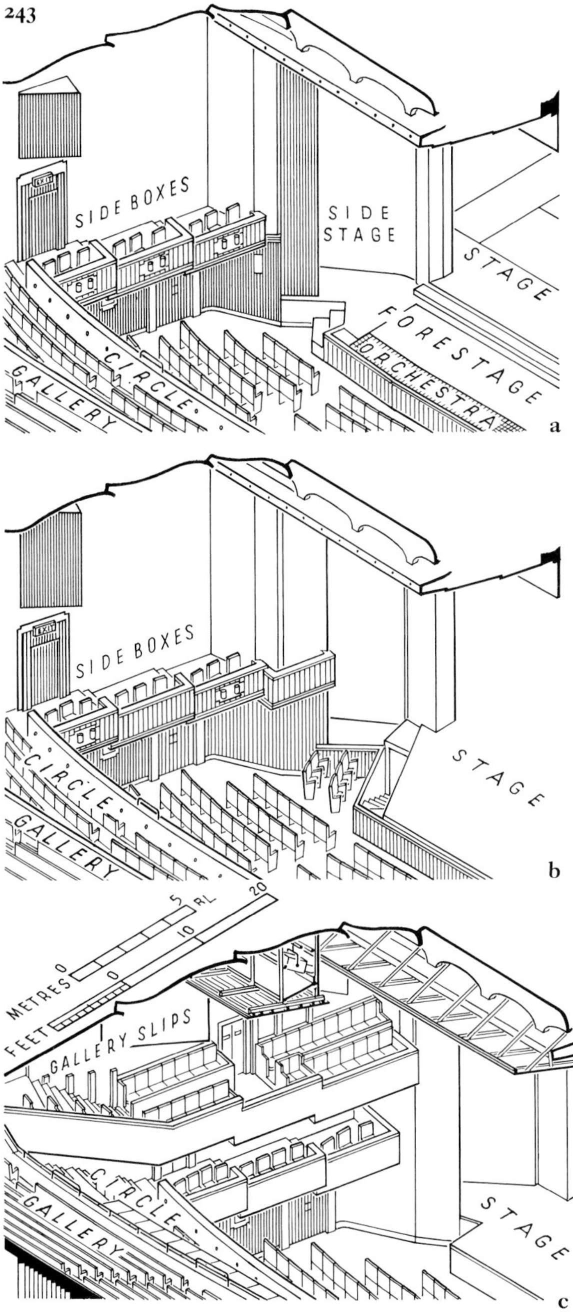
SIDE BOXES
SIDE STAGE
STAGE
FORESTAGE
ORCHESTRA
CIRCLE
GALLERY
a
SIDE BOXES
STAGE
CIRCLE
GALLERY
b
METRES
FEET
RL
GALLERY SLIPS
CIRCLE
GALLERY
STAGE
c

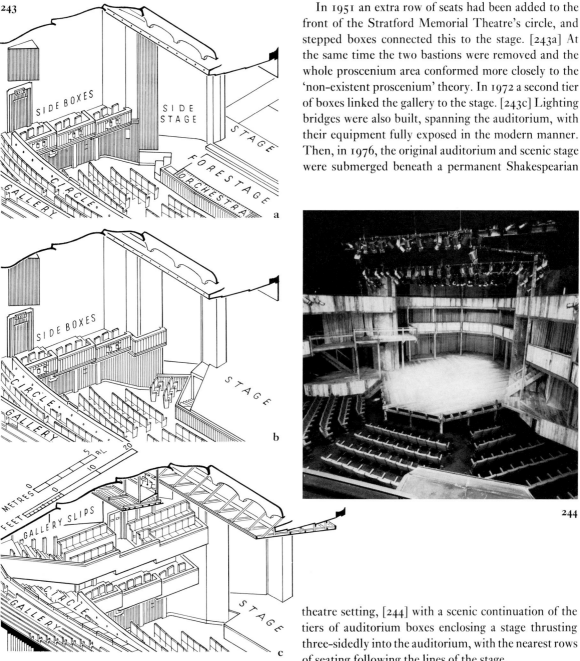

In 1951 an extra row of seats had been added to the front of the Stratford Memorial Theatre's circle, and stepped boxes connected this to the stage. [243a] At the same time the two bastions were removed and the whole proscenium area conformed more closely to the 'non-existent proscenium' theory. In 1972 a second tier of boxes linked the gallery to the stage. [243c] Lighting bridges were also built, spanning the auditorium, with their equipment fully exposed in the modern manner. Then, in 1976, the original auditorium and scenic stage were submerged beneath a permanent Shakespearian theatre setting, [244] with a scenic continuation of the tiers of auditorium boxes enclosing a stage thrusting three-sidedly into the auditorium, with the nearest rows of seating following the lines of the stage.

244

In this one buiding, we thus have an illustration of the drastic changes which have taken place within the forty years since the theatre was opened, culminating here, for the time being at least, in the total disappearance of the picture-frame. To see how this came about we must retrace our steps.

243 Shakespeare Memorial (now Royal Shakespeare) Theatre in
- **a**: 1951
- **b**: 1962
- **c**: 1972

244 in 1976

25 The open stage

Adolph Appia and the Festival Auditorium, Hellerau. Copeau and the Vieux Colombier. Permanent architectural settings. Reinhardt's Redoutensaal, Vienna. The Mermaid, Blackfriars. Fire regulations and the open stage. Front-of-house lighting. La Junta High School theatre.

The renaissance of Shakespearian stages with their permanent architectural surrounds had far-reaching effects. An early example was the Festival Auditorium at Hellerau, designed by Heinrich Tessenow in 1910–12. [245–246] This was a single hall containing both stage and auditorium, separated only by a sunken orchestra pit. The walls and ceiling were covered with transparent fabric, behind which were lights, so that the whole room glowed: a system devised by A. von Salzmann. The stage settings were simple steps, platforms, and pillars designed and lit by Adolph Appia.

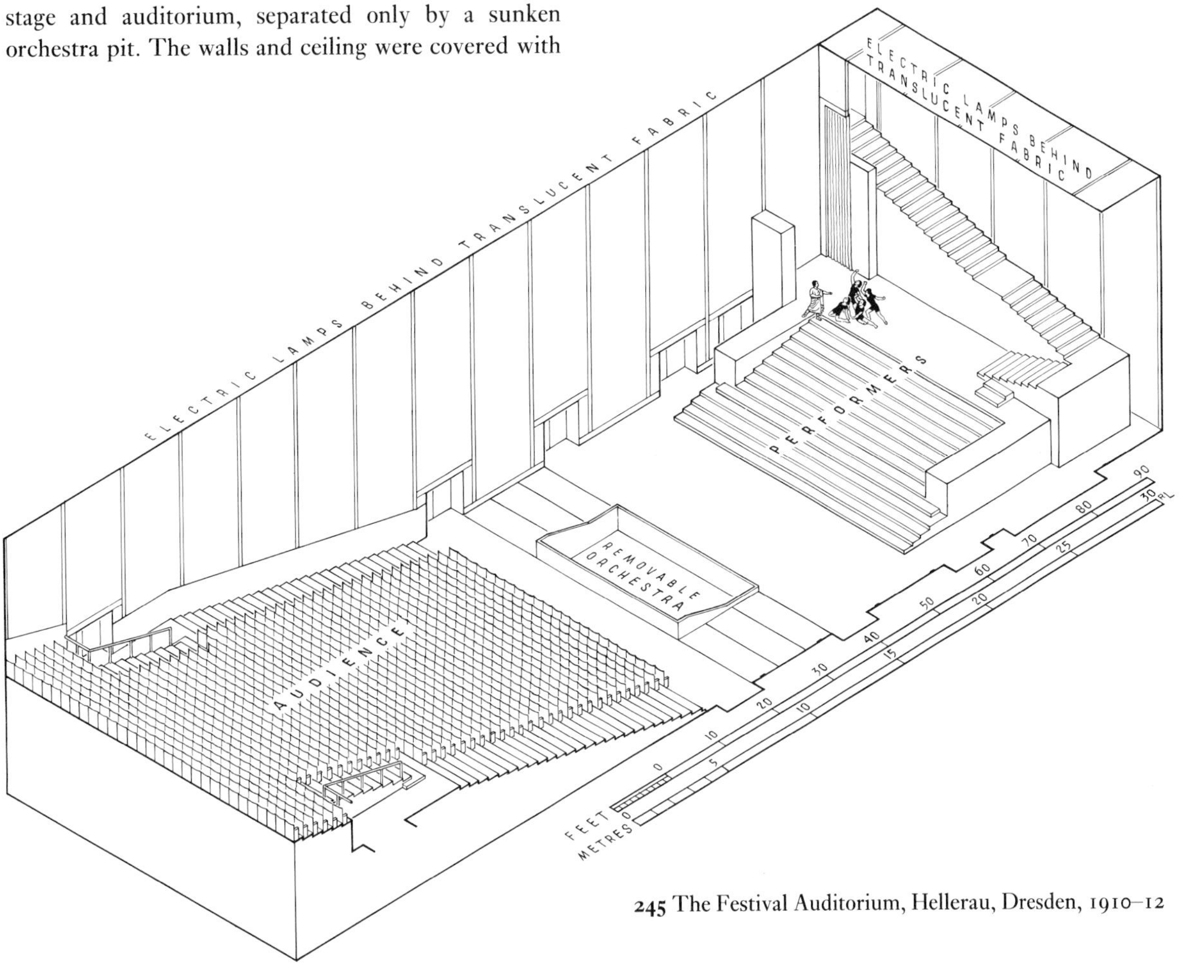
ELECTRIC LAMPS BEHIND TRANSLUCENT FABRIC
ELECTRIC LAMPS BEHIND TRANSLUCENT FABRIC
PERFORMERS
REMOVABLE ORCHESTRA
AUDIENCE
FEET
METRES
0
10
20
30
40
50
60
70
80
90
0
5
10
15
20
25
30
PL

245 The Festival Auditorium, Hellerau, Dresden, 1910–12

246 Hellerau.
Setting for *L'Annonce faite à Marie*

247 The Vieux Colombier, Paris
a: Stage in 1913
b: Theatre in 1920
c: Stage in 1930
248 the original music hall; **249** interior of the 1920 theatre

248

249

In 1913 Jacques Copeau adapted a small, proscenium-style music hall [248] in the Rue du Vieux Colombier, Paris, as a theatre, [247a] believing that by simplifying the scene to its bare essentials it was possible to concentrate attention on the thoughts and actions of the performers. His stage was separated from a rectangular auditorium by a light, triple-arched screen, beyond which was an inner proscenium, the space between forming a simple forestage.

In 1917–18 Copeau experimented with a permanent 'Elizabethan'-style setting, built on the stage of the Garrick Theatre in New York, which formed the basis for his reconstruction of the Vieux Colombier in 1919–20. [247b] The new stage, built in concrete, was now open to the auditorium, being separated from the seating only by three sets of three steps each. [249] At the rear, flights of steps led to a central stepped bridge, beneath which was an alcove. Entrances to the stage were limited to three doors in the stage wall right, with a further opening above giving access to the upper levels. Trapped areas were built into the forestage, and sections of the mainstage were made of wood, so that these could be removed to allow for scenic variations. All stage lighting was by lamps installed in octagonal units attached to the roof arches in the auditorium, and designed to conform with the architectural decor.

While this architectural setting provided the basic acting levels and entrances which Copeau required, it imposed its own limitations on the productions, both scenically and in the patterns of movement on the stage. Although many ingenious scenic variations were contrived – by the use of drapes or panels hung from steel girders or attached to the permanent structure, or by the introduction of additional stairs or platforms – the basic, monochrome setting was nevertheless usually visible. In some instances the scenic items introduced for a particular play would have made possible a wider range of production movement, but the lack of variation contributed to the eventual closure of the theatre in 1924.

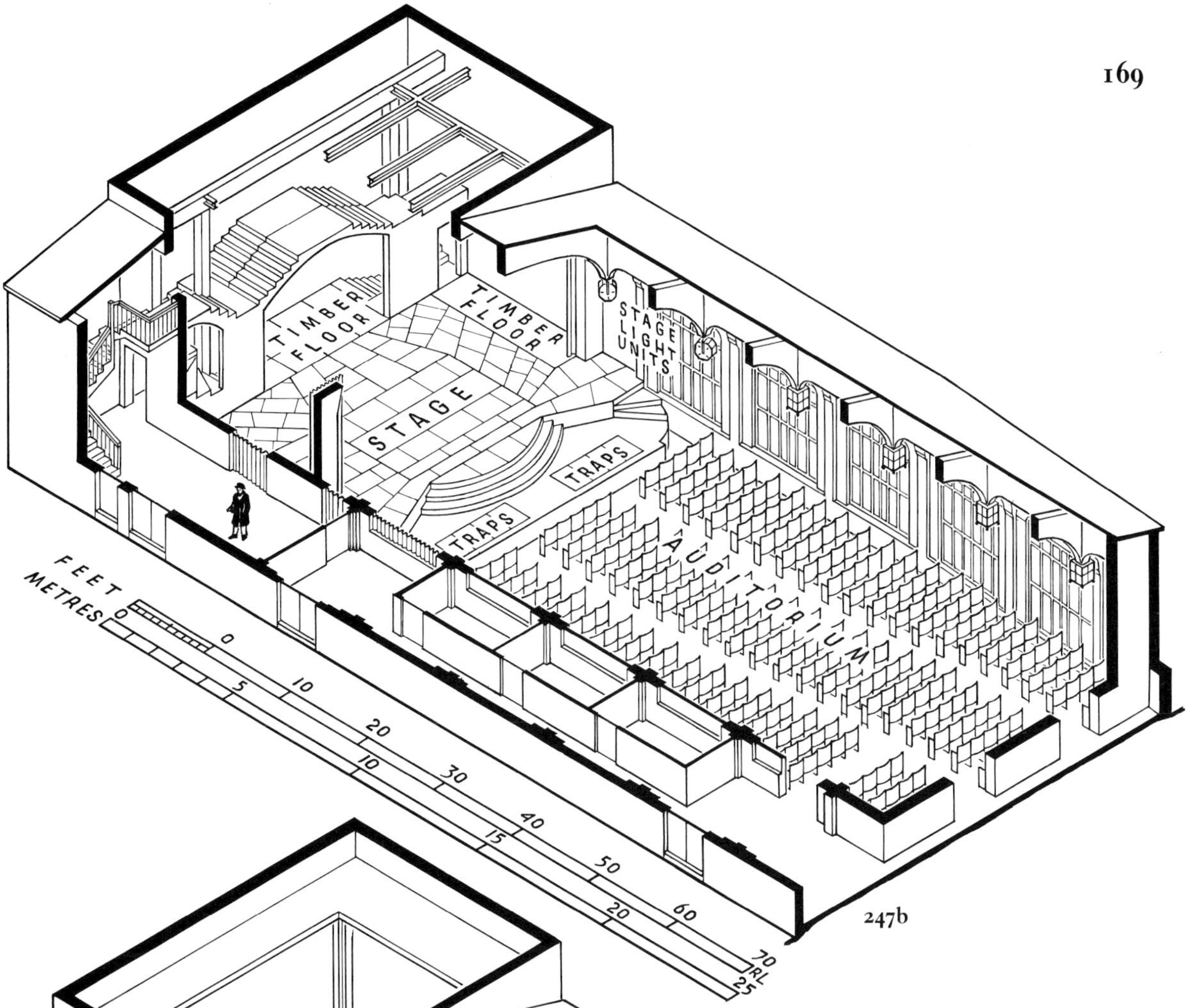
TIMBER FLOOR
TIMBER FLOOR
STAGE LIGHT UNITS
STAGE
TRAPS
TRAPS
AUDITORIUM
FEET
METRES
0 10 20 30 40 50 60 70
0 5 10 15 20 25
RL

247b

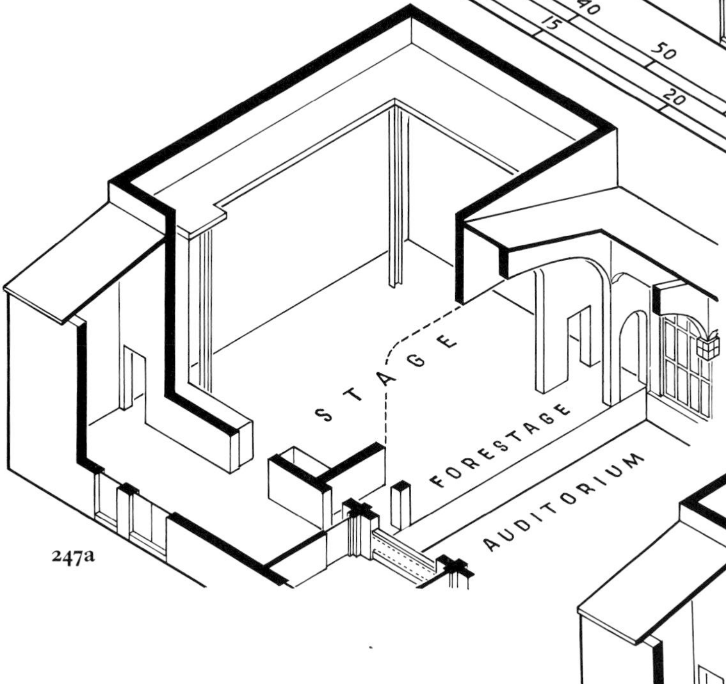
STAGE
FORESTAGE
AUDITORIUM

247a

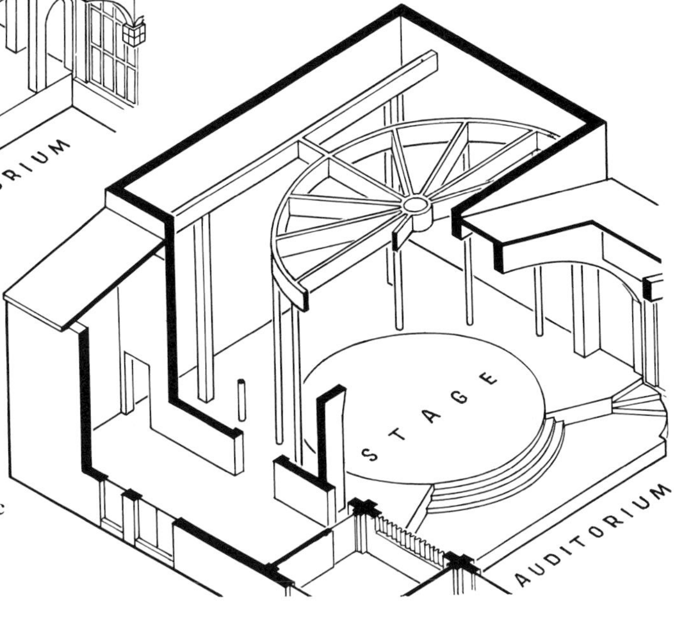
STAGE
AUDITORIUM

247c

250 Redoutensaal, Vienna

In 1922 Reinhardt presented plays in the Redoutensaal in the Hofburg, Vienna. [250] At one end of this Baroque ballroom was a 4 feet (1.22m) high stage, backed by curving screens and incorporating an existing balcony with a flight of stairs. Some 600 persons were seated on the flat floor of the hall, an arrangement which would hardly have provided ideal sight-lines.

When Terence Gray removed the proscenium from the Barnwell Theatre in 1926, he created what was in effect an open-end stage, an innovation sometimes ascribed to the Mermaid Theatre, Blackfriars, of 1959. This was based on earlier reconstructions of a Shakespearian stage – the first built in 1951, at the home of Bernard Miles, with a wedge-shaped stage flanked by doors with arched openings above, on which the actor was set amid the audience; the second, a three-sided arrangement of stage and audience set in the Royal Exchange in 1953. [251]

The eventual Blackfriars Mermaid [252] was built in the shell of a long, rectangular warehouse, which

251 The Mermaid in the Royal Exchange

The Mermaid, Puddle Dock, London, 1959:
252, 253

restricted the extent to which the seating could enclose the stage. This was raised only 9 inches (0.23m) above the lowest level of the auditorium floor, which was stepped up in one continuous tier to seat some 500 within an overall depth of 65 feet (19.81m). [253] A manually-operated revolve was set centrally in the stage, with a trap in front leading to an under-stage passage. At the rear was a central recess with a balcony over. There was a simple flying system, for rolled cloths or lifting properties, above the rear portion of the stage, which was approached through the central recess or by two openings at each end of the rear wall.

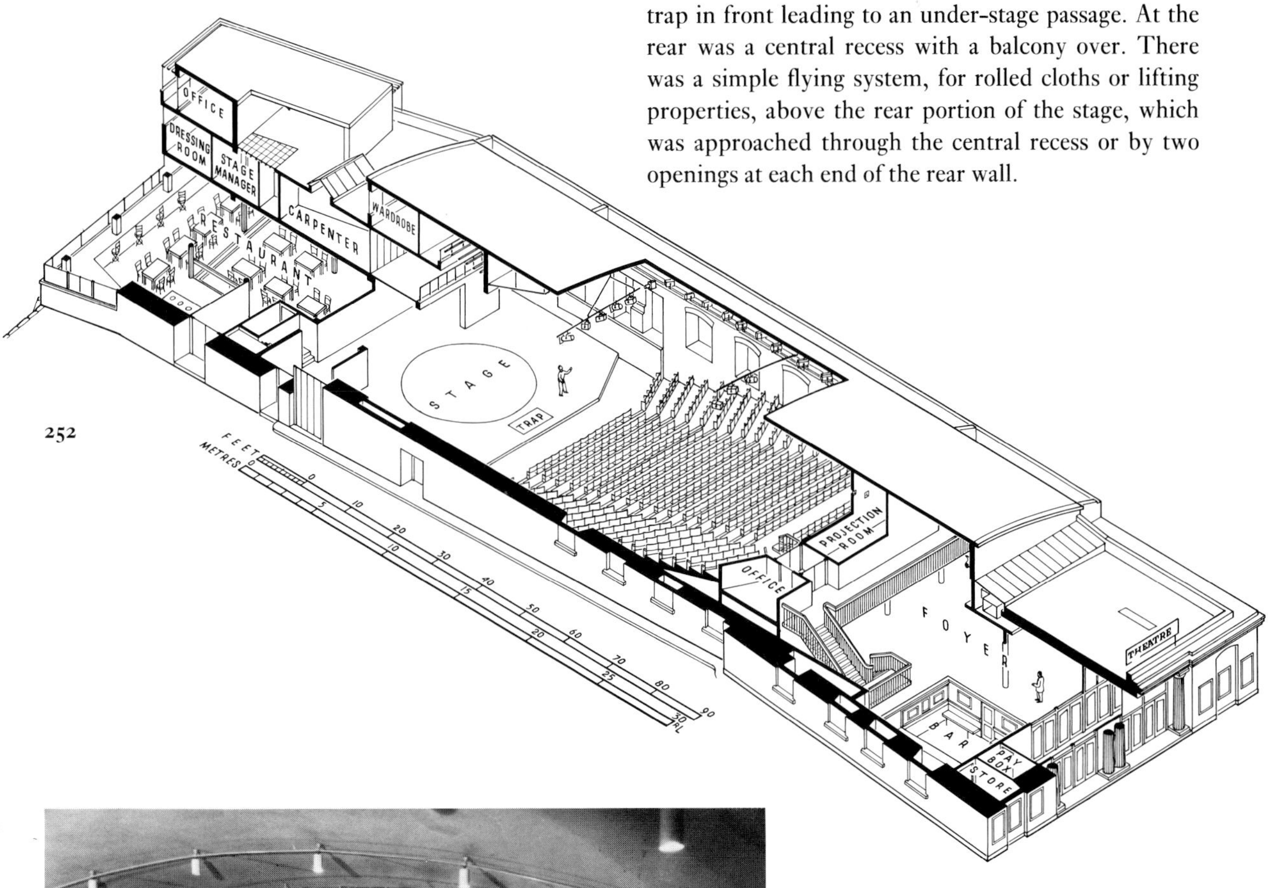
OFFICE
DRESSING ROOM
STAGE MANAGER
RESTAURANT
CARPENTER
WARDROBE
STAGE
TRAP
PROJECTION ROOM
OFFICE
FOYER
BAR
PAY BOX
STORE
THEATRE
FEET
METRES

252

253

Unlike the Vieux Colombier, the permanent architectural features of the Mermaid were kept to a minimum, and free-standing screen settings were used, points of entry to the scene proper being scenically contrived for each play. By this means a greater degree of flexibility in presentation was achieved, as the openings in the rear wall could be completely obscured by the scenery or be brought into use as occasion demanded. The Mermaid had no front curtain, and all settings were in full view of the audience from the moment they entered the auditorium, any changes being carried out as part of the action of the play, or during the intervals.

Fire regulations in Britain had previously required the separation of a stage with scenery from the auditorium by a fire-resisting curtain in new buildings seating more than 400. When the Mermaid was conceived, it was intended that only limited use would be made of scenery, but this did not work out in practice, and has not done so elsewhere. With the safety of an audience still of paramount importance, restrictions are now more firmly enforced regarding the materials from which scenery may be constructed in the open theatres: as a result it is being suggested that it might be more economic to include a fire curtain as an integral but visually unobtrusive feature of such open stages.

Although the Mermaid had its genesis in a Shakespearian reconstruction, the plan of the existing warehouse imposed a directional pattern which owed little to the Shakespearian theatre, and the relationship of stage to auditorium differed little from that of the standard picture-frame theatre, except that the frame concealing the working areas of the stage was omitted. Reconstructed within a new office-block, a new Mermaid opened in 1981. [254]

WRESTLING

The use of electricity for stage lighting had resulted in an increased movement of equipment into the auditorium, with spotlights placed on balcony fronts, or set behind louvres in the auditorium walls or ceiling. With the advent of the open stage, both stage machinery and lighting units were open to the view of the audience, and in the Mermaid no attempt was made to conceal the various lighting units hung from battens.

The suspension of such units above an audience is, however, open to question, both from the aesthetic point of view and on grounds of safety for patrons. Although the replacement of naked lights by electricity has undoubtedly reduced the fire hazard, the risk is still present, and the widespread use of materials capable of producing toxic fumes (not only on the stage but in the seating materials of the auditorium) has made the necessity of containing fires and smoke even more important that it was when fire curtains were first introduced.

The Senior High Schoool at La Junta, Colorado (1963–64), fits into an hexagonal pavilion. [255] A wedge-shaped open stage projects into the seating, the front six rows being parallel with the three sides of the main stage. This is backed by an inner stage some 17 feet (5.18m) deep, approached through an open arcade. Above is a gallery, the front portion above the open arcade being at a slightly lower level than the remainder, to which it is connected by two flights of steps.

Both stage and gallery extend along the side walls to form narrow side stages, which at stage level are connected across the auditorium between the front and rear sections of seating. The theatre thereby makes provision for the Shakespearian inner and upper stages, and

RL

254 (*left*) The new Mermaid, 1981. Arranged with arena stage

255 (*above*) Senior High School Theatre, La Junta, Colorado

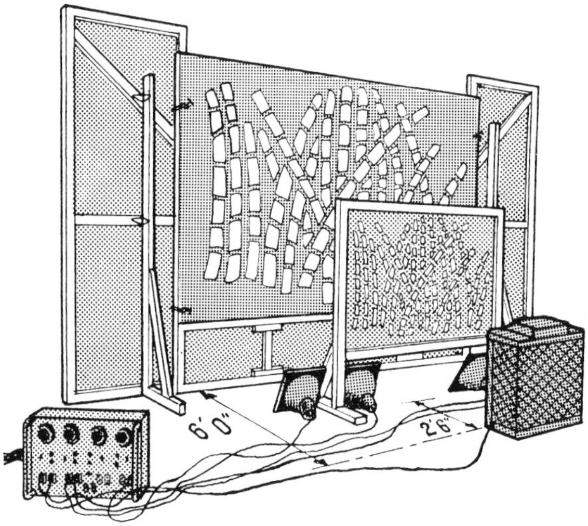
6'0"
2'6"

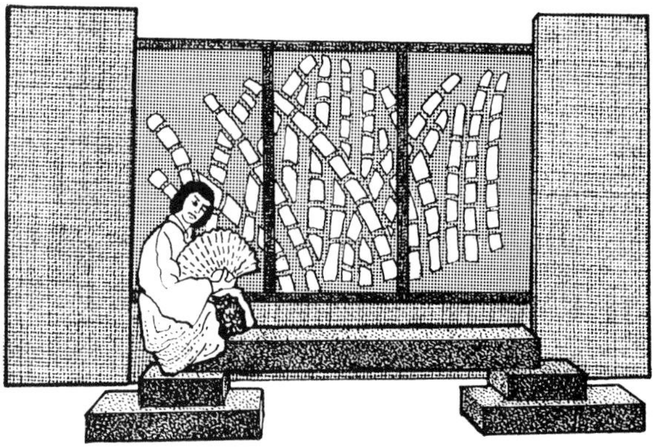

256a Rear projection unit

to the standard pattern of movement which both these and the main stage permit is added the possibility of penetration into and enclosure of the audience by the performers. Although no doors are provided for entry to the stage, these can be introduced by scenic openings, whilst light screens can be used as masking units to conceal the movement of actors in areas considered 'backstage' for a particular production.

The insertion of translucent panels into the three openings of the arcade permits the introduction of colour and imagery from a rear-projection unit. [256] The stage lighting is fixed to catwalks in the roof space, readily accessible to the technicians from their lighting and sound controls at the ends of the side galleries. A partly-sunk orchestra pit can be floored over to add to the depth of the main stage. The 52 feet (15.85m) depth from front stage to rear seating has a capacity of 379.

256b Setting for *Madam Butterfly*

26 Three-sided thrust stages

Guthries's Thrie Estaitis. The Festival Theatre, Stratford, Ontario. Limitations of production patterns. Sight-line problems. The Festival Theatre, Chichester. Tyrone Guthrie Theatre, Minneapolis.

A feature of the Elizabethan stage which these theatres have not achieved is the ability to place an actor at the central focal point of an enclosing audience, as was possible in the Swan and other early Elizabethan theatres. The projecting stage with an audience on three sides formed the basis of numerous projects, and eventually found simple expression in Tyrone Guthrie's adaptation of the Assembly Hall, Edinburgh, in 1948 for a performance of *The Thrie Estaitis* of Sir David Lyndsay. [257]

The stage, built in the centre of one side of the hall, and enclosed on three sides by an audience seated in the body of the hall and in the galleries, was backed by a raised gallery with stairs on either side and an arched recess beneath, before which was set the king's throne. Actors approached the stage through the gangways, and a sense of scenic spectacle was achieved with banners and heraldic devices carried by the performers.

RL

257 Assembly Hall, Edinburgh. *The Thrie Estaitis*

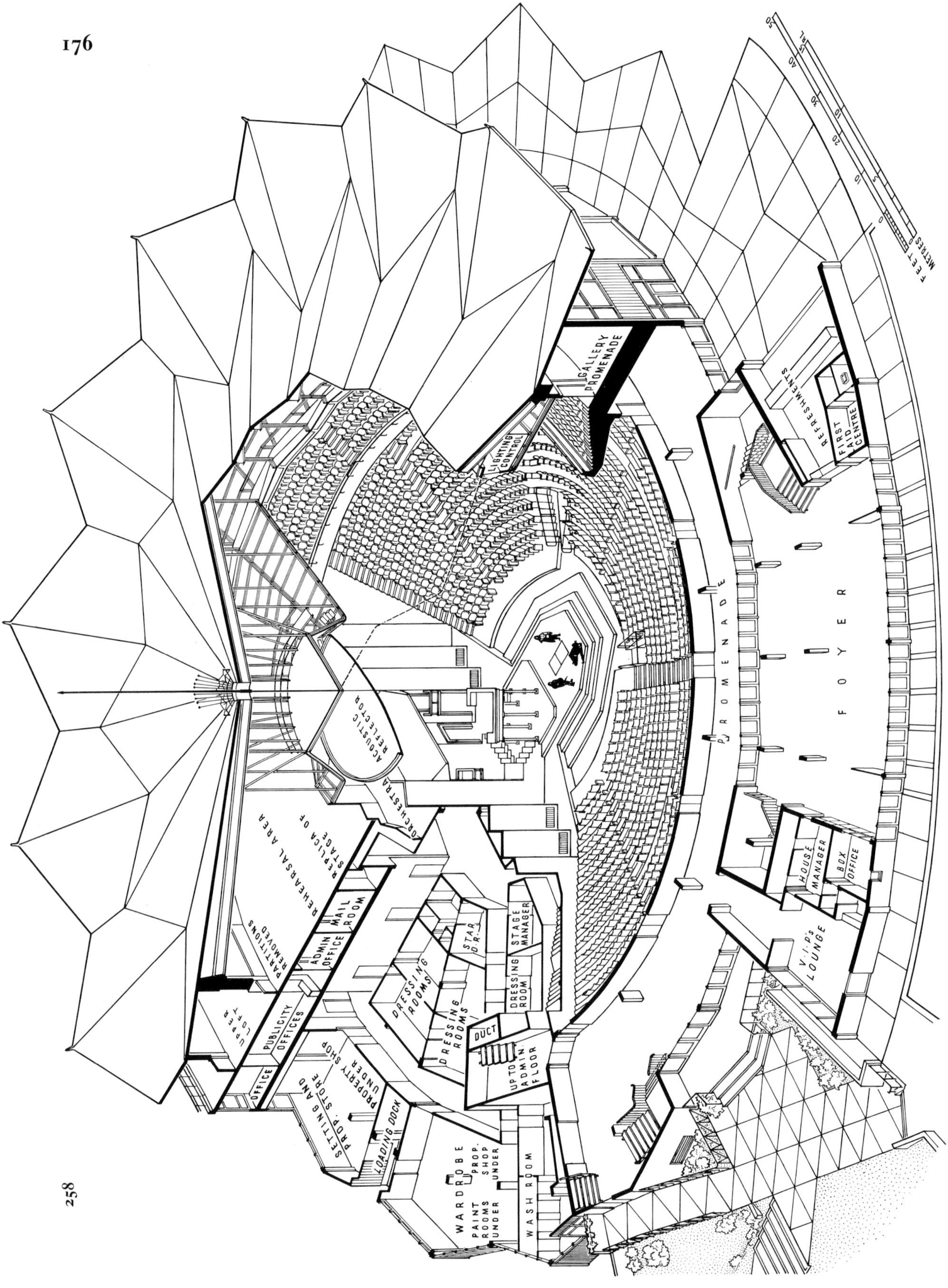
GALLERY PROMENADE
LIGHTING CONTROL
REFRESHMENTS
FIRST AID CENTRE
PROMENADE
FOYER
ACOUSTIC REFLECTOR
ORCHESTRA
REHEARSAL AREA
REPLICA OF STAGE
PARTITIONS REMOVED
ADMIN OFFICE
MAIL ROOM
UPPER LOFT
PUBLICITY OFFICES
OFFICE
HOUSE MANAGER
BOX OFFICE
V.I.P.'s LOUNGE
STAR D.R.
STAGE MANAGER
DRESSING ROOMS
DRESSING ROOMS
DRESSING ROOM
DUCT
UP TO ADMIN. FLOOR
PROPERTY SHOP UNDER
SETTING AND PROP. STORE
LOADING DOCK
WARDROBE
PROP. SHOP UNDER
PAINT ROOMS UNDER
WASH ROOM
FEET
METRES

This experiment led to the eventual construction of the Festival Theatre in Stratford, Ontario (1957). [258] Here the stage forms the central focus of a 'circular' auditorium, [259] providing seating for 1,400 in a single flight of steps, with a further 858 in a balcony, the stage being so designed that the audience looks down on it. [260] Two ramps lead to the advanced corners of the stage, further entrances being made from a central doorway at the rear and from two raised doorways on either side, giving access by stairs both to the main stage and to a projecting balcony raised on columns above the rear stage. The space beneath provides for an inner recess. Two smaller balconies project above the side doors, with their own entries.

The Shakespearean Festival Theatre, Stratford, Ontario, 1957
258; **259**;
260 the original stage

259

260

An orchestra gallery was situated above the rear stage wall, hidden from the audience but open to a circular sound reflector above the stage. But movement on the stage between the various entrances was both limited and repetitive, and in 1963 the rear stage wall was designed [261] to spread the same units over almost twice the original width, giving greater flexibility of movement in much the same way that the limitations of the Swan had been corrected at the Globe [102].

While this theatre shows that a much larger audience may be seated within an acceptable distance from the actor than is possible in a directional picture- or end-stage arrangement, it also indicates that such a thrust stage is more restrictive to the movement of actors, in that their points of entry and exit are both fixed and limited compared with the many variations that can be created by the use of movable scenery on an end stage.

At Stratford, Ontario, as in Reinhardt's Grosses Schauspielhaus, the audience could see the actors 'in the round', in contrast with the two-dimensional relationship of the picture or 'relief' stage; but it must also be appreciated that the Greeks had found that an actor needed a directional relationship with his audience if he was to be able to make full use of all his faculties, and performers have claimed that it is only possible to 'hold' the audience from the base of such thrust stages: in any other position they can only make contact with a small section at any one time.

In Ancient Greece it was the 'sculptural' chorus which occupied the orchestra, and with Reinhardt it was his crowds – while the Crucible Theatre, Sheffield, is at its most successful when used for performances of snooker. At Stratford, Ontario, the seating was taken too far round the stage, so that the end sections of seat-

261 The Festival Theatre, Ontario. The 1963 stage

262 The Festival Theatre, Chichester

ing at both levels have their view of the actors restricted by the stars and balconies, a problem which was recognized by the pricing of these areas as the cheapest seats. (Similar problems existed at both Epidaurus [39] and the Elizabethan Swan [97–9]).

The Festival Theatre, Chichester (1962), avoids this problem to a large extent by a limitation of the arc, with a consequent reduction of seating to 1,360. [262] The scenic balcony, stairs, and rear wall to the stage are demountable and may be arranged in a number of ways. The stage is raised above floor level, and the upper balcony is continued along the side walls of the hexagonal auditorium, so that actors may make their entrances from behind the audience or through similar vomitories (used by the audience) to those at Stratford.

In Minneapolis, the Tyrone Guthrie Theatre was opened in 1963. [263] Here, the seating is arranged asymmetrically at ground and balcony levels, the latter having a projecting and receding front, and sweeping

263 Tyrone Guthrie Theatre, Minneapolis

down to stage level on one side. This may well have overcome a drawback of the Stratford theatre, where the seats at the lower level have a good, intimate relationship with the stage, but the balcony seats, even in the front row, feel cut off from the stage below.

At Minneapolis there are no permanent acting levels backing the stage, the rear wall being removable to permit the movement of furniture, properties, or scenic items onto the playing area; but as the arc of seating is comparable to that at Stratford, the same sight-line problems are present. As at the Vieux Colombier, the need to adapt the permanent stage structure by the addition of scenic items led to alterations being undertaken at Stratford in 1976, [264] when the middle balcony was adapted so that it could be removed to leave a central opening.

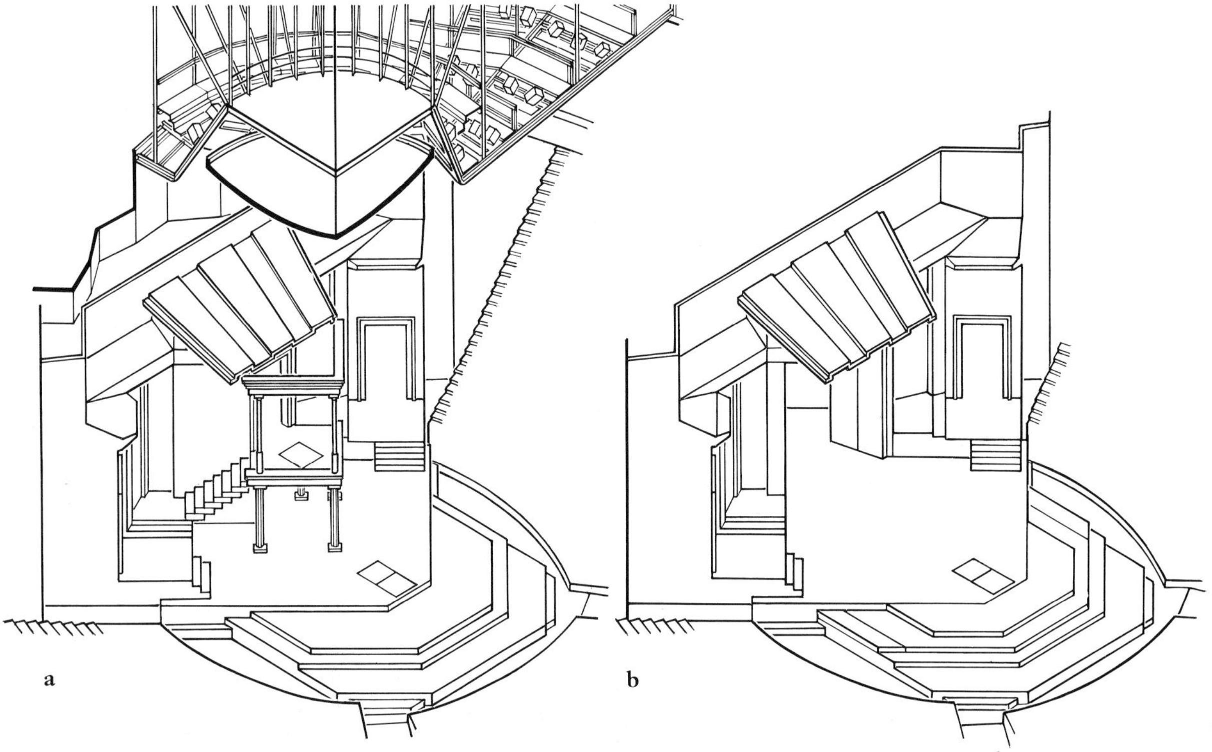
a
b

264 The Festival Theatre, Ontario. The stage of 1976 with **a**: balcony; **b**: central opening

27 The pictorial thrust stage

Civic Theatre, Malmo. Flexible auditoria. Problems of scenic machinery. Sarah Lawrence College, New York.

In spite of Reinhardt's problems with the Grosses Schauspielhaus, further attempts to combine a scenic stage with a thrust stage continued to be made, one of the most successful being the Municipal Theatre at Malmo, Sweden (1944). The theatre [265] with its spacious foyers and restaurant stands in an open park. Here the excessive projection of Reinhardt's stage was reduced to an 'open horseshoe', extending no more than 30 feet (9.14m) into the auditorium. The seating followed the lines of the projecting stage before opening out to become the arc of a circle, with its centre based near the front of the forestage. [266] In this way both stages may be viewed by some two-thirds of the audience, without their having to turn in their seats.

The whole auditorium can seat 1,595, but it is designed so that its shape and volume may be changed to seat totals of 553, 597, or 1,257, depending on the nature of the performance. [267] These alterations are achieved by the removal of some seats and by the use of screens hanging from tracks in the auditorium ceiling; these are housed in a storage compartment on the prompt side of the stage. The two smaller sizes of auditorium are seldom used, but the full auditorium may also become a concert hall when special reflectors

266
The Municipal Theatre, Malmo

182

The Municipal Theatre, Malmo, Sweden, 1944; **265**; **267**

265

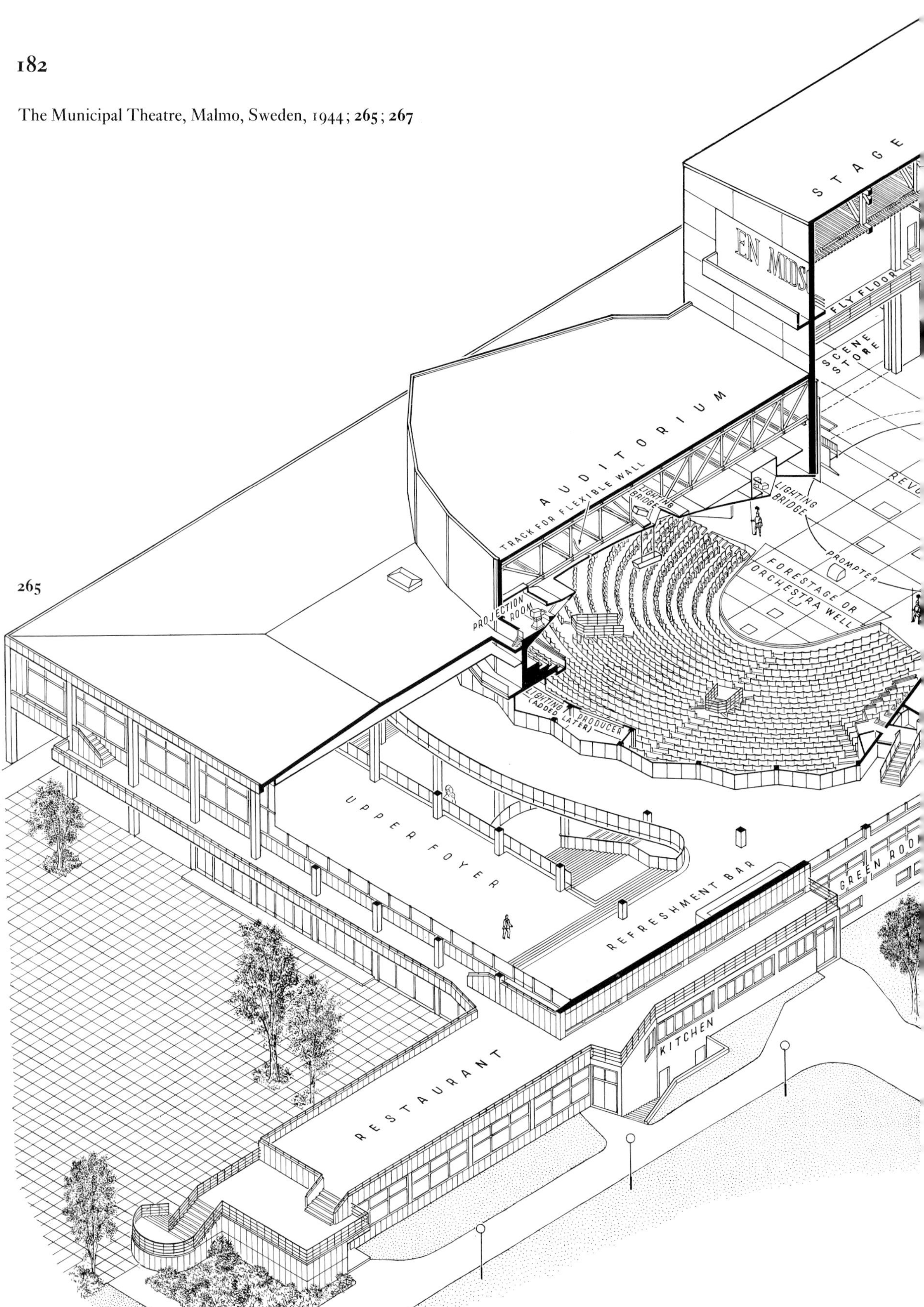
STAGE
FLY FLOOR
SCENE STORE
AUDITORIUM
TRACK FOR FLEXIBLE WALL
LIGHTING BRIDGE
LIGHTING BRIDGE
PROMPTER
FORESTAGE OR ORCHESTRA WELL
PROJECTION ROOM
LIGHTING (ADDED LATER)
PRODUCER
UPPER FOYER
REFRESHMENT BAR
KITCHEN
RESTAURANT

267

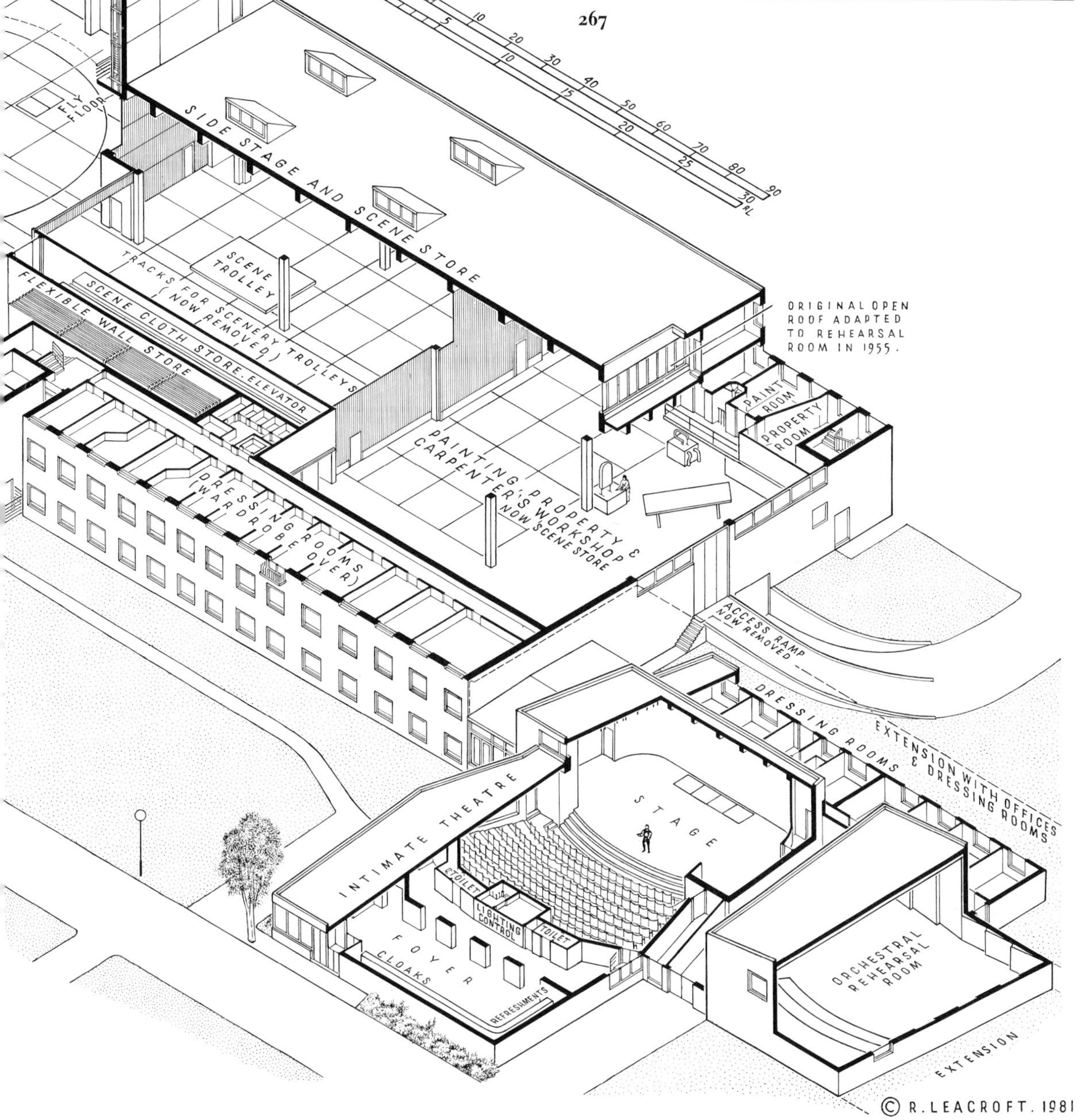
LOADING GALLERY
FLY FLOOR
FEET
METRES
0 10 20 30 40 50 60 70 80 90
0 5 10 15 20 25 30
SIDE STAGE AND SCENE STORE
SCENE TROLLEY
TRACKS FOR SCENERY TROLLEYS (NOW REMOVED)
FLEXIBLE WALL STORE
SCENE CLOTH STORE: ELEVATOR
ORIGINAL OPEN ROOF ADAPTED TO REHEARSAL ROOM IN 1955.
PAINT ROOM
PROPERTY ROOM
DRESSING ROOMS (WARDROBE OVER)
PAINTING, PROPERTY & CARPENTER'S WORKSHOP
NOW SCENE STORE
ACCESS RAMP
NOW REMOVED
DRESSING ROOMS
EXTENSION WITH OFFICES & DRESSING ROOMS
INTIMATE THEATRE
STAGE
TOILET
LIGHTING CONTROL
TOILET
FOYER
CLOAKS
REFRESHMENTS
ORCHESTRAL REHEARSAL ROOM
EXTENSION
© R. LEACROFT. 1981

are introduced above the stage. The seating is arranged on one continuous slope, save for four rows on a small gallery across the rear, connected at each end to the main body of seating by six small boxes stepping down to the lower level.

The forestage is built in four sections, which can be raised or lowered together or independently, and the whole may be lowered to floor level to take an additional 100 seats, or further to form an orchestra well for 70 musicians. The proscenium opening can vary from 72 feet (21.94m) to 39 feet (11.89m) in width, and is equipped with a steel fire curtain. The stage has a fly tower over the central portion, with a double-purchase counterweight system. [231b]

Front-of-house lighting is concealed behind openings in the auditorium ceiling, the original lighting fittings having been replaced by a further lighting bridge. A projection room is situtated at the back of the auditorium above the ceiling, and additional control rooms have been built at the rear.

In contrast to the limited backstage areas in the Belgrade Theatre [233], provision was made for the use of some forty scenic wagons, which could be run off-stage through rolling shutters on to large side stages, and, on the prompt side, into carpenters' and painters' workshops. However, these wagons have since been removed, together with the tracks on which they ran, as they proved too limiting, noisy, and difficult to manoeuvre. Today the workshops have become additional scene stores, and a new workshop has been built elsewhere, serving a total of six stages in the city complex.

On a smaller scale, the theatre at Sarah Lawrence College, Bronxville, New York (1952), [268, 269], has a stepped auditorium accommodating 500, seated around a trapeze-shaped stage projecting some 18 feet (5.49m) in front of a normal picture stage, this open portion being removable to provide an additional 35 seats or a sunken orchestra pit. There are two rows of seats to each step of the auditorium floor, with 3 feet 6 inch (1.07m) wide gangways. Alternate rows of seats may be replaced by tables for cabaret productions, and the chairs adjoining the stage swivel so that the audience can readily view whichever portion of the stage is in use.

Sarah Lawrence College,
Bronxville, New York
268; 269

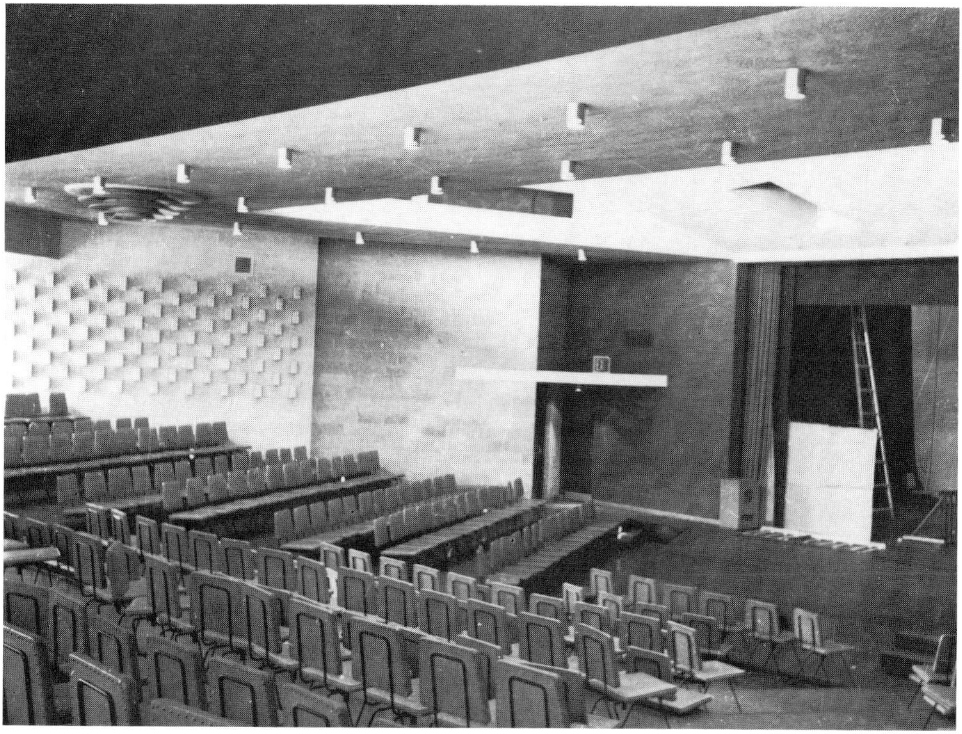

268

269

28 Theatres in the round

Okhlopkov's Realistic Theatre and 'Mother'. The Penthouse Theatre, Seattle. The Playhouse and Alley Theatre, Houston. S. Erasmo, Milan. Circular, octagonal, and rectangular stages. Casa Manana, Fort Worth. Victoria Theatre, Stoke on Trent. Royal Exchange, Manchester. Norman Bel Geddes and 'Theatre No. 14'. Problems of 'in-the-round' production.

In the early 1930s, Nicolai Okhlopkov, the director of the Realistic Theatre, Moscow, used a simple rectangular hall with a balcony at one end, in which he expressed similar ideas to those of Adolph Appia, who had asked for 'a bare and empty room' in which platforms and tiers of seats could be arranged and rearranged for each production. Okhlopkov set a stage down one wall, jutting out at the centre and at either end, and seated his audience in the bays. He set square platforms corner to corner in the centre of the hall, with the audience around them. Bridges were built over the heads of the audience, and for Gorky's *Mother* a circular stage in the middle of the hall was connected by gangways to a raised platform surrounding the walls. Okhlopkov's work was seminal to two developments in Europe and America: theatre in the round and flexible theatres.

RL

270 *Mother* at the Realistic Theatre, Moscow

The central stage provided for *Mother* [270] set the pattern for similar acting areas completely surrounded by an audience who, like the exponents of the thrust stage, wished to see the actors 'in the round'. In 1932 the School of Drama at the University of Washington, Seattle, experimented with a surrounding audience of sixty. Adaptation of existing premises in 1935 gave their Penthouse Theatre a more permanent home with a capacity of 140, replaced in 1940 [271, 272] by a new theatre seating 185.

This theatre is elliptical, with a stage of the same shape, enclosed by three rows of seats. It is approached by four ramps from doors in the auditorium wall, used both by actors and audience. The auditorium is enclosed by a corridor-like foyer, off which open the dressing rooms, furniture and property stores, cloaks, kitchen, and box office. While the maximum intensity of light is concentrated on the actors, a degree of illumination is also allowed to spread over the audience.

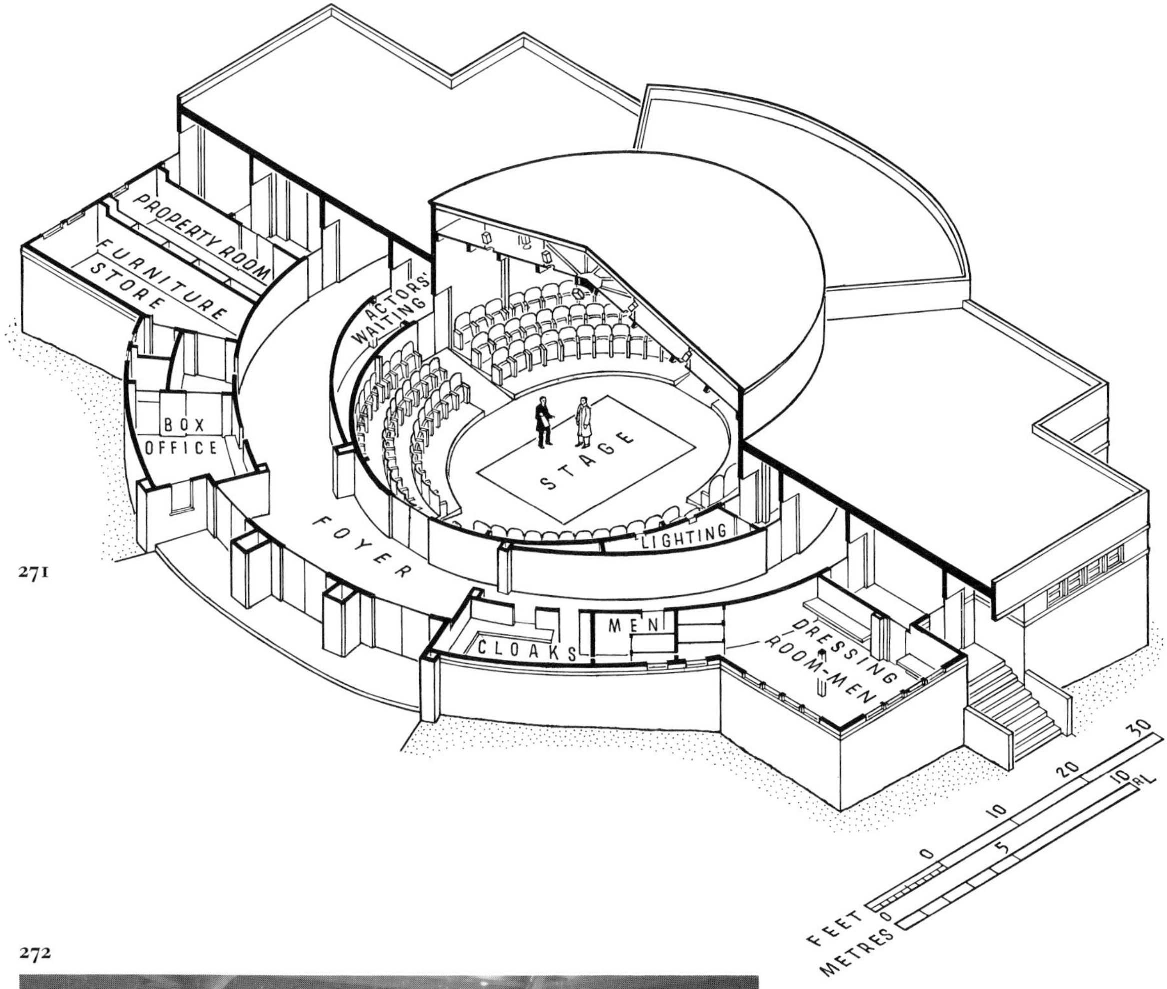
PROPERTY ROOM
FURNITURE STORE
ACTORS' WAITING
BOX OFFICE
STAGE
FOYER
LIGHTING
MEN
CLOAKS
DRESSING ROOM-MEN
FEET
METRES
0
10
20
30
0
5
10

271

272

The Penthouse Theatre, Seattle, Washington, 1940
271; 272

273 The Playhouse Theatre, Houston, Texas, 1950; 274 interior with scenic stage

The Playhouse Theatre in Houston, Texas, as built in 1950 [273, 274] had a circular stage surrounded by five concentric rows of seats, originally seating 306, the stage being built as a revolve 6½ inches (0.17m) high. Three sloping ramps led from doors, approached from concentric passages giving access to a 'backstage' assembly area for actors, properties, furniture, and scenery. Above this was the lighting, sound, and stage manager's control room. In contrast to the Penthouse Theatre the walls, floor, and ceiling were painted black to control reflected light.

A variation on the circular stage was employed in the Teatro S. Erasmo in Milan (1953). Here [275] an octagonal stage was flanked by seating for 250 on opposing sides. On the opposite axis were two curtained entrances, one of which was used for furniture and scenic items. In direct contrast, Nina Vance's original Alley Theatre [276] had a rectangular stage. As this theatre was adapted from an existing warehouse, the size of the stage was conditioned by four columns sup-

274

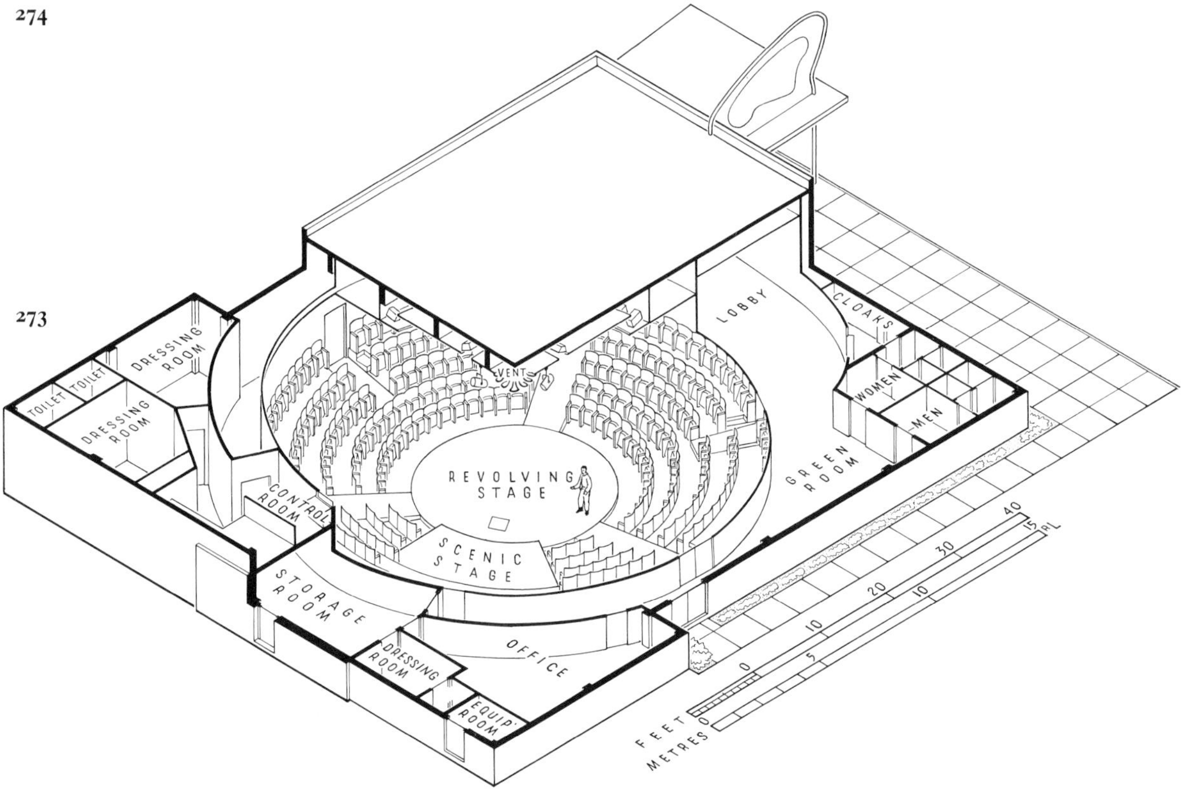

LOBBY
CLOAKS
DRESSING ROOM
TOILET
TOILET
DRESSING ROOM
VENT
WOMEN
MEN
REVOLVING STAGE
GREEN ROOM
CONTROL ROOM
SCENIC STAGE
STORAGE ROOM
OFFICE
DRESSING ROOM
EQUIP' ROOM
FEET
METRES
0
10
20
30
40
0
5
10
15

273

porting the roof. An egg-crate grid made it possible to light the actors without blinding the audience, and to achieve a decisive break between the lit stage and the surrounding patrons seated in darkness. The seating was in four rectangular blocks like the arms of a Greek cross.

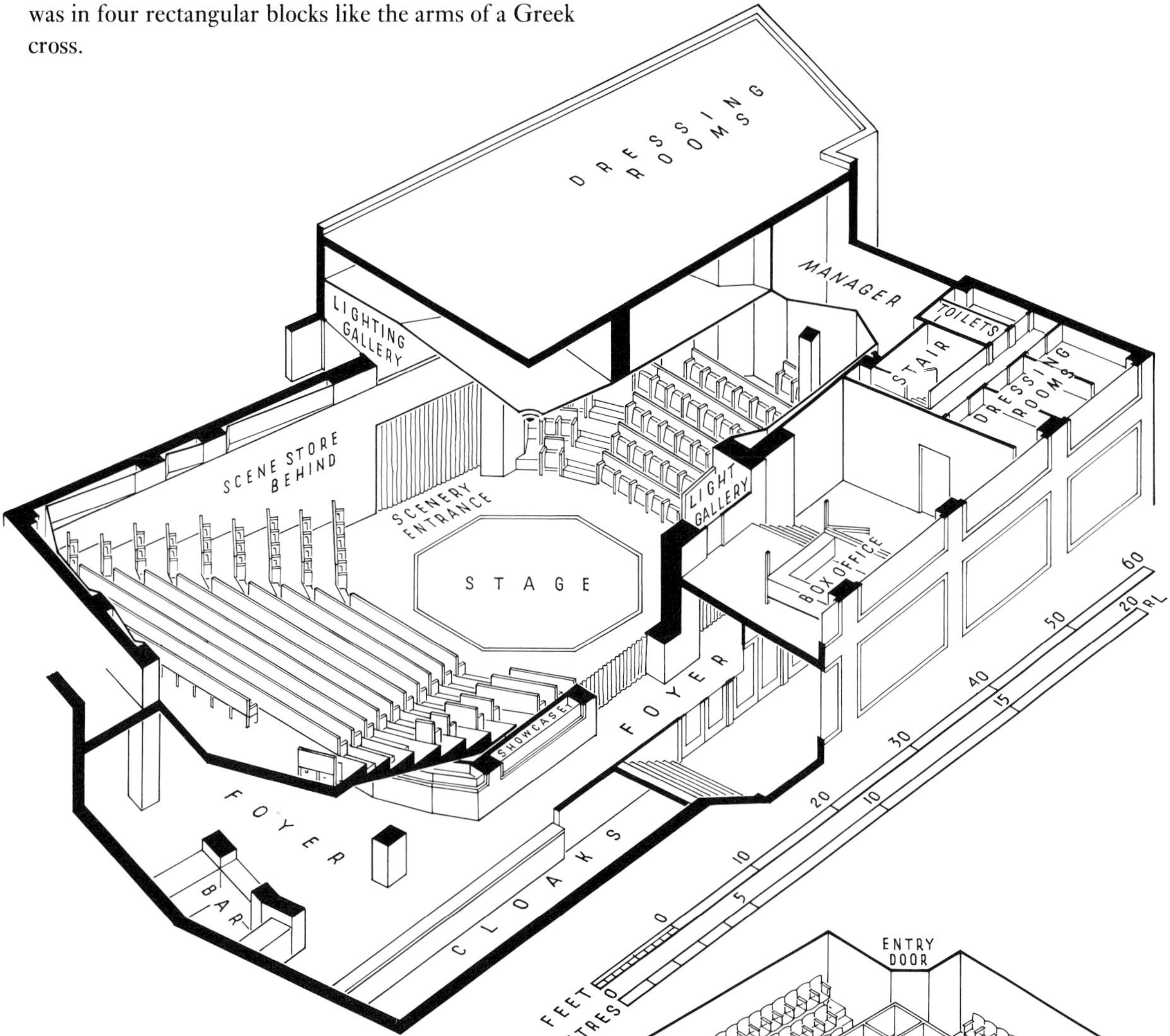
DRESSING ROOMS
MANAGER
LIGHTING GALLERY
TOILETS
STAIR
DRESSING ROOMS
SCENE STORE BEHIND
SCENERY ENTRANCE
LIGHT GALLERY
STAGE
BOX OFFICE
FOYER
SHOWCASE
FOYER
BAR
CLOAKS
FEET
METRES
0
10
20
30
40
50
60
0
5
10
15
20
RL

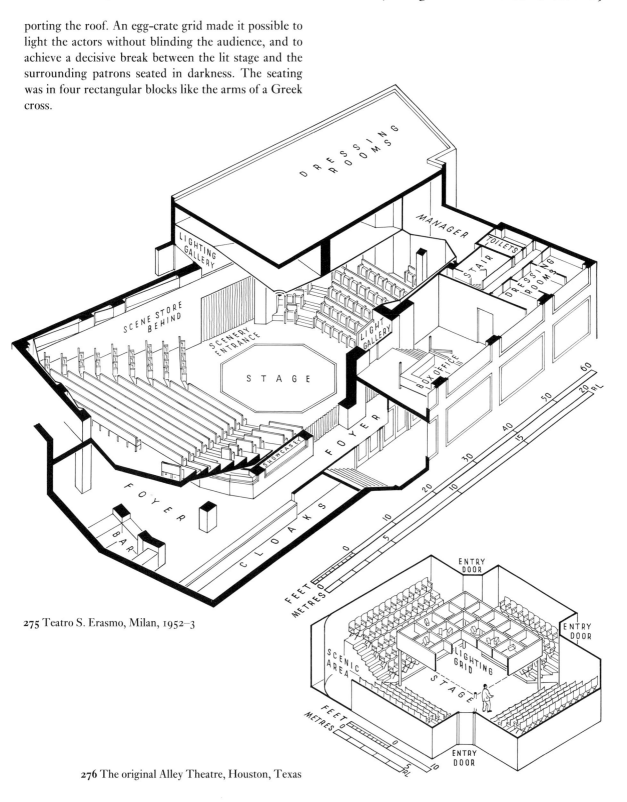

275 Teatro S. Erasmo, Milan, 1952–3

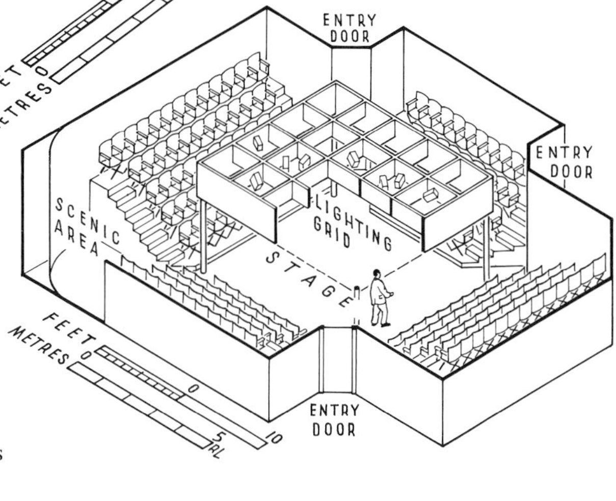
ENTRY DOOR
ENTRY DOOR
SCENIC AREA
LIGHTING GRID
STAGE
FEET
METRES
0
0
5
10
RL
ENTRY DOOR

276 The original Alley Theatre, Houston, Texas

An advantage over the circular and elliptical theatres was that the entry doors were close to the acting area, where they played a more direct part in the action – an advantage surprisingly omitted from the rebuilding of this theatre in 1968. When an actor has to make an entrance down the length of a gangway, the dramatic value of surprise cannot be used, and the tempo of the performance is consequently controlled by the length of time it takes to traverse the distance between the entry doors and the stage – a distance of 46 feet (14.02m) in the vast Casa Manana Theatre, Fort Worth, Texas, of 1958. [277]

The rectangular acting area is favoured by many exponents of this form of open stage, as conforming more closely to the characteristics of the 'normal' living room which is often required for plays originally written for the picture-frame stage. This shape was used by Stephen Joseph in his Studio Theatre adaptations of existing halls, [278a] and in 1962 for his permanent Victoria Theatre, Stoke on Trent, [279] where the

277 Casa Manana Theatre, Fort Worth, Texas

278 'Studio Theatre' adaptation of
a : Wycliffe School Hall, Leicester
b : old Vaughan College Hall, Leicester

a

b

blocks of seating on all four sides of the acting area were later extended by bridging over the entry ways. His adaptation in 1958 of the Vaughan College Hall, Leicester, [278b] however, followed the pattern seen at S. Erasmo, Milan, but with minimum seating on either side, an arrangement which has also been adopted at the newest Mermaid [254] for the presentation of a play about all-in wrestling, for which theatre in the round is an ideal solution.

The Royal Exchange Theatre, Manchester (1976), has a seven-sided auditorium and stage erected within the existing Exchange Hall. [280] Entrances at each corner are shared by stage and audience, and the surrounding hall serves as an actors' assembly area. Because of constructional problems inherent in the original building, only 450 seats are provided at floor level in five rows, three being lifted above the hall floor on raised steps. An additional row of low bench-seats defines the actual stage area, which can be increased by removing these and the two rows of seats at floor level. The remaining seats, totalling 700, are disposed in two galleries, with two rows in each – the outermost row consisting of tall stools, to overcome sight-line limitations. There are lighting bridges at ceiling level, with addi-

279 Victoria Theatre, Stoke on Trent, Staffs

tional lighting at the gallery levels controlled from a panel in the upper gallery. Provision is made for limited flying of scenery.

In most theatres in the round settings are restricted to the use of items of furniture, to low screens or three-dimensional planes or levels, or to scenic items hung above the eye level [284d]. The Casa Manana, Fort Worth, [277] was designed for the presentation of spectacular musicals. For scenery it relied on frame-like structures through which the action might be viewed, and on decorating the large, circular pelmet hung above the stage containing lighting and sound equipment. Any changes of furnishing or scenery are made in full view of the audience, a necessity which here has been transformed into a virtue. This theatre is enclosed within a geodesic dome, which is brought into dramatic use by flooding the internal surface with different coloured lights to set the mood.

This idea had formed the basis of a 1914 scheme by Norman Bel Geddes, which he updated in 1922. [281] His 'Theatre No. 14' was designed as a circular dome in which a central, circular stage of 30 feet (9.14m) diameter was separated by a moat from a surrounding balcony of six rows of seats, for an audience of 800. As in his previously described project [215], the stage could be lowered to the basement, where it was replaced by a platform ready set with scenery. It was approached by a flight of steps leading up from a circular corridor, off which opened all the dressing rooms and the green room, as well as the offices for the director and stage

280 Royal Exchange Theatre, Manchester

281 Norman Bel Geddes. Theatre No. 14, 1922

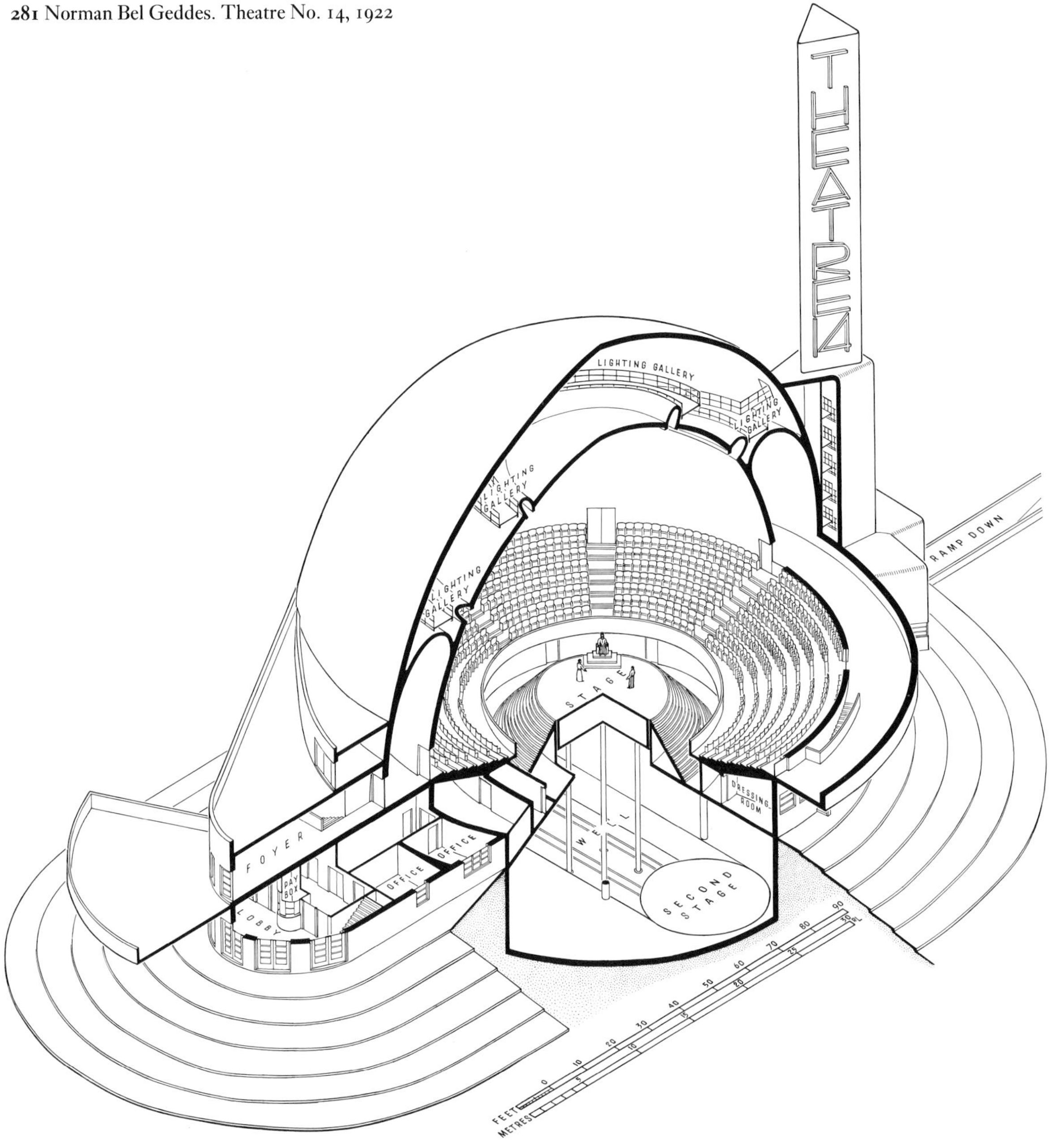
LIGHTING GALLERY
LIGHTING GALLERY
LIGHTING GALLERY
LIGHTING GALLERY
RAMP DOWN
STAGE
WELL
SECOND STAGE
DRESSING ROOM
FOYER
OFFICE
OFFICE
PAY BOX
LOBBY
FEET
METRES

manager. Stage lighting was concealed in the dome and around the front of the balcony, the dome itself acting as a totally enclosing cyclorama – which would no doubt have created insuperable acoustic problems had the project been realized.

But here was an attempt to achieve the best of both worlds: the intimacy of single-space enclosure of actor and audience, together with scenic spectacle. Nevertheless the size and arrangement of scenery on this stage would have been seriously limited if adequate sight-lines were to be maintained. Bel Geddes had indicated that 'scenery would be restricted to what is commonly called properties', and one cannot avoid wondering if the expensive machinery provided would have been fully employed. His own sketch of *King Lear* shows no more than a throne on three low steps and some seats. An indication of statues surrounding the auditorium is suggested, to be achieved perhaps by the use of projected slides.

The round is an ideal form for circuses, gymnastics, wrestling, boxing, and the antics of clowns – which suggests that productions intended for presentation in the round should be devised to make the most of such possibilities. But too often even those plays written to be performed in this way have not broken free from picture-frame conventions, and in such cases, or when picture-frame plays are adapted, production patterns are limited by the fixed positions of the entrances and exits, and their distance from the acting area. Limitations are also placed on the movements of performers, and on the use of furnishings and scenery which may restrict the view of members of the audience.

As the original purpose of breaking free from the picture-frame was the wish to return to a simpler set of conventions, unencumbered by the problems created by the use of realistic settings, one should perhaps accept the conventions which these stages impose, and make the most of the intimate relationship between actor and audience which they certainly offer. This relationship is considered to be of the greatest importance by the Gimi-speaking people of the Eastern Highlands of Papua New Guinea, where dramas representing legends and social topics affecting the community are presented 'in the round' inside the houses in the villages. No member of the audience is denied a full view, because the actors often reverse their positions and repeat a part of the drama so that their faces may be seen by everyone.

But the desire for scenic illusion is an important element of theatre, and one which will, almost inevitably, raise its head eventually, whatever form of stage is used. Even in the extreme strongholds of escape from the picture-frame which these theatres in the round represent, the desire to include scenery has thus proved too strong in at least two of the theatres mentioned above: in 1958 the Houston Playhouse Theatre was adapted by the removal of a segment of seating to include a small platform, [274] while one corner of the Houston Alley Theatre was fitted with a small cyclorama before which scenery could be placed. [276]

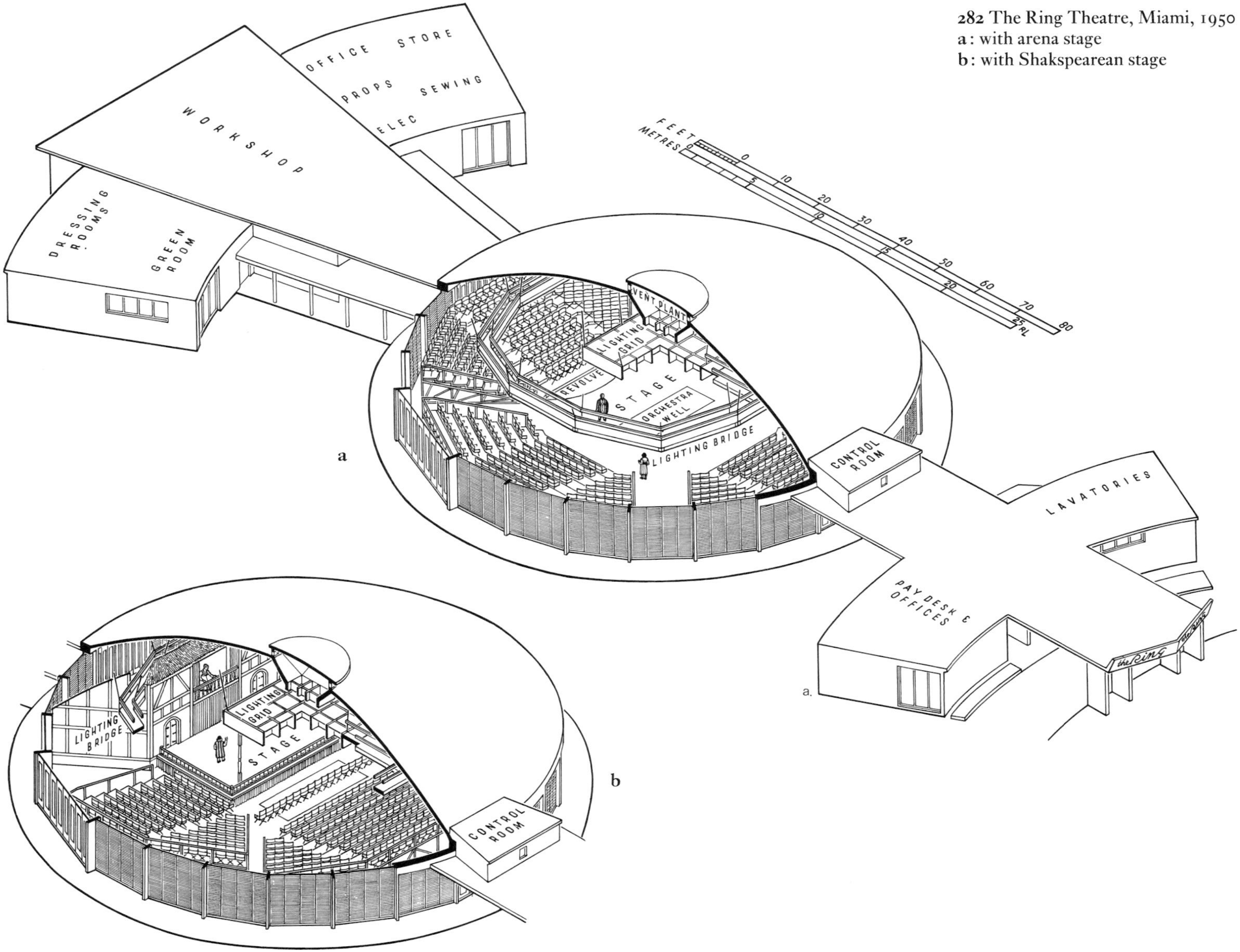
WORKSHOP
OFFICE
STORE
PROPS
SEWING
ELEC
DRESSING ROOMS
GREEN ROOM
FEET
METRES
VENT PLANT
LIGHTING GRID
REVOLVE
STAGE
ORCHESTRA WELL
LIGHTING BRIDGE
CONTROL ROOM
LAVATORIES
PAY DESK & OFFICES
the Ring
a
LIGHTING BRIDGE
LIGHTING GRID
STAGE
CONTROL ROOM
b

282 The Ring Theatre, Miami, 1950
a: with arena stage
b: with Shakspearean stage

29 Flexible theatres

Royce Hall, California. The Ring Theatre, Miami. Corn Exchange, Leicester. Studio One, Baylor University, Waco, Texas. The Loeb Drama Center, Harvard University. Computers and winches. National Theatre, Mannheim. The Questors, Ealing. The Bolton Octagon. The Waco Civic Theatre.

The idea of changing the relationship between stage and seating to suit each play was taken up in the 1940s at the University of California, where a classroom in Royce Hall was used for this purpose. Rearrangement of seating units can readily be carried out on a small scale, but the larger the hall and the audience, the more difficult the problem becomes.

In the flexible Ring Theatre of 1950 at the University of Miami, [282] the auditorium consisted of a single domed building with separate wings for administration, workshops, and dressing rooms. The theatre could be arranged with a central stage with seating for 900, or as a picture-type stage with a revolve, which could have an open stage projecting forward in varying degrees, with three sections of seating enclosing it.

The orchestra pit in the centre of the building could be used with a forestage for operatic or musical comedy productions, and it was also possible to build an Elizabethan stage with inner and upper stages and flanking doors. Over the central acting area was a pendant lighting grid, connected to a surrounding lighting bridge. Conversion from an arena stage to classical, Elizabethan, or modern scenic forms was more readily achieved in a project for converting the Corn Exchange in Leicester in 1959. [283, 284] Here the canopy additionally acted as a sounding board.

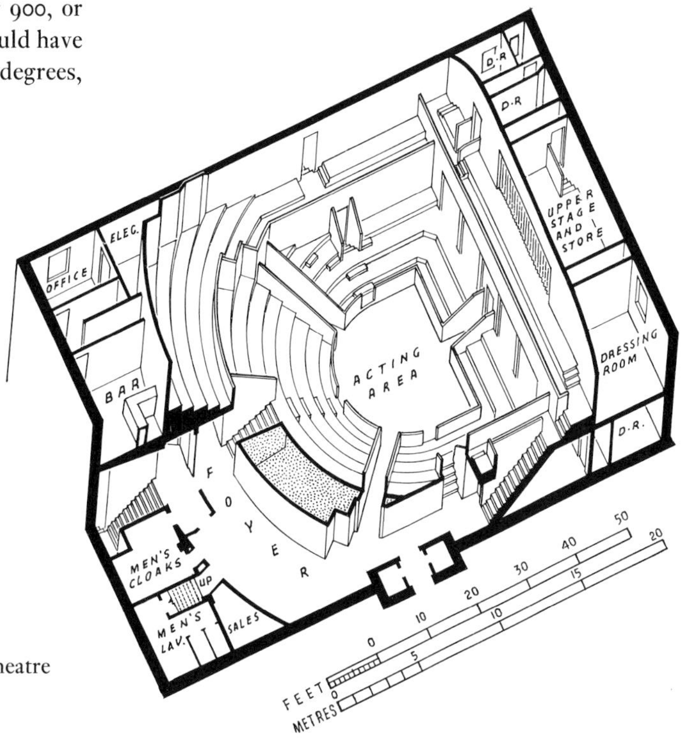
D·R
D·R
UPPER STAGE AND STORE
ELEC.
OFFICE
DRESSING ROOM
ACTING AREA
BAR
D·R.
FOYER
MEN'S CLOAKS
UP
MEN'S LAV.
SALES
FEET
METRES
0
10
20
30
40
50
5
15
20

283 Corn Exchange, Leicester. Project for flexible theatre

a

b

c

d

284 Corn Exchange, Leciester. Project arranged as
a : arena stage
b : classical stage
c : Elizabethan stage
d : modern scenic stage

Studio One at Baylor University, Waco, Texas (1941), [285] had a picture stage with cyclorama and gridiron, but the auditorium side walls were replaced by flanking stages, separated from the main stage by movable screens: when these were open, all three stages formed a continuous unit. The rectangular auditorium had a flat floor for approximately three-quarters of its depth, the rear portion having four steps suitable for seats. The unfixed seats could swivel, so that the audience could follow the action of the performance moving from one stage to another.

The rear wall was connected to a foyer by a wide opening, above which a gallery opened off an upper room. These openings and the steps in front formed the basis for an Elizabethan tiring house, with the audience now facing in the opposite direction, seated on the main floor and the surrounding stages. The auditorium could also become the stage of a theatre in the round. A control room was situated on a pendant gallery above the auditorium floor.

In contrast to these manually-operated theatres, the Loeb Drama Center, Harvard, of 1960, [286, 287] relied on analogue computers for the movement of stage and seating units. The main theatre had a rectangular auditorium with 556 seats on a single slope, divided by a cross-gangway into two groups. The major, rear group of 402 seats was permanently fixed on a stepped concrete floor, while the minor group was supported on two motorised platforms which stood on a lift unit, built in four sections.

285 Studio One, Baylor University, Texas

In the lowest position of this unit, the seats continued the auditorium slope, but when the lift was raised the platforms could swing to face each other across a pro-

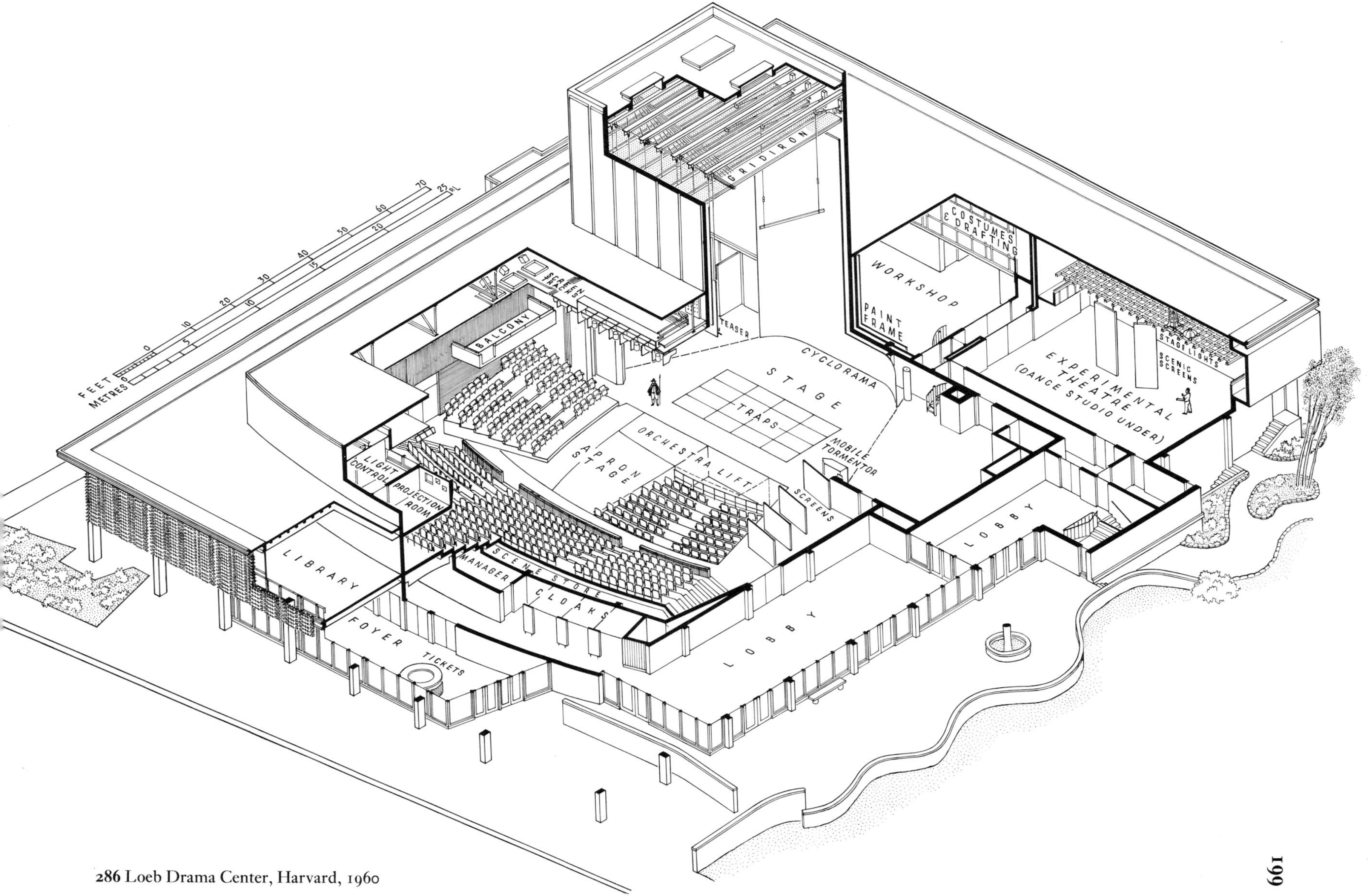
GRIDIRON
COSTUMES & DRAFTING
WORKSHOP
PAINT FRAME
EXPERIMENTAL THEATRE (DANCE STUDIO UNDER)
STAGE LIGHTS
SCENIC SCREENS
TEASER
CYCLORAMA
STAGE
TRAPS
MOBILE TORMENTOR
SCREEN TRACKS
BALCONY
ORCHESTRA LIFT
APRON STAGE
SCREENS
LIGHT CONTROL
PROJECTION ROOM
LIBRARY
MANAGER
SCENE STORE
CLOAKS
FOYER
TICKETS
LOBBY
LOBBY
LOBBY
FEET
METRES
0 10 20 30 40 50 60 70
0 5 10 15 20 25

286 Loeb Drama Center, Harvard, 1960

Loeb Drama Center; 287; 288 287

jecting open stage, formed by the central sections of the lift, one of which could sink to form an orchestra well. The seating platforms could also swing completely round on to the main stage, additional seating being introduced to the side areas to form a theatre in the round.

The size of the proscenium opening can be adjusted by the use of a flexible border or 'teaser' and a mobile 'tormentor', to alter the height and width respectively. [288] The main picture stage has side storage space for wagons, and the acting area, which is trapped in sixteen sections, can be totally enclosed by a cyclorama with a permanent rear portion and two mobile side wings. The normal pulley and counterweight flying system is here replaced by thirty electrically controlled winches, fixed to the walls above the gridiron. Lines can be taken from these to any point above the grid where a pulley block might be hung.

288

The winches can be used separately or in groups to deal with large scenic units. Further winches operate the front curtain and the proscenium teaser, and all these and the movement of the cyclorama side wings are operated from a single mobile control console. It is claimed that this system, designed by George Izenour, allows greater flexibility in the hanging and flying of scenery than was possible under the old system of sets of lines, especially when the all-enclosing cyclorama is used, but practice suggested that more lines were needed. Once again it has been found, as Herr Rudolph earlier experienced, that mechanical control is seldom so finely sensitive as a manual system.

The projecting stage is designed to be used in conjunction with the main stage or as a separate unit; if the latter, the proscenium opening can be closed by the front curtain or by scenic units incorporating appropriate entrances. As it is level with the cross gangway, it can also be approached through doors in the side walls of the auditorium. When the orchestra lift is dropped, it leaves a small island stage which can be approached by steps from beneath the main stage.

The balconies on either side of the proscenium were intended for use with the open stage, as additional acting areas, but such use would appear to be limited, each balcony being unseen from the seating on its own side of the auditorium. In the picture stage arrangement, the side areas are masked by screens hanging from ceiling tracks, the side galleries then becoming lighting perches. The theatre-in-the-round arrangement has proved less than satisfactory, as the audience seated on the main stage find themselves in a different environment from those in the auditorium.

Nor does much thought seem to have been given to the provision of assembly areas, or entrances for the actors using the open stages. Here, as in so many open-stage theatres, it would seem to be considered sufficient to provide an open space or platform and surround it with seating, scant consideration being given to the mechanics of production.

In the National Theatre at Mannheim (1955–57), the smaller theatre [289] was designed as an experimental hall capable of adaptation to various actor-audience relationships, as well as for opera, ballet, concerts, and lectures. There is no fly tower, the whole room or chamber having a single-level ceiling composed of a series of panels, sections of which can be opened as lighting louvres. Provision is also made for hanging scenic items.

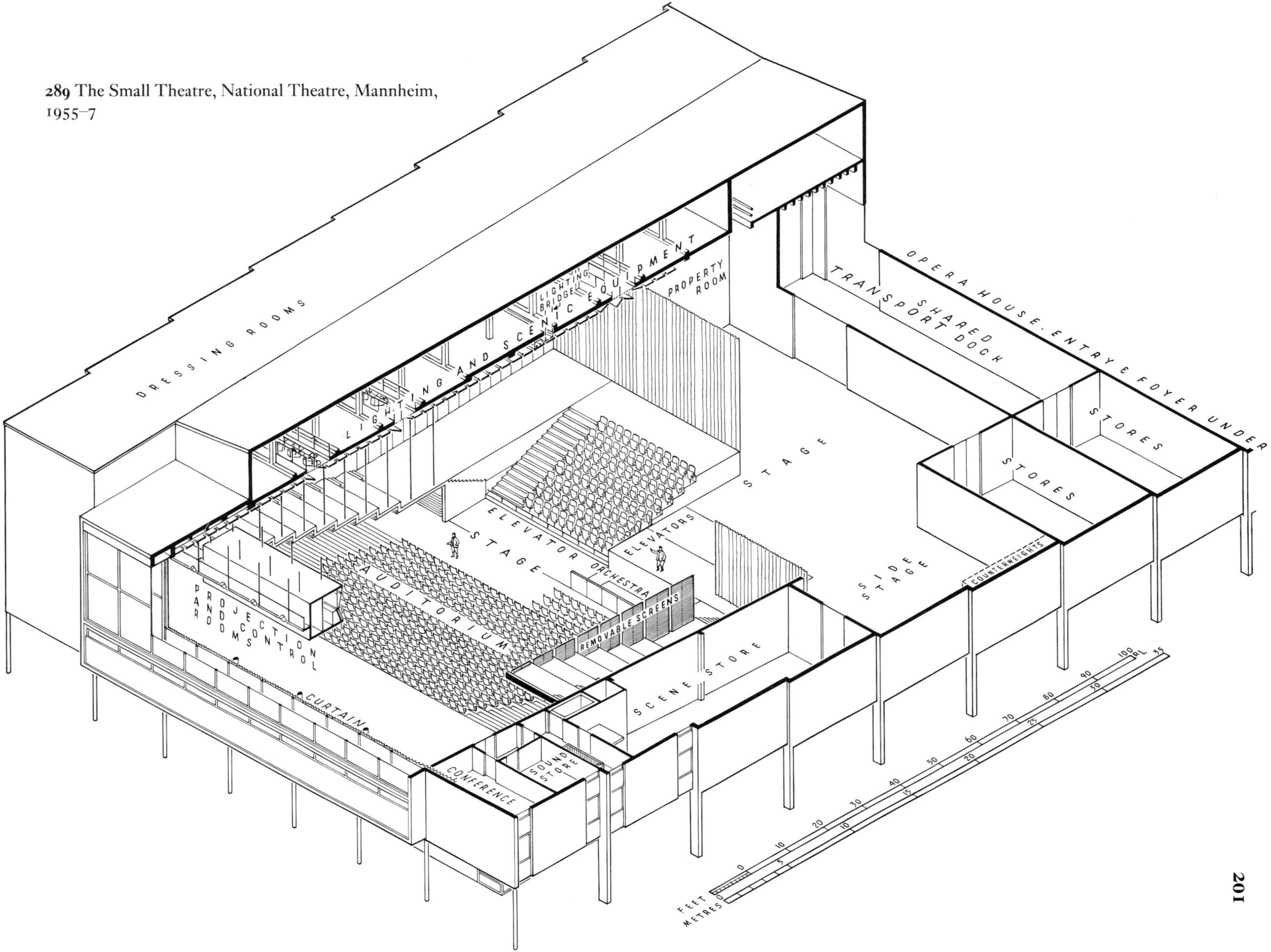
DRESSING ROOMS
LIGHTING BRIDGE
LIGHTING AND SCENIC EQUIPMENT
PROPERTY ROOM
OPERA HOUSE. ENTRY & FOYER UNDER
SHARED TRANSPORT DOCK
STORES
STORES
STAGE
SIDE STAGE
COUNTERWEIGHTS
ELEVATORS
ELEVATOR STAGE
ORCHESTRA
REMOVABLE SCREENS
AUDITORIUM
PROJECTION AND CONTROL ROOMS
CURTAIN
SCENE STORE
SOUND STORE
CONFERENCE
FEET
METRES
0
10
20
30
40
50
60
70
80
90
100
5
10
15
20
25
30
35

289 The Small Theatre, National Theatre, Mannheim, 1955–7

One half of the hall is designed as an auditorium, [290] the other being the stage. Audience entries are at the mid-way position on either side. The auditorium has some 600 permanent seats on a single slope, enclosed on each side by suspended steps providing side stages and access to lighting, projection, sound control, and stage-management cubicles in a long bridge across the rear of the hall. These side stages can be screened off by panels, the space behind being used to accommodate lighting units. The front part of the stage is equipped with three hydraulically operated lifts.

As originally designed, the hall could be adapted for use in a variety of ways. Three variations on a picture stage were possible: with an orchestra pit; with steps to the main stage; or with a large forestage. It was also possible to arrange the stage with an audience on two or four sides. Apart from the opening production of Schiller's *Die Räuber*, arranged in the manner shown in the upper half of the reconstruction, the theatre is normally arranged as a picture stage.

While both this and the Loeb Center theatre were designed with a bias towards the picture stage, the Questors Theatre, Ealing (1964), [291] was a miniature version of the Grosses Schauspielhaus, with seven or (in places) eight rows of seating giving a capacity of 346 seats encircling a horseshoe stage projecting from a main stage occupying the full width of the building. [292a] The projecting stage can be approached through three vomitories in the auditorium, which may be covered to provide additional seating; or the stage can, if required, be removed altogether, the floor beneath being stepped to permit more seating to be introduced facing the main stage. The rear stage wall is curved and plastered as a cyclorama, with a covered lighting pit in front and a cross-passage behind.

As first designed, a proscenium arrangement could be created by the use of a temporary frame and removable side panels. The side seats, which would have had a poor view of the picture stage, were to have been concealed by curtains, but are now covered with black cloth. Theatre in the round could be formed by the addition of seating rostra on the main stage, but the original arrangement, shown on the reconstruction, was unsatisfactory, and has since been amended, as may be seen from the photograph. [292b] Lighting units are not concealed, but are supported on four bridges spanning the hall, connected by a lighting gallery around the walls to a control room at the rear of the auditorium.

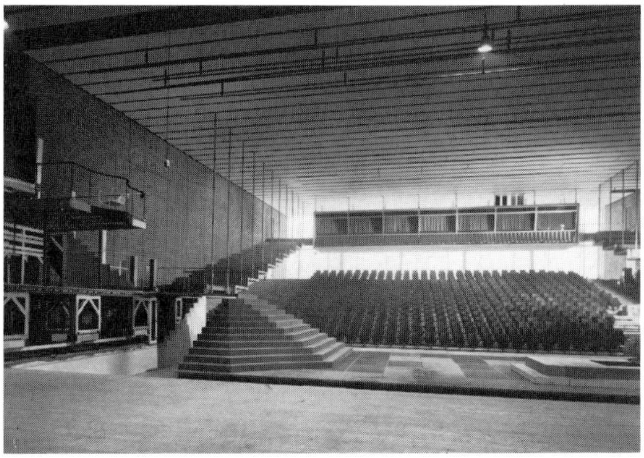

290 The Small Theatre, Mannheim

The Questors Theatre, Ealing, London, 1964: **291**
292a as thrust stage
292b: as arena stage

292a

292b

291

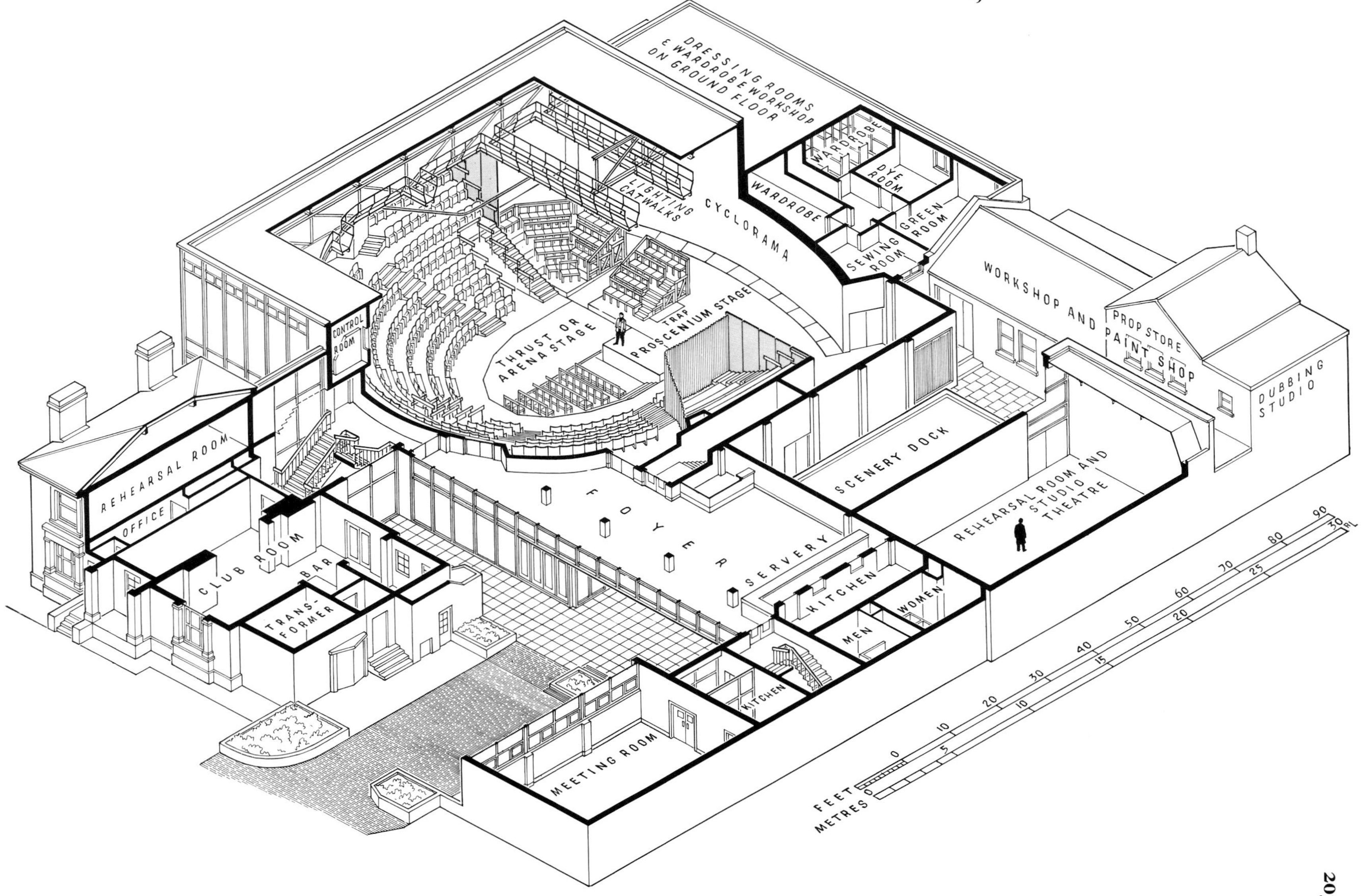
DRESSING ROOMS
& WARDROBE WORKSHOP
ON GROUND FLOOR
WARDROBE
DYE ROOM
WARDROBE
GREEN ROOM
SEWING ROOM
LIGHTING CATWALKS
CYCLORAMA
CONTROL ROOM
THRUST OR ARENA STAGE
TRAP
PROSCENIUM STAGE
WORKSHOP AND
PROP STORE
PAINT SHOP
DUBBING STUDIO
SCENERY DOCK
REHEARSAL ROOM AND STUDIO THEATRE
REHEARSAL ROOM
OFFICE
CLUB ROOM
BAR
TRANS-FORMER
F O Y E R
SERVERY
KITCHEN
WOMEN
MEN
KITCHEN
MEETING ROOM
FEET
METRES
0
10
20
30
40
50
60
70
80
90
0
5
10
15
20
25
30
RL

293

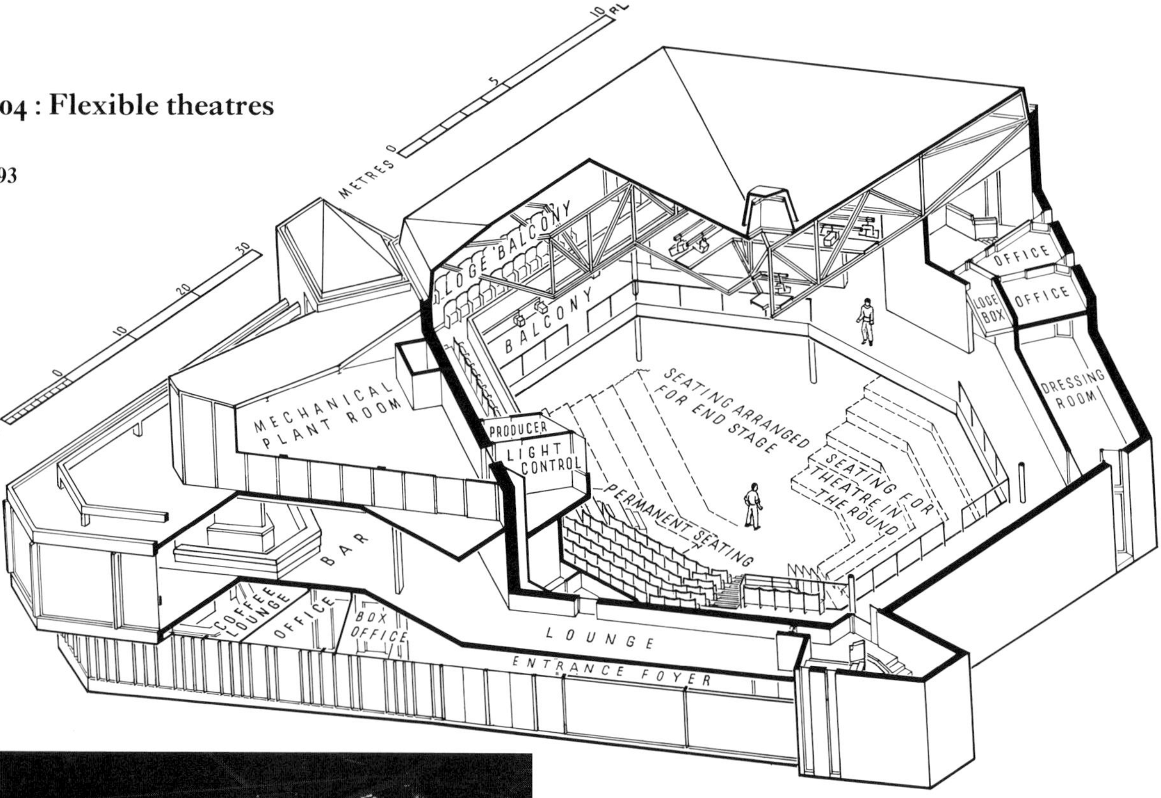
METRES 0 5 10
FEET 0 10 20 30
LOGE BALCONY
BALCONY
OFFICE
OFFICE
LOGE BOX
DRESSING ROOM
MECHANICAL PLANT ROOM
PRODUCER
LIGHT CONTROL
SEATING ARRANGED FOR END STAGE
SEATING FOR THEATRE IN THE ROUND
PERMANENT SEATING
BAR
COFFEE LOUNGE
OFFICE
BOX OFFICE
LOUNGE
ENTRANCE FOYER

294

The Octagon Theatre, Bolton, 1967:
293;
294 end stage
295 arena stage
296 thrust stage

295

296

LAV

While it is possible to create a picture stage without a fly tower at the Questors, the potential of the Bolton Octagon (1967) [293] is limited to open stage forms. Within an hexagonal auditorium, the stage and seating may be rearranged to create a theatre in the round [295] seating 422; a thrust stage [296] seating 322; or an end stage [294] with an audience of 356. Both end and thrust stages have been used with elaborately built constructivist settings comprising numerous acting levels and staircases, which together provide a reasonable degree of flexibility of production movement. An open lattice roof contains lighting galleries, and lighting equipment may also be hung on the gallery fronts.

Amateur theatres such as the Questors, or the Civic Theatre at Waco, Texas (1958), must be sufficiently flexible to permit the groups involved to experiment with their productions. The Waco Theatre [297] offers flexibility largely as a result of its limited seating capacity – 150, on folding canvas chairs – and by omitting all those features which, while encouraging one use, would detract from another. Its unfixed seating can be rearranged within the hall in any position required.

Internally, the hall is a single volume subdivided by two projecting pavilions, each with a door obliquely facing the larger area of the hall. This has an ovoid pit sunk 3 feet (0.91m) below the main floor, to which it

297 Civic Theatre, Waco, Texas, 1958

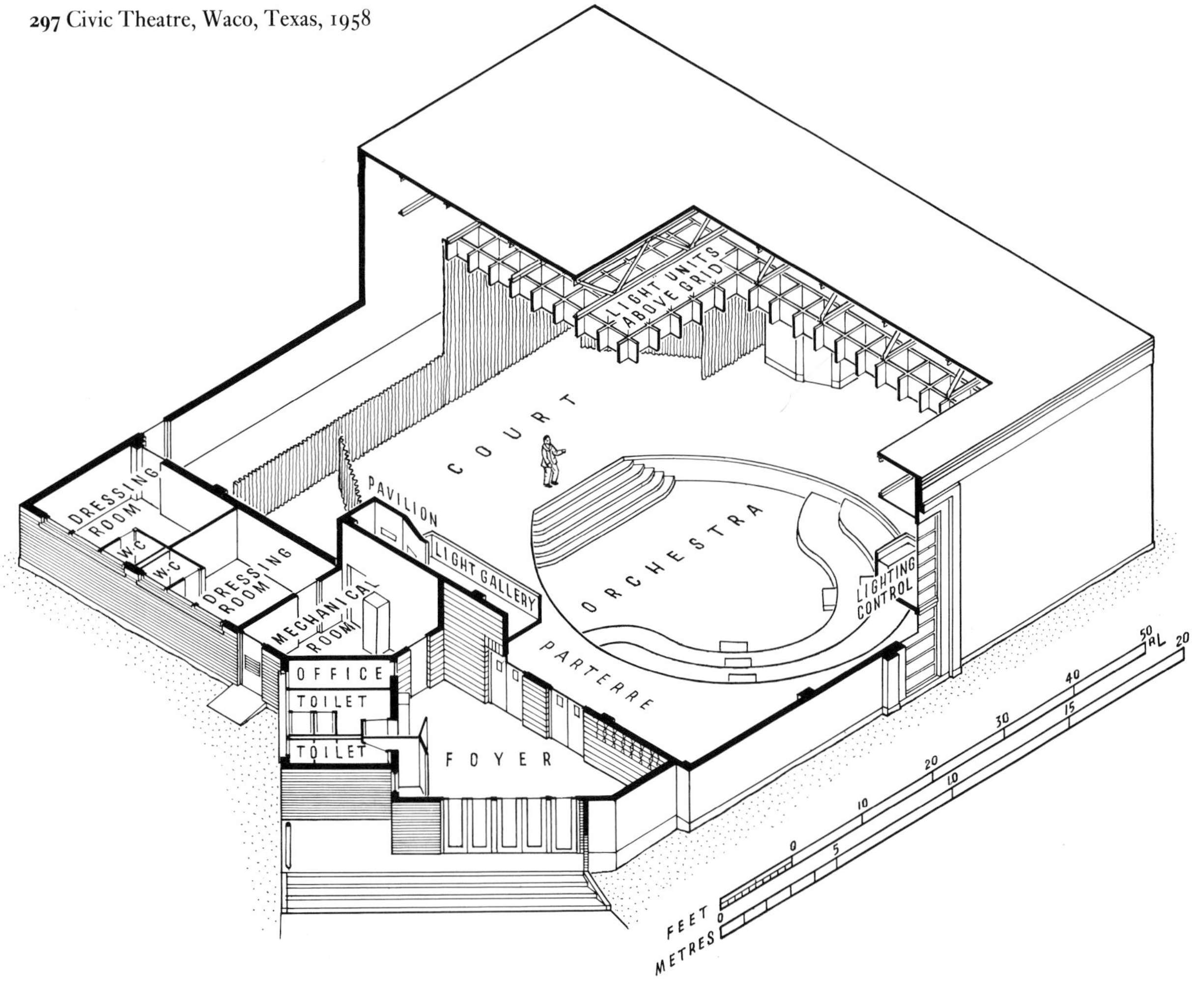
LIGHT UNITS ABOVE GRID
COURT
PAVILION
LIGHT GALLERY
ORCHESTRA
LIGHTING CONTROL
DRESSING ROOM
W.C
W.C
DRESSING ROOM
MECHANICAL ROOM
OFFICE
TOILET
TOILET
FOYER
PARTERRE
FEET
METRES
0
10
20
30
40
50
0
5
10
15
20

is connected at the 'stage' end by a flight of steps and at the opposite end by two wide steps or terraces. Linking the pavilions around the 'auditorium' is a gallery, used for lighting units, with a lighting console on the central axis. The unity of the hall is emphasized by a rectangular, open-grid ceiling above both 'stage' and 'auditorium', designed to permit lighting units to be hung above it on special fittings, so that the grid conceals the light source.

Conventional staging may be presented by using curtains to form 'proscenium' wings, [298] and open staging may be achieved in the well or on the surrounding 'parterre'; but in these instances actors make their entrances through the audience. Even when used as a picture stage, however, there is little sense of separation between actor and audience, since the 'stage' floor reaches out and encircles the audience, and the ceiling grid provides a positive link.

298 Waco Civic Theatre

30 Experimental drama studios

St. Mary's, Twickenham. First Studio and Vandyck Studio, Bristol University. Norman Bel Geddes's 'large empty room'. George Izenour's Yale project. Manual and mechanical adaptations. The Loeb Drama Center. Midland, Texas.

The adaptable theatre at St. Mary's Training College, Twickenham (1963), [299–301] is a rectangular hall which can be arranged as a theatre in the round, as a thrust stage, or as a picture stage. A cyclorama surrounds the room, with an additional track subdividing the enclosed space. The central area is trapped in 4 feet (1.22m) squares, eight units wide by twelve units long, giving access to an under-floor area of head-room height. Removal of these units and their supporting

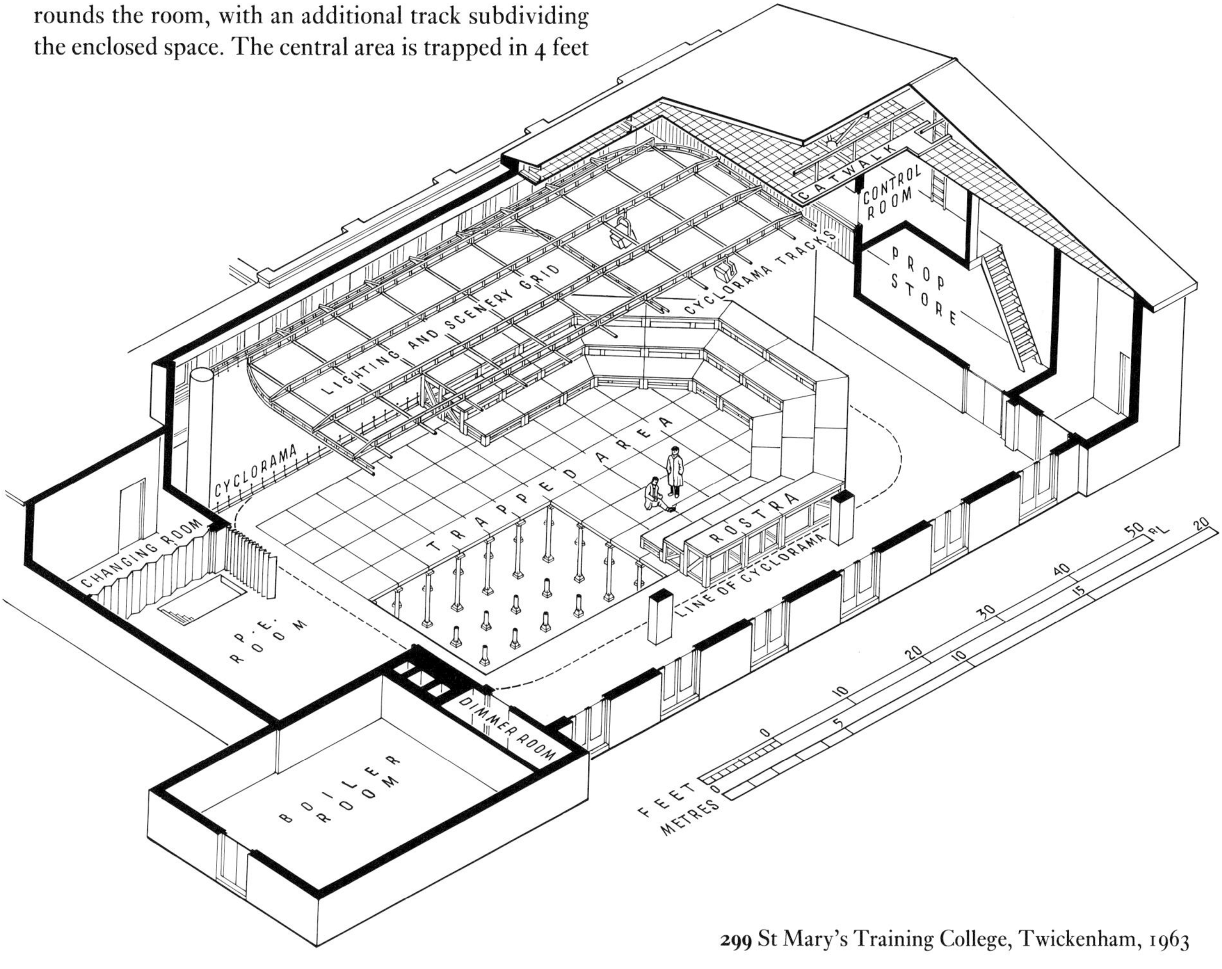
CATWALK
CONTROL ROOM
PROP STORE
CYCLORAMA TRACKS
LIGHTING AND SCENERY GRID
CYCLORAMA
TRAPPED AREA
ROSTRA
LINE OF CYCLORAMA
CHANGING ROOM
P.E. ROOM
DIMMER ROOM
BOILER ROOM
FEET
METRES
0
10
20
30
40
50
5
10
15
20

299 St Mary's Training College, Twickenham, 1963

300–1 St. Mary's Training College

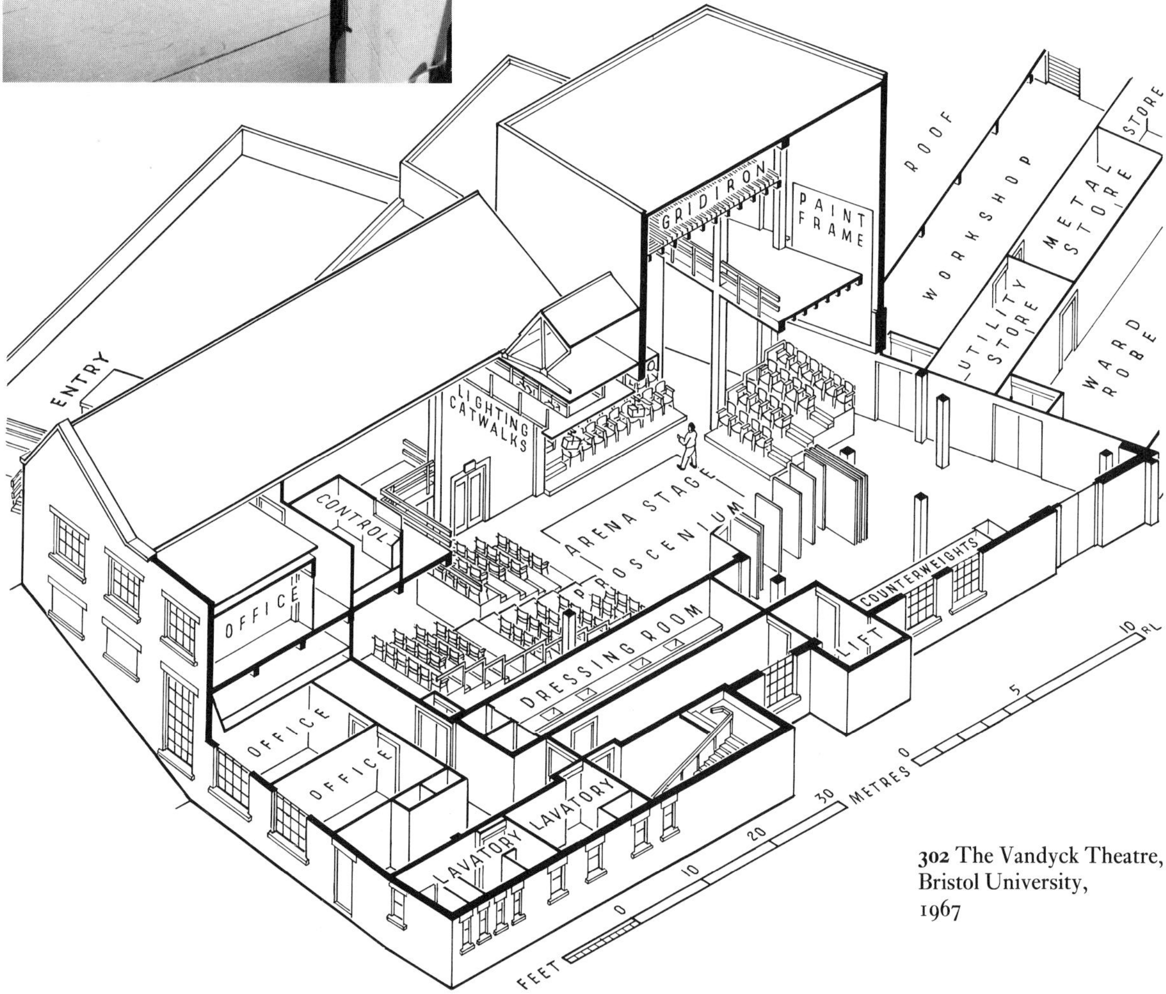
ENTRY
LIGHTING CATWALKS
GRIDIRON
PAINT FRAME
ROOF
WORKSHOP
STORE
METAL STORE
UTILITY STORE
WARD ROBE
CONTROL
OFFICE
ARENA STAGE
PROSCENIUM
DRESSING ROOM
COUNTERWEIGHTS
LIFT
OFFICE
OFFICE
LAVATORY
LAVATORY
FEET 0 10 20 30
METRES 0 5 10
RL

302 The Vandyck Theatre, Bristol University, 1967

columns makes possible a variety of levels or an orchestra pit. A range of rostra are available for building up the seating levels required to accommodate three rows of seats.

Where drama schools wish to present plays from the historical repertoire in an actor-audience relationship appropriate to a specific period, then it should be possible to create an appropriate pattern in their studios. In 1951 the Drama Department at Bristol University adapted an existing squash court to form such a studio theatre, thus permitting performances with proscenium, thrust, or arena staging. The later Vandyck Studio of 1967 [302] permits similar patterns within wider limits – this time, those of an adapted printing works.

Too many drama schools, however, have studios which limit experiment to predetermined forms. If flexibility is important to professional actors, it is essential among students of the theatre, who should be encouraged in the creation of new and experimental forms. In 1950 Norman Bel Geddes suggested that

The proper theatre for an educational institution is one where the auditorium and stage are in one large empty room. The entire ceiling of this room is a gridiron. Consequently everything within the room can be moved about mechanically or manually, but in any event, easily.

Such a studio project was designed by George Izenour for the Drama Department at Yale in 1955. [303] The hall was to be some 92 feet (28.04m) by 60 feet (18.29m), with a 2 feet (0.61m) square grid of open channels at a height of 18 feet (5.59m) in which roller hangers, supporting screens, could run. An access area above provided space where special lighting units could stand, projecting light through the grid or being lowered on telescopic stands to whatever height was required. The central area of the studio floor was divided into 45 eight feet (2.44m) square lifts, operated by hydraulic pistons driven by electrically operated pumps.

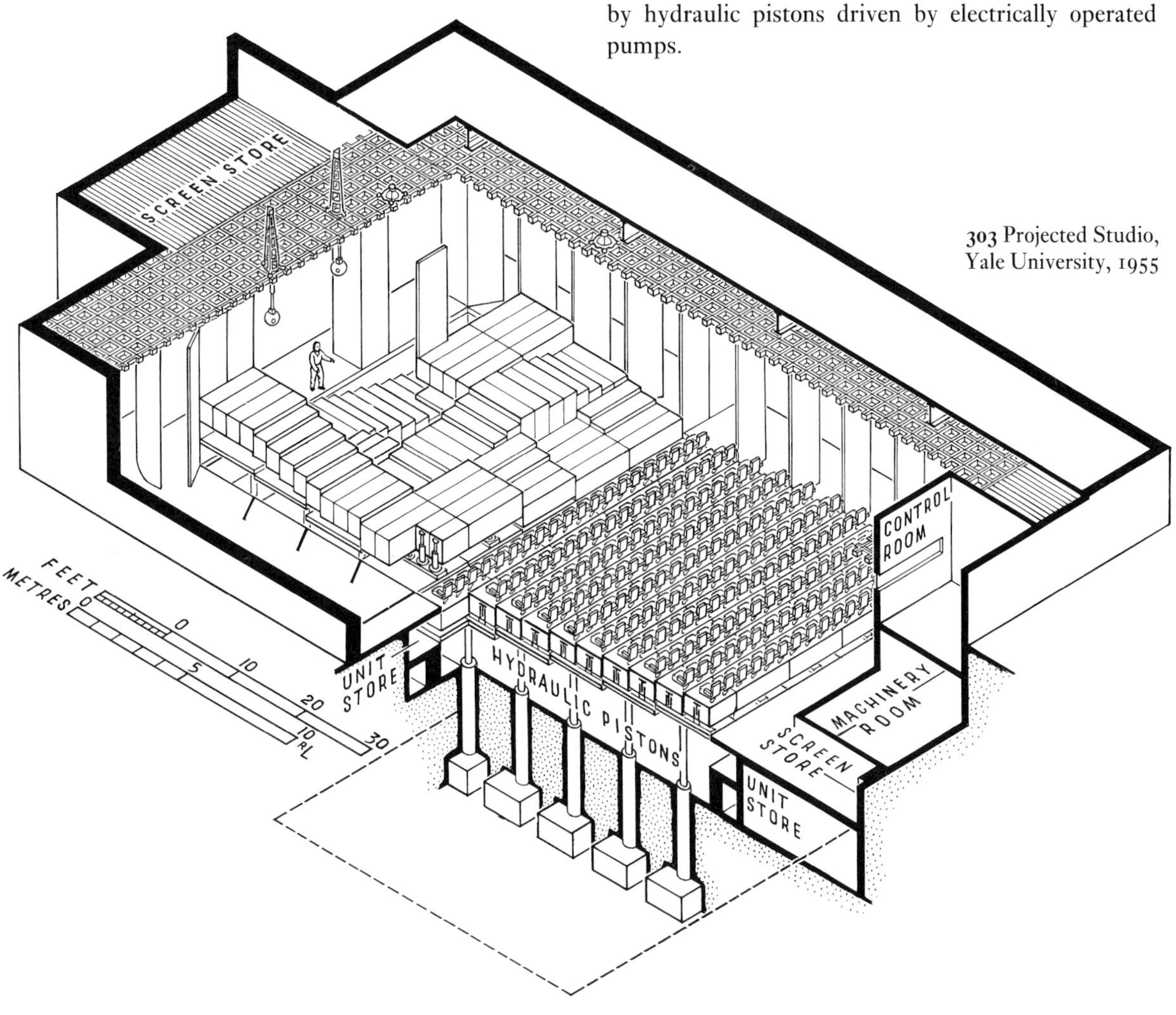
SCREEN STORE
CONTROL ROOM
FEET
METRES
0
0
5
10
20
10
30
UNIT STORE
HYDRAULIC PISTONS
MACHINERY ROOM
SCREEN STORE
UNIT STORE

303 Projected Studio, Yale University, 1955

The whole system was to be connected to an analogue computer, in turn linked to a one-inch scale model on which the operator could work out any combination of levels and units to provide the necessary acting levels and steps for seating. Any predetermined arrangement could be transferred to the floor, which could duplicate the model within five minutes. Each platform had two female sockets into which chairs could be inserted. As a result it was possible to produce a wide variety of stage-seating relationships which, together with the use of opaque and translucent screens, could create whatever environment was desired.

A simpler version of this highly mechanized system, incorporating the channel grid for scenery and lighting, but omitting the trapped floor, was installed in the experimental studio at the Loeb Drama Center. [286, 304] This try-out room was designed to have as little positive architectural character as possible. Walls, ceiling, and a gallery on three sides are all painted black to provide a neutral effect. Rostra and folding sections of stepped seats and free-standing units complete the furnishings, making possible many combinations of stage, seating, and screens. The environments created are modelled by light, shade, and colour.

Studio spaces have also been included in or added to a number of recent British theatres, including the Questors [305] and the Haymarket, Leicester. [306] A similar experimental room is included in the new theatre complex at Midland, Texas (1978). [323] An upper balcony and catwalks provide housing for and access to lighting equipment, permitting a variety of lighting angles and positions. The space is surrounded by black drapes in such a way that entrances may be provided to the enclosed space at any point.

304 Experimental theater, Loeb Drama Center (see fig. 286)

305 Studio Theatre, The Questors (see fig. 291)

306 Studio Theatre, The Haymarket, Leicester

31 Courtyard theatres

Reconstruction of the Fortune Theatre, University of Western Australia, Perth. Christ's Hospital Arts Centre, Horsham. The Georgian and tennis-court prototypes. The Cottesloe, National Theatre.

An open-air theatre in the University of Western Australia, Perth (1964), was designed as a reconstruction of the Shakespearian Fortune, with a rectangular stage viewed largely from three sides. [307] The Christ's Hospital Arts Centre at Horsham (1974) was designed to be used for drama teaching, school produc-

307 New Fortune Theatre, Perth, W. Australia, 1964

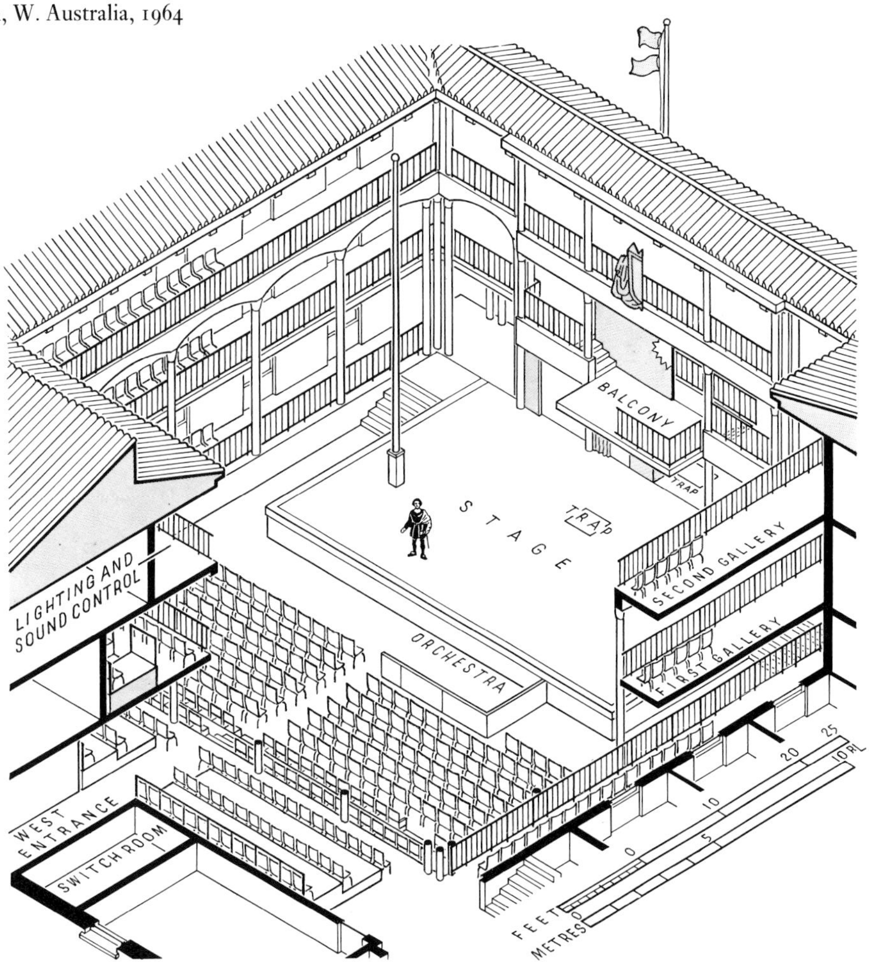
BALCONY
TRAP
STAGE
TRAP
SECOND GALLERY
FIRST GALLERY
LIGHTING AND SOUND CONTROL
ORCHESTRA
WEST ENTRANCE
SWITCH ROOM
FEET
METRES
0
5
10
20
25
0
5
10

Christ's Hospital Arts Centre, Horsham, 1974: **308**; **309**

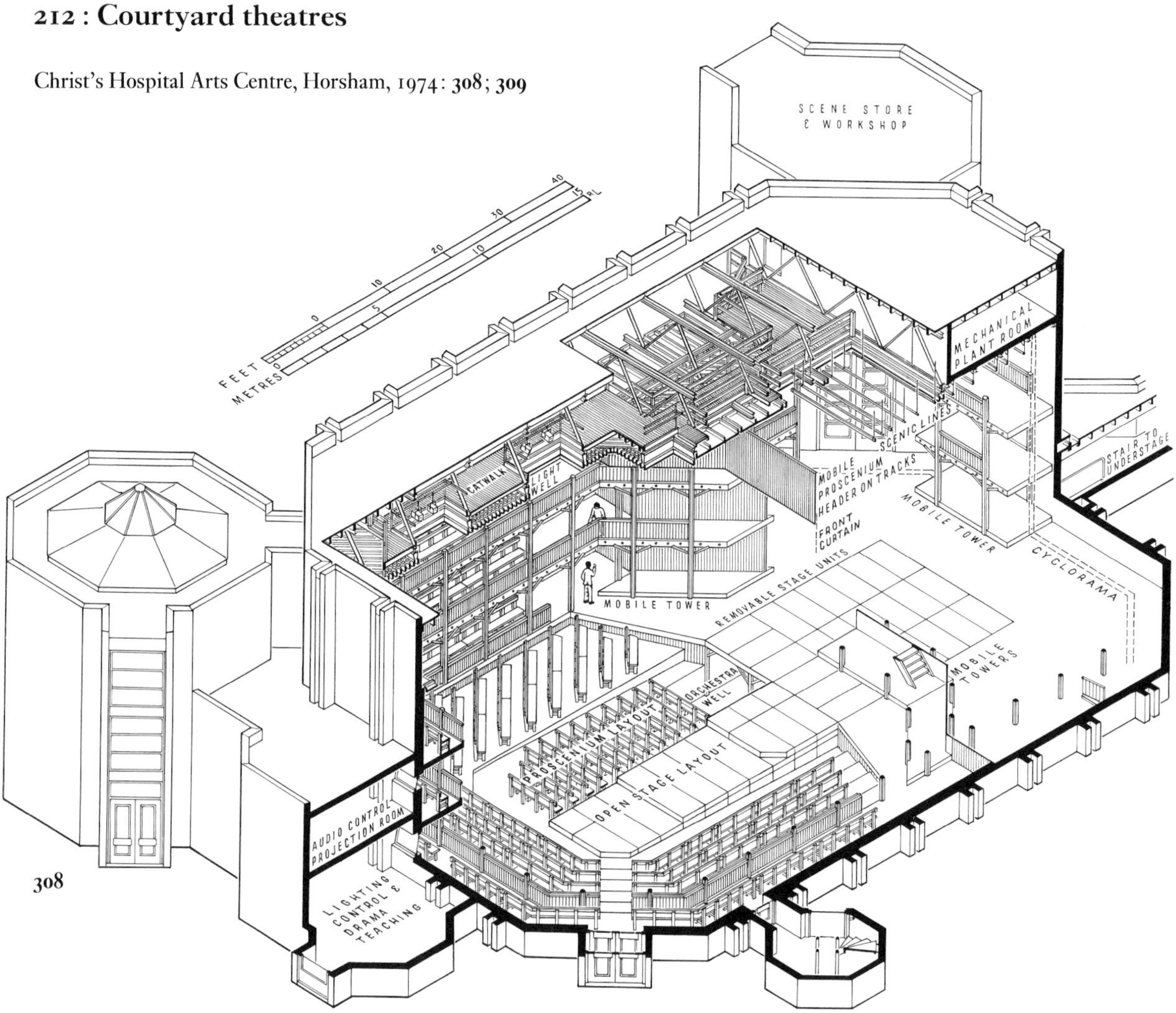
SCENE STORE
& WORKSHOP
MECHANICAL
PLANT ROOM
FEET
METRES
CATWALK
LIGHT
WELL
SCENIC LINES
MOBILE
PROSCENIUM
HEADER ON TRACKS
FRONT
CURTAIN
MOBILE TOWER
CYCLORAMA
STAIR TO
UNDERSTAGE
MOBILE TOWER
REMOVABLE STAGE UNITS
MOBILE
TOWERS
ORCHESTRA
WELL
PROSCENIUM LAYOUT
OPEN STAGE LAYOUT
AUDIO CONTROL
PROJECTION ROOM
LIGHTING
CONTROL &
DRAMA
TEACHING

308

309

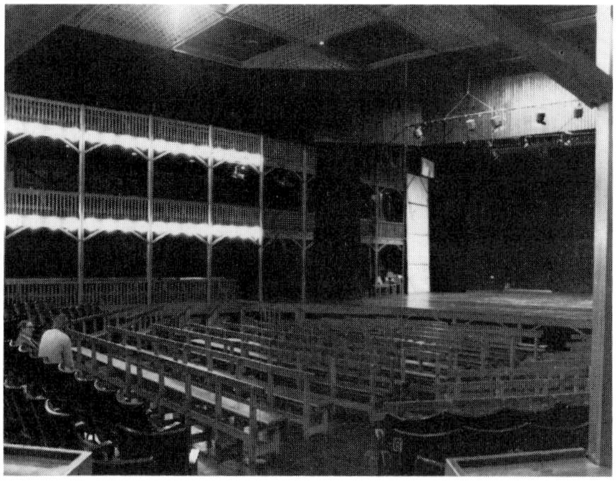

tions, visiting companies, concerts, and as a cinema. [308] But, like St. Mary's and many other educational theatres, it provides student experience only within predetermined forms. Here these consist of an open-end stage made up of modular (but heavy) sections, convertible to a picture stage by the use of a mobile proscenium unit [309] equipped with curtain tracks. Basic scene flying is provided above the end-stage area.

The auditorium is enclosed on three sides by two permanent galleries, each with a single row of seats, and the enclosure may be completed on the fourth side by four mobile towers, but these, being heavy and difficult to move, are seldom used. They can be put to scenic use on the end and picture stages, but when not required they occupy most of the available storage space. The main auditorium seating, on stepped rostra, can be rearranged to suit the various theatre forms, which include a thrust stage. A grid of open and closed squares forms the ceiling, and permits the fixing and adjustment of lighting units for use with all forms of staging.

The Cottesloe unit of the National Theatre (1977) has a similar courtyard pattern with three tiers of galleries on three sides, a fourth side being contemplated. The theatre [310] may be adapted in a number of ways: as an end stage with the main section of the seating filling the pit, or with the front row at stage level rising at the rear to first floor level. [311, 312]

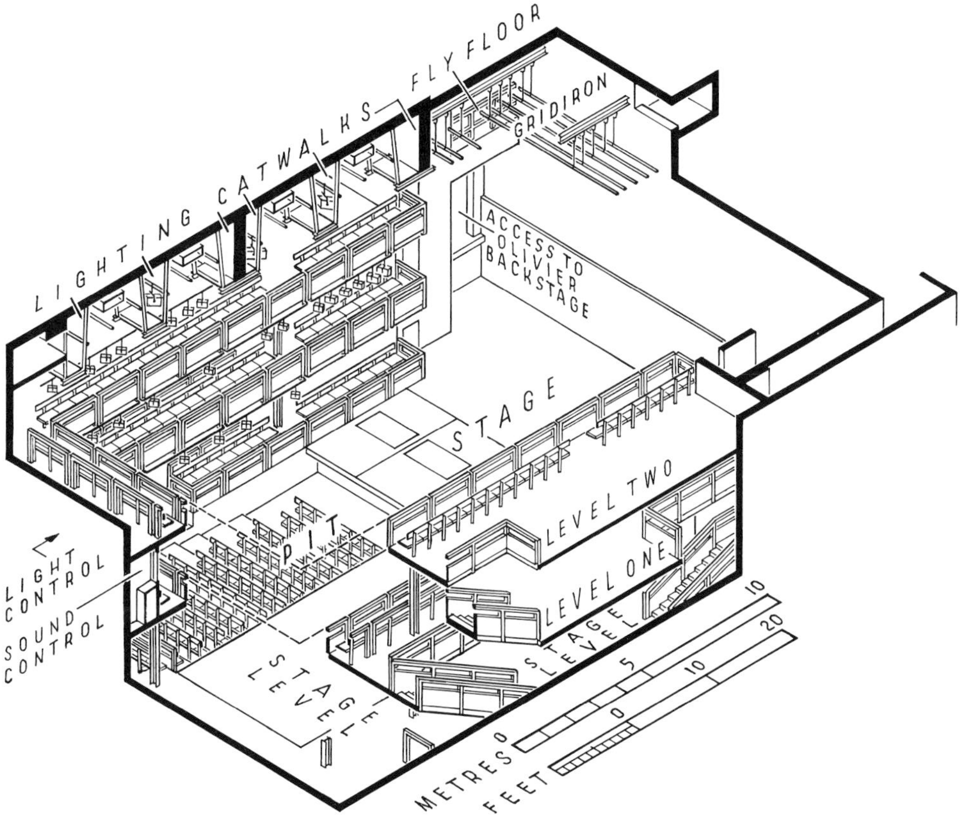
FLY FLOOR
LIGHTING CATWALKS
GRIDIRON
ACCESS TO OLIVIER BACKSTAGE
STAGE
LEVEL TWO
PIT
LEVEL ONE
LIGHT CONTROL
SOUND CONTROL
STAGE LEVEL
STAGE LEVEL
METRES 0 5 10
FEET 0 10 20

310

311

The Cottesloe, National Theatre, London, 1977
310
311

By moving seats to the end stage, a theatre in the round may be formed, which it was originally intended should be enclosed by the 'fourth wall' of galleries. The open pit can be floored over level with the stage providing a continuous acting area, devoid of seats, where actors and audience may mingle in the medieval manner, the latter moving around or sitting on the floor as occasion demands.

These 'courtyard' theatres are based on a return to the principles expressed by such Georgian playhouses as that at Richmond [140]. But these were still expressing the problems inherent in the original tennis-court theatres [114], which, as we know from Pepys, were far from satisfactory for many of their audience. Exponents of the courtyard arrangement claim that it offers new theatrical experiences, but it should be possible to achieve these without returning to the problems which existed in the tennis-court and Georgian prototypes. Side galleries are not well suited to the use of end stages, even when these are no longer fitted with perspective scenes.

312 The Cottesloe with end stage

32 The open picture stage

The Kalita Humphreys Theater, Dallas. Integration of stage and auditorium. Restrictions imposed by positive architectural forms. The Haymarket, Leicester. Fire curtains and audience participation. The Olivier, National Theatre. Sight-lines and wide stages. Flying systems.

Given that a combination of thrust stage and scenic stage makes for difficulties in seating an audience, if all are fully to appreciate both the capabilities of the actors and the visual characteristics of the scenery, then perhaps it becomes necessary to rearrange the scenic stage itself.

The Kalita Humphreys Theater in Dallas, Texas (1959), is one theatre in which this has been attempted. [313] It is a comparatively small theatre, originally seating 404 on a single stepped floor, with an additional 40 seats in a lighting gallery. The wedge-shaped rows of seats enclose a 40 feet (12.19m) diameter circular

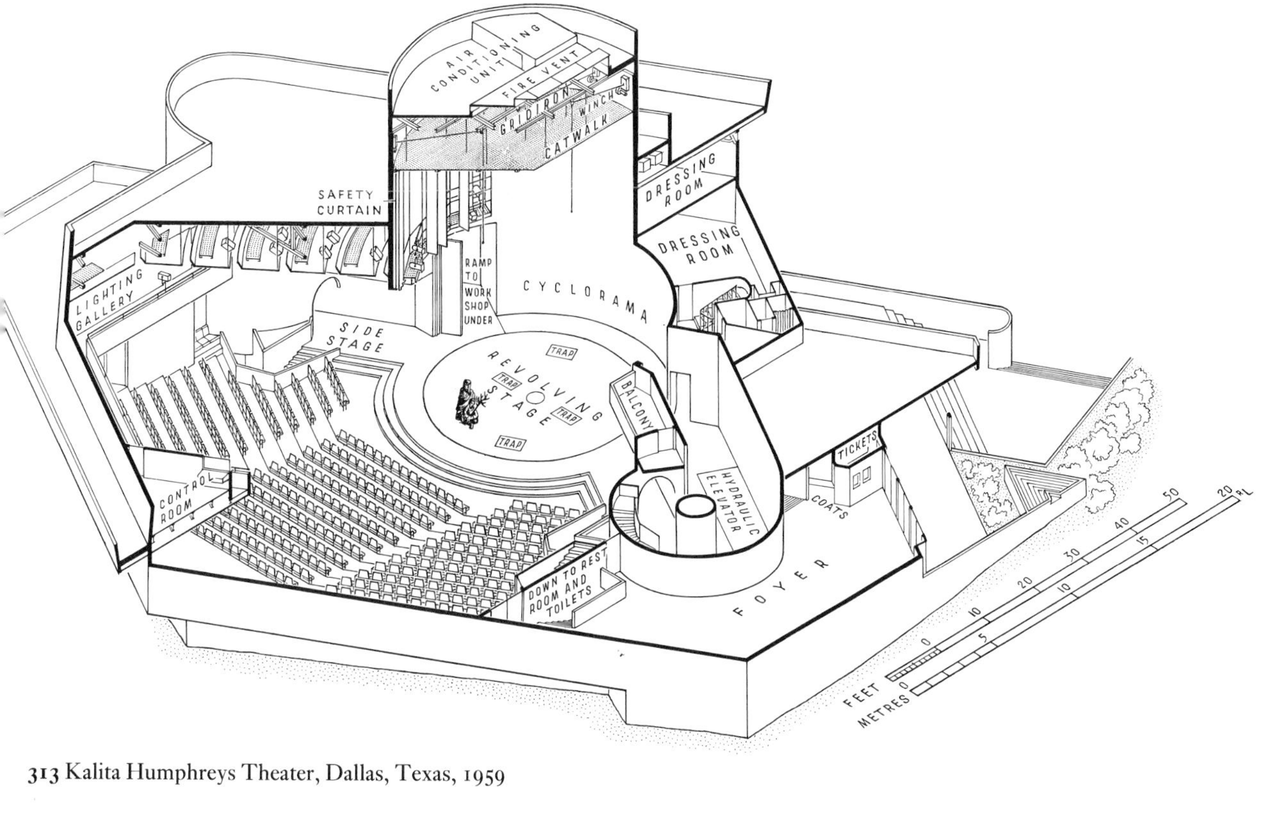
AIR CONDITIONING UNIT
FIRE VENT
GRIDIRON
WINCH
CATWALK
SAFETY CURTAIN
DRESSING ROOM
DRESSING ROOM
LIGHTING GALLERY
RAMP TO WORK SHOP UNDER
CYCLORAMA
SIDE STAGE
TRAP
REVOLVING STAGE
TRAP
TRAP
TRAP
BALCONY
TICKETS
CONTROL ROOM
HYDRAULIC ELEVATOR
COATS
DOWN TO REST ROOM AND TOILETS
FOYER
FEET
METRES
0
10
20
30
40
50
0
5
10
15
20

313 Kalita Humphreys Theater, Dallas, Texas, 1959

314 Kalita Humphreys Theater

stage incorporating a revolve, and raised no more than 15 inches (0.38m) above the lowest level of the auditorium floor, to which it can be connected by steps. [314] A total width of 70 feet (21.34m) is achieved by the addition of side stages, with balconies over, partly enclosing the outer ends of the front seating.

There is no proscenium, the side walls of the auditorium continuing as the rear wall or cyclorama of the circular stage – an arrangement which gives a satisfactory impression of unity between stage and auditorium. The nearest seats are some 3 feet (0.91m) from the stage, so that all the audience may look down on a stage which appears to be an extension of the auditorium floor.

Owing to the permanent nature of the cyclorama, the only points at which concealed entry can be made are from behind the side walls, or through archways at the ends of the side stages. However, additional scenic entrances can be built as required, though concealing elements must connect these to the side walls. It could be argued that a proper use of light and dark, as suggested by Bragdon (p. 145), would eliminate the need for these, since the actor should be able to approach a stage area in darkness, to be revealed in a controlled area of light. The auditorium had, however, been painted in light tones to create a unity of space, and the high degree of light reflection in spill from the ceiling lighting louvres and from the stage itself made such precise lighting control impossible.

Above the stage is a concrete drum forming a fly tower, the rear portion of which, carried down to stage level, acts as the cyclorama. At the front, its lower edge forms a kind of 'proscenium' opening, 18 feet (5.49m) above stage level, housing front and fire curtains. These latter make a full use of scenery possible, but side access for scenic items is difficult, as the normal stage wings are replaced by a ramp and a hoist, leading to a basement scene store with very little headroom.

On this circular stage, a normal counterweight flying system would have been difficult to install, and to overcome this problem George Izenour first introduced his electric winches, similar to those at the Loeb Drama Center. Unfortunately, the normal use of a proscenium frame for concealing the flown scenery is here negated by the forward sweep of the drum, so that even from the rear seats the scenic items are revealed. In the first season alone the scene designers found the dominant architectural shape of the circular stage and drum too emphatic, and restricting on the designs that could be placed within it.

The Haymarket Theatre, Leicester
315 (*left*)
316 (*below*)

Both here and at the Haymarket, Leicester (1973), [315] which owed much to Dallas for its design, the provision of this 'concealing' feature was largely conditioned by the need to enclose the projecting stage within a fire curtain. A problem is, however, caused by the use of a fire curtain in this situation. In the normal picture-frame arrangement, the stage would be separated from the auditorium by an orchestra well, with the acting area usually well upstage of a tormentor, so that the likelihood of anyone being trapped beneath a suddenly descending fire curtain is minimal. Not so with these new arrangements, where the audience may even be encouraged to participate in some productions, and both actors and participating audience could be caught beneath a curtain whose main purpose is to descend rapidly in an emergency.

The Leicester Haymarket overcomes the problem of seating a larger audience of 703 by the introduction of a balcony with five rows of seats, the ends of which step down to link it to the stage. [316] The seats are harmoniously arranged in three facets reflecting the lines of the wedge-shaped stage, which projects some 20 feet (6.10m) into the auditorium. Like the Dallas theatre, the stage is connected to the auditorium floor by two broad steps, and there is a 'non-existent' proscenium opening some 42 feet (12.80m) wide, with side stages and balconies expanding the total stage width to some 70 feet (21.34m). Unlike Dallas, adequate wings for the storage of scenes are provided with direct access to a large paint room and workshop. Here, too, there are problems of masking related to the 'proscenium opening'.

The Olivier unit of the National Theatre (1976) is the largest of these combined pictorial-open stages, seating 1,160 in a similar manner to that at the Haymarket, Leicester, with 518 seats in the main balcony and 158 in two intermediate balconies linking the upper and lower blocks of seating. [317] Two small boxes, each seating five persons, flank either side of an approximately 58 feet (17.68m) wide 'non-existent' proscenium opening. Both stage and fly tower project some 30 feet (9.14m) into the auditorium in a similar three-sided pattern to the Haymarket, but here the seats are set out in concentric curves. A drum revolve constructed in two halves is intended to be used for raising pre-set scenes from the basement, additional scenery being run on from three rear stages when the separating fireproof shutters are raised. As in the Dallas theatre, access for actors has been found to be severely limited.

Unlike Benjamin Wyatt, who related the width of

317 The Olivier, National Theatre, London

his picture frame to the cost of filling the stage with actors and scenery, the great width of openings in many contemporary subsidized theatres takes little note of such problems, and in many cases architects are satisfied to provide good sight-lines for the full-width opening, forgetting that these will be far from perfect when more limited settings are used. The same problem arises when various portions of a full-width setting are used, which happen to be on one side of the stage out of sight of the audience on the opposing side.

At Leicester a counterweight flying system was installed, with a variant on the winch system of spot lines above the forestage. The Olivier Theatre has power-operated scenic hooks, which can be worked singly or in groups by a centrally controlled computer, and were designed to fly three-dimensional scenic items rather than cloths. A number of single spot lines are also provided, and these may be positioned anywhere on the 90-feet (27.43m) high grid.

As Kinsila predicted in 1917 (p. 148) the fly tower, originally introduced to permit cloths to be flown without creasing or rolling, has today become less relevant as storage space. Nevertheless the possibility of moving scenic items vertically above the stage must still be given consideration as one means of defining the vertical dimension of stage space, and where painted scenery is still considered essential to the traditional set – as for example, in opera and ballet – a degree of flying must still be catered for.

At the Barbican Theatre, lack of space at stage level has precluded the introduction of scene stores, but hopefully the problem has been remedied by the inclusion of a double-height fly tower with a gridiron some 110 feet (33.53m) above the stage.

It will be appreciated that what at first glance appear to be open stages are in reality picture stages drawn forward into the auditorium, and as a result the concealing purpose of the 'picture frame' is defeated – suggesting that, if a fly tower is considered necessary, the frame should be provided in a normal relationship with the auditorium, when it can operate in a properly concealing manner.

Today, however, with the acceptance that scenic and lighting units may be hung in full view of an audience and be taken for granted, there might seem to be little purpose in providing this 'unit of concealment' – although, such are the arbitrary fashions of the theatre world, this present revealing habit may well give way once again to a fancy for concealment.

33 The single-chamber theatre

The amateur theatre in the United States. Midland, Texas. Multi-purpose uses of single-chamber theatres. Projected backgrounds as an integrated architectural feature. Western Springs, Illinois. Intimate relationship of audience and three-dimensional actors in a scenic setting.

In the first decades of the century it was the amateur theatre, inspired by the Munich Künstler theatre, which, through its own 'little' and civic theatres, became notable for experimental presentations of drama. It is perhaps no coincidence that it is again the amateur theatre in the United States which has, in recent years, contributed new ideas in theatre architecture.

Unlike the examples discussed above, a number of theatres have been built in which the omission of a fly tower has resulted in the development of a scenic open stage. An early example, from 1957, was the Midland Community Theater, Texas, [318] which had its stage and seating for 400 arranged in the same space with no proscenium or picture-frame separation. The stage

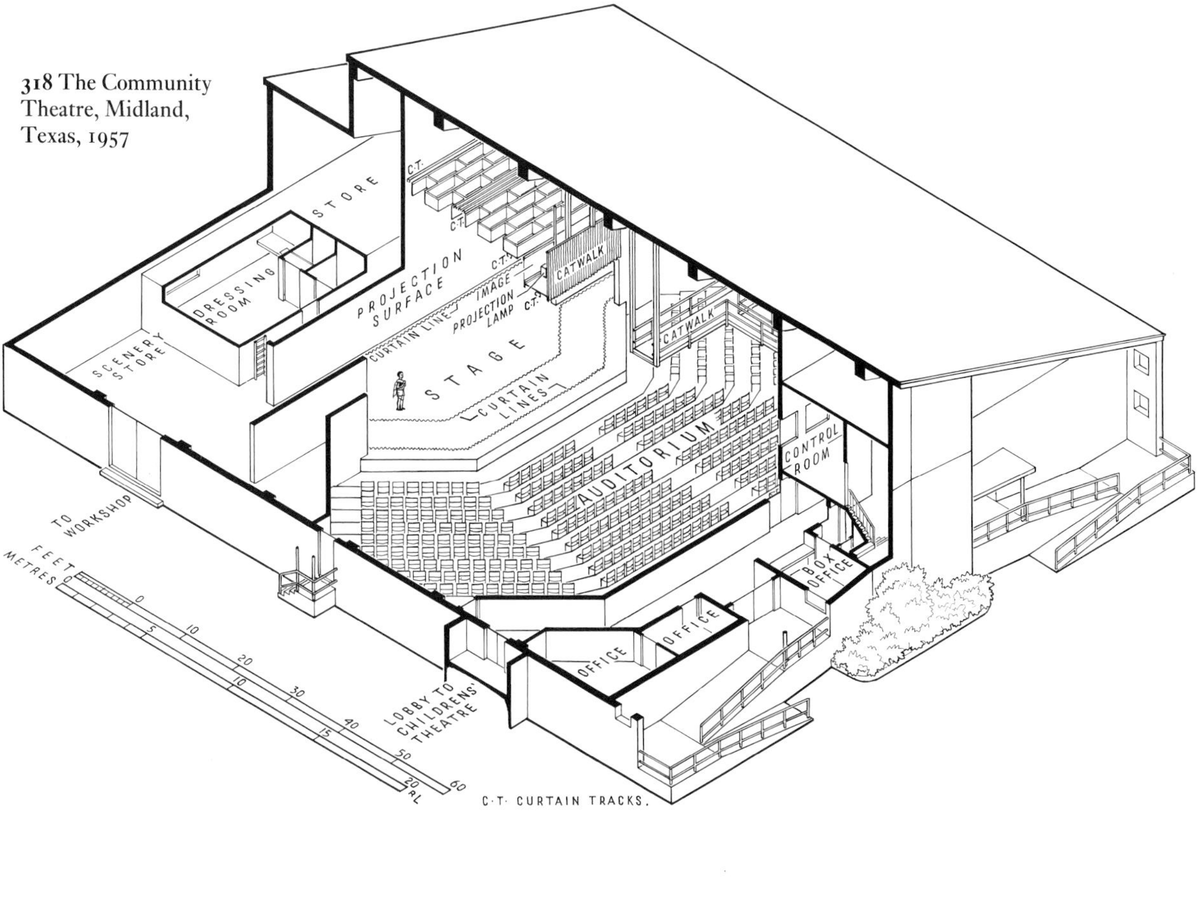
STORE
DRESSING ROOM
SCENERY STORE
PROJECTION SURFACE
C.T.
IMAGE
PROJECTION LAMP
CATWALK
CURTAIN LINE
STAGE
CURTAIN LINES
AUDITORIUM
CONTROL ROOM
BOX OFFICE
OFFICE
OFFICE
LOBBY TO CHILDRENS' THEATRE
TO WORKSHOP
FEET
METRES
0
10
20
30
40
50
60
5
15
C·T· CURTAIN TRACKS.

318 The Community Theatre, Midland, Texas, 1957

was enclosed by the side walls of the auditorium, which angled-in to form a 'non-existent' opening. [319] There was no actual ceiling to the auditorium, apart from the roof over the whole building, painted black on its underside. [320]

Two lighting catwalks spanned the auditorium, one of which followed the line of the trapeze-shaped stage front, and, in providing support for the front curtain, might be said to act as a 'proscenium' top, if it were not for the fact that, being painted black like the roof above, it played little part in the stage picture. Because there was no false ceiling, and consequently no lighting

319

Midland Community Theatre: 319; 320

320

louvres, there was no light spill or reflection.

The overall width of the stage was 48 feet (14.63m), reduced by a pair of brick wings 18 feet (5.49m) upstage to 36 feet (10.97m). The stage was backed by a plastered wall acting as a screen for projected backgrounds, and was ceiled with an open grid some 22 feet (6.71m) above stage level, which served both as a masking element and for supporting lighting units.

Spot lines for individual pieces of scenery could be dropped in, but the need for flying scenery on a large scale was dispensed with as no backcloths or drops were used, their place being taken by backgrounds projected from the stage catwalk, [321] and by the use of plain or painted curtains running on a series of curtain tracks

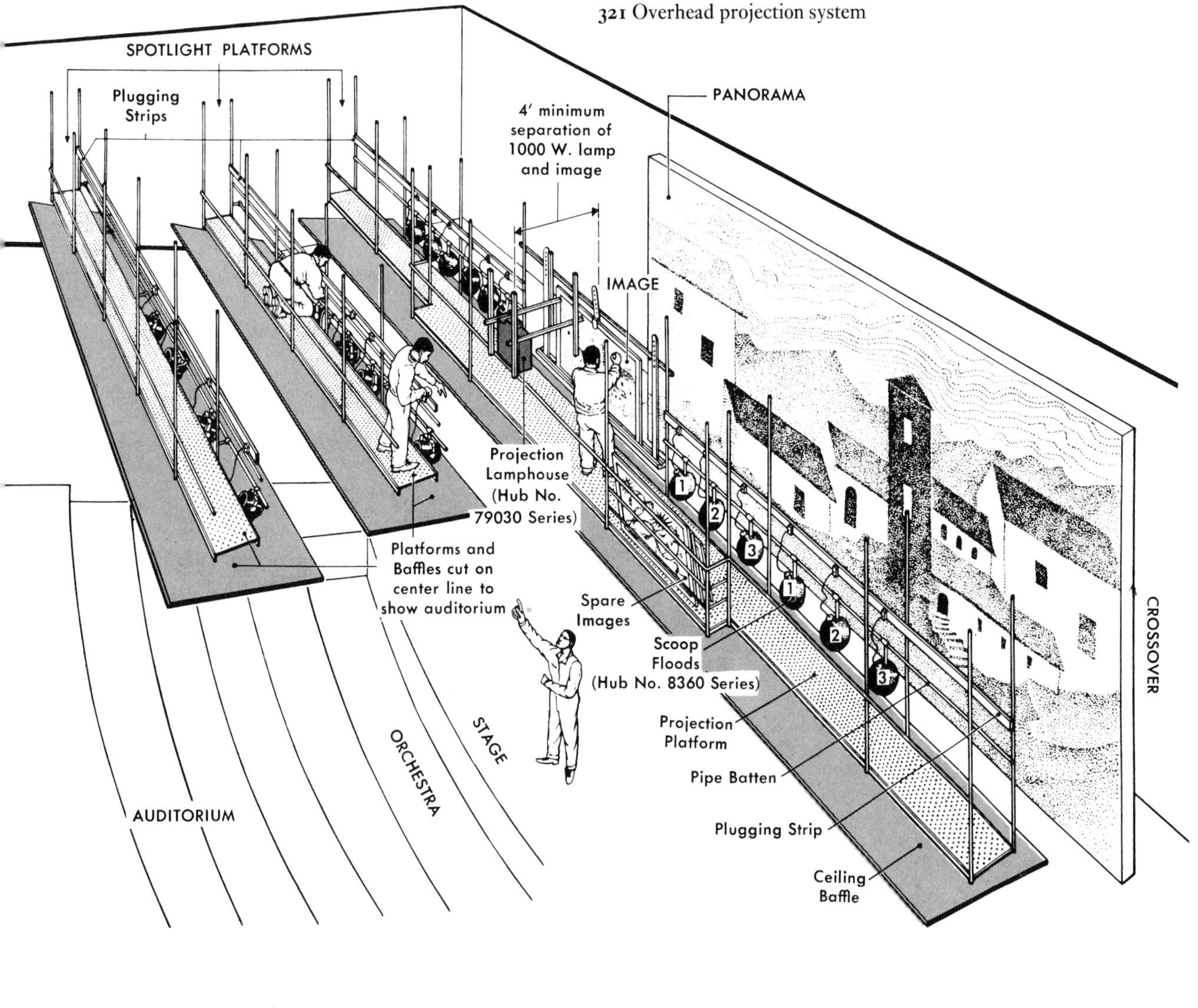
SPOTLIGHT PLATFORMS
Plugging Strips
4' minimum separation of 1000 W. lamp and image
PANORAMA
IMAGE
Projection Lamphouse (Hub No. 79030 Series)
Platforms and Baffles cut on center line to show auditorium
Spare Images
Scoop Floods (Hub No. 8360 Series)
Projection Platform
Pipe Batten
Plugging Strip
Ceiling Baffle
CROSSOVER
STAGE
ORCHESTRA
AUDITORIUM

321 Overhead projection system

BILLIS
BATH CLUB

322 Midland Community Theatre, Setting for *South Pacific*

spanning the stage. [322] Adequate wing space enabled built-up scenic units to be stored and run on stage on wagons.

For musical shows that normally need a large cast, and a correspondingly large area, the whole width of the stage was used, but more intimate settings were related to the inner wings. This single-chamber theatre was equally useful for lectures or trade demonstrations. The furthest seats were some 44 feet (13.41m) from the stage, and all the audience could look down on the stage floor, which was considered to be an important visual element: so it was raised no more than 2 feet (0.61m), and was kept as dark as possible to reduce light-bounce affecting the projected backgrounds.

In 1978 this theatre was replaced by a new building [323] seating 515 in concentric curves enclosing a projecting stage. The rearmost seat is now only 38 feet (11.58m) from the stage, but here the catwalks are hidden behind panels. The same use is made of projected scenery, and scene wagons may be run on from the side stages on two tracks set in the stage floor. Better facilities are now provided for the audience, together with a large scene shop, extending the full width of the stage and connected to it at either end through sound locks, so that it can be used during performances.

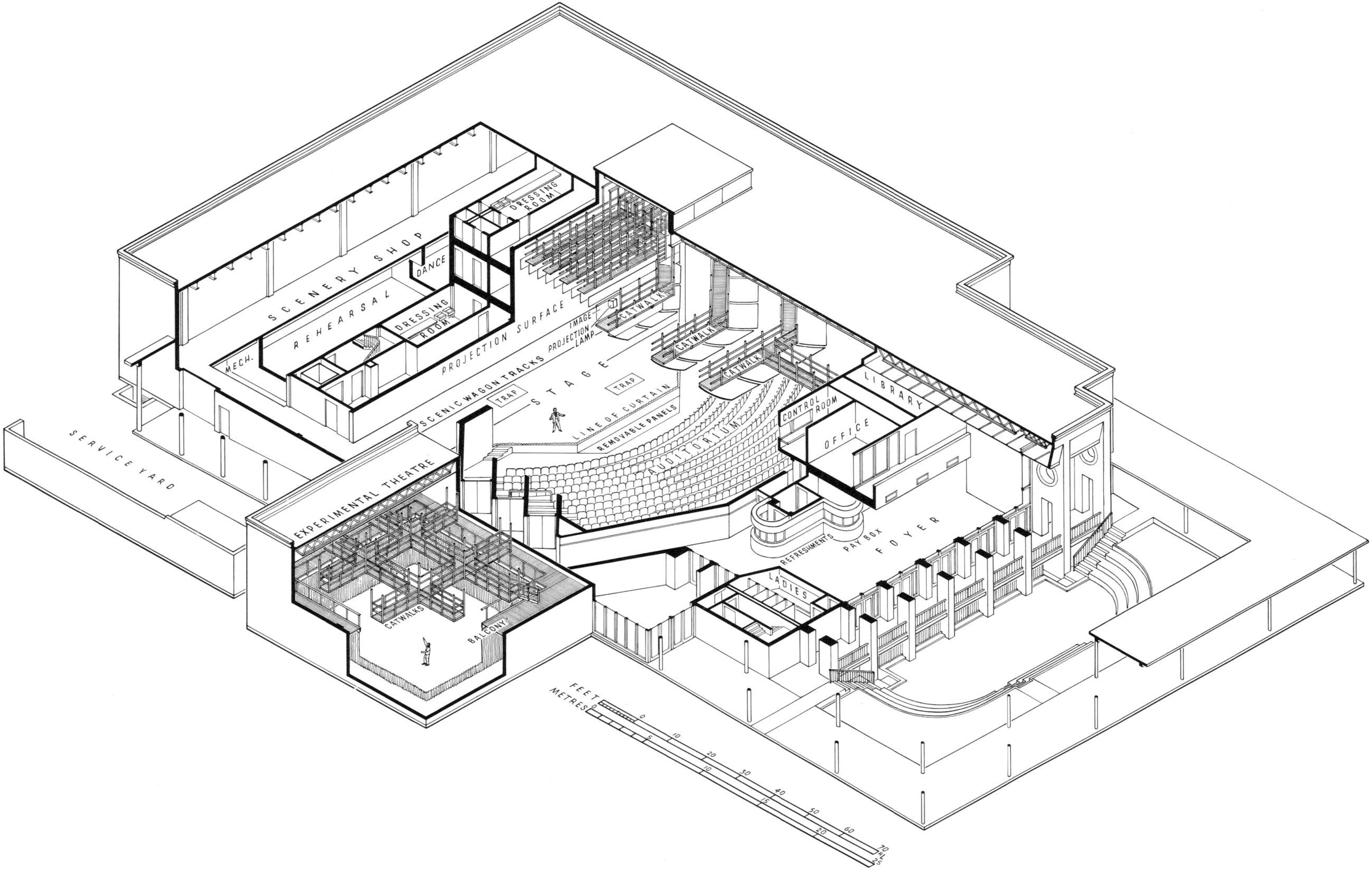
SCENERY SHOP
DRESSING ROOM
DANCE
REHEARSAL
DRESSING ROOM
MECH.
PROJECTION SURFACE
IMAGE
PROJECTION LAMP
CATWALK
CATWALK
CATWALK
SCENIC WAGON TRACKS
STAGE
TRAP
TRAP
LINE OF CURTAIN
REMOVABLE PANELS
AUDITORIUM
CONTROL ROOM
LIBRARY
OFFICE
REFRESHMENTS
PAY BOX
FOYER
LADIES
EXPERIMENTAL THEATRE
CATWALKS
BALCONY
SERVICE YARD
FEET
METRES
0
10
20
30
40
50
60
70
0
5
10
15
20
25

323 New Community Theatre, Midland, Texas, 1978

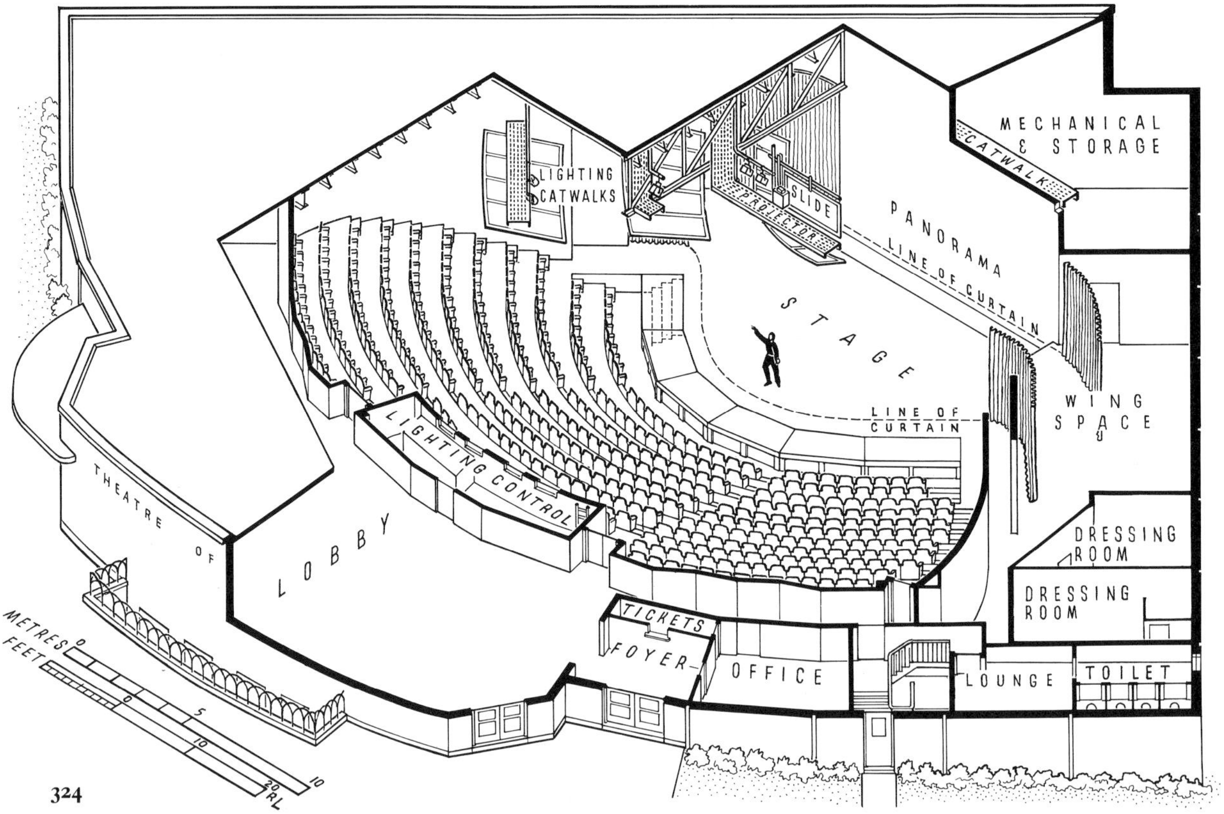
MECHANICAL & STORAGE
CATWALK
LIGHTING CATWALKS
SLIDE
PROJECTOR
PANORAMA
LINE OF CURTAIN
STAGE
LINE OF CURTAIN
WING SPACE
LIGHTING CONTROL
THEATRE OF
LOBBY
DRESSING ROOM
DRESSING ROOM
TICKETS
FOYER
OFFICE
LOUNGE
TOILET
METRES 0 5 10
FEET 0 10 20
RL

324

325

Reminiscent of Norman Bel Geddes's 'Theatre Number 6', [215] at least in plan, the Theatre at Western Springs, Illinois (1961), was designed diagonally across a square, with a 52-feet (15.85m) wide stage. [324] This curves forward to be enclosed by eleven concentric rows of seating, the furthest seat being no more than 28 feet (8.53m) from the stage.

Once again the stage is backed by a plastered wall for projected backgrounds, achieved by direct projections of light and shadow, superimposed on colour washes from floodlights. [325, 326] Since these backgrounds may be easily changed during the progress of the performance, the need for individual, expensive backcloths is eliminated – together with the need for a fly tower, both savings being particularly relevant to amateur and small community projects.

The planes of the auditorium ceiling continue above the stage with a clear height of 15 feet (4.57m). These mask catwalks spanning both auditorium and stage, and provide access to (and support for) the lighting units and scenic projector. The stage is 2 feet (0.61m) high, and the seats are raked steeply so that the dimensions of the stage floor may be appreciated by the audience of 417. Unlike the end stages in the Redoutensaal or the Mermaid theatres, the actor advancing to the front of these stages may be fully appreciated 'in the round' by his enclosing audience, without the necessity of placing him on a thrust stage.

Here, then, we have a theatre where the actor may retain his directional command of his audience with the intimate relationship that Garrick had in Old Drury. At the same time we have a stage that permits the use of settings that all may see, together with a range of production patterns which may vary as often as the scene presented.

RL

326

Community Theatre, Western Springs, Illinois, 1961:
324; 325; 326

Conclusions

The earliest form of Greek theatre had a directional relationship between the audience on their timber benches and the actors on their rectangular or trapeze-shaped *orchestras*. This relationship was only strengthened by the introduction of entrance doorways beyond the orchestra, which then became an integral part of the dramatic form. It was the development of the geometrically-perfect circular *orchestra* which created the standard Greek *cavea*, with its focus on the *orchestra* at just the time that the actors had moved back to their raised *logeion*.

This movement of the actors made the new theatre form out of date by the time it was built – in a similar manner to that in which the Theatre Royal, Leicester, continued to reflect the Georgian and Restoration theatres, with their side circles and slips. These may well have been suitable when the actor was on his proscenium stage within the auditorium, but not by the time this theatre was built, when the actor was being pushed, protesting, behind the picture-frame, so creating a stage for which it was almost impossible to design settings that all the audience could see.

It has been suggested that the Georgian theatres were a poor precedent for the courtyard theatre – equally, that the Greek theatre was a poor precedent for the modern thrust stage, as used by Reinhardt and others. The modern return to this thrust stage owes much to the suggestion – now open to question (p. 178) – that an actor should once again be placed in the midst of his audience for maximum dramatic command, the example cited at the 'Conference on the Architecture of New Theatres' held in York in 1960 being the Shakespearian theatre as exemplified by de Witt's Swan, whose form derived more from the arrangement of an audience set to view three-dimensional bull- and bear-baiting than from its theatrical relationship of actor to audience.

This suggestion, however, placed the emphasis solely on the relationship of the actor to his audience, and completely ignored the limited production patterns inherent in movement to, across, and from such a stage. It would seem that even the Elizabethans found the thrust stage of the Swan inhibiting, and we have suggested that in their later theatres they made provision for the greater flexibility offered by the directional end stage of the second Globe.

The late nineteenth century moves for a return to open-staging were made with the main object of presenting Shakespeare's plays in a Shakespearian setting, and to this end the one known visual example – the Swan – was a legitimate model. But this purpose has long since been lost sight of, and the thrust stage is now built for the presentation of modern productions which call for much more than the mere placing of an actor in the midst of his audience. It is interesting to note that the Stratford Theatre, Ontario recreated the same problem that had bedevilled the Greeks, when they gave over the outermost *kerkides* to strangers, latecomers, and women.

If we are to learn from past experience, we should note that the Greeks started with a directional bias for their basic actor-audience relationship, an approach which was maintained in such theatres as those of Argos and Pergamon. The Elizabethans moved from the thrust stage of the Swan to the end stage of the second Globe, and Sir Christopher Wren, faced with the problems of combining both open stage and scenic illusion, chose a predominantly directional arrangement for his seating in Drury Lane. Even without scenery, the end stage has the advantage of offering direct address by an actor to the whole audience. but with scenery it is the only open-stage pattern that does not create problems of blocked sight-lines caused by scenic units and actors alike.

It may now be beginning to be appreciated that a *stage* is not simply a platform set before or in the midst of an audience, but is in fact a three-dimensional volume which not only includes offstage areas of assembly for actors and scenery, but also requires adequate entrances for actors, arranged to permit the maximum range of production patterns, separate entrances for the audience, and a galaxy of lighting units, each positioned at an ideal distance from (and at an ideal angle to) the actors on the stage.

Starting from such an 'abstract' spatial concept of the full use of a stage, the architect may incorporate such lighting masks, acoustic reflectors, and similar essential features of the enclosing environment of actor and audience, in order that they too form part of the stage machine: from such a fundamental, non-preconceived approach will stem new solutions to theatre design.

Whatever the form of future theatres – with audiences set before or around the actors; with actors above or below their audiences on raised or sunken stages; with audiences seated on a single slope of seating, with directional balconies, or in surrounding Elizabethan-type galleries – the most important element is the drama itself, and this may well be most satisfactorily conveyed under the simplest of conditions. [327] If scenic illusion is to be added, then the best settings are not always those which rely on the most elaborate and expensive machinery, since this all too often limits and inhibits the designer's concepts. Biggest and most expensive is not necessarily best.

327 *Oliver Twist* at the 'George Inn', Southwark, London, 1944

Notes to the Illustrations

1. *Frontispiece*: Delos, Greece. *Orchestra*, water channel, and *prohedria* benches.
2. Buffalo dance by Okippe Indians, after a painting in the University of California.
3. Threshing floor near Bassae, Greece. Original theories regarding early circular orchestras were based on the shape of such threshing floors.
4. Theatral, area, Palace of Gournia, Crete, *c*.1650 BC.
5. Theatral area, Palace of Knossos, Crete, *c*.1600–1400 BC.
6. Lato, Crete. Reconstruction of the eighth–seventh century BC theatral area in the *agora*.
7. Lato. General view of *agora* and temple of Artemis.
8. Lato. Detail of eastern section of steps.
9. Spectators on stand, after a vase painting by Sophilus, *c*.580–70 BC.
10. Steps on the processional way, Eleusis, Greece. A late example, dating from the end of the fourth or early third centuries BC, of a trapezoidal arrangement of stone steps may be seen in the *agora* at Morgantina, Sicily. (AJA, LXI, pl. 53. LXII, pl. 35).
11. Theatral area in the Sanctuary of Dionysus, Ikaria, *c*.mid-fifth century BC.
12. Rhamnous, Greece. View of rectangular *cavea* from the *orchestra*, Remains of stone *prohedria* thrones, dated by Bulle to the fourth century BC (right foreground), and *stelai* bases (centre front).
13. Thorikos, Greece. a) late sixth century BC theatre with timber benches. b) fifth century BC reconstruction in stone with enlarged *orchestra*. c) fourth century BC extension of *cavea*.
14. Thorikos. *Orchestra* and 'dressing rooms' from west.
15. Thorikos. *Orchestra*, temple base, and *cavea* from east.
16. Chaeronea, Greece. Elliptical rock-cut seats.
17. Greek dancers at Delphi.
18. Theatre of Dionysus, Athens, phase I. The stones at A and B are the extant remains of the first retaining wall (see fig. 21). The natural rock outcrop, possibly used as an early scenic device, may be seen at the bottom left of the *orchestra*. Most earlier reconstructions of this theatre have been bedevilled by the insistence on the inclusion of a circular *orchestra*, with the extant stones fitting the perimeter. These attempts have created their own problems, which do not exist when a more natural evolution is accepted.
19. Reconstruction of the late fifth century BC theatre at Corinth (after P. Arnott, *Greek Scenic Conventions*).
20. Temporary stage for *phlyax* comedy.
21. Theatre of Dionysus, Athens: the straight retaining wall with post grooves. In front may be seen the extant stones of the earlier wall (A on fig. 18).
22. Pergamon, Asia Minor. Stone sockets for timber posts.
23. Theatre of Dionysus, Athens, phase II. Temporary timber scenic structures in front of straight retaining wall. The central *prohedria* benches are shown with stone seats on vertical stone risers, while the outer benches are shown with timber seats on stone risers, the latter being marked with subdivisions on their upper faces. The remainder of the seating is shown as timber benches with vertical boards to hold back the earth, which the audience may have kicked with their heels to show their displeasure, as described by Pollux.
24. Early theatre at Oropus, Greece (after P. Arnott). The reconstruction shows the stone steps (fig. 43) which are presumed to have replaced earlier timber benches. A similar, but much later, arrangement of trapezoidal steps may be seen below the semicircular seats of the later third century BC theatre at Morgantina, Sicily. These steps relate to a pressed earth orchestra of *c*.325 BC. (AJA, LXIV, pl. 91, fig. 3).
25. Oropus. *Skene* with *breccia* wall, left and post holes beneath later wall, right: 2,3,4,5,6.
26. Orestes and Iphigenia in Tauris, after a Campanian vase painting.
27. Timber *skene* on vase painting from Tarentum.
28. Theatre of Dionysus, Athens, phase III, including *stoa*, and temporary *paraskenia* setting based on the vase paintings.
29. Eretria, Greece. Late fifth century BC timber and mud-brick *skene*, and *cavea* built of timber scaffolding on the flat site.
30. Theatre of Dionysus, Athens. General view of *cavea* to Acropolis.
31. Theatre of Dionysus, Athens. *Prohedria* thrones and

central throne for the priest of Dionysus; probably dating from the second or first centuries, but thought to copy the fourth century BC originals.

32. Eretria. The Hellenistic theatre, with stone *proskenion* and *episkenion*. The *cavea* seating is shown as stone blocks resting on the earth without the usual footrests. *Prohedriai* have not been included as there is no evidence as to their number and position. Fragments of thrones were found, which may have been sited in the *orchestra* as at Oropus (fig. 43). It is likely that there were portals leading to the *parodoi*, as at Epidaurus (fig. 39), but these have been omitted as there is insufficient evidence for their accurate reconstruction. Two stone recesses on either side of the *episkenion* have been interpreted as bases for *periaktoi*.
33. Eretria. View of the *skene* from the east.
34. Eretria. The *orchestra* with exit from Charon's tunnel.
35. Epidaurus, Greece. Production in 1954 of the *Hippolytus* of Euripides, with early-style *skene*. (Water colour by Richard Leacroft.)
36. *Cavea* ends: a) Megalopolis; b) Athens; c) Epidaurus.
37. Megalopolis, Greece. *Prohedria* benches and *cavea* end.
38. Epidaurus. *Cavea* end.
39. Epidaurus. Restored outer *kerkides* and portals. (Photo: Robert Leacroft.)
40. Argos, Greece. The fan-shaped *cavea*.
41. Pergamon. The fan-shaped *cavea*. Note post holes (fig. 22) to extreme right.
42. Typical theatre of the early Hellenistic period.
43. Oropus. General view from west of polygonal stone *cavea*, the restored *proskenion* of *c*.200 BC, and thrones in the *orchestra*.
44. Oropus. *Proskenion* and western *parodos*.
45. A late Hellenistic theatre, similar to Epidaurus, with painted scenery in the *thyromata* and between the columns of the *proskenion*. Vestigial *paraskenia* form slightly projecting ends to the *proskenion*. (From Leacroft, *The Buildings of Ancient Greece*).
46. Sikyon, Greece. Rock-cut ramp to *logeion*.
47. Priene, Asia Minor. Late Hellenistic theatre. Compare the stone seating with that shown at Eretria (fig. 32): here the seating slabs are supported on stone 'posts' in the manner of timber benches, and stone footrests are supported on stone risers which hold back the earth.
48. Priene. General view from north.
49. Priene. *Logeion* with stone supports for timber flooring.
50. Priene. *Proskenion*: note holes for wedges holding *pinakes* behind the half-columns.
51. Priene. *Prohedria* benches and thrones, with central altar to right, and later *prohedria* bench four rows directly above. Note stone 'posts' to general seating.
52. The Greek theatre according to Vitruvius.
53. Eretria. Charon's tunnel: view to centre of *orchestra*.
54. Theatre of Dionysus, Athens, showing the paved Roman *orchestra*, protective wall, and the sculptured Bema of Phaedrus or front to the low Roman stage. Beyond are the remains of the Lycurgan *proskenion* and *paraskenia*, and, further, the straight retaining wall.
55. Delphi, Greece. Paved Roman *orchestra* and protective wall.
56. Perge, Asia Minor. Protective balustrade.
57. Miletus, Asia Minor. Removal of front seats to create 'sunken *orchestra*'.
58. Theatre of Pompey, Rome, 55 BC. Model in the Museo Civilta Romana.
59. Theatre of Marcellus, Rome, 13–11 BC. Conjectural reconstruction.
60. Aspendos, Asia Minor. Vaulted passage leading to vomitoria.
61. Reconstruction based on the theatre of Aspendos. A procession of priests carries the god's seat into the *orchestra*. The curtain on the right would have extended across the stage. (From Leacroft, *The Buildings of Ancient Rome*).
62. Aspendos, Asia Minor. General view of the second century AD theatre. Stone corbels with holes for *velarium* masts may be seen on the right.
63. Verona, Italy. Amphitheatre. (Photo: Maurizo Lotti.)
64. Mystery of Elche, Spain. Araceli descending from the dome of S. Maria. (Photo: courtesy of the Folger Shakespeare Library and the Patronato Nacional del Misterio de Elche.)
65. Mystery of Elche, Spain. Details of the Granada. (From *L'Illustration*, 18 September 1897.)
66. The Martyrdom of S. Apollonia, by Jean Fouquet, *c*.1452–6.
67. Piran Round, Cornwall. Conjectural reconstruction of the setting for Day One of the Cornish *Ordinalia*.
68. Piran Round, Cornwall. View to north entry with pit and trench in foreground.
69. The Valenciennes Passion Play, 1547. Conjectural reconstruction. Liturgical-dramatic rituals are known to have taken place in Ancient Egypt, but they required no specific theatre building being almost certainly performed in the temple precinct. Professor H. W. Fairman has drawn an analogy between the possible methods of staging these legends and the arrangement of 'mansions' illustrated at Valenciennes.
70. The Villingen Passion. Sketch plan of 1585–1600, showing the mansions in the Market Place. (Originally thought to be the Donaueschingen Passion.)
71. The Lucerne Passion, 1583. Conjectural

reconstruction based on Cysat's stage plan for Day One.
72. A medieval pageant.
73. Isabella's Triumph, Brussels, 1615, The car of the Nativity. (Crown Copyright, Victoria and Albert Museum.)
74. *Ballet comique de la Reyne*, Petit Bourbon, Paris, 1591. (Courtesy of the Trustees of the British Museum.)
75. The Great Hall, Penshurst Place, Kent, with dais at near end and screens beyond. Retainers' tables and benches have been moved aside to provide three tiers of seats enclosing the open *platea* or 'place'.
76. The Great Hall, Penshurst, with small stage adjoining screens. (After Garret Christmas's design for Dekker's *London's Tempe*, 1629.)
77. Penshurst, with stage in the form of a 'city'.
78. Penshurst, with practical mansions and curtained throne.
79. Medieval practicable mansions illustrated in the fourteenth century Tèrence des Ducs. Compare these 'doll's house'-like structures with the Serlian perspective scenes.
80. Setting for the *Andria* of Terence, 1493.
81. Serlio's design for a temporary Court theatre, 1545.
82. Serlio's *Tragic Scene*. (Model by Richard Leacroft.)
83. Serlio's *Comic Scene*. (Model by Richard Leacroft.)
84. Serlio's *Satyric Scene*. (Model by Richard Leacroft.)
85. Teatro Olimpico, Vicenza, Italy. A. Palladio, 1580–4.
86. Teatro Olimpico. General view. (Photo: L. Chiovato, Vicenza.)
87. Teatro Olimpico. Rear view of scene to right of central vista. Note oil lamp in upper opening. (Sketch by Richard Leacroft.)
88. Teatro Olimpico. The central vista. (Photo: Si. C.C.A., Vicenza.)
89. Teatro Olimpico, Sabbioneta. V. Scamozzi, 1588.
90. Strolling players with platform stage, after a sixteenth century painting by P. Breughel.
91. Commedia dell'Arte platform stage and actors, after Callot.
92. Serlian-style vista, after the Curzio Gonzaga, 1592.
93. Royal Tennis Court. (Courtesy of the University of Oxford Tennis Court.)
94. Hôtel de Bourgogne, Paris. Conjectural reconstructions, a) of the original theatre of 1548 with curtained mansions on stage; b) after the alterations of 1647 with Serlian-style perspective vista; c) *c.*1717, based on sketch plans drawn by Sir James Thornhill.
95. Hôtel de Bourgogne. Etching by le Blond after A. Bosse. (Courtesy of the Bibliothèque Nationale, Paris.)
96. The Swan, after de Witt.
97. The Swan, 1594–6. General view. Cut away reconstruction. A combination of features from the bull- and bear-baiting yards and the screens of the medieval halls.
98. The Swan. View after de Witt.
99. The Swan. Aerial view.
100. The second Globe Theatre (left) and the Hope or Bear Garden (right), after Hollar's *Long View of London*, 1647.
101. The Swan, with medieval style mansions.
102a & b. The second Globe Theatre, 1614. Revised version of the reconstruction in *Development of the English Playhouse* (fig. 29), with only one door of entry to the yard, now centrally placed under My Lord's Room.
103. Teatro Farnese, Parma, Italy. G. B. Aleotti, E. Bentivoglio, and G. B. Magnani, 1618–20. Conjectural reconstruction of the theatre, arranged for the first production in 1628. The Ladies of the Court sat on the left-hand side, and the Gentlemen on the right. A third and fourth gallery, filled with people, were painted in perspective on the upper portions of the walls and on the ceiling, together with a vista of the heavens filled with gods, goddesses, and cupids supporting the great chandeliers which lit the theatre.
104. Teatro Farnese. a) View of stage. b) Auditorium. (Photos: ed. Alinari, courtesy of the Superintendent of Art and History, Parma.)
105. Teatro Farnese. View of auditorium from the stage, showing timber structure of proscenium: compare with fig. 156. (Photo: Edward Craig.)
106–7. The Tudor Hall, Whitehall, adapted by Inigo Jones for the performance of *Florimène*, 1635, illustrating the rectangular pattern imposed by the existing hall, and the subdivision into two separate but connected parts by the masking frontispiece.
108. Inigo Jones: unknown theatre, maybe Phoenix, Drury Lane.
109. Cockpit in Court, Whitehall, Inigo Jones and John Webb, *c.*1660. General view, including the machine room within the existing roof space.
110. Cockpit in Court, Whitehall. Detail of stage and *frons scaenae*, adapted to the limitations of the existing cockpit.
111. Teatro SS. Giovanni e Paolo, Venice, 1639, after a drawing of 1654.
112. Salle des Machines, Paris, G. Vigarani, 1662. Plans from Diderot, *Encyclopédie*, 1772.
113. Comédie Française, Paris. F. d'Orbay, 1689.
114. Lincoln's Inn Fields Theatre, 1661, after a reconstruction by Edward A. Langhans (see *Essays in Theatre*).
115. Theatre Royal, Drury Lane. Sir C. Wren, 1674. An updated reconstruction from *The Development of the English Playhouse* (fig. 63), including a frontispiece

based on the *Ariane* design, which reduces the width of the vista, but provides greater wing space for the movement of wings and shutters. In 1709 the stage is known to have been 'full of Trap-Doors', and these have now been included (dotted) in accordance with a plan of a theatre at Hampton Court Palace, described by G. Barlow.

116. Theatre Royal, Drury Lane. General view of cut-open model.
117. Theatre Royal, Drury Lane. Interior, with stage boxes based on Hogarth's painting of Gay's *Beggar's Opera*.
118. Theatre Royal, Drury Lane. R. Adam, 1775.
119. Theatre Royal, Drury Lane, 1775. The figures have been corrected to relate to scaled drawings by Robert Adam.
120. Stage design by Giuseppe Bibiena. 1719.
121. Teatro Scientifico, Mantua, Italy. A. G. Bibiena, 1769.
122. The Margravine's Opera House, Bayreuth. G. and C. Bibiena, 1744–8. View of the stage.
123. The Margravine's Opera House, Bayreuth. Auditorium and Royal Box. (This and 122, courtesy of the Bavarian Administration of Staatlichen, Schlosser, Garten und Seen.)
124. Manoel Theatre, Valetta, Malta, 1731–2. Auditorium.
125. Manoel Theatre. Proscenium ceiling.
126. Manoel Theatre. View from box.
127. La Scala, Milan. G. Piermarini, 1778. After the alterations of 1830.
128. Teatro Regio, Turin. B. Alfieri, 1740. Section from Diderot, *Encyclopédie*.
129. Theatre Royal, Covent Garden, in 1794. H. Holland (from R. Wilkinson's *Theatrum Illustrata*, 1825).
130. Theatre Royal, Covent Garden. R. Smirke. Old Price Riots of 1809.
131. Court Theatre, Drottningholm, Sweden. C. F. Adelcrantz, 1766. a) Stage and auditorium. b) Machinery above and c) below stage.
132. Theatre at Imola, Italy. C. Morelli, 1779–80, from G. Saunders, *A Treatise on Theatres*. Section & plan.
133. Theatre at Lyons. J. G. Soufflot, 1754.
134. The Grand Theatre, Bordeaux. V. Louis, 1773–80.
135. The Grand Theatre, Bordeaux. Present-day auditorium. (Courtesy of the Municipal Archives of Bordeaux.)
136. The Theatre, Besançon. C. N. Ledoux, 1778.
137. The Theatre, Besançon. Auditorium after the alterations of 1836 and 1857. (Photo: Studio Meusy.)
138. Theatre Royal, Drury Lane. H. Holland, after the alterations of 1797. Compare with fig. 93, *Development of the English Playhouse*.
139. Theatre Royal, Drury Lane. (Crown Copyright Victoria and Albert Museum, Theatre Museum.)
140. The Georgian Theatre, Richmond, Yorks, 1788. Auditorium. The model shows the pit as it would originally have been with backless benches. As first restored, the benches were designed to conform to evidence obtained from the Sparrow Hill Theatre, Loughborough (fig. 143), the only concession to modern problems being the duplication of the pit entrance on the OP side (fig. 103a, b, *Development of the English Playhouse*). These 'Georgian' conditions were found unacceptable to modern audiences, and have since been amended. It is interesting to note, however, that the 1 foot 11 inches (0.58m) measurement back to back of the original restoration, was generous compared to those noted on a plan of 1799 for an unknown theatre, in the recently acquired collection of Winston drawings, which was brought to my attention by Dr. James Fowler of the Theatre Museum. Here, both pit and boxes have 9 inch (0.22m) benches, with $8\frac{1}{2}$ inch (0.21m) benches in the gallery. All are spaced 1 foot (0.30m) apart.
141. The Georgian Theatre, Richmond. Stage with machine room under.
142. The Georgian Theatre, Richmond. Exterior. (Water colour by Richard Leacroft.)
143. Sparrow Hill Theatre, Loughborough, Leics, 1822.
144. Sparrow Hill Theatre, Loughborough. Exterior in 1949.
145. The Theatre, Vadstena, Sweden, 1826. The stage. (Photo: Siöwall, Vadstena.)
146. The Theatre, Vadstena. Auditorium (Photo: Siöwall, Vadstena.)
147. The Theatre, Wisbech, Cambs, 1793.
148. Fisher's Theatre, North Walsham, Norfolk, 1827. The stage.
149. Fisher's Theatre, North Walsham. Auditorium.
150. The great bespeak for Miss Snevellicci. (Phiz illustration to *Nicholas Nickleby*.)
151. The Theatre Royal, Ipswich, Suffolk. R. Fulcher. a) The theatre in 1803. b) After the alterations of 1815. c) After the alterations of 1887, when the front of the pit was widened to the full width of the building and the new exits were formed, and of 1888, when the roof over the stage was raised to permit scenes to be flown. (Reconstructions based on information compiled by the manager, H. R. Eyre.)
152. Theatre Royal, Ipswich. The auditorium in 1822. A water colour by the scenic artist, W. Burgess. (Courtesy of Suffolk County Records.)
153. Theatre Royal, Bristol. T. Paty, 1766. The gallery. See fig. 76, *Development of the English Playhouse*.
154. Theatre Royal, Bristol. Still from *The Charge of the Light Brigade*. (Courtesy of United Artists Corp. Ltd.)
155. Theatre Royal, Bury St. Edmunds. W. Wilkins, 1819.

156. Theatre Royal, Bury St. Edmunds. Stage prior to the reconstruction of 1965, showing the timber-framed proscenium wall and barrel loft (top right). (Photo: J. McM. Abbott, RIBA.)
157. Theatre Royal, Bury St. Edmunds. The restored auditorium of 1965. (Photo: Steve Stephens.)
158. Theatre Royal, Drury Lane. B. Wyatt, 1812. See fig. 106, *Development of the English Playhouse*.
159. Haymarket Theatre, London. C. J. Phipps, 1880. (Mander and Mitchenson Theatre Collection.)
160. Theatre Royal, Leicester. W. Parsons, 1836. Auditorium.
161. Theatre Royal, Leicester. The stage after the alterations of 1888.
162. Theatre Royal, Leicester. Upper scene grooves. (Photo: R. Hunt.)
163. Normansfield Hospital Theatre, Teddington, London. Roller cloth (top left), and upper grooves (top right).
164. Theatre Royal, Bath. Scene barrels.
165. Theatre Royal, Bath. Prompt-side fly gallery with rollers and hemp lines.
166. Theatre Royal, Leicester, with fly tower of 1888.
167. Hemp line flying system.
168. Her Majesty's Theatre, London. The grid with timber roller and later wire lines.
169. Palace Theatre, London (formerly the New English Opera House of 1891).
170. The Opera House, Paris. C. Garnier, 1861–75. The fly gallery.
171. The Opera House, Paris. Stage cellar.
172. The Opera House, Paris. The four mezzanine floors and cellar beneath the stage.
173. Court Theatre, Vienna. G. Semper and Baron Hasenauer, 1888. View of flying bars above stage.
174. Court Theatre, Vienna. The gridiron.
175. Court Theatre, Vienna. Understage machinery. (Figs 170–5 from Sachs, *Modern Theatre Stages*.)
176. Backstage at a continental theatre. (After Laumann, *La Machinerie au Théâtre*.)
177. Wagner Opera House, Bayreuth. O. Brueckwald, 1876.
178. Wagner Opera House, Bayreuth. Auditorium, from Sachs, *Modern Theatres and Opera Houses*.
179. The People's Theatre, Worms. O. March, 1889. Auditorium with orchestra well. From Sachs, *Modern Theatres and Opera Houses*. (Figs. 179–80)
180. The People's Theatre, Worms. Auditorium with forestage.
181. Asphaleia stage, from Sachs, *Modern Theatre Stages*.
182. The Auditorium Building, Chicago. Asphaleia stage, from Sachs, *Modern Theatre Stages*.
183. Theatre Royal, Drury Lane. Hydraulic bridges of 1896 lowered for the 'lock scene' in the play *Low Water*.
184. Theatre Royal, Drury Lane. Hydraulic bridges of 1896 set for a scene in *White Heather*.
185. Theatre Royal, Drury Lane. Electric bridges of 1898. (Nos. 183–5, Theatre Museum, Victoria and Albert Museum.)
186. a) A wing and border setting. b) A box setting.
187. The Court Opera House, Munich. Project by Karl Lautenschlaeger for a revolving stage, from Sachs, *Modern Theatre Stages*.
188. Brandt's 'Reform Stage', after Kinsila, *Modern Theatre Construction*.
189. Theatre Royal, Ipswich. Detail of footlights, from the Eyre scrapbook.
190. 'Lighting the footlights', from the Eyre scrapbook. (Nos. 189, 190, courtesy of Suffolk County Records.)
191. Gas batten with three colour medium. A: Wood frame of batten. B: Sheet-iron whitened to reflect light. C: Lines to work medium. D: Ropes to carry batten. E: Iron guard with wires. From F. Lloyds, *A Practical Guide to Scene Painting*.
192. Fortuny lighting system, from H. Carter, *New Spirit in Drama and Art*.
193. Fortuny sky dome, from H. Carter, *New Spirit in Drama and Art*.
194. A mobile sky dome.
195. The Schauspielhaus, Dresden. W. Lossow and M. H. Kühne, 1913–14.
196. The Ziegfeld Theatre, New York. J. Urban and T. W. Lamb, 1926.
197. The Royal Opera House, Leicester. C. J. Phipps, 1876–7. In the reconstruction the right-hand side of the auditorium is as indicated on the original drawings, while the left-hand side shows the auditorium as surveyed in 1960, and includes the proscenium wall and stage alterations of 1903 and 1906.
198. The Auditorium Building, Chicago. D. Adler and L. Sullivan, 1886–9. The auditorium, from Birkmire's *American Theatres*.
199. Karl Immermann's setting for *Twelfth Night*, Dusseldorf, 1840.
200. Freiherr von Perfall's setting for *King Lear*, Munich, 1889.
201. William Poel's *Measure for Measure* at the Royalty Theatre, 1893. (Courtesy of the Society for Theatre Research.)
202. Max Krüger's reconstruction of the Swan.
203. The Maddermarket Theatre, Norwich. N. Paul, 1921. Setting for *The Knight of the Burning Pestle*. (Courtesy of the theatre management.)
204. The Shakespearean Festival Theatre, Ashland, Oregon. J. A. Edson and R. Hay, 1959.

205. The Greek Theatre, Bradfield College, Reading, Berks, 1890.
206. The Künstler Theatre, Munich. M. Littmann, 1907–8.
207. The Künstler Theatre, Munich. Auditorium, from M. Littmann, *Das Münchner Künstlertheater*. It should be noted that the plan reproduced in this book shows 20 full rows of seats and a 3m-wide orchestra pit, while the section conforms to the photographs with 21 rows of seats and a 2m-wide pit.
208. The Künstler Theatre, Munich. Stage with setting by Julius Diez for Reinhardt's *Twelfth Night*, 1909.
209. The Little Theatre, New York. H. C. Ingalls and F. B. Hoffman. 1912.
210. People's Opera House, Paris. Davioud and Bourdais, 1875. Section and plan.
211. The Little Theatre, John Adam Street, London. A. B. Hayward and Maynard, 1910.
212. Grosses Schauspielhaus, Berlin. H. Poelzig, 1919–20. Reconstruction with seating arranged (left) for picture stage, and (right) with thrust stage.
213. Reinhardt's production of *Danton's Death*.
214. Grosses Schauspielhaus, Berlin. Interior, from Sayler, *Max Reinhardt and his Theatre*.
215. Norman Bel Geddes, 'Theatre No. 6', 1922.
216. The Barnwell Theatre, Cambridge, *c*.1816.
217. Festival Theatre, Cambridge. E. Maufe, 1926.
218. Festival Theatre, Cambridge. Auditorium, from C. H. Ridge, *Stage Lighting*.
219. Festival Theatre, Cambridge. Setting by Doria Paston for *Salomé*.
220. Palace Theatre of Varieties, Leicester. F. Matcham, 1901.
221. Palace Theatre of Varieties, Leicester. Auditorium. (Photo: Fisher and Potter.)
222. Royal Adelphi Theatre, London. T. H. Wyatt, 1858. (Courtesy of the Theatre Museum, Victoria and Albert Museum.)
223. Century (Adelphi) Theatre, London. E. Runtz, 1901. (Courtesy of the Theatre Museum, Victoria and Albert Museum.)
224. Adelphi Theatre, London. Prior to the alterations of 1930.
225. Adelphi Theatre, London. After the alterations of 1930.
226. Adelphi Theatre, London. E. Schaufelberg. 1930. (Courtesy of *Architects' Journal*.)
227. The Playhouse, Oxford. F. G. M. Chancellor of F. Matcham and Co., 1938.
228. London Theatre Studio, Islington, M. Breuer, 1937. (Photo: courtesy of *Architects' Journal*.)
229. Shakespeare Memorial Theatre, Stratford-upon-Avon. Scott, Chesterton and Shepherd, 1932.
230. Shakespeare Memorial Theatre, Stratford-upon-Avon. Interior of 1932.
231. Counterweight flying systems: a) single-purchase; b) double-purchase.
232. A 'non-existent' proscenium opening, from *Civic Theatre Design*.
233. Belgrade Theatre, Coventry. A. Ling, 1958.
234. Belgrade Theatre, Coventry. Interior, with 'non-existent' proscenium and forestage. (Photo: P. W. and L. Thompson.)
235. Belgrade Theatre, Coventry. Auditorium with side boxes. (Photo: P. W. and L. Thompson.)
236. Circle with side boxes, from *Civic Theatre Design*.
237. Rear wall boxes and side boxes, from *Civic Theatre Design*.
238. The Forum Theatre, Billingham, Cleveland. Elder Lester Associates, 1968.
239. a) b) The Forum Theatre, Billingham. (Photos: Courtesy of the Department of Planning, Cleveland County Council.)
240. Eden Court Theatre, Inverness. Law and Dunbar-Nasmith, 1976.
241. Eden Court Theatre, Inverness. View from rear boxes. (Photo: courtesy of the Architects.)
242. The Barbican Theatre, London. Chamberlin, Powell, and Bon, 1982.
243. Shakespeare Memorial (now Royal Shakespeare) Theatre. a) after the alterations of 1951 by B. O'Rorke; b) 1962; c) the alterations of 1972 by R. Harvey.
244. The Royal Shakespeare, as altered for the 1976 season. (Photo: J. Cocks Studio.)
245. The Great Hall of the Dalcroze School at Hellerau, Dresden. H. Tessenow, 1910–12. With setting by Adolph Appia for the scene in *Hades* from Gluck's *Orpheus and Euridice*.
246. Setting by Salzmann for Paul Claudel's *L'Annonce faite à Marie*, after *The Stage Year Book 1914*.
247. The Vieux Colombier, Paris. a) The stage in 1913: F. Jourdain. b) Theatre in 1919–20: L. Jouvet. c) Stage in 1930 for La Compagnie des Quinze: A. Barsacq.
248. The Vieux Colombier. Interior of original music hall.
249. The Vieux Colombier. Interior of the 1919–20 theatre. (Nos. 248–9 from *Revue d'Histoire du Théâtre*.)
250. Redoutensaal, Vienna, 1922, with setting for Reinhardt's production of Goethe's *Clavigo*.
251. The Mermaid, in the Royal Exchange, London, 1953. Drawing by Michael Stringer. (Courtesy of Lady Miles.)
252. The Mermaid, Puddle Dock, London. E. L. W. Davies, 1959.
253. The Mermaid. Interior with stage. (Photo: Raymond

Moore, reproduced by courtesy of the Gordon Fraser Gallery Limited.)

254. The new Mermaid, Puddle Dock, London. Seifert and Partners, 1981. Theatre arranged with seating set up on stage for the arena presentation of *Trafford Tanzi*. Permanent seating in foreground.

255. Senior High School Theatre, La Junta, Colorado. Shaver and Company (Theatre Consultant, James Hull Miller), 1963–4. (Drawing by Richard Leacroft for *Hub Bulletin*, 109, 'The Open Stage'.)

256. a) James Hull Miller's rear projection unit. b) Setting for *Madam Butterfly*. (Drawings by Richard Leacroft for *Hub Bulletin*, 107, 'Little Theatres from Modest Spaces', and 109, 'The Open Stage'.) Linnebach developed a system for projecting designs, painted on glass slides, without the use of lenses onto the cyclorama of his Dresden Schauspielhaus (fig. 195). At the same time Mark Hasait of the Dresden State Opera was using a projection system based on Javanese shadow puppets, similar to that now being used by James Hull Miller. (See also figs. 321–2).

257. Assembly Hall, Edinburgh, 1948. Tyrone Guthrie's production of *The Thrie Estaitis*.

258. The Shakespearean Festival Theatre, Ontario. R. Fairfield, 1957.

259. The Shakespearean Festival Theatre, Ontario. Auditorium. (Photo: H. Nott, courtesy of theatre publicity.) It is claimed that more itimate productions can be achieved on this thrust stage than is possible in a proscenium theatre, but in a practical comparison between a performance experienced in the front row of this circle compared with a similar position in the Royal Theatre, Northampton (C. J. Phipps, 1884), the latter won 'hands down'.

260. The Shakespearean Festival Theatre, Ontario. Original stage. (Photo: P. Smith, courtesy of theatre publicity.)

261. The Shakespearean Festival Theatre, Ontario. The 1963 stage. (Photo: Stratford Festival Archives.)

262. The Festival Theatre, Chichester. Powell and Moya, 1962. (Photo: courtesy of *Architect's Journal*.) For a graphic description of the problems involved in attempting direct address on this stage see Joyce Grenfell's *In Pleasant Places*, pp. 18–19.

263. Tyrone Guthrie Theatre, Minneapolis. R. Rapson, 1963. (Photo: R. A. Wilson, courtesy of theatre publicity.)

264. The Shakespearean Festival Theatre, Ontario. The stage of 1976 with a) balcony; b) central opening.

265. The Municipal Theatre, Malmo, Sweden. E. Lallerstedt, S. Lewerentz, and D. Hellden, 1944.

266. The Municipal Theatre, Malmo. (Drawing by Richard Leacroft for Army Bureau of Current Affairs, No. 110, M. E. Edition, *The Theatre and You*, 1946.)

267. The Municipal Theatre, Malmo. Auditorium. (Photo: Anders Mattsson, courtesy of the theatre.)

268. Center of Dramatic Art, Sarah Lawrence College, Bronxville, New York. M. Breuer, 1952. Auditorium and stage.

269. Sarah Lawrence College, New York. Auditorium with lighting control above.

270. Realistic Theatre, Moscow, *c.*1930. Okhlopkov's production of *Mother*.

271. The Penthouse Theatre, University of Washington, Seattle. C. F. Gould. 1940.

272. Penthouse Theatre, Seattle. Interior.

273. The Playhouse Theatre, Houston, Texas. B. F. Greenwood, 1950.

274. The Playhouse Theatre, Houston. Interior with added scenic stage.

275. Teatro S. Erasmo, Milan. A. Carminali and C. De Carli, 1952–3.

276. The Alley Theatre, Houston, Texas. The original theatre.

277. Casa Manana Theatre, Fort Worth, Texas. G. King and Associates, 1958.

278. Stephen Joseph's 'Studio Theatre' adaptation of a) Wycliffe School Hall, Leicester; b) old Vaughan College Hall, Leicester, 1958.

279. Victoria Theatre, Stoke on Trent, Staffs, 1962. Rehearsal of *Doctor Fergo Rides Again*. (Photo: Don McNeil, courtesy of the theatre management.)

280. Royal Exchange Theatre, Manchester. Levitt Bernstein Associates, 1976. (Photo: Picture Coverage Ltd., courtesy of the architects.)

281. Norman Bel Geddes, 'Theatre No. 14', 1922.

282. The Ring Theatre, University of Miami. R. M. Little and M. I. Manley, 1950: a) with arena stage; b) with Shakespearian stage.

283. The Corn Exchange, Leicester. R. Leacroft, 1959. Project for a flexible open-stage theatre.

284. The Corn Exchange, Leicester. Project arranged as: a) arena stage; b) classical stage; c) Elizabethan stage; d) modern scenic stage.

285. Studio One. Baylor University, Waco, Texas. W. Tammings, 1941. View with picture stage to left and control gallery above.

286. Loeb Drama Center, Harvard, Massachusetts. H. Stubbins, 1960. Reconstruction showing auditorium arranged (left) for an apron stage and (right) for a proscenium stage. (See fig. 304 for photograph of the experimental theatre.)

287. Loeb Drama Center. Auditorium with control and observation rooms above. (Photographs 286–7,304, taken prior to opening date.)

288. Loeb Drama Center. General view of stage with masking screens to left of photograph.
289. The Small Theatre, National Theatre, Mannheim, W. Germany. G. Weber, 1955–7. Reconstruction showing (left) the seldom-used arena style seating and (right) the picture stage with orchestra.
290. National Theatre, Mannheim. The small auditorium with control bridge at rear. (Photo: A. Pfau, courtesy of *Architectural Review*.)
291. The Questors Theatre, Ealing, London. N. Branson of W. S. Hatrell and Partners, 1964. The reconstruction shows the theatre arranged (left) with an arena stage, and (right) as a proscenium stage.
292. The Questors Theatre, Ealing. Arranged as a) a thrust stage; b) a theatre in the round.
293. The Octagon Theatre, Bolton, Lancs. G. Brooks, 1967.
294. The Octagon Theatre, Bolton. Arranged as end stage.
295. The Octagon Theatre, Bolton. As arena stage.
296. The Octagon Theatre. Bolton. Arranged as a thrust stage. (Nos. 294–296: photos by Winter and Kidson, courtesy of the Dept. of Planning and Development, Bolton Metropolitan Borough.)
297. Civic Theatre, Waco, Texas. Wiedemann and Salmond (Theatre Consultant, James Hull Miller), 1958.
298. Civic Theatre, Waco. The theatre arranged as a proscenium stage. When this photograph was taken James Hull Miller was demonstrating the possibilities of his overhead projection system. The 'slide' and lamp would normally be hidden (see fig. 321).
299. Experimental Studio, St. Mary's Training College, Twickenham, London. Sir A. Richardson, Houfe, and Partners, 1963.
300–1. St. Mary's Training College, Twickenham. Studio arranged for lecture with control room window in upper part of photographs.
302. The Vandyck Theatre, Bristol University. Dept. of Architecture, 1967. Reconstruction with (left) arena stage and (right) end or picture stage.
303. Projected Experimental Studio, Yale University. George C. Izenour, 1955. Reconstruction arranged as an end stage.
304. Experimental Theater, Loeb Drama Center, Harvard, 1960. (See fig. 286.)
305. Studio Theatre, the Questors, Ealing (see fig. 291).
306. Studio Theatre, the Haymarket, Leicester, 1973.
307. New Fortune Theatre, University of Western Australia, Perth. M. Clifton, 1964. Left: the theatre arranged for the first production of *Hamlet*. Right: the basic theatre, with orchestra.
308. Christ's Hospital Arts Centre, Horsham, Sussex. HKPA, 1974. Reconstruction arranged (left) as proscenium stage and (right) as thrust stage.
309. Christ's Hospital Arts Centre. Proscenium layout.
310. The Cottlesloe, National Theatre, London. Denys Lasdun and Partners (Theatre Consultant: Iain Mackintosh), 1977. Reconstruction arranged (left) as end stage and (right) as continuous level floor acting area.
311. The Cottesloe, National Theatre, London. Auditorium with pit filled in and seats rising to first floor level.
312. The Cottesloe, National Theatre, London. End stage in use for a rehearsal.
313. Kalita Humphreys Theater, Dallas, Texas. F. L. Wright, 1959. Reconstruction as built in 1959. Additional rehearsal rooms, public areas, and offices added in 1968.
314. Kalita Humphreys Theater, Dallas. Auditorium with side stage. Note lack of masking above stage.
315. The Haymarket Theatre, Leicester. Leicester Architects's Dept., 1973.
316. The Haymarket, Leicester.
317. The Olivier, National Theatre, London, Denys Lasdun and Partners, 1976. (Photo: Denys Lasdun and Partners.)
318. The Community Theatre, Midland, Texas. Theatre consultant: James Hull Miller, 1957.
319. Community Theatre, Midland, Texas. The stage with setting related to inner brick wing walls.
320. Community Theatre, Midland, Texas. Auditorium with catwalks and control room.
321. James Hull Miller's overhead projection system. (Drawing by Richard Leacroft for *Hub Bulletin*, 109, 'The Open Stage'.
322. Community Theatre, Midland, Texas. Setting for *South Pacific*, using both built and projected scenery. (Photo: Rubin's, courtesy of theatre publicity.)
323. New Community Theatre, Midland, Texas. Frank Welch Associates, 1978. Note experimental theatre.
324. Community Theatre, Western Springs, Illinois. G. Orth, 1961.
325. Western Springs. Setting for *Dark of the Moon*. (Photo: courtesy of theatre publicity.)
326. Western Springs. Setting for *Strange Bedfellows*, 1962. (Drawing by Richard Leacroft for *Hub Bulletin*, 109, 'The Open Stage'.)
327. 'The George Inn', Southwark, London. The Tabard Players perform *Oliver Twist* in the inn yard, 1944.

The models illustrated in Figs. 75–8, 89, 97–9, 106–7, 109–10, 116–17, 140–1, and 160–1, were made by students of the Leicester School of Architecture, from reconstructions prepared by Richard Leacroft. These models are now in the collection of the Leicestershire Museum Education Service. All photographs, except those attributed to other sources, and Nos. 17, 148, 149, 227, 278b and 327, are by Richard Leacroft.

Bibliography

Sections 1–4

Anti, C., *Teatri Greci Arcaici*, Rome, 1947.
——, *Nuove Ricerche sui Teatri Greci Arcaici*, Padova, 1969.
Arnott, P., *Greek Scenic Conventions in the 5th. Century B.C.*, Oxford, 1962.
Beare, W., *The Roman Stage*, London, 1968.
Bieber, M., *The Greek and Roman Theater*, Princeton, 1961.
Boyd-Hawkes, *Gournia,* Philadelphia, 1908.
Demargne, J., 'Fouilles a Lato en Crete, 1899–1900', *Bulletin de Correspondence Hellenique*, 1903, pp. 206–32.
Dilke, O. A. W., 'Greek Theatre Cavea', *Annual of the British School at Athens*, XLIII, 1948, pp. 125–92.
——, 'Details and Chronology of Greek Theatre Caveas', *Annual of the British School at Athens* XLV, 1950, pp. 21–62.
Dinsmoor, W. B., *The Architecture of Ancient Greece*, London, 1950.
——, 'The Athenian Theater of the Fifth Century': *Studies presented to D. M. Robinson*, St. Louis, I, 1951. pp. 309–330.
Eretria., *American Journal of Archaeology*, VII, 1891, pp. 253–80; X, 1895, pp. 338–46; XI, 1896, pp. 317–31.
Evans, Sir A., *Palace of Minos, Knossos*, London, 1921.
Fiechter, E. von, *Antike griechische Theatergebaude*, Stuttgart, 1930–7.
——, *Das Theater In Eretria*, Stuttgart, 1937.
——, *Das Theater in Oropos*, Stuttgart, 1930.
——, *Das Theater in Sikyon*, Stuttgart, 1931.
Flickinger, R. C., *The Greek Theater and its Drama*, Chicago, 1936.
Gebhard, E., 'The Form of the Orchestra in the Early Greek Theater', *Hesperia*, XLIII, 1974, pp. 428–40.
——, *The Theater at Isthmia*, Chicago–London, 1973.
Gerkan, A. von, *Das Theater von Epidauros*, Stuttgart, 1961.
——, *Das Theater von Priene*, Munich, 1921.
Ginouvès, R., *Le Théâtron à Gradins droits et l'Odéon d'Argos*, Paris, 1972.
Hackens, T., 'Thorikos, 1963, le Théâtre', *L'Antiquité Classique*, XXXIV, 1965, pp. 39–46.
——, 'Le Théâtre', *Thorikos 1965*, III, 1967, pp. 74–96.
Hammond, N. G. L., 'The Conditions of Dramatic Production to the Death of Aeschylus', *Greek, Roman, and Byzantine Studies*, XIII, no. 4, Winter 1972, N. Carolina, pp. 387–450.
Hanson, J. R., *Roman Theater-Temples*, Princeton, 1959.
Hutchinson, R. W., *Prehistoric Crete*, London, 1962.
Ikaria. *American Journal of Archaeology*, IV, 1888, p. 421; V, 1889, p. 9.
Leacroft, H. and R., *The Buildings of Ancient Greece*, Leicester & New York, 1966.
——, *The Buildings of Ancient Rome*, Leicester & New York, 1969.
Leacroft, R., 'Actor and Audience', RIBA Athens Bursary Report, *RIBA Journal*, LXIII, Aug. 1956, pp. 414–23.
Miller, W., 'Thorikos – The Theater of', *Papers of the American School*, IV, p. 23 ff.
Morgan, M. H., *Vitruvius: The Ten Books of Architecture*, New York, 1960.
Morgantina. *American Journal of Archaeology,* LXI, 1957, p. 152; LXII, 1958, pp. 161–2; LXVI, 1962, pp. 137–8; LXIV, 1970, pp. 363–4.
Petrakos, B., *O Oropos kai to leron tou Amphiaraou*, Athens, 1968.
Pickard Cambridge, A. W., *Theatre of Dionysus in Athens*, Oxford, 1946.
Sicyon. *American Journal of Archaeology*, V, 1889, pp. 267–81; VII–VIII, 1891–2, pp. 281–2, 388–409.
Sifakis, G. M., *Studies in the History of Hellenistic Drama*, London, 1967.
Stillwell, R., *Corinth: the Theatre,* Harvard, 1952.
Thallon Hill, I., *The Ancient City of Athens*, London, 1953.
Travlos, J., *Pictorial Dictionary of Ancient Athens*, London, 1971,
Webster, T. B. L., *Greek Theatre Production*, London, 1956.
Wycherley, R. E., *How the Greeks Built Cities*, London, 1962.

Section 5

Arnott, P. D., 'The Origins of Medieval Theatre in the Round', *Theatre Notebook*, XV, 1960–1, pp. 84–7.
Blakemore Evans, M., *The Passion Play of Lucerne*, New York, 1943.
Chambers, E. K., *The Medieval Stage*, 2 vols., Oxford, 1903.
Craik, T.W., *The Tudor Interlude*, Leicester, 1958.
Fairman, H. W., *The Triumph of Horus*, London, 1974.
Nagler, A. M., *The Medieval Religious Stage*, New Haven, 1976.
Neuss, P., 'The Staging of the Creacion of the World', *Theatre Notebook*, XXXIII, 1979, pp. 116–25.
Ordish, T. F., *Early London Stages*, London, 1894.
Paris, P., 'Les Fétes de L'Assomption a Elche (Espagne)', *L'Illustration*, 18 Sept. 1897, pp. 226–7.
Patronato Nacional del Misterio de Elche, *El Misterio de Elche*, Elche, 1974.
Ratcliffe, D. F., 'The Mystery of Elche in 1931', *Hispania*, XV, 1932, pp. 109–16.
Schmitt, N. C., 'Was there a Medieval Theatre in the Round', *Theatre Notebook*, XXIII, 1968–9, pp. 130–42; XXIV, 1969–70, pp. 18–25.
Shoemaker, W. H., *The Multiple Stage in Spain during the Fifteenth and Sixteenth Centuries*, Princeton, 1935.
Southern, R., *The Medieval Theatre in the Round*, rev. ed., London, 1975.
Tydeman, W., *The Theatre in the Middle Ages*, Cambridge, 1978.
Wickham, G., *Early English Stages*, 2 vols., London, 1959, 1972.

Sections 6–8

Barlow, G., 'The Hôtel de Bourgogne According to Sir James Thornhill', *Theatre Research International*, I, 1976, pp. 86–98.
Campbell, L. B., *Scenes and Machines on the English Stage*, London, 1923.
Chambers, E. K., *The Elizabethan Stage*, 4 vols., Oxford, 1923.
Duchartre, P. L., *The Italian Comedy*, London, 1929.
Deierkauf-Holsboer, S. W., *Le Théâtre de l'Hôtel de Bourgogne*, 2 vols., Paris, 1968.
——, *Le Théâtre du Marais*, 2 vols., Paris, 1954.
Eccles, M., 'Martin Peerson and the Blackfriars', *Shakespeare Survey*, XI, pp. 104 ff., Cambridge, 1958.
Galloway, D., *The Elizabethan Theatre*, London, 1969.
Hodges, C. W., *The Globe Restored*, London, 1953.
Hosley, R., 'A Reconstruction of the Second Blackfriars', in Galloway, D., op. cit., pp. 74–88.
Illingworth, D., 'Documents inédits et nouvelles précisions sur le Théâtre de l'Hôtel de Bourgogne', *Revue d'Histoire du Théâtre*, XXII, 1970, pp. 125–32.
——, 'L'Hôtel de Bourgogne: une salle de théâtre "à l'italienne" à Paris en 1647', *Revue d'Histoire du Théâtre*, XXIII, 1971, pp. 40–9.
Kernodle, G. R., *From Art to Theatre*, Chicago, 1943.
Leacroft, R., 'Serlio's Theatre and Perspective Scenes', *Theatre Notebook*, XXXVI, 1982, pp. 120–22.
Leclerc, H., *Les Origines Italiennes de l'architecture Théâtrale Moderne*, Paris, 1946.
Magagnato, L., *Il teatro Italiano del Cinquecento*, Venice, 1954.
Mongrédien, G., *Daily Life in the French Theatre*, London, 1969.
Niemeyer, C., 'The Hotel de Bourgogne, France's First Popular Playhouse', *Theatre Annual*, 1947, pp. 64–80.
Peccati, G., *Il Teatro Olimpico, Sabbioneta*, Mantua, 1950.
Pozzo, A., *Rules and Examples of Perspective Proper for Painters and Architects*, London, 1707.
Puppi, L., *The Olimpic Theatre*, Neri Pozzo Ed., 1965.
Prouty, G., *Studies in the Elizabethan Theatre*, USA, 1961.
Roy, D. H., 'La Scène de l'Hôtel de Bourgogne', *Revue d'Histoire du Théâtre*, XIV, 1962, pp. 227–35.
Sabbattini, N., *The Practice of Building Scenes and Machines of the Theatre*, Ravenna, 1637–8.
Sarlos, R. K., 'Development and Decline of the First Blackfriars Theatre', in Prouty, G., op. cit, pp. 139–77.
Schiavo, R., *A Guide to the Olimpic Theatre*, Vicenza, 1981.
Serlio, S., *Tutte l'opere d'architettura et prospettiva, Il secondo Libro*, Paris, 1545.
Villiers, A., 'L'ouverture de la scène á l'Hôtel de Bourgogne', *Revue d'Histoire du Théâtre*, XXII, 1970, pp. 133–41.
Wiley. W. L., 'The Hôtel de Bourgogne', *Studies in Philology*, LXX, Dec. 1973, pp. 1–114.
Zorzi, G., 'Le Prospettive del Teatro Olimpico di Vicenza', *Arte Lombarda*, X, 2, 1965, pp. 70–97.

Sections 9–10

Boswell, E., *The Restoration Court Stage*, London, 1932.
Bourdel, N., 'L'establissement et la construction de l'hotel des comediens français', *Revue d'histoire du Théâtre*, VII, 1955, pp. 145–72.
Campbell, L. B., *Scenes and Machines of the English Stage*, London, rep. 1960.
Carrick, E., 'Theatre Machines in Italy, 1400–1800', *Architectural Review*, July 1931, Aug. 1931.
——, 'The Theatre of Parma', *Theatre Arts*, XV, March 1931, pp. 201–8.

——, 'Wooden Theatres of the Seventeenth Century', *Wood*, Aug. 1939, pp. 328–32.
Craig, E., *Baroque Theatre Construction*, Bledlow Press, 1982.
Diderot, D., *Encyclopédie*: Theatre Architecture and Stage Machines, x, 1772.
Dumont, G. P. M., *Parallele de Plans des plus belles salles de spectacles. c.*1774, rep. New York, 1968.
Hawley, J., and Jackson, A. S., 'Scene Changing at the Palais Royal (1770–1781)', *O.S.U. Bulletin*, VIII, 1961, pp. 9–23.
Keith, W. G., 'A Theatre Project by Inigo Jones', *Burlington Magazine*, XXXI, no. 173, pp. 61–70; no. 174, pp. 105–11.
——, 'John Webb and the Court Theatre of Charles II', *Architectural Review*, LVII, no. 2, 1925, pp. 49–55.
Lawrenson, T. E., *The French Stage in the Seventeenth Century*, Manchester, 1957.
Leacroft, R., 'The Introduction of Perspective Scenery and its Effect on Theatre Forms', *Theatre Notebook*, XXXIV, 1980, pp. 21–4.
Leclerc, H., *Les origines Italiennes de l'architecture théâtrale moderne*, Paris, 1946.
Nagler, A. M., *Theatre Festivals of the Medici*, New Haven, 1964.
Nicoll, A., *Stuart Masques and the Renaissance Stage*, London, 1937.
——, *The Development of the Theatre*, London, 5th ed., 1966.
Rowan, D. F., 'A Neglected Jones/Webb Theatre Project', in Galloway, D., *The Elizabethan Theatre*, II, 1970, pp. 60–73.
——, 'The Cockpit in Court', in Galloway, D., *The Elizabethan Theatre*, I, 1969, pp. 89–102.
Southern, R., *Changeable Scenery*, London, 1952.
Wickham, G. W., 'The Cockpit Restored', *New Theatre Magazine*, Bristol, VII, no. 2, Spring 1967, pp. 26–35.

Sections 11–13

Adam, R. and J., *The Works in Architecture of Robert and James Adam*, II, London, 1779.
Algarotti, F., *Essays on the Opera*, London, 1767.
Barlow, G., 'Hampton Court Theatre, 1718', *Theatre Notebook*, XXXVII, 1983, pp. 54–63.
Beijer, A., *Bilder från Slottsteatern På Drottningholm*, Malmo, 1940.
——, *The Court Theatres of Drottningholm and Gripsholm*, rep., New York, 1972.
Bell, H., 'Contributions to the History of the English Playhouse', *Architectural Record*, XXXIII, 1913, pp. 359–68.
Boydell, P., 'The Manoel Theatre, Malta', *Theatre Notebook*, XII, 1957–8, pp. 91–3.
Carter, R., 'The Drury Lane Theatres of Henry Holland and Benjamin Dean Wyatt', *Journal of the Society of Architectural Historians*, XXVI, no. 3, Oct. 1967, pp. 200–16.
d'Welles, J., *Le Grand Théâtre de Bordeaux*, Paris, 1949.
Dumont, G. P. M., *Parallele de Plans des plus belles salles de spectacles*, *c.*1774, rep., New York, 1968.
Ferrero, V. M., *Filippo Juvarra, Scenografo e architetto Teatrale*, rep., New York, 1970.
Godfrey, W. H., 'The Apron Stage of the eighteenth century as illustrated at Drury Lane', *Architectural Review*, XXXVII, no. 219, Feb. 1915, pp. 31–5.
Glasstone, V., 'The Influence of Victor Louis', *Architectural Review*, CLXIX, no. 1007, Jan. 1981, pp. 36–45.
Hillestrom, G., *Drottningholmsteatern, Förr och nu*, Stockholm, 1956.
Hume, R. D., *The London Theatre World, 1660–1800*, Carbondale, Ill., 1980.
Langhans, E.A., '*The Theatres*', in Hume, R. D., op. cit., pp. 35–65.
——, 'Conjectural Reconstructions of the Vere Street and Lincoln's Inn Fields Theatres', *Essays in Theatre*, Vol. 1, No. 1, Nov. 1982, pp. 31–5.
——, 'The Vere Street and Lincoln's Inn Fields Theatres in Pictures', *Educational Theatre Journal*, XX, no. 2, May 1968, pp. 171–85.
Leacroft, R., 'The Introduction of Perspective Scenery and its Effect on Theatre Forms, II, *Theatre Notebook*, XXXIV, 1980, pp. 69–73.
Leclerc, H., 'Au Théâtre de Besançon', *Revue d'Histoire du Théâtre*, X, 1958, pp. 103–27.
Louis, V., *Salle de Spectacle de Bordeaux*, Paris, 1782.
Nicoll, A., *The Garrick Stage*, Manchester, 1980.
Marani, E., *Il teatro di Antonio Bibiena in Mantova e il palazzo accademico*, Mantua, 1979.
Saunders, G., *A Treatise on Theatres*, London, 1790.
Sawyer, P., *The New Theatre in Lincoln's Inn Fields*, London, 1979.
Secchi, L. L., *Il Teatro alla Scala, 1778–1978*, Rome, 1977.
Sheppard, F. H. W., *The Theatre Royal, Drury Lane, and the Royal Opera House, Covent Garden* (*Survey of London*, XXXV), London, 1970.
Summers, M., *The Restoration Theatre*, London, 1934.
'Il Teatro scientifico di Mantova', *Architettura : Cronache e Storiaii*, April 1966, pp. 822–7.

Sections 14–16

Buckle, J. G., *Theatre Construction and Maintenance*, London, 1888.

Contant, C., *Parallèle des principaux théâtres modernes de l'Europe*, 1860, rep., New York, 1968.

Leacroft, R., 'Nineteenth-Century Theatrical Machinery in the Theatre Royal, Bath', *Theatre Notebook*, XXX, 1976, pp. 21–4.

——, 'The Remains of the Theatres at Ashby de la Zouch and Loughborough', *Theatre Notebook*, IV, 1949, pp. 12–21.

——, 'The Remains of the Fisher Theatres at Beccles, Bungay, Lowestoft, and N. Walsham', *Theatre Notebook*, V, 1950, pp. 82–7.

——, 'The Remains of the Old Theatre, Wisbech', *Theatre Notebook*, XXXII, 1978, pp. 68–75.

——, 'The Theatre Royal, Leicester, 1836–1958', *Trans. of the Leicester Arch. and Hist. Soc.*, XXXIV, 1958, pp. 39–52.

Mackintosh, I., *Pit, Boxes and Gallery: the Story of the Theatre Royal, Bury St. Edmunds*, National Trust, 1979.

Pudney, J., 'Nordic Encounter – Vadstena', *Theatre Arts*, XXX, no. 4, April 1946, p. 239 and plates.

Sachs, E. O., 'Modern Theatre Stages', nos. 1–30, *Engineering*, LXI–LXII, 17 Jan. 1896–23 Apr. 1897.

Southern, R., 'Interesting Matter Relating to the Theatre Royal, Ipswich', *Architectural Review*, C, Aug. 1946, pp. 41–4.

——, 'Progress at Richmond, Yorkshire', *Theatre Notebook*, IV, 1949–50, pp. 9–12.

——, *The Georgian Playhouse*, London, 1948.

——, 'The Picture-Frame Proscenium of 1880', *Theatre Notebook*, V, 1950–1, pp. 59–61.

Wyatt, B. D., *Observations on the Design of the Theatre Royal, Drury Lane*, London, 1813.

Sections 17–20

Adler, D., 'The Chicago Auditorium', *Architectural Record*, Apr.–June 1892, pp. 415–34.

Bab, J., *The Theatre in the German Language Area since the World War*, in Dickinson, T. H., op. cit., pp. 121–78.

Birkmire, W. H., *The Planning and Construction of American Theatres*, London, 1896.

Birnstingl, H. J., 'Modern Theatre Design', *Architectural Review*, Nov. 1922, pp. 134–9.

Carter, H., *The New Spirit in Drama and Art*, London, 1912.

Dickinson, T. H., *The Theatre in a Changing Europe*, London, n.d.

Lloyds, F., *Practical Guide to Scene Painting*, London, 1875.

Kahn, E. J., 'Ziegfeld Theatre', *Architectural Record*, LXI, no. 5, May 1927, pp. 385–93.

Kinsila, E. B., *Modern Theatre Construction*, New York, 1917.

Lossow, W., *Das Neue Königliche Schauspielhaus*, Dresden, Darmstadt, 1914.

Moderwell, H. K., *The Theatre of To-Day*, London, 1915.

Morin, R. L., 'Design and Construction of Theatres', *The American Architect and Architectural Review*, CXXII, 1922; CXXIII, 1923.

'New Court Theatre, Dresden', *Architectural Review* (USA), II, no. 11, Nov. 1913, pp. 269–72, pls. 78–81.

Pridmore, J. E. D., 'The Mechanical Development of the Modern German Stage', *Architectural Review* (USA), II, Nov. 1913, pp. 263–8.

——, 'The Perfect Theatre', *Architectural Record*, XVII, Feb. 1905, pp. 101–17.

Rees, T., *Theatre Lighting in the Age of Gas*, London, 1978.

Royal Opera House, Leicester. *Leicester Weekly Post*, 25 Aug. 1877. *Leicester Chronicle and Leicestershire Mercury*, 25 Aug. 1877. *Leicester Advertiser*, 25 Aug. 1877.

Sachs, E. O., and Woodrow, E., *Modern Opera Houses and Theatres*, 3 vols., London, 1896–8.

Simonson, L., *The Art of Scenic Design*, New York, 1950.

Theatre Royal, Plymouth. *Architects' Journal*, 13 Oct. 1982. pp. 63–87.

Wolff, J. F., *Das Bühnensystem das Neuen Königliche Schauspielhaus zu Dresden*, Berlin, n.d.

'Worms Theatre, *The Builder*, 15 Dec. 1894, pp. 425–34.

'Ziegfeld Theatre', *Architectural Forum*, XLVI, May 1927, pp. 414–21.

Sections 21–24

Adelphi Theatre. *The Sketch*, 6 Mar. 1901, pp. 270–1; 11 Sept. 1901, pp. 297–8. *The Tatler*, 11 Sept. 1901, p. 523. *The Builder*, 25 Dec. 1858, p. 871; 7 Sept. 1901, p. 217. *Architects' Journal*, 3, Dec. 1930, pp. 824, 828–30. *Architect and Building News*, 5 Dec. 1930, pp. 760–3; 19 Dec. 1930, pp. 825–9. *Illustrated London News*, 18 Dec. 1858. *Survey of London*, XXXVI, pp. 245–50.

'Belgrade Theatre', *Architects' Journal*, 29 July. 1964, pp. 299–302.

Bentham, F., *New Theatres in Britain*, London, 1970.

Bragdon, C., 'Towards a New Theatre', *Architectural Record*, Sept. 1922, pp. 170–81.

Carter, H., *The Theatre of Max Reinhardt*, London, 1914.

Craig, E. G., *The Art of the Theatre*, 5th. imp., London, 1957.

——, *The Theatre Advancing*, London, 1921.

Craig, E., *Gordon Craig*, London, 1968.

——, 'Gordon Craig and Bach's St. Matthew Passion', *Theatre Notebook*, XXVI, 1971–2, pp. 147–151, pls. 1–4.

Festival Theatre, Cambridge. *Theatre World*, VII, no. 34, Nov. 1927, p. 22-3, 29. *Architect and Building News*, 7 Jan. 1927, p. 12 ff.

Fuerst, W. R., and Hume, S. J., *Twentieth-Century Stage Decoration*, 2 vols., London, 1928.

Glasstone, V., *Victorian and Edwardian Theatres*, London, 1975.

Gray, T., 'On Modernising the Theatre', *Drama*, XI, no. 2, Nov. 1932, pp. 19–20.

Grosses Schauspielhaus. *Architectural Review*, CXXXIII, June 1963, pp. 400–5. *Monatsheft fuer baukunst*, Wasmuth, Berlin, Jahr 5, Hefte 1–2, p. 1 ff.

Hamilton, C., 'The Advent of the Little Theatre', *Bookman*, USA, XXXV, May 1912, pp. 239–49.

Ivill, R., 'Cambridgeshire Theatres of the Past', *Cambs., Hunts and Peterboro. Life*, Sept. 1975, pp. 22–3.

Jellicoe, G. A., *The Shakespeare Memorial Theatre*, London, 1933.

Leacroft, R., *Civic Theatre Design*, London, 1949.

Little Theatre, London. *The Builder*, 10 June 1910, p. 783; 12 Nov. 1910, pp. 581–3; 20 Mar. 1914, pp. 357, 359.

Little Theatre, New York. *American Architect*, CI, no. 1895, 17 Apr. 1912, pp. 176–8. *Architecture* (N. York), XXV, no. 4, 15 Apr. 1912, pp. 49–58, pls. 41–5.

Littmann, M., *Das Münchner Künstlertheater*, Munich, 1908.

London Theatre Studio. *Architects' Journal*, LXXXVI, 29 July 1937, pp. 186–8.

MacArthur, D., 'New York's Smallest Professional Theatre', *Theatre Annual*, XX, 1963, pp. 1–19.

Marshall, N., *The Other Theatre*, London, 1947. (Festival Theatre, see pp. 53–71.)

Monck, N., 'The Maddermarket Theatre and the Playing of Shakespeare', *Shakespeare Survey*, XII, 1959, pp. 71–5.

Palace Theatre of Varieties, Leicester. *Leicester Daily Post*, 18 June 1901, p. 5. *Leicester Chronicle and Leicestershire Mercury*, supplement, 22 June 1901, p. 3.

Pichel, I., *Modern Theatres*, New York, 1925.

Porter, E., 'Old Cambridge Theatres', *Cambs., Hunts and Peterboro. Life*, May 1969, pp. 26–8.

Ridge, H., *Stage Lighting*, Cambridge, 1930.

——, *Stage Lighting*, London, 1936.

Rose, E., *Gordon Craig and the Theatre*, London, n.d.

Sayler, O. M., *Max Reinhardt and his Theatre*, New York, 1924.

Schöne, G., 'The Munich Künstlertheater and its First Season', *Apollo*, Nov. 1971, pp. 396–401.

Shakespeare Memorial Theatre. *Architect and Building News*, 22 Apr. 1932, pp. 91–117.

Speight, R., *William Poel and the Elizabethan Revival*, London, 1954.

Urban, J., *Theatres*, New York, 1929.

Washburn-Freund, F. E., 'The Stage and Arts in Germany', *Stage Year Book*, 1909, pp. 112–9.

Sections 25–27

Adams, D., 'A Proscenium Stage Sans', *Sightline*, XI, no. 1. Spring 1977, pp. 5–12.

Aikens, J. R., 'This Unworthy Scaffold – The Story of the Festival Stage', Stratford, Ontario, 1972.

Chichester Festival Theatre. *Architect and Building News*, 4 July 1962, pp. 9–14. *Architectural Design*, Nov. 1962, pp. 530–5. *Architects' Journal*, 4 July 1962, pp. 25–40.

Davies, E. L. W., 'Building the Mermaid', *House of Whitbread Journal*, Autumn 1959, pp. 33–7.

Grenfell, J., *In Pleasant Places*, London, 1979, pp. 118–19.

Macgowan, K., *The Theatre of Tomorrow*, New York, 1921.

Macgowan, K. and Jones, R. E., *Continental Stagecraft*, London, 1923.

Malmö State Theatre. *Byggmastaren*, 18 Sept. 1935, pp. 161–72; no. 10, 1942, pp. 130–4; no. 22, 1944, pp. 398–417.

Malmö New City Theatre and Concert Hall, *Architect and Building News*, 20 April 1945, pp. 39–44.

Mermaid Theatre, Puddle Dock. *Architect and Building News*, 24 June 1959, pp. 819 ff. *Architecture and Building*, Aug. 1959, pp. 292–5.

Miller, J. H., 'Little Theatres from Modest Spaces', *Hub Bulletin*, *107*, Chicago, 1962.

——, 'The Open Stage', *Hub Bulletin*, *109*, Chicago, 1964.

Rapson, R., 'Tyrone Guthrie Theatre, Minneapolis', *Architectural Design*, XXXIV, Aug. 1964, pp. 394–8.

Raymond, A., 'The Théâtre du Vieux-Colombier in New York', *Journal of the American Institute of Architects*, Aug. 1917, pp. 384–7.

Scales, R., 'The Balcony scene at the Other Stratford', *Sightline*, X, no. 2, pp. 34–9.

'Shakespearean Festival Theatre, Stratford', *Journal of the Royal Architectural Institute of Canada*, XXXIV, July 1957, pp. 267–74.

'Tyrone Guthrie Theatre, Minneapolis'. *Tabs*, XXI, Dec. 1963, pp. 32–8. *Progressive Architecture*, XLIV, Dec. 1963, pp. 98–105.

'Vieux-Colombier, La Scène de', *Revue d'Histoire du Théâtre*, 1948–9, pp. ix–xvi, 171–2.

Volbach, W. R., *Adolph Appia*, Connecticut, 1968.

Washburn-Freund, F. E., 'The Theatrical Year in Germany', *Stage Year Book*, London, 1914, pp. 81–96.

Sections 28–33

Amery, C. (ed.), 'National Theatre', *Architectural Review*, CLXI, no. 959, Jan. 1977.

Bentham, F., 'The New Questors Theatre', *Tabs*, XXII, June 1964, pp. 5–10

——, 'Five Theatre Exercise' (incl. Christ's Hospital, Horsham), *Sightline*, IX, no. 2, Autumn 1975, pp. 10–9.

——, 'A Tale of Two Cities' (incl. Haymarket, Leicester), *Tabs*, XXXI, no. 4, Dec. 1973, pp. 138–48.

——, 'Two for Posterity and One Not' (incl. Olivier, Eden Court, and Royal Exchange), *Sightline*, X, no. 2, Autumn 1976, pp. 15–27.

Boyle, W. P., *Central and Flexible Staging*, Los Angeles, 1956.

Branson, N., 'The Questors Theatre', *Adaptable Theatres*, London, 1962, pp. 25–9.

——, 'The Questors, Ealing', *Architect and Building News*, CCXX, 30 Aug. 1961, pp. 318–21.

Brett, R., 'The Olivier Flying System', *Sightline*, XIII, no. 1, pp. 49–54.

Brundig, V. E., 'Possibilities of the Adaptable Theatre', *Adaptable Theatres*, London, 1962, pp. 71–3.

Carter, H., *The New Theatre and Cinema in Soviet Russia*, London, 1924.

Corry, P., 'The Bolton Octagon', *Tabs*, XXVI, no. 1, March 1968, pp. 4–9.

Emmet, A., 'A Case for an Adaptable Theatre', *Tabs*, XV, Dec. 1957, pp. 10–14.

Geddes, N. Bel., 'Symposium on Theatre Planning', *Educational Theatre Journal*, II, March 1950.

——, *Horizons*, New York, rep., 1977.

Gillison, G., 'Living Theater in New Guinea's Highlands', *National Geographic*, CLXIV, August 1983, pp. 146–69.

Glasstone, V., 'A Triumph of Theatre: the Barbican', *Architects' Journal*, 18 Aug. 1982, pp. 31–44.

Gyseghem, A. V., *Theatre in Soviet Russia*, London, 1943.

Ham, R., 'Buildings Update: Leisure', *Architects' Journal*, 12 Aug. 1981, pp. 309–23; 19 Aug. 1981, pp. 355–68.

Haymarket Theatre, Leicester. *Architects' Journal*, 20 Mar. 1974, pp. 607–22.

Isaacs, E. J. R., *Architecture for the New Theatre*, New York, 1935.

Izenour, G., 'An Experimental Theatre', *Perspecta*, Yale, Jan. 1959, pp. 67–72.

Jones, M., *Theatre in the Round*, New York, 1951.

Joseph, S., *New Theatre Forms*, London, 1968.

Kalita Humphreys Theater, Dallas. *Architectural Forum*, CXII, March 1960, pp. 130–5. *Architectural Record*, CXXVII, Mar. 1960, pp. 161–6.

Land, D., 'Harvard's Loeb Drama Center', *Theatre Design and Technolgoy*, no. 1, May 1965, pp. 12–18.

Leacroft, R., 'The Open Stage', *Architectural Review*, CXXV, no. 747, April 1959, pp. 255–62.

——, 'Actor and Audience, Pt. 2: a Study of Experimental Theatres in the U.S.A. and Canada', *Journal of the RIBA*, April 1963, pp. 145–55; May 1963, pp. 195–204.

——, 'The Theatre in Leicester', *Tabs*, XVII, Sept. 1959, pp. 9–17.

Loeb Drama Center. 'The Theater Automatique', *Architectural Forum*, Oct. 1960, pp. 90–8. 'Work of Hugh Stubbins', *Architectural Record*, Oct. 1959, pp. 178–82.

Macleod, J., *The New Soviet Theatre*, London, 1943.

National Theatre, *Architects' Journal*, CLXV, no. 2, 12 Jan. 1977.

Octagon Theatre, Bolton. 'Hexagonal Auditorium in New Bolton Theatre', *Architect and Building News*, CCXXXIII, 31 Jan. 1968, pp. 169–73.

Parkey, J., 'Flying at the Barbican Theatre', *Sightline*, XVI, no. 2, pp. 72–3.

Questors Theatre, Ealing. *Architects' Journal*, 29 July 1964, pp. 291–7.

Ring Theatre, University of Miami. *Progressive Architecture*, Aug. 1953, pp. 114–7.

Royal Exchange Theatre, Manchester. *Architectural Review*, CLX, no. 958, Dec. 1976, pp. 356–62.

Russell, A., 'The Barbican Theatre Flying System', *Sightline*, XVI, no. 2, pp. 68–71.

St. Mary's Training College, Twickenham. 'Adaptable Theatre', *Tabs*, XXI, no. 1, April 1963, pp. 31–6.

Silverman, M., *Contemporary Theatre Architecture*, New York, 1965.

Villiers, A., *Le Théâtre en Rond*, Paris, 1958.

Woodham, R., 'The Vandyck Theatre, Bristol University', *Tabs*, XXVI, no. 3, Sept. 1968, pp. 12–16.

General

Allen, J., *A History of the Theatre in Europe*, London, 1983.

Aloi, R., *Architetture per lo spettacolo*, Milan, 1958.

Altman, G., *Theater Pictorial*, Univ. of California, 1953

Baur-Heinhold, M., *Baroque Theatre*, London, 1967.

Cheney, S., *Stage Decoration*, New York, 1928.

——, *The Theatre*, New York, 1929.

Gascoigne, B., *World Theatre*, London, 1968.

Hartnoll, P., *A Concise History of the Theatre*, London, 1968.

Izenour, G. C., *Theater Design*, New York, 1977.

Leacroft, R., *The Development of the English Playhouse*, London, 1973.

Mackintosh, I., and Ashton, G., *The Georgian Playhouse*, Hayward Gallery Catalogue, London, 1975.
Nagler, A. M., *Sources of Theatrical History*, New York, 1952.
Nicoll, A., *The Development of the Theatre*, rev. ed., London, 1966.
Oenslager, D., *Stage Design*, New York, 1975.
Pevsner, N., *A History of Building Types: 6, Theatres*, London, 1976.
Simonson, L., *The Art of Scenic Design*, New York, 1950.
——, *The Stage is Set*, New York, rep. 1946.
Sonrel, P., *Traité de Scénographie*, Paris, 1943.
Tidworth, S., *Theatres*, London, 1973.

Index